This original collection of essays offers an account of key moments and themes in the history of the Czech Lands from the time of the rise of the Přemyslide dynasty in the ninth century to the fall of socialism in 1989. The essays, commissioned specially for this volume, are written by prominent scholars almost all teaching and researching in the present-day Czech Republic. There is no comparable book in English on the subject.

Along with eleven historical essays on socio-political lines are four contributions which focus broadly on the arts, sciences and education, emphasizing political, economic and other aspects. Of these, two concentrate on the reigns and courts of Charles I/IV (1346 [1355]–1378) and of Rudolf II (1576–1612). Two further essays consider the worlds of the university and of science in the period 1800–1914 and 1800–1930 respectively, as parts of the educational system of the Habsburg monarchy and in the context of the Czech–German bilingualism that pervaded the political and cultural atmosphere of the Czech Lands. The co-existence and encounters between Czechs and Germans are embedded in Czech history and are therefore emphasized throughout the book, while the conflicts between the two nationalities in the nineteenth and twentieth centuries are examined in a separate chapter. Lastly, pursuing the 'ethnic' theme, there are essays on both the little-explored question of Czech–Jewish relations and on the sensitive Czech–Slovak question.

Bohemia in History

Bohemia in History

EDITED BY

MIKULÁŠ TEICH

CAMBRIDGE UNIVERSITY PRESS

PUBLISHED BY THE PRESS SYNDICATE OF THE UNIVERSITY OF CAMBRIDGE
The Pitt Building, Trumpington Street, Cambridge CB2 1RP, United Kingdom

CAMBRIDGE UNIVERSITY PRESS
The Edinburgh Building, Cambridge, CB2 2RU, United Kingdom
40 West 20th Street, New York, NY 10011–4211, USA
10 Stamford Road, Oakleigh, Melbourne 3166, Australia

First published 1998

Printed in the United Kingdom at the University Press, Cambridge

Typeset in 10½ on 12½pt Baskerville   [SE]

A catalogue record for this book is available from the British Library

Library of Congress Cataloguing in Publication data applied for

ISBN 0 521 43155 7 hardback

Contents

Maps and illustrations

Notes on contributors

JAN HAVRÁNEK is Professor of Modern Czech History at Charles University, Prague. He was Fellow of the Woodrow Wilson Center for International Scholars. His main research on the history of Prague University in the nineteenth and twentieth centuries has been conducted at the Institute for University History of Charles University. His numerous publications include books and articles on the modern social, political and intellectual history of Central Europe.

FRANTIŠEK KAVKA is Emeritus Professor of Czech History at Charles University, Prague. In 1970 he was obliged to give up his academic activities to which he was able to return in 1990. He has published widely on late medieval history. His recent book is *The Rule of Emperor Charles IV (1355–1378)* (Prague, 1993).

DUŠAN KOVÁČ is Director of the Institute of Historical Studies at the Slovak Academy of Sciences in Bratislava. He is Chairman of the Slovak National Committee of Historians. His numerous publications deal with Central European history of the nineteenth and twentieth centuries, especially with Czech–Slovak relations and the question of national minorities.

HELENA KREJČOVÁ is Head of the Department of Jewish Studies at the Institute of Contemporary History of the Czech Academy of Sciences in Prague. Her main area of interest is the history of the Czech–Jewish assimilation movements and the fate of Czech Jews from 1938 to the present.

JAN KŘEN is Director of the Institute of International Studies at Charles University, Prague. He is author of several books on the modern history of

Bohemia. Recently he published a critique of Czech communist historiography *Bílá místa v našich dějinách* [Blanks in our history] (1990) and *Historické proměny češství* (Historical metamorphoses of Czechdom) (1992).

JIŘÍ KROUPA is Reader in Theory and History of Arts and Head of the Department of History of Arts at Masaryk University in Brno. His special field of interest is eighteenth-century cultural history and the history of the arts in their social and functional context. His principal works are *Alchymie štěstí Pozdní osvícenství a moravská společnost 1770–1810* [Alchemy of happiness: The late Enlightenment and Moravian society] (1987); *'Lieu de plaisance' a barokní Morava* ['Lieu de plaisance' and Baroque Moravia] 3 vols. (1994); *Metodologie dějin umění* (Methodology of the history of the arts), I (1996).

ROBERT KVAČEK is Professor of Czech and Czechoslovak History at the Philosophical Faculty of Charles University, Prague. His numerous books deal with political and cultural history of the nineteenth and twentieth centuries, including the latest *Obtížné spojenectví. Československo a Francie 1937–1938* (Troubled alliance. Czechoslovakia and France 1937–1938) (1989).

JOSEF MACEK was Director of the Historical Institute of the Czechoslovak Academy of Sciences in Prague until 1969. Foreign language editions of his books include *Il Rinascimento italiano* (1971), *Jean Hus et les traditions hussites* (1973), *Machiavelli e il machiavellismo* (1980), *Histoire de la Bohême* (1984) and *Michael Gaismair* (1988). Posthumously published so far two parts of his seven-part *Jagellonský věk v českých zemích (1471–1526)* (The Jagiellon era in the Czech Lands) (1992, 1994).

VLADIMÍR MACURA is Director of the Institute of Czech Literature of the Czech Academy of Sciences in Prague. He has published in the field of the semiotics of culture and the theory of literature, including *Šťastný věk* (The happy age) (1992), *Masarykovy boty* [The Boots of President Masaryk] (1993) and *Znamení zrodu České národní obrození jako kulturní typ* [The sign of genesis: Czech national revival as a cultural type], new enlarged edition (Jinočany, 1995).

ZDENĚK MĚŘÍNSKÝ is Reader in Czech Medieval History and Medieval Archaeology at the Masaryk University in Brno. He is author of monographs and studies in Slavonic archaeology and historical archaeology. He also directed a number of excavations in Moravia, e.g. in Rokštejn and Strachotín.

JAROSLAV MEZNÍK is Professor of Medieval History at the Masaryk University in Brno. He was persecuted and imprisoned in the period of 'normalization' before 1990. His research is concerned with the history of Bohemia and Moravia in the fourteenth and fifteenth centuries. His most recent book is *Praha před husitskou revolucí* [Prague before the Hussite Revolution] (1990).

MILAN OTÁHAL was a Research Fellow of the Historical Institute of the Czechoslovak Academy of Sciences in Prague until 1970 when he was obliged to discontinue his scientific work to which he was able to return in 1990. His field of interest is modern Czech history. His recent publication is *Opozice, moc, společnost 1969–1989 Příspěvek k dějinám 'normalizace'* [Opposition, power, society 1969–1989 Contribution to the history of 'normalization'] (1994).

JOSEF PETRÁŇ is Professor at Charles University, Prague, Director of the Institute of History – Archives of Charles University and Member of the Council of the Czech Learned Society. His interests centre on Czech history from the sixteenth to the eighteenth centuries. His numerous books include *Dějiny hmotné kultury* (The history of material culture), I/1–2 (1988).

LYDIA PETRÁŇOVÁ, PhD, is a historian at the Institute of Ethnology of the Czech Academy of Sciences in Prague. She has published several books on the history of culture of everyday life and on historical anthropology, including *Československo, obrazy země a dějin* [Czechoslovakia, pictures of the country and its history] (1990).

IRENA SEIDLEROVÁ has published on the history of physics and technology. She co-authored recently (with J. Dohnálek) *Dějiny betonového stavitelství v českých zemích do konce 19. století* [The history of concrete building in the Czech Lands until the end of the nineteenth century] (1991).

JIŘÍ SLÁMA is Reader in Archaeology at Charles University, Prague. His interests concern the early Middle Ages and the beginnings of the Czech state. Among his publications are *Střední Čechy v raném středověku* [Central Bohemia in the early Middle Ages], vols. I–III (1977–1990) and he co-authored with P. Charvát *Vyvraždění Slavníkovců* (The Slaughter of the Slavník dynasty) (1992).

FRANTIŠEK ŠMAHEL is Professor of Medieval History at Charles University, Prague, Director of the Historical Institute of the Czech Academy of Sciences in Prague, and Editor-in-Chief of the *Český časopis historický*. His is Fellow of the British Academy, Corresponding Fellow of the Royal Historical Society, and Honorary Foreign Member of the American Historical Association. He has numerous publications in several languages on the history of Czech culture and religious movements. His most recent publications include the four-volume *Husitská revoluce* [The Hussite revolution] (1993) and *Zur politischen Präsentation und Allegorie im 14. und 15. Jahrhundert* (1994).

MIKULÁŠ TEICH is Emeritus Fellow of Robinson College Cambridge and Honorary Professor of the Technical University Vienna. He has recently edited, with Roy Porter and Bo Gustafsson, *Nature and Society in Historical Context* (1997).

ALICE TEICHOVA is Emeritus Professor of Economic History at the University of East Anglia in Norwich and Honorary Fellow of Girton College Cambridge. She received Honorary Doctorates from the University of Uppsala and the University of Vienna. Recently she edited, with Herbert Matis, *Österreich und die Tschechoslowakei 1918–1938 Die wirtschaftliche Neuordnung in Zentraleuropa in der Zwischenkriegszeit* (Vienna, 1996).

OTTO URBAN was Professor of Czech and Medieval History at Charles University, Prague, and Fellow of the Collegium Budapest. He authored numerous books and articles. His book *Česká společnost 1848–1918* [Czech society 1848–1918] (1982) was published in German *Die tschechische Gesellschaft 1848–1918* (1994).

JOSEF VÁLKA is Professor of Czech History at the Philosophical Faculty of Masaryk University in Brno. His numerous studies in several languages on culture from the fifteenth to the eighteenth centuries in the Czech Lands and in Central Europe include *Dějiny Moravy / středověká Morava* [The History of Moravia/medieval Moravia] I (1991).

Acknowledgements

It is a great pleasure to offer thanks to colleagues and friends who have given advice in the early/later stages of the project: Dr Jaroslav Folta, Dr Eduard Kubů, Professor Milan Myška, Dr Milan Otáhal, Dr Libuše Otáhalová, Professor Jaroslav Pátek, Professor Václav Průcha, Dr Irena Seidlerová, Dr Josef Smolka, Professor František Šmahel.

I acknowledge gratefully the assistance given to me by Clarissa Campbell Orr in linguistic matters, and Dr Mary Stewart in the field of German literary history. I am indebted to Dr Con Coroneos for his helpful copy-editorial suggestions. I offer my warmest thanks to William Davies of Cambridge University Press for his constant interest and patient support of the project. But it is to Professor Alice Teichova that my debt is incalculable – without her I could not possibly have completed the editing of the book.

Sadly two contributors, Josef Macek (1922–1991) and Otto Urban (1938–1996), died before the publication of the book. To their memory and to the memory of František Graus (1921–1989), the editor of a previous collection in which the attempt was made to assess the state of research and reflection in Czech historiography, this work is dedicated.

M.T.

Editorial note

As Robert Evans pointed out in his influential *The Making of the Habsburg Monarchy 1550–1700* (Oxford, 1979) 'Bohemia' is not a simple notion. Largely but not exclusively in this book it is co-extensive with 'Czech Lands', encompassing historically the Kingdom of Bohemia, the Margravate of Moravia and (the duchies of) Silesia. They were constituent parts, with Slovakia and Subcarpathian Ruthenia, of Czechoslovakia between 1918 and 1939, and again (without Subcarpathian Ruthenia) between 1945 and 1992. The links in the histories of the Czech Lands and Slovakia are addressed particularly in chapters 13, 15 and 18.

Names of some towns in Czech and German

Czech	German	
Brno	Brünn	
České Budějovice	Budweis	
Hradec Králové	Königgrätz	
Cheb	Eger	
Chomutov	Komotau	
Jachymov	Joachimsthal	
Jihlava	Iglau	
Kroměřiž	Kremsier	
Kutná Hora	Kuttenberg	
Litoměřice	Leitmeritz	
Mikulov	Nikolsburg	
Minstrberk	Münsterberg	Ziębice (Polish)
Mladá Boleslav	Jungbunzlau	
Most	Brüx	
Olomouc	Olmütz	
Opava	Troppau	
Ostrava	Ostrau	
Plzeň	Pilsen	
Prostějov	Prossnitz	
Stará Boleslav	Altbunzlau	
Terezín	Theresienstadt	
Ústí nad Labem	Aussig	
Vranov nad Dyjí	Frain	
Vratislav	Breslau	Wrocław (Polish)
Znojmo	Znaim	
Žatec	Saaz	

Introduction

MIKULÁŠ TEICH

With history it is possible to do almost anything – only to elude it is not possible.

František Graus (ed.), *Naše živá i mrtvá minulost* [Our living and dead past] (Prague, 1968), p. 8.

I

This collection appears later than planned for reasons that afflict multi-authored publications whose individual chapters are delivered at different times. As it happens, *Bohemia in History* is published in the year of memorable anniversaries. That is, 650 years after the foundation of the University of Prague, the oldest in Central Europe; 380 years after the (Second) Defenestration of Prague which led to the end of Czech statehood and the beginning of the Thirty Years War; 150 years after students of the University of Prague with the more radical sections of the population had urged the need for fundamental political and social changes in the existing feudal order; 80 years after the establishment of the First Czechoslovak Republic and 60 years after its demise; 50 years after the Communist Party of Czechoslovakia achieved monopoly of power and 30 years after the unsuccessful attempt to reform the system within – towards 'a socialism with a human face'.

The starting point of this volume was a letter from Prague that I received in Cambridge in December 1989 – a month after the events in Czechoslovakia described as the 'Velvet Revolution'. The letter came from the Historical Institute of the Czechoslovak Academy of Sciences where I had been a research worker since 1954 until my leaving the country into a virtually enforced emigration in 1968.[1] In the letter this was acknowledged, an apology offered for the wrongs that had affected my life professionally and privately, and a wish expressed to put them right. I was invited to come to Prague to discuss these matters, including possibilities of future co-operation with the Historical Institute. After Alice Teichova obtained a similar letter of apology from the Paedagogical Faculty of Charles University (where she had been Head of the Department of History), we travelled to Prague following an absence of nearly twenty-two years at the end of January 1990. Since then, old contacts with Czech colleagues have been renewed and new ones established. On the one hand, this paved the way for close co-operation of Czech economic historians with Alice Teichova, including their participation in the international research project 'The economic role of Austria in interwar Central Europe' under her direction. On the other hand, the visit eventually actuated collaboration of social, political and cultural historians in taking stock of 'the state of the art' in the manner of the previous remarkable attempt *Naše živá i mrtvá minulost*, a collection of eight essays on Czech history published in 1968. It was edited by František Graus who wrote the introductory essay, bearing the same title as the book, from which the chapter quotation has been taken.

Notwithstanding that thirty years have passed since its appearance, the slim volume remains valuable reading for the content, thematic treatment and quality of its individual essays. Its purpose was to readdress critically the enduring mythicization of some themes in Czech historiography: the beginning of statehood (D. Třeštík); the Hussite movement (F. Šmahel); the aftermath of the Battle of the White Mountain (J. Petráň); the national revival (M. Hroch); the formation of the nation without a state (J. Kořalka); right-wing radicalism and the First World War (B. Loewenstein); the First Republic, 1918–1938 (V. Olivová). The contributions were ostensibly influenced by and committed to a discerning Marxist method of interpreting the past. *Naše živá i mrtvá minulost*, so to speak a scholarly introspection, should be taken account of by serious students of the intellectual underpinnings of the process in Czechoslovakia, which culminated in what has become known as 'Prague Spring of 1968' and whose history has yet to be written.[2] Significantly František Šmahel, who discusses the Hussite movement in both books, begins his contribution to *Bohemia in History* as follows:

It does not always pay to be the first or to refuse to toe the line. History displays a host of cautionary examples of both these cases. Bohemia did not pay for nonconformity in 1968 alone. An anomaly *sui generis* was constituted by the Hussite movement, this Reformation before the Reformations and revolutions before the revolutions.

II

Neville Chamberlain's notorious reference to 'a quarrel in a far-away country between people of whom we know nothing' (27 September 1938) has occasionally been viewed as a folly of an ignorant provincial English businessman, turned into a politician who by chance became a prime minister. Be that as it may, in Britain and elsewhere the state of affairs regarding knowledge of Czech and, for that matter, Slovak history has not changed materially for the better since Chamberlain's fateful pronouncement sixty years ago.

The eighteen informative and interpretative essays assembled in *Bohemia in History* should help to redress the balance. They are based on synthesis of authors' and other scholars' work. Chiefly along socio-political lines they identify major moments in the past of the Czech Lands from the time the Přemyslide dynasty began to rise to power in the ninth century to the fall of socialism in 1989. Four essays focus broadly on the arts, sciences and education in interaction, as the case may be, with political, economic and other spheres. Of these, two concentrate on the reigns and courts of Charles I/IV (1346 [1355]–1378) and Rudolf II (1576–1612) respectively. Two further essays consider the worlds of university and science. One discusses them in the framework of the higher educational system of the Habsburg monarchy from about 1800. The other looks at the world of science in the context of Czech–German bilingualism, from about 1800 to 1930, pervading the political and cultural atmospheres of the Czech Lands drawing into its wake the threat of their division or outright dismemberment along blurred ethnic lines. The coexistence and the encounters of Czechs and native Germans are embedded in the history of the Czech Lands and, as such, are paid attention to in the essays of the volume throughout. The conflicts between them in the nineteenth and twentieth centuries are examined in a separate contribution. Lastly, pursuing the 'ethnic' theme, there are two essays on the little explored Czech–Jewish relationship and the consequential 'Slovak Question'.

The first essay by Jiří Sláma sheds light on the origin of 'Bohemia' and its Czech equivalent 'Čechy' which, in fact, is a plural. Bohemia, which embraces the western part of the present-day Czech Republic, derives its name from the Celtic tribe Boii whose members appeared to have resided on the territory of Bohemia between the first century BC and the first century AD only to be pushed out by successive waves of Germanic and Slavic settlers. 'Bohemia' is recorded in Frankish annals since the ninth century. As to 'Čechy', the expression appears earliest as 'česki muži' (Czech men) in an Old Slavic tenth-century source.

Between the tenth and thirteenth centuries, Bohemia and Moravia were transformed under the Přemyslides into an important medieval state. In the second essay Zdeněk Měřínský and Jaroslav Mezník trace this by no means linear process involving, among others, alignments as well as tensions with the throne of the Roman (German) Empire. The rising influence of the Přemyslide state derived from the availability of silver which began to be mined in the thirteenth century. Silver mining brought German-speaking miners, thus reinforcing the influx of German colonists which began in the twelfth century and decisively affected the ethnical composition of the Czech Lands.

After the extinction of the Přemyslides (1306), influential magnates turned to Emperor Henry VII of Luxemburg. His eldest son, John, after being married at the age of fourteen to Elizabeth, the youngest sister of the last Přemyslide, was elected King of Bohemia (1310–1346). Though due for reappraisal – Měřínský and Mezník speak of him as this 'knightly and intelligent king'[3] – it is the reign of his eldest son Charles (dubbed 'the golden age' by older historiography) which attracts attention.

It is František Kavka who focuses on Charles's consummate political and diplomatic acumen. Beyond that, he brings out that Charles was the driving spirit that animated the immense artistic, architectural and urban planning activities that were to transform Prague into a northern Rome. Such a town had to be home to a university which, as expressly stated in the Founding Charter of 7 April 1348, was to serve the intellectual needs of the denizens of the Kingdom of Bohemia:[4]

So, in order that our loyal inhabitants of the realm, incessantly hungering after the fruits of learning, may not be constrained to beg for alms in foreign countries, but may find set out a welcoming table in our realm, and also that those who are distinguished by natural sagacity and talent may through knowledge and science become skilled in learning and may no longer be obliged, but hold it even superfluous in their pursuit of learning, to travel about in far-off lands of the world, to seek out foreign nations, or to beg in foreign countries for the satisfaction of their aspirations for knowledge, but in order that they may reckon it for their own glory to summon others from abroad to the sweet savour and bid them share in their pleasure.

Within five decades or so, the situation that the Masters and students from Bohemia had only one vote in the administration of the university against the three votes of the Masters and students from abroad became a major issue, involving national, political and doctrinal concerns. In 1409 a royal act, known as the Decree of Kutná Hora, inverted the existing status in favour of the *natio Bohemorum*. At the centre of the university party, demanding the change, was Jan Hus (*c.* 1370–1415) whose name is inseparably linked with 'the Reformation before the Reformations and revolution before the revolutions' which is the point at issue raised by F. Šmahel. After examining the multifarious dimensions of the Hussite movement – social, national, revolutionary, doctrinal, spiritual and cultural – Šmahel discerns 'contours of long-term processes' which, within 100 years of Hus's death at the stake in Constance, transformed the Kingdom of Bohemia into 'a monarchy of the estates'.

'Until recently', writes Josef Macek, 'the contribution of the estates to the Czech statehood and culture has been played down'. He saw it as his task to remedy the situation by providing a comprehensive seven-part account of the period 1471–1526, known as the 'Jagiellon era' in the history of the Czech Lands.[5] Josef Macek completed his offering to *Bohemia in History* literally just before his death, and thus it may be read as a summary of his seasoned *magnum opus*. The period was one of political change. In the absence of prelates in political life, burghers became the third political force besides lords and knights. Macek notes that there were 190 meetings of the Diet between 1471 and 1526 in which the lesser nobility and burghers took active part. 'If one assumes democratization', he continues, 'to mean the gradual awakening to political and public activity of these sections of the population previously (partially or completely) excluded from it, then the meetings of the Diet in Bohemia were doubtless a form of a process of democratization.' The meetings of the Diet (and the sittings of the Land Court) took place in the largest state room in Europe – in the vast Late Gothic Vladislav Hall of the Prague Castle, built between 1481 and 1500. Macek's verdict: political power and the ambience in which it functioned were in accord.

From the fifteenth century, in keeping with the major role they played in state affairs, the estates were calling for the King of Bohemia to live permanently in Prague. Perhaps because he wished to comply with this demand or for more personal reasons, Rudolf II took up residence in the Prague Castle in 1583. 'Around 1600 – after two centuries – Prague regained its significance as an important political and cultural centre in Europe.' This is how Josef Válka begins his far-ranging essay in which he reclaims the failed ruler and unlucky military man to a paramount position as a patron of the arts and learning. In Rudolf's perception, artistic and scientific pursuits were no disparate quests. Indeed, as Válka shows, the major and minor painters, sculptors, architects, astronomers and alchemists who served Rudolf II and other patrons were realizing his programme (or they believed that they were doing just that): to penetrate into the hidden meaning of the Cosmos. This ambition provides the clue, for example, to the efforts of the Imperial Astronomer to Rudolf II and one of the very great figures of the Scientific Revolution, Johannes Kepler

(1571–1630), to search for the mathematical harmony of the Universe. It illustrates that in Bohemia, as elsewhere in Europe, science and magic were by no means separate spheres in the time of transition of the Renaissance to the Baroque.

In his major work on the emergence of the Habsburg monarchy Robert Evans describes the Defenestration of Prague (23 May 1618) as 'that tragicomic charade which hoped to eliminate by medieval means the two chief representatives (Martinic and Slavata) of a king (Ferdinand II) so recently elected with an overwhelming majority.'[6] Moreover, he finds it somehow absurd to call 'an hour-and-a-half's skirmishing between makeshift armies on a featureless plateau just west of Prague' (8 November 1620) the 'Battle of the White Mountain'.[7] The problem is that, apart from the Hussite movement, no other event in the history of the Czech Lands has attracted more scholarly and popular attention than the uprising/rebellion of the estates and the war 1618–1620. Addressed by Josef Petráň in *Naše živá a mrtvá minulost*, in this volume he returns at length, with Lydia Petráňová, to the Battle of the White Mountain. The authors discuss how the defeat of the rebel armies in the Battle of the White Mountain has lent itself to myth-making as a medium for history-centred Czech patriotism/nationalism from the seventeenth century to the present. The authors' underlying approach is summarized as follows:

A society which needs to define itself almost purely in terms of its past – either because it feels threatened or because it is uncertain of its own strength – seeks support in ideology or historical myth. The myth of the White Mountain and every other myth as a historical fact possessed in various historical situations and in different societies an adaptive function, whether in a positive or a negative sense.

Although Bohemia and Moravia (the eastern part of the Czech Republic named after the river Morava rising in the Sudeten Mountains and flowing south to the Danube) have coexisted in a common state for nearly 900 years, there are particular political, cultural and other aspects of the history of Moravia which historiography has tended to neglect. This applies, for example, to the study of the Enlightenment from the Moravian perspective which is the topic of Jiří Kroupa's contribution. His concern is not so much whether the Moravian Enlightenment possesses distinctive features but to provide evidence for its institutional, scholarly and literary existence, including ideas which had moved the Moravian *Aufklärer*, such as patriotism, virtue and happiness. What Kroupa offers is an additional mosaic in the build-up of Europe's Enlightenment.

In Czech historiography, the period from about 1800 to about 1850 has been associated with the process of 'national revival' (*národní obrození*), which laid the foundations of modern Czech culture. It has often been described as a near miracle – a notion which Vladimír Macura approaches in his essay iconoclastically. For one thing, Macura stresses that the national revival has not only narrow native roots but has to be looked at in its wider Josephinian and French Revolution contexts. For another thing, Macura points to the contrast between the high cultural aspirations of the national(ist) project and the low level of national consciousness of Czech interest-groups which a small band of 'revivalists' strove to influence. 'This problem', Macura finds, 'led to

an orientation towards language, towards the production of culture in the sphere of philology, and hence to the primacy of the verbal form over the content of a message, over originality in the realm of ideas. This trend resulted naturally in the artificiality of cultural production and, with it, a blurring of the boundaries between the true and the false, between illusion and reality.

For Otto Urban, Czech society comes into its own as a functional modern national and civil society between 1848 and 1918. He examines this process through its social, economic, political, ethnic and cultural aspects and their actual relationships in the context of domestic and international problems of the Habsburg monarchy. The change was striking: economically the Czech Lands became the most important region of the Habsburg monarchy. No less conspicuous was that by 1900 illiteracy, among both ethnicities, virtually disappeared. Urban notes that this gave emphasis to the viewpoint, before 1914, that 'Czech society became gradually "rooted" in Austria and learned to use the existing possibilities of the system'. It underlined the conduct of 'official' Czech politics whose spokesmen, by and large, possessed neither the willingness nor the ability to formulate a programme of state independence, in accord with the undoubtedly existing national feeling and aspirations of the Czechs.

The Great War 1914–1918 transformed the situation. Among the few politicians who believed that there was more to it than a rivalry between the great powers and that it opened a window of opportunity for the establishment of an independent state was Tomáš (Thomas) Garrigue Masaryk (1850–1937). He was professor of philosophy at the independent Czech branch of the University of Prague and founder of the tiny Czech People's (Realist) Party (1900) – metamorphosed into the Czech Progressive Party (1906) – which represented in the Reichsrat (Imperial Parliament). After the outbreak of the Great War, Masaryk left Prague and went abroad in December 1914 only to return four years later in December 1918 as President of the Czechoslovak Republic – an independent state. What happened in the intervening years Urban describes as follows:

[Masaryk] assumed the war to be a great conflict between the modern democratic and republican principle and the old aristocratic and monarchistic principle. In this spirit he reformulated, in the summer of 1915, the Czech political programme along decisively maximalist lines . . . For a long time, this programme was only an idea and its realization depended on the result of the war, on the attitude of the victorious parties and on a number of other circumstances. The collapse of Russian tsarism in 1917 and the revolutionary chaos that followed in Russia, influenced pervasively further developments, and also contributed in the end to the fall of the Central European monarchies and their political systems. After 1917, therefore, Czech political activity abroad grew substantially. But, at the same time, the Czech domestic political scene was becoming gradually active and the maximalist political programme was gaining more open followers. By the time of the defeat of the Central Powers in the autumn of 1918, this programme was accepted by all decisive political forces in Czech society.

In keeping with Maria Theresa's dictum about education always being a political matter, the Austrian state exercised control over it to a degree which included the universities. Did this extend to imposing breaks on the academic freedom to research and publish? It is Jan Havránek's contention that this was not the case. He ascribes the academic liberties to the rise of the social prestige of university professors and examines the factors which helped to produce this change during the nineteenth century. They enabled university professors – who were state officials – to make *ex cathedra* political statements 'which was tolerated by the state, and attempts to restrain this liberty were as a rule resisted by the academic community as a whole'.

In 1961 a book appeared on the history of mathematics, astronomy, physics and chemistry in Bohemia and Moravia up to the end of the nineteenth century. It was co-authored by six scholars who in their accounts fully respected the bilingual framework within which science in the Czech Lands had evolved.[8] Irena Seidlerová, who participated in the earlier collaborative venture, explores in the present volume the pursuit of science in bilingual institutional and academic settings in the Czech Lands into the 1930s when, as she deplores in her conclusion, the mutual ignorance of the Czech-speaking and German-speaking scientific communities was total. Thus

a science student at the Czech Charles University in Prague did not know who lectured in his discipline at the German University in Prague, whose building was sometimes less than 100 metres away. Even Czech university teachers and researchers often had no idea that in their works they actually cited a colleague from the Brno German Technische Hochschule. Not only from the viewpoint of science was this a very sad affair.

As brought out by Robert Kvaček, there were two 'national question' issues which became festering sores that continued to debilitate

Czechoslovakia from its beginning in 1918 to her crippling in 1938. They concerned the attitude to the new state of indigenous Germans who found themselves to be a 'national minority', and of Slovaks pronounced to be 'Czechoslovaks'. Officially, Czechoslovaks made up, during the period, about 67 per cent of the total population (under 15 million) of Czechoslovakia which, though established as a nation-state and consecrated by the Versailles settlement, was only slightly less variegated ethnically than Austria-Hungary from which it descended as the sole enduringly democratic successor state.[9]

The German-speaking population constituted the largest minority but was it a minority if one acknowledges that the concept of a unitary Czechoslovak nation ('Czechoslovakism'), realised from two – Czech and Slovak – branches, proved to be unsustainable? Given that Czechs made up about 52 per cent and Slovaks about 16 per cent of Czechoslovakia's total population, the German-speaking populace constituted hardly a minority (over 22 per cent). Be that as it may in retrospect, there can be no doubt that democratic Czechoslovakia, more than any other state that signed the Minority Protection Treaty (1919), had observed the conditions laid down by it.

Behind the flawed conception of Czechoslovakism stood President Masaryk who exercised paramount influence on the affairs of the state from a position of authority which he held continuously for seventeen years of its twenty-year existence. Czechoslovakism had much to do with Czech 'appropriation' of Czechoslovakia which, as Kvaček notes, 'gave rise to conflicts and misunderstandings which could have been avoided, or at least diminished and blunted, had there been a greater degree of sensitivity on the Czech part towards the other nationalities'.

Yet what emerges from Kvaček's account is that the claim to self-determination by Germans and Slovaks in democratic Czechoslovakia was 'instrumental' rather than 'pivotal' to developments that culminated in the Munich Agreement, heralding her doom. While mobilizing broad sections of the German and Slovak population, the principle of national self-determination – fuelled by economic and social grievances – became a weapon in the hands of the authoritarian leaderships of the Sudeten German Party and the Slovak People's Party, lastly intent on the undermining of the democratic political structure of Czechoslovakia.

It was their right-wing orientation that created the lines of contact with Hitler Germany, determined to nullify the Versailles system of which Czechoslovakia constituted an integral part. Kvaček observes that Hitler's Germany assailed Czechoslovakia

with campaigns designed to demonstrate oppression of ethnic minorities and danger of bolshevism. The propaganda met with international response where it

suited one's own enmity towards Czechoslovakia, or where it could be used in bringing political pressure to bear on her government.

Bowing to the pressures of democratic Great Britain and France accommodating Nazi Germany and fascist Italy, the Czechoslovak government,
which was not consulted, accepted the Munich Agreement signed by
Neville Chamberlain, Edouard Daladier, Adolf Hitler and Benito Mussolini
on 29/30 September 1938.

As a result of the dictate, Germany annexed about 37 per cent of the
Czech Lands with more than 3.5 million people; nearly one fifth were ethnic
Czechs. But, as Robert Kvaček concludes,

There was more to it than depriving Czechoslovakia of a part of her territory. The
blow dealt to Czechoslovakia at Munich had as a consequence the setting off an
internal transformation which marked the end of democracy in Czechoslovakia.
'Munich' also badly hit Czechoslovakia's economy and robbed her of independent
foreign policy. Reaching beyond the Czechoslovak context 'Munich' did severe
damage to democracy worldwide and finally disrupted the international order
established after 1918. In the climate 'Munich' had ushered in, Germany found no
difficulty to destroy Czechoslovakia completely in March 1939.

According to Richard Overy, the distinguished authority on the Nazi
economy, Hitler was primarily instrumentalist in his approach to economic
policy. 'For him the economy', Overy writes, 'was not simply an arena for
generating wealth and technical progress; its *raison d'être* lay in its ability to
provide the material springboard for military conquest'.[10] For this statement
Alice Teichova provides chapter and verse in her article on the German economic policy in the 'Protectorate of Bohemia and Moravia'. This was the
name given to truncated Czech Lands after their occupation by German
troops entering Prague on 15 March 1939. The Protectorate existed for over
six years until remnant German military units withdrew to the West confronted, as they were, with a rising of Prague citizens (5 May 1945) and the
arrival of the Red Army (9 May 1945) but not before killing many Czechs.[11]

The choice to declare the Czech Lands as a Protectorate was deliberate.
As Teichova points out, the creation of the French Protectorate in Tunis
(1881) and its administration served the Nazis as a model for a semi-colonial
regime in the Czech Lands. In the short term the Czechs were to be tolerated as long as they were prepared to carry out the directives of the German
masters in the interest of the war effort. 'Fundamentally', she emphasizes,
'economic realities – the crucial importance of Czech war production – set
limits to mass terror and, in conjunction with ruthless strikes against opposition and resistance, led to a stick-and-carrot policy.' With regards to the
Czechs the racial programme, implemented *vis-à-vis* the Jewish population

in the Czech Lands, was to be delayed until after the war was won but then to be pursued no less implacably.

The forty-five years from the liberation of Czechoslovakia in 1945 to the end of coɩ ɪmunist rule in 1989 are examined by Milan Otáhal. The period is marked by three internal events which attracted wide attention in the outside world.

First was the 'victorious February of 1948' – denoted as such by the Communists for their victory in the struggle for power, by 25 February 1948, which led to 'the removal from power of those representatives of political parties who tried to stop the communist advance with quite inadequate means. That is, by relying on elections, on the parliament and on USA support'.

Second was the 'Prague Spring of 1968' – the by-name for the short period when critics of the Soviet-type system, within the Communist Party of Czechoslovakia with mass support, tried to reform it.

As to the third event, the 'Velvet Revolution of 1989', Otáhal observes that following the forcible suppression of the 'Prague Spring' the official ideas of socialism were losing attractioɩ : all the more when any attempt at reform within the framework of the ɩ ɩommunist Party was branded as counter-revolutionary. Under these ɩ ɩrcumstances, the movement to reform/transform Czechoslovak society evolved outside the Communist Party and in opposition to its leadership. The dissent's leading figure became Václav Havel (born 1936) under whose influence the notion of 'non-political politics' was accepted as its guiding principle. As Otáhal points out, students were not part of the dissent, yet it was their manifestation in Prague on 17 November 1989 which unpremeditatedly ushered in the 'Velvet Revolution'. Remarkably, they appear not to have been involved in subsequent negotiations between Ladislav Adamec, the Prime Minister of the Federal Government, and the representatives of the Civic Forum which led to the transfer of power to the Civic Forum, and eventually to Václav Havel's election as President of Czechoslovakia.

As amply demonstrated in the essays no serious history of the Czech Lands can leave out the German connection. Jan Křen sees (Czech) literature on Czech–German relations focusing, on the whole, on the Czech component. Therefore he has chosen to concentrate 'particularly on Germans in Bohemia (*Deutschböhmen, Sudetendeutsche*),[12] and on the uncertainties, splits and changeability of their national identity, connected as they were with turns in the national-political programme. There were more twists and turns in their development than in that of the Czechs – one of the underestimated causes of domestic nationality conflicts.'

While Křen addresses himself to the nineteenth and twentieth centuries,

of interest are František Graus's observations concerning the early growth
of Czech national awareness in medieval Bohemia, a growth which was not
parallelled by an evolution of German national self-ide_tification in the
German-speaking population in Bohemia. In retrospect or _ can discern the
beginning of ominous Czech–German antagonism sowing the seeds of dis-
astrous consequences for both Czechs and Germans in the Czech Lands.[13]

The descendents of the German-speaking settlers of the thirteenth and
fourteenth centuries participated in turn as players, victors and victims in
events that paved the road to Munich in 1938 and their expatriation from
their homeland after 1945. It is the restitution of their property, including
the right of their return, which has become a sensitive issue for the Czech
and German governments.

The main purpose of Helena Krejčová's article is to give a necessarily
compressed account of the history of Jews in the Czech Lands spanning the
period from the tenth century to 1945, including the division of the ways in
which they were drawn closer either to the Germans or to the Czechs. What
emerges from her narrative is that Prague was one of the great centres of
Jewish (Hebrew) learning from the end of the twelfth century until the
1730s.[14] It also ser_es to remind us that Bohemia, during 1899–1900, experienced a ritual _urder trial (Hilsner Affair) in which T. G. Masaryk
involved himself because he felt that 'the ritual superstition is a terrible
indictment of the Czech nation'.[15] Another theme developed in her article
is that the road from Munich via the occupation of Prague led to the Terezín
ghetto which became a transfer point for Jews (mainly from the
Protectorate) to concentration camps in the East.

Not long ago a knowledgeable Western student of Czech and Slovak
history wrote: 'Arguably, neither [Masaryk and Beneš] fully understood
what being Slovak really meant.'[16] While this attribute could be extended to
other Czech politicians and intellectuals (be they bourgeois or communist),
the problem is to explain it. Without an explanation, it is not possible to
understand how and why the Federative State of Czechs and Slovaks split
on 31 December 1992/1 January 1993, into the Czech Republic and
Slovakia.

The historical background of the process(es) that eventually, despite
intermittent close ties between Czechs and Slovaks, gave rise to the separation is discussed by Dušan Kováč who in his study weaves the political, linguistic, religious, intellectual and constitutional threads of the story. He
starts by stating that Czechs and Slovaks are two distinct nations with two
distinct languages 'easily comprehensible to both nations'. Kováč draws
attention to the fact that while Czechs had developed into a nation against
the background of having had their own state, the Slovaks had not. They

were for 1,000 years part of the Hungarian state. 'Thus', writes Kováč, 'the historically separate development of the ethnically and linguistically close Czechs and Slovaks has been the decisive element in their differentiation.'

Kováč stresses that the foundation of the common state of Czechs and Slovaks, after the fall of the Austro-Hungarian monarchy, was the optimal solution for both nations. He underlines this by quoting the memorable pronouncement by the leader of Slovak Catholics, Andrej Hlinka, made even before the war came to an end (May 1918): 'Let us not avoid the question and admit frankly that we are for the Czechoslovak orientation. The thousands years' marriage with the Magyars has been a failure. We have to part.'

The establishment of the democratic republic opened the way for unprecedented national, educational, cultural and social progress in inter-war Slovakia. This positive side of its existence is not in question. The negative side was Prague centralism fuelled by Czechoslovakism which opposed the idea of Slovak autonomy. As Kováč points out, autonomist objectives began to dominate political life in Slovakia during the 1930s.

The problem of full Czech–Slovak equality remained despite impulses in favour of it, which came from the Slovak uprising against the clerico-fascist Slovak State in August 1944 and after the restoration of the Czechoslovak Republic in 1945. In fact, neither under the postwar presidency of Beneš nor under his communist successors the situation was solved in a manner that would satisfy the political representation of both nations. It was a fateful legacy which, as Kováč puts it,

revealed itself fully when the activities of democratic institutions were restored after November 1989. It was not only the constitutional issue but the question of mutual relations in general that contributed to the deep crisis that arose between Czechs and Slovaks and the dissolution of the common state in 1992.

III

Recently emphasis has been placed on the historico-philosophical pre-occupations of the Czechs (extending over 150 years and possibly unique in the European context) with finding grounds that vindicate their national existence and, indeed, give it a deeper meaning.[17] To all intents and purposes, modern debate on this question was initiated by T. G. Masaryk in articles and books in the 1890s.[18] In them he developed a broad interpretation of the Czech national revival at the end of the eighteenth century and during the first half of the nineteenth century, which became both influential and consequential in ideological and political struggles in the Czech Lands (and to a lesser extent in Slovakia) until the end of the communist era.

In 1895 for Masaryk – his emphasis varied at different stages of his life and events – the Czech national revival resulted from two intertwined strands. One concerned with the German-channelled European Enlightenment ideas, and the other rooted in the religious humanism of the Czech Reformation, set in motion by the Hussite movement.

Naturally, the enthusiastic struggle for revival and for cultural awakening had to be founded on a unified philosphical outlook. All mental work, all practical effort requires a clear and firm philosophical foundation. Otherwise, life would become but a series of isolated episodes, and no thoughtful, authentic person could tolerate such an existence. The philosophical perspective can take many forms, but every thinking individual must have an ultimate philosophic base.

Our awakeners, too, needed this foundation and discovered it in German philosophy. It is an irony of fate that German philosophy provided the groundwork for an anti-German national movement. In order to build a Czech culture, our awakeners used German philosophy, and even French and English thought came to us primarily through German mediation.

This, then, is the historic significance of German Enlightenment insofar as it served our awakeners towards the last part of the eighteenth century . . . Enlightened, humanist philosophy was in perfect accord with our yearning for progress and education. German philosophy and science thus repaid an old debt. The Czech Reformation movement had spilled over onto German soil and had fertilized it for the growth of new ideas. Thousands upon thousands of Czech exiles, the finest flower of a suppressed people, enriched German blood and German spirit. In its turn, the German philosophy of the eighteenth and nineteenth centuries repaid its debt to the Czech people and helped our awakeners rouse the nation from its long torpor. In a sense, the German, English, and French Enlightenment was a development and elaboration of the leading ideas of the Czech Reformation.[19]

Masaryk's position on the salient historical significance of the Czech Reformation for the making of the modern Czech nation was rejected as devoid of historical substance by contemporary representative Czech academic historiography: calmly by Jaroslav Goll (1846–1929) and polemically by Josef Pekař (1870–1937).[20] This question developed into a celebrated controversy, between Masaryk and Pekař, whose comprehension requires the awareness that it turned on interrelated questions such as: what constitutes historical facts, can they be value-free, and what is the cognitive status of historical and historico-philosophical analysis (theory) for political action (practice)? They feature in Jaroslav Marek's broad inquiry into the status of history as a scholarly (scientific) discipline. For one thing, Marek declares historical knowledge to be a philosophical, theoretical problem in itself. For another thing, Marek sees philosophy entering Pekař's positivist cast of mind, and affecting his practice as a historian, through his antagonism to what he regarded as speculative history tied to the Enlightenment and Romanticism.[21]

It was Pekař's criticism that Masaryk, in disregard/ignorance of facts established by unbiased scholarship, went beyond them and imputed a 'meaning' to national history which Pekař considered as a doubtful exercise in itself. Even if we accept Pekař's point about the dubiousness of the search for the meaning of history, it would be naïve to view him as a white knight of pure, value-free historical knowledge. For example, he was by no means free of political and social philosophy of history in his critique of the harmful consequences of the Hussite movement for Czech history. When all is said and done, Pekař was 'reluctant to accept revolutionary ideas and political parties that proclaimed a new democratic and social order'.[22] And it is this attitude that led him, before 1918, to reject the notion of a Czech (Czechoslovak) state outside the Habsburg monarchy, promoted by Masaryk. It is no accident that Pekař's name is not to be found among the 222 Czech writers and representatives of Czech culture who signed an open letter by mid-May in 1917 addressed to the Czech members of the Reichsrat. Sitting as they were on the fence, the deputies were urged to defend Czech national interests with the view of a future 'democratic Europe of self-legislating and free nations'.[23]

As it turned out, Czechoslovakia alone among the successor states remained a bourgeois democracy during its twenty years of effective independence. It is also no accident that Pekař, no friend of radical social and political change, was approached by representatives of the Right to be the candidate for the presidency in the succession to Masaryk.[24]

Given the weight of the Masaryk–Pekař controversy in the past, it is worthy of note that the contributors to the volume – except for the Petráňs – take virtually no notice of it. The perspective is to search not for a 'meaning' of Czech history, but to make sense of it, i.e., to understand it. As to the historiographical method, there is a clear shift from the still perceptible Marxist point of view in *Živá a mrtvá minulost* towards a variety of approaches extending from traditional history writing to 'semiohistory' in *Bohemia in History*.

It is near at hand to look briefly, in the two books, at the respective treatments of the Hussite Revolution and the Battle of the White Mountain, arguably the two major landmarks in the history of Bohemia up to the early seventeenth century. They have been persistently in the foreground of interest to Czech historians and non-historians for their real or perceived national and international connotations.

Compared with his previous account, the most significant change in Šmahel's contribution to *Bohemia in History* pertains to the raising of the question whether the Hussite Revolution, in the context of fifteenth-century Bohemia, was an anomaly. His discussion and his affirmation that the upheaval was indeed an anomaly is of wider interest than just to historians of the Reformation. Essentially, Šmahel's examination addresses the general issue whether the history of great movements in the development of human thought and action, such as the Reformation, conform to a norm. This connects with the question whether, in Europe, there was one Reformation proceeding in phases or whether there were more Reformations.[25]

What of the White Mountain problematic? Without going into further detail, what is common to both essays on the subject is the call to discern between historical reality and myth when it comes to evaluating concretely, from the specific Czech national point of view, the extent of adversities and sufferings which befell the Czech Lands in the Counter-Reformationary aftermath of the Battle of the White Mountain during 1620–1781. It concerns the perception of the political, religious, national, social, economic and cultural consequences in the period denoted in Czech historiography and literature as the 'Period of Darkness' (*obdobi temna*). A crucial concept in the raising of Czech national consciousness in the nineteenth century, it continued (despite doubts about its general validity) to have a national(ist) connotation in Czech politics long into the twentieth century.

In particular the constitutional follow up became a major theme in Czech historical and political literature which had largely adopted a negative view: Czech statehood was suppressed. Unhistorically, it was taken to have been restored after 300 years when the Czechoslovak Republic came into being in 1918. Within two decades, after the Munich Agreement and as a bitter fruit of it, the new state ceased to exist. Not surprisingly, the roads to the White Mountain and Munich, including the repercussions, have evoked comparisons. Thus historical parallels have been drawn between the failures by the leaders of the uprising and that of the Republic (President Beneš) to assess realistically the contemporary international state of affairs. Whereas the former counted on outside Protestant assistance which did not materialize, the latter believed that the Western democracies would not abandon democratic Czechoslovakia in order to appease anti-democratic Nazi Germany which occurred. The censure that in both situations the country's representatives misjudged the role of power politics and self-interest is not unjustified. Yet there are those who forget this background to the Munich Agreement while criticizing Beneš's policies and blaming him for the events that generated it. To omit to pay any attention to the ubiquitous anti-Soviet component in the ideology and policies of Chamberlain and Daladier that brought them to Munich to sit down with Hitler and Mussolini and sign the Agreement, heralding the end of Masaryk's republic, is to be economical with historical truth. Surely this is to marginalize the broader international political and military framework of deliberate diplomatic moves not to involve the Soviet Union that allowed the conclusion of the Munich Agreement.[26]

Placed into national and international context, the Munich Agreement represents a landmark in the history of Bohemia (Czechoslovakia) of significance akin to that of the Hussite Revolution and the Battle of the White Mountain. It is of more than passing interest that this was acknowledged, in 1977, in a *samizdat* analysis of the 'Prague Spring' as follows: 'The Munich period and the war years are also in my opinion the key to comprehending everything that has happened and the way it has happened since then to the present.'[27] After 1989 a scholarly debate over this subject has not developed. This has something to do with uncertainties, in Czechoslovak historical context, in how to make sense of the communist era, including the 'Prague Spring'. How to deal with a time period lasting almost forty years, which seemingly had not blunted the population's attachment to socialism after the end of one-party rule?[28] Was this an accidental interregnum in Czechoslovak history? Was the movement underlying the 'Prague Spring' a historical anomaly – not unlike the Hussite movement – as hinted by Šmahel? This broaches the general issue of what is 'normal' and 'anomalous' in history.[29]

It goes without saying that a volume such as this has to be selective. What emerges retrospectively is that the Hussite Revolution, the Battle of the White Mountain, the Munich Agreement and the 'Prague Spring' stand out as historical events that transcend the home dimension. These and other events of lesser or no international significance happened because they were caused to happen. In dealing with them there is no need to search for a 'meaning'. In words of a great historian the object is 'to understand and explain *why* things turned out the way they did, and how they hang together'.[30]

Notes

1 After the invasion of Czechoslovakia by military units of the Soviet Union and its allies (Poland, Hungary, German Democratic Republic and Bulgaria) on 21 August 1968, I left the country to take up a one-year Exchange Fellowship that had previously been arranged between the Czechoslovak Academy of Sciences and the American National Academy of Sciences. As my wife, Alice Teichova who accompanied me to the USA, and I profoundly disagreed with the intervention of the Soviet bloc, we chose not to return after the expiry of the Fellowship in May 1969. We then proceeded to Cambridge (England) where we

were offered short-term visiting posts at King's College and University College (now Wolfson College) respectively.

2 In a footnote on the last page of the work, F. Graus stresses that his introductory essay was completed on 20 March 1967 and that the other seven authors, while acquainted with it, had not based their account on it. The whole manuscript was delivered to press on 3 November 1967. It is not without interest that this offering to anti-dogmatic Marxist historiography was brought out in 1968 by Svoboda, the publishing house of the Central Committee of the Communist Party of Czechoslovakia. Even before the reprobations and purges during the 'normalization' period after the suppression of the 'Prague Spring', J. Válka published a perceptive review: 'Živá a mrtvá minulost', *Dějiny a současnost*, 5, 11 (1969), ii–iv. That the collection remained unknown in the West is not unexpected. What surprises is that, as far as one can make out, it had no place in 'underground' debates about approaches to Czech history during the 'normalization' period. Here the two-volume *samizdat* (typewritten manuscript) collection, published in 1986 and 1987, *Pojetí českých dějin* [Conception of Czech history] may be singled out. An ambitious contemporary inquiry into the history of Bohemia from the end of the eighteenth century to the Nazi occupation in 1939 was Podiven's *Češi v dějinách nové doby (Pokus o zrcadlo)* [Czechs in modern history (An attempt to mirror their past)]. Originally intended as a *samizdat* publication, it appeared after the 'Velvet Revolution' in 1991. Podiven is a pseudonym derived from *údiv* (astonishment/amazement) and adopted by three authors – Petr Pithart (jurist), Petr Příhoda (psychiatrist) and Milan Otáhal (historian) – who collaborated under difficult conditions for fourteen years. Nor does *Živá a mrtvá minulost* attract attention in the still rather sporadic post-1989 discussions on interpretations of the past of the Czech Lands.

3 Known as the Knight-errant King and supporting the French side, the blind John died in the Battle at Crécy. 'King Edward did all honour to the dead king, placed his body in his own tent and then sent it to Germany for burial. It was on this memorable occasion that the Black Prince assumed the crest and insignia of his fallen enemy; and the three ostrich feathers and the motto *Ich dien* may be regarded as the first direct link between England and Bohemia.' Cf. R. W. Seton-Watson, *A History of the Czechs and Slovaks* (Hamden, 1965), p. 26.

4 Quoted from the English version of the Founding Charter printed as a fly sheet by the Charles University publishing house Karolinum (nd). The original was taken away from Charles University Archives in 1945 and is missing. For the published version of the original, see V. Hrubý (ed.), *Archivum Coronae regni Bohemiae* (Prague, 1928), II, p. 68–9.

5 In 1526, after the Battle of Mohács in which the childless Jagiellon King Louis II of Bohemia and Hungary lost his life in fighting the Turks, Charles's V younger brother who ruled over the hereditary Austrian domains (*Erblande*) became King Ferdinand I of Bohemia and Hungary (1526–1564). Thus 1526 began to be regarded as the year in which 'Habsburg monarchy' – the entity linking Austria, Bohemia and Hungary – was born.

6 R. J. W. Evans, *The Making of the Habsburg Monarchy 1550–1700 An Interpretation* (Oxford, 1979), p. 66.

7 *Ibid.*, p. 68.

8 J. Folta, Z. Horský, L. Nový, I. Seidlerová, J. Smolka and M. Teich, *Dějiny exaktních věd v českých zemích do konce 19. století* [History of exact sciences in the Czech Lands up to the end of the 19th century] (Prague, 1961), with Russian and English summaries.

9 According to the census of 1930, the national distribution of population in Czechoslovakia was (percentages): Czechoslovaks (66.91), Ruthenians (3.79), Germans (22.32), Magyars (4.78), Jews (1.29), Poles (0.57).

10 R. J. Overy, *War and the Economy in the Third Reich* (Oxford, 1994), p. 1.

11 Perhaps 5,000; cf. W. V. Wallace, *Czechoslovakia* (London and Tonbridge, 1977), p. 248.

12 Of comparative recent origin, the term *Sudetendeutsche* (Sudeten Germans) came into use after 1918. Before then Germans in Bohemia were known as *Deutschböhmen* (German Czechs). The term is used in eighteenth-century literature where it is differentiated from *Stockböhmen* (true-born Czechs). Cf. F. v. Hartig, *Kurze historische Betrachtungen ueber die Aufnahme und den Verfall der Feldwirthschaft bey verschiedenen Voelkern* (Prague–Vienna, 1786), pp. 381, 407–8; J. A. v. Riegger, *Skizze zu einer statistischen Landeskunde Böhmens* (Leipzig and Prague, 1793–4), pp. 102f. The Joint-Czech Historical Commission recently published in Czech and German an outline of German-Czech history since the nineteenth century in which the not customary term 'böhmische Deutsche' as the translation of 'čeští Němci' (Czech Germans) is to be found. Cf. *Konfliktgemeinschaft, Katastrophe, Entspannung Skizze einer Darstellung der deutsch-tschechischen Geschichte seit dem 19. Jahrhundert Konfliktní společenství, katastrofa, uvolnění Náčrt výkladu německo-českých dějin od 19. století* (Munich, 1996), p. 17. There is a question to be answered: how come that we do not meet *Deutschslowaken, Deutschungarn, Deutschpolen, Deutschrussen* but *Slowakeideutsche, Ungarndeutsche, Polendeutsche, Russlanddeutsche?* Has this not something to do with the latter not having identified themselves with Slovakia, Hungary, Poland, Russia to the same extent (if at all) as *Deutschböhmen* did with Bohemia? As long as this will not receive attention from Czech and German historiography, separate 'Sudeten German history' – which the Commission rejects – will throw its shadow.

13 Es enstand ein allgemeiner deutsch-tschechischer Gegensatz, in dem die Gewichte viel zu ungleich verteilt waren, als daß ein echter Ausgleich wirklich möglich gewesen wäre. Schon in der Hussitenzeit drohte die Sprache zum ausschließlichen Symbol zu werden, die alles andere überdeckte. Eine verhängnisvolle Entwicklung hatte sich angebahnt, die oft durch die Komik des 'Taferlstreites' für den oberflächlichen Betrachter ihre wahre Tragik verbarg. Eine echte Tragik, mit Schuld und Unschuld auf beiden Seiten und ohne Möglichkeit einer echten Neutralität. Eine Tragödie, in der ein großer Einsatz an Mut, Opferwillen, an gemeinsamen Leiden und Schaffen verspielt wurde.

Eine Tragik, in der sich der Einzelne oft unschuldig in eine Schuld verstrickte, eine Tragödie, die sich abspielte und deren Szenen nicht mehr wiederholbar sind.

See F. Graus, 'Die Bildung eines Nationalbewußtseins im mittelalterlichen Böhmen (Die vorhussitische Zeit)', *Historica*, 13 (1966), 5–49 (pp. 48–9). Cf. also F. Graus, *Die Nationenbildung der Westslawen im Mittelalter* (Sigmaringen, 1980), *passim*.

Illustrations 10 and 14 are mirror images of human tragedies in the Czechoslovak border regions connected with the flight/expulsion of the Czech population in 1938 and expatriation of the German population in 1945.

14 It is of more than passing interest that the portraits and biographical sketches of two Jewish learned rabbis, Jonathan Eybenschütz and David Oppenheimer, were incorporated into one of the representative publications of the Enlightenment in Bohemia: *Abbildungen Boehmischer und Maehrischer Gelehrten und Kuenstler nebst kurzen Nachrichten von ihrem Leben und Wirken*, 4 parts (Prague, 1773–82); *Effigies virorum eruditorum atque artificum Bohemiae et Moraviae, una cum brevi vitae operumque ipsorum enarratione*, 2 parts (Prague, 1773–5). It was edited by the Piarist historian [M.] A. Voigt (1733–87), who eight years before the Toleration Patent of 1781 justified the inclusion remarkably as follows:

> Toleration must be upheld in the Republic of Scholars more so than in any other society. We would commit a sin against this contract unanimously agreed between true scholars and against the thinking of our philosophical age if we would leave out a few worthy native scholars from our list. This only because they belong to a religious community which though different from ours has, on the contrary, at all times nourished in its midst great men of genius and enlightened heads.
>
> Cf. *Abbildungen*, pt. 1. pp. 118–22.

15 Quoted by I. Herben, *T. G. Masaryk*, 5th edn (Prague, 1946), p. 87. For a brief critical assessment of Masaryk's views on the 'Jewish Question', see M. A. Riff, 'The ambiguity of Masaryk's attitudes on the "Jewish Question", in R. B. Pynsent (ed.), *T. G. Masaryk (1850–1937*, vol. 2: *Thinker and Critic* (Basingstoke and London, 1989), pp. 77–87; cf. also S. Beller, 'The Hilsner Affair, anti-Semitism and the individual in the Habsburg Monarchy at the turn of the century', *ibid.*, pp. 52–76. It is perhaps worthy of note that in one of the recent, altogether rare, examinations of the Hilsner Affair, the historian B. Černý refers to the Czech writer Jiří Gruša suggesting a link between Franz Kafka's *Trial* and Hilsner's trial. Cf. B. Černý, *Justiční omyl (Hilsneriada)* [Judicial error (the Hilsner Affair)] (Prague, 1990), p. 121.

16 W. V. Wallace, 'Masaryk and Beneš and the creation of Czechoslovakia: a study in mentalities', in H. Hanak (ed.), *T. G. Masaryk (1850–1937)*, vol. 3: *Statesman and Cultural Force* (Basingstoke and London, 1989), pp. 71–85 (p. 78).

17 M. Havelka (ed.), *Spor o smysl českých dějin 1895–1938* [The controversy about the meaning of Czech history 1895–1938] (Prague, 1995), p. 7. In this section I draw on some of my previous work. Cf. M. Teich, 'Bohemia: from darkness into light', in R. Porter and M. Teich (eds.), *The Enlightenment in National Context* (Cambridge,

1981), pp. 141–63, 215–17, 247–53; M. Teich, 'The meaning of history: Czechs and Slovaks', *The Historical Journal*, 39 (1996), 553–602.

18 *Česká otázka* [The Czech question] (1895); *Naše nynější krise* [Our present crisis] (1895); *Jan Hus* (1896); *Karel Havlíček* (1896).

19 T. G. Masaryk, *The Meaning of Czech History* (ed. with intro. R. Wellek, trans. P. Kussi) (Chapel Hill, 1974), pp. 17–18. There have been attempts to present Václav Havel, now the President of the Czech Republic, as Masaryk's spiritual heir. This certainly does not obtain when it comes to comparing Masaryk's positive and Havel's negative attitude to the Renaissance and the Enlightenment. Cf. V. Havel, 'The end of the modern era', *The New York Times*, 1 March 1992.

20 J. Pekař, 'Masarykova česká filosofie' [Masaryk's Czech philosophy], *Český časopis historický*, 18 (1912), 170–208.

21 J. Marek, *O historismu a dějepisectví* [On historism and historiography] (Prague, 1992), p. 168. The book was to be published in 1969. As was the case with other works of historical scholarship, its publication was prevented by the oppressive political system instituted as part of the backlash ('normalization'), prompted by the downfall of the 'Prague Spring'. The delay has not affected Marek's balanced, albeit concise treatment of the Masaryk–Pekař debate. This receives attention by contributors to Eva Kantůrková (ed.), *Pekařovské studie* [Pekař studies] (Prague, 1995), especially by the philosopher M. Machovec, 'Ke sporu mezi Masarykovou a Pekařovou filosofií českých dějin' [On the controversy between Masaryk's and Pekař's philosophy of Czech history], pp. 179–87. Originally this collection appeared in 1987 as a *samizdat* production to commemorate the 50th anniversary of Pekař's death. Cf. also Karel Kučera, 'Masaryk and Pekař: their conflict over the meaning of Czech history and its metamorphosis', in S. B. Winters (ed.), *T. G. Masaryk (1850–1937)*, vol. 1. *Thinker and Politician* (Basingstoke and London, 1989), pp. 88–105; M. Hauner, 'The meaning of Czech history: Masaryk versus Pekař', in Hanak (ed.), *Masaryk*, III, pp. 24–42; M. Kučera, *Pekař proti Masarykovi* [Pekař versus Masaryk] (Prague, 1995).

22 Kučera, 'Masaryk and Pekař', p. 105.

23 Cf. O. Urban, *Česká společnost 1848–1918* [Czech society 1848–1919] (Prague, 1982), p. 610.

24 The events surrounding the offer to Pekař and his rejection deserve more attention. According to an admittedly hostile account, Pekař eventually declined, pleading old age, loss of memory and ill-health. Cf. J. Pachta, *Pekař a pekařovština v českém dějepisectví* [Pekař and pekařism in Czech historiography] (Prague, 1950), p. 54. Martin Kučera believes that despite serious reservations *vis-à-vis* Masaryk's closest collaborator and choice Edvard Beneš (1884–1948), Pekař was not prepared to oppose him, on behalf of the extreme Right, in the presidential election of 1935. See his *Pekař proti Masarykovi*, p. 66. This made way for Bohumil Němec (1873–1966), the distinguished plant physiologist cum politician, to attempt unsuccessfully to attain the presidency. See also A. Gašparíková-Horáková, *U Masarykovcov Spomienky osobnej archivárky T. G. Masaryka* [with the Masaryks: reminiscences of T. G. Masaryk's personal archivist] (Bratislava,

1995), pp. 262, 265. For this reference I owe Eduard Kubů thanks.

25 See B. Scribner, 'A comparative overview', in B. Scribner, R. Porter and M. Teich (eds.), *The Reformation in National Context* (Cambridge, 1994), pp. 215–16. Cf. also F. Kavka, 'Bohemia', *ibid.*, pp. 149–50.

26 Here it is apposite to cite an old friend of Masaryk, R. W. Seton-Watson, not known for being in sympathy with the Soviet Union:

> Russia advised Prague to appeal to the League under Article XI or XVI, and was preparing for action though circumspectly, so as to give no excuse for the launching of an anti-Bolshevist campaign in the West . . . M. Litvinov's outspoken speech at the League assembly a week earlier, in which he advocated collective action and announced not only the readiness of the Russian army chiefs to confer with the French and Czech staffs, but even Russia's intention of joining the French in defence of Czechoslovakia. It is not too much to affirm that the attitude of Russia was clear and consistent throughout the crisis, whereas that of the two Western Powers was inexplicable on any other showing than that from the first they had no intention of helping Czechoslovakia, for otherwise their neglect of the first steps towards military cooperation in case of need would have been sheer insanity.
>
> See Seton-Watson, *A History of the Czechs and Slovaks*, pp. 366–7.

27 P. Pithart, *Osmašedesátý* [The year 1968], 3rd edn (Prague, 1990), p. 44. Following the *samizdat* edition, the book was published in Cologne under the pseudonym J. Sládeček in 1980. Up to 1968 the author taught constitutional law at Charles University in Prague, he was a signatory of Charter 77, and Prime Minister of the Czech Republic within the binational Federative State of Czechs and Slovaks (16 February 1990–2 July 1992). As mentioned in note 2, Pithart was one of the trio concealing identity under the pseudonym Podiven.

28 On 24 and 25 November 1989, the Research Institute of Public Opinion conducted a poll to determine the feelings and opinions of 260 persons from Prague and 450 persons across the country. Of these, 47% favoured 'something between socialism and capitalism', 45% approved of socialism and only 3% preferred capitalism. See 'Občané o politické situaci' [Citizens on the political situation], *Rudé Právo*, 27 November 1989.

29 It appears that the problem of anomaly/norm relationship in history is of great interest to Czech historians at present. A conference on 'Czechoslovakia: contingency or historical inevitability' was convened on 12 and 13 October 1993 by the Historical Institute of the Czech Academy of Sciences in Prague. See the papers in *Moderní dějiny*, 2 (1994), 7–195. This does not extend to treatments of the 'Prague Spring' which tend to be ahistorical. For an account of the 'Prague-Spring' limited to the year 1968, see J. Pauer's *Prag 1968 Der Einmarsch des Warschauer Paktes Hintergründe-Planung-Durchführung* (Bremen, 1995).

30 E. Hobsbawm, *Age of Extremes The Short Twentieth Century 1914–1991* (London, 1994), p. 3.

1

Boiohaemum-Čechy

JIŘÍ SLÁMA

Prehistory

Scattered archaeological findings indicate that the most ancient evidence of human beings in the Bohemian basin date from the Lower Palaeolithic epoch, more than half million years ago. This area's geographical situation, distinguished by a chain of border mountain ranges enclosing it all round, was very aptly described at the beginning of the twelfth century by the Czech Canon Cosmas (*c.* 1045–1125), author of the earliest chronicle of Bohemia written in Latin, *Chronica Boemorum*.[1] From the standpoint of physical anthropology, these humans belonged to the species of *Homo erectus*, one of the stages in the development of the present human type. The presence of the latter can be discerned some 35,000 years ago in a somewhat sudden manner over extensive territories throughout the entire Old World. Small hunting bands of *Homo sapiens* were undoubtedly responsible for the Upper Paleolithic cultures on Bohemian territory.

A truly radical transformation of the history of preliterate Bohemia occurred in consequence of new population groups arriving in Bohemia from the south-east, at the end of the sixth millennium BC. They introduced Neolithic agricultural civilization influenced by the achievements of human groups living in Asia Minor and the Near East. Differences in the way of life between the agricultural newcomers and the autochthonous hunters and fishermen were so far-reaching that specialists do not hesitate to resort to the term 'Neolithic revolution', radically changing all aspects of life of the period. For Europe, the Near East continued to be a source of new knowledge and inventions even in the following epochs, when sophisticated civilizations with the first written records emerged in the latter area not only in Mesopotamia and Egypt but, after a certain time, in other regions as well. One of the chief discoveries of this kind was undoubtedly the production and processing of metals. Non-European written records (especially from Asia Minor), outlining, at least for the second millennium BC, the earliest geographical diffusion of Indo-European languages, allow the assumption that the first Indo-Europeans, the most ancient territory of whom is usually sought north of the Black Sea and the Caucasus mountains, may be expected on Bohemian territory as early as the end of the 3rd millennium BC.

Roughly the same period of time witnessed the earliest origins of the most ancient civilization of the European continent, that of the Aegean, which progressed to the creation of its own writing system over a rather short period of time. Thus the first segment of Europe approached the threshold of history. With respect to the history of prehistoric human groups in the rest of Europe – including the territory of Bohemia – the gradual transfer of the major centre of civilization from the Aegean and Greece westward to the Apennine peninsula, during the first millennium BC was of far greater significance. In the second half of that millennium, the region in question saw the emergence of the powerful and advanced Roman state which, having held under its sway the earlier individual cultural centres of the whole Mediterranean, now by a series of military conquests proceeded to penetrate into hitherto prehistoric Europe.

This expansion, fuelled by political and economic power, was initiated by Julius Caesar's conquests of the territory of modern France in the fifties of the first century BC, and climaxed around the turn of the century with the occupation by the imperial legions of all lands west of the Rhine and south of the Danube. These events shortened the distance between the territory of Bohemia and the Roman world and, in consequence of this, events in the Bohemian basin in which the Roman imperial policy played an integral part in the early Christian era, started to attract the attention of contemporary writers. Thanks to their records, the population groups then resident on Bohemian territory shed their anonymity and we may quite safely assign them to the Celtic milieu.

Celtic tribes: the Boii

A number of hitherto unresolved problems burden the ethnogenesis and the earliest history of the Indo-European Celts who occupied, over the last centuries of the pre-Christian era, vast territories from the Atlantic coast via Central Europe and the Balkans as far as Asia Minor. From the fifth century BC, news of them gradually filtered into the Greek and Roman world. At the beginning of the following century, Celtic armed bands crossed the Alps from upper Danubian regions, heading for Italy. It took the fresh Roman republic more than two centuries and a considerable effort to win the battle with these dangerous intruders. Nor did the Celts remain unknown to the Greeks as groups of the former crossed the Carpathian basin and reached the Balkans, advancing even as far as Central and Eastern Anatolia where they lived for several centuries to come. St Paul the Apostle addressed one of his epistles to these Celts of Asia Minor in the first half of the Christian era.

The Celtic episode in the history of Bohemia, constituting most probably the eastern fringe of the oldest Celtic area, lasted for the five centuries terminating the pre-Christian era and represented without any doubt the apex of the preceding prehistorical development. From reports by Greek and Roman writers it emerges that the Celts lived in a tribal society. In addition to the institutions of the chieftain and tribal organization, this society was dominated by aristocratic kinship and a warrior elite. The importance of the latter grew especially in occupied territories where the Celts had to keep autochthonous groups at bay. Nevertheless, the generally higher cultural level of the Celts brought about gradual assimilation of these earlier ethnic groups on the territories where the Celts settled in overwhelming numbers. The Celts were the first inhabitants of prehistoric Central Europe who could exploit to the full the economic advantages following from widespread use of iron for the production of tools and weapons. The Celtic period witnessed not only the marked rise in technology levels of a number of arts and crafts, and the introduction of a number of discoveries, such as the use of the potter's wheel in ceramic production, iron ploughshares on wooden bases, and grinding corn between stone wheels, but also the establishment of specialized production sites from which blacksmiths, potters, jewellers, glassmakers, and other mastercraftsmen and women supplied their products to wide customer circles. All this led to the development of exchange activities and, later on, to the introduction of trade when, from the end of the second century BC Celtic groups initiated the minting of gold and silver coins, at first imitating Macedonian staters. The general development level reached by Celtic society and by its economy resulted ultimately in the Celts of Western Europe building extensive and heavily fortified central sites. These were observed by Julius Caesar, who referred to them by the distinctive Latin term *oppidum*. Such sites were probably handicraft, commercial, administrative and religious centres. In Bohemia, however, their building might have been accelerated from the end of the second century BC by the threat represented by Germanic tribes migrating from their homeland situated north of Bohemia, in Jutland and northern Germany.

The earliest Germanic–Celtic clashes were noted by some authors of the then distant Greek and Roman world. Poseidonius of Apamea, a Greek philosopher living *c.* 151–35 BC, is quoted by Strabo the geographer (66 BC–21 AD) to the effect that some time before 113 BC the Celtic Boii succeeded in repelling an attack of the Germanic Teutoni and Cimbri tribes, somewhere in the Hercynian Forest. Though we can hardly be certain of the location of this conflict – the 'Hercynian Forest' was a descriptive term of Greek and Roman geographical thought denoting an extensive area north of the Danube from the sources of this river as far as the Carpathian Mountains – this battlefield is most frequently sought in the region from the Upper Rhineland to the Bohemian basin. After their victory, the Boii left their settlement areas for a period of some duration, for reasons which remain unknown. During the period *c.* 100–50 BC they went to Hungarian Danubia, settling down in the territories of the later Roman provinces of Illyricum and Pannonia. The Boii referred to here belonged to one of the most important Celtic tribes, whose existence is attested to at several European sites.[2] An old Celtic tradition locates their homeland in the territory of Gallia (France), and adjacent upper Danubia. In the fourth century BC internal strife and pressures within the community induced some groups to take up arms and go to Italy where they clashed with the armies of the young Roman republic. As late as the second century, groups of Boii lived in the Po Plains in the vicinity of present-day Bologna whose name still preserves Celtic linguistic traces. In the following era the Boii of this territory succumbed fairly quickly to Romanization. Nevertheless, a part of them managed to preserve their identity by migrating back to the north, most probably into central Danubia. There they formed an alliance with the Celtic Taurisci tribe, as well as with some Boii who came subsequently from the Hercynian Forest. In their new settlement zones, however, the Boii suffered a crushing defeat from the Dacian king Burebista, whose extensive empire included the left side of the lower Danube, around 60 BC. From that time on, Upper Pannonian territories devastated by the war bore the characteristic denomination of 'Boiic desert'. Such a designation was undoubtedly somewhat exaggerated as written sources attest to the presence of residual Boii groups there as late as the second century AD. At any rate, the fortunes of the Boii were at an especially low ebb in the first century BC. The survivors took the westward course upstream the Danube and settled down somewhere in central Gallia in Julius Caesar's times. There, of course, they constituted hardly more than a shadow of the former power and glory of the tribe and did not produce any more significant historical record in their new residential areas.

At least a part of Boiic history must have taken place in Bohemia, and the Boii are the first ethnic group inhabiting Bohemian territory to be recorded. Of course, they were not exclusively the residents. In addition to the autochthonous population groups, they had the Celtic Volcae-Tectosages tribe for neighbours. In the course of its history, the latter tribe, shrouded in myths and sagas as early as the Greek and Roman age, also split, the individual segments taking refuge in various territories both inside and outside Europe (in Greece and Asia Minor). The growing pressure of Germanic groups started the slow dislodgement of the Celtic groups then resident on Bohemian territory as early as the first half of the final century BC. The fall of Celtic power over Bohemia, however, did not occur until the very end of that century. A new factor coming into play was Roman military penetration as far as the Rhine and Danube rivers which, together with the Germanic northern front, enclosed the Celtic groups of Central Europe from the south and west.

Germanic tribes

An event of prime importance for the history of Bohemian territory was the victory of the imperial legions under the command of Nero Claudius Drusus over the Germanic Marcomanni tribe somewhere in the Main river basin 9 BC. Retreating towards the east, the defeated Germanic groups finally reached territories occupied by the residual Boii groups. Historians and archaeologists converge in locating the areas of their settlement in central and northern Bohemia as well as in eastern Bavaria. Upon their arrival, Germanic warriors did away with Celtic political power and subverted the economic base of Celtic society. At present we are unable to estimate the time for which the Boii survivors lived on in Bohemia under Germanic rule. The assertion of P. Cornelius Tacitus, the Roman historian (c. 55–c. 120), concerning the eviction of the Boii population by the Marcomanni is probably an exaggeration. The Germanic newcomers took over not only some of the technological know-how of the Celtic groups but also the name of the land which they occupied. This name, referred to by the Classical authors Strabo, Velleius Paterculus and Tacitus, was 'land of the Boii' or 'Boiohaemum'.[3] This designation, denoting the land for the millennium to come, lives to this day in Romance and Germanic languages (Bohemia, Bohême, Böhmen). From the viewpoint of social history, the entry of the Germanic groups into the development of Bohemia constituted a distinct reversal of the tide of history. The preceding Celtic society had all but reached the threshold of statehood. A comparable level of social development was attained by Bohemia for the second time only after nine centuries in a completely different political situation.

The Marcomanni groups who came to Bohemia were ruled by a chief called Marbod (Marobudus of the Roman sources), who had lived in his childhood as a hostage at the Roman imperial court. Classical records say that this Germanic 'king' – a barbarian rather by birth than by attitude, as they have it – inhabited in Boiohaemum a splendid residence with an adjacent fort. This settlement unit was known as Marobuduum and was especially popular among Roman merchants who brought valuable southern commodities there. Up to now, the persistent efforts of specialists to find the site of Marobuduum have failed. Using his Germanic army which, according to Roman sources, numbered more than 70,000 warriors as his main means of persuasion, Marbod extended his overlordship to a number of neighbouring Germanic groups, creating thus a rather heterogenous tribal union. In addition to Bohemia, his sphere of influence is likely to have included the lower Labe (Elbe) river regions, present-day Poland and Moravia, reaching as far as the Roman frontier on the Danube in the south. Marbod thus had again to cope with a situation he had previously sought to avoid by the resettlement of his tribe to Boiohaemum, that of a common frontier with the Romans. It need hardly be said that Rome must have viewed with suspicion a realm of this size so close to territories freshly conquered by its legions. Nevertheless, a military campaign against Marbod with a force of *c.* 120,000 legionnaires was averted only by a large-scale rebellion in the Roman province of Pannonia in 6 AD. Ultimately, however, Marbod's power was subverted by internal strife among the Germanic groups. In 19 AD, a Germanic chief named Catualda occupied Marbod's residence with his warriors, sending Marbod off to exile. He met the same fate two years later, having been deposed by Vibilius, chief of the Hermunduri tribe.

By a peculiar twist of fate, both Marbod and Catualda took refuge with the Romans, ending up as lifelong exiles in the Empire. The Romans posted the military retinues of both these chiefs somewhere in the area of present-day south-west Slovakia, keeping a watchful eye on them.

Imperial interest in events on the territory of Boiohaemum waned after the collapse of Marbod's power. After the three decades when Boiohaemum entered history, writers of the Classical world diverted their attention to other issues and the land reverted to prehistory. For eight centuries to come, elements of material culture once again become the chief source for writing the history of the Bohemian basin.[4] Over the first century AD, archaeological evidence bears out the weakening of commercial contacts with the Roman milieu as well as a certain depopulation of the territory of Bohemia. The first half of the second century AD saw a certain increase in the quantity of Roman imports brought to Bohemia. Nevertheless, the Roman influence over territories situated at greater distances from the frontier declined, especially after the Marcomannic wars (166–180), in which the Germanic warriors, crashing through the Roman military border in middle Danubia, had advanced as far as northern Italy before their onslaught could be brought under control. This, of course, was relevant to Bohemia, although isolated imports from the Empire such as coins do turn up every now and then. On the other hand, contacts between Bohemia and Germanic groups living in the middle part of the Elbe area and in Thuringia grew stronger, especially from the fourth century AD. The Bohemian basin was bypassed by the tempestuous events of the Migration period of the fourth to sixth centuries when the Roman domination of the former provinces gave in and even the Empire itself collapsed. In this direction, one of the decisive factors is likely to have been constituted by the ranges of border mountains, barring access to the land. At the close of the fifth century, Bohemia played host to a Germanic tribe, the Langobards, who passed through from the north towards south Moravia and Danubia, but archaeological data indicate that at that time, the population density of Germanic Bohemia declined. A fundamental change in the settlement of the land came about in the first half of sixth century with the advent of new population groups – the Slavs.

The first Slavs

The Slavs, who were among the speakers of Indo-European languages, emerged as an ethnic unit only in the Migration period. At that time they lived over extensive territories situated south, north and north-east of the Carpathian mountain ridge. At this earliest period of their history, they were divided into two groups, the western Sklavinoi and the eastern Antoi. Historical sources shed no light on their massive expansion from Transcarpathia eastwards to the Russian plains, southwards to the Balkan peninsula and westwards into Central Europe, with the exception of their penetration of the Balkans, then held by the Byzantine Empire. The Slavic expansion went on in several directions and unlike other migrations, such as those of the Germanic groups which moved on for centuries, proceeded at rather a quick pace. This is attested to by the considerable stylistic uniformity of the earliest Slavic artefacts. Unlike the military campaigns of Celtic and Germanic groups, which were set in motion by warrior groups commanded by their chiefs and kings, Slavic penetration of Central Europe assumed the character of agricultural colonization.

The first Slavic settlers passing through southern Poland westwards and coming to Bohemia via Moravia appeared on this territory some time in the first half of the sixth century. The Slavs appeared on the Central European stage with a material culture coresponding, by and large, to archaeological

assemblages of the pre-Celtic periods. In Bohemia, they ultimately incorporated and assimilated individual groups of the earlier Germanic settlers,
borrowing from them a number of local river and mountain toponyms.
Philological experts have attributed Celtic origins to some of these names.

Following the first wave of Slavic immigrants, a second one came from
Danubia some fifty to seventy-five years later; unfortunately, the chronology
of early Slavic material culture lacks the precision which would allow more
exact dating. The immigrants in this second wave may have been descendants of the Antoi who advanced from Transcarpathia between the Black
Sea and the Carpathian mountain range into lower Danubia. From there
they turned into the interior of the Balkan peninsula; on this front,
Byzantine resistance was weakened by the deployment of imperial troops
in the Mediterranean, by local depopulation brought about by the preceding turbulent Migration-period events, by the consequences of bubonic
plague which had swept the Classical world, then under Emperor Justinian
(527–565), as well as by the brigandage of nomadic Avars who joined in
attacking Byzantine territories after their migration into the Carpathian
basin in 567. In some cases, the Byzantine administration might have
attempted to employ the incoming Slavs for operations against the Empire's
enemies such as, for instance, the Langobards. On the territories of former
Roman provinces Slavic groups came into contact with the fully fledged
civilization of the Classical world, as well as with the administrative and military organization of the Byzantine Empire. This resulted in a considerable
rise of their economic and cultural level and had an impact on their social
structures. These are the very first Slavic groups to display unmistakable evidence for the existence of tribes. At a date around 600, some of the Balkan
Slavic groups followed the Danube westwards and arrived at the territory
of Bohemia via southern Slovakia and Moravia. The motive for their
departure may perhaps be sought in the destabilization brought about by
Avaric incursions and perhaps also in the Byzantine counter-offensive at the
close of the sixth century, which diverted for a certain time the pressure of
invaders of the Byzantine realms. It is interesting to note that the Balkan
origin of the Slavic newcomers to Bohemia was known to some authors of
Czech medieval literature several centuries later. The first wave of Slavic
immigrants occupied only the most fertile areas of Bohemia; in the later
phase, the incoming groups settled the whole territory as far as the border
mountains, albeit in a dispersed fashion. As against the first Slavic colonists,
the general cultural level of this second-wave people was visibly higher.
After a gap of some 600 years they again started building hillforts and they
lived in a tribal organization.[5]

Historical records do shed some light on the events which took place in the Bohemian basin in the first half of the seventh century. At that time, Slavs residing in the north-west border range of the Avar khanate rose in revolt against their Avar masters, and proceeded to create their own independent territory, led by a Frankish merchant named Samo (623–658). The location of this realm is much debated. Its centre is most frequently sought in south-western Slovakia and the adjacent Moravian and Austrian territories; at any rate, however, Bohemia must have constituted one of its border regions. In 631, Samo's warriors inflicted a crushing defeat on Frankish troops at a site called Wogastisburc. Unfortunately, the exact position of this locality connected with a historical event of great importance remains unknown. The defeat of the invaders brought an end to the attempts of the Frankish Empire to extend its influence eastwards as far as the Byzantian border. These trends came back to life some 150 years later.[6]

The political situation of Central Europe displayed profound changes from the close of the eighth century. In several campaigns its western part was conquered and incorporated into the Frankish Empire by Charlemagne (768–814). This expansion, aimed at Bavaria and present-day Austrian and Hungarian Danubia, where it extinguished the Avars' power, brought the border of the Frankish Empire into direct contact with Slavic groups resident in Bohemia. For the whole ninth century, Frankish emperors who had brought back to life the ancient title 'Roman Emperor' (designating the highest lay representative of Western Christianity from *c.* 800), aimed at the subjugation of their eastern Slavic neighbours. In a number of military campaigns they repeatedly invaded both Bohemia and Moravia. In the course of the ninth century, the latter region saw the emergence of a mighty Slavic empire which by the mid tenth century was called Great Moravia by Constantine VII Porphyrogenétos, a cultured Emperor of Byzantium. Relationships between Great Moravian and Frankish power set the stage for the history of Bohemia in the ninth century.

Duces: the Přemyslides

The same period which ushered in more intensive contacts between Slavic groups also witnessed the emergence of an elite group referred to in the sources as *duces*, who rose to dominant positions in the political and military spheres. The archaeological contribution to the study of this sustained emergence is represented by investigations of hillforts and all kinds of walled sites. Excavations have indicated that within the precincts, *duces* built residences enclosed by palisades and consisting of a group of structures. The burials of these *duces*, some of whom were richly provided with jewellery (although at the beginning this included only male ornaments associated with the wearing of swords and spurs), weapons, and other valuable objects of Western European, Great Moravian and even non-European origin, are an eloquent testament to contact between the 'ducal' milieu and neighbouring and distant civilizations.

In the earliest phase of its existence the function of the 'Duke of the Land' (the term used by the earliest sources for the chief ruler of Bohemia) was not hereditary and clearly limited by the deliberations of the assembly of all free inhabitants of the duchy. All *duces* of the land took care to attach to themselves a group of selected warriors – a military retinue, which constituted the crack troops in all military operations. Dependent only on the *duces*, this retinue gradually assumed the role of forwarding their ambitions, irrespective of the interests of the free inhabitants of the ducal domains.[7]

The references to Czech *duces*, turning up every now and then in Frankish sources, clearly indicate their important social position. These *duces* by and large took a common course of action in decisive political events. A case in point is the adoption of Christianity by fourteen Czech *duces* at the court of King Ludwig the German at Regensburg, in January 845. This collective decision of the *duces* may well have been motivated by their desire to deprive the Franks of a pretext for military incursion into Bohemian territory. Things were put into proper perspective by the hostile Frankish action the very next year. This made the Czech *duces* see that they calculated wrongly and they gave up Christianity.

In the absence of a common enemy the alliance among the *duces* loosened, and they became strong rivals. Powerful enough to subdue a weaker neighbour, none of these *duces* succeeded in unifying the entire Bohemian basin. In spite of that, power became concentrated in the course of the ninth century. In 872, for example, an alliance of six Czech *duces* challenged a Frankish incursion under the command of Liutbert, Archbishop of Mainz, which was heading for the lower Vltava river region. Compared with 845, the number of allies had clearly decreased. The six *duces* of 872 included Bořivoj, the first member of the Přemyslide dynasty ever to be documented by history who ruled during the 870s and 880s. Next to nothing is known about the origins of this lineage, the scions of which held the Czech throne until 1306. Unquestionably, Bořivoj turned up at the very moment when influence of the power of the adjacent Great Moravia came to a climax in Bohemia.[8]

The written sources hint that Bořivoj, perhaps together with other Czech *duces*, had to acknowledge his formal dependence on Svatopluk (871–894), the ruler of Great Moravia. At some point during the 870s, however, Přemyslides began to be regarded as the leading aristocratic family in Bohemia. Their power base was constituted by a not very sizable duchy situated at the very heart of Bohemia. This territory underwent a number of radical changes under the Přemyslide Bořivoj, apparently with Moravian help. This included the suppression of the power of the assembly (hitherto the dominant body in decisions to be taken in major issues involving the Slavonic community); the establishment of the hereditary ducal function and limiting it to one single lineage; gradual enserfment of the population; forced exaction of a variety of dues from villagers; and the emergence of a primitive organization to serve as a means of control over the entire population. In this manner the Přemyslide domain acquired features of a true early medieval state. All these transformations came to a climax when Bořivoj converted to Christianity, around 880, at the court of Svatopluk of Great Moravia. In addition to having played the role of the exclusive vehicle of cultural and spiritual values, Christianity constituted an indispensable tool for early state-building on account of its struggle against the pagan ideology of the preceding social structure.[9]

Up to about 935, the above-mentioned Přemyslide dynastic territory of central Bohemia provided the stage for the whole history of this ambitious family. The remaining territories of Bohemia were administered by other *duces* who, however, formally acknowledged their dependence on the Přemyslides, apparently from Bořivoj's times. None of them managed to create a domain such as that held by the Přemyslides in central Bohemia. The focal point of the Přemyslide dynastic domain was the Castle of Prague, the chief residence of the ruling member of the family. By the end of the ninth century, Prague became the place of residence of the country's ruler, keeping this privileged position until the modern age. In a very short time Prague also became an ecclesiastical centre, the official residence of the representative of the Regensburg episcopal see to whose jurisdiction Bohemia belonged. From Bořivoj's times, the wood and clay architecture of the Castle was joined by the first stone churches, where in the tenth century the first Czech martyrs and saints were buried.

Below the Castle ramparts lay the most important market in Bohemia, strategically situated on a major overland route which crossed the European continent from west to east and continued farther into Asia. A series of 'frontier forts' built at distances between 26 and 34 km from Prague approximated the circular borderline of the Přemyslide domain. Most of these forts, usually presided over by members of the lineage who did not hold the ducal office, were close to important communication arteries. This ingenious positioning had no counterpart in Bohemia and may be viewed as an embryonic stage of the administrative organization which specialists refer to as the 'castle system'. In effect, in the Central European context, it constitutes the most ancient institution of public and legal character.

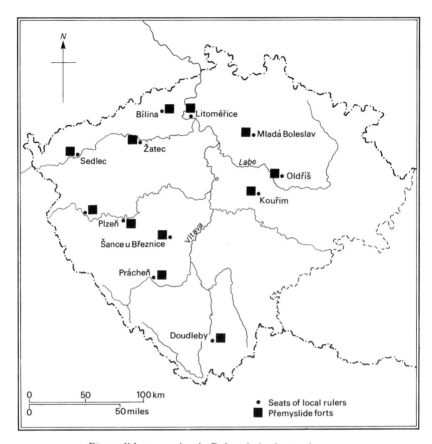

1. Přemyslide expansion in Bohemia in the tenth century.

The power structure of Bohemia just described lasted from the close of the ninth century, throughout the reigns of Bořivoj I, his sons Spytihněv I (?895–915) and Vratislav I (915–921) as well as of his grandson Václav [Wenceslas] (921–935) and matched the political situation emerging in Central Europe from the end of the ninth century. In that region Great Moravia and the East Frankish Empire faced serious difficulties: Great Moravia had collapsed altogether and the Empire had disintegrated into several independent duchies. This situation did away with threats from outside the Bohemian basin. A new factor on the scene concerned the nomadic Magyar tribes who, after settling in the Carpathian basin, spent the first half of the tenth century raiding territories from the Balkans to Western Europe. By and large, Bohemia enjoyed protection from such dangers behind her border mountains, though the Magyars passed through several times. Moreover, the Přemyslides sought to consolidate their positions by friendly relations with the Duke of Bavaria. A re-orientation of the political and strategic situation followed after 919 when the ambitious Henry, Duke of Saxony, was elected Emperor. Henry quickly restored the coherence of the Empire (from the time of his rule, the Empire was increasingly referred to as the German Empire – *regnum Teutonicorum*), embarking upon a course of expansion against the eastern Slavic neighbours. All this made the threat of an armed incursion into Bohemia merely a question of time.

The danger materialized in 929. At that time, Henry's army overwhelmed the Přemyslide troops, advanced as far as Prague and dictated the terms of Duke Wenceslas's capitulation. This military and political failure exposed the need for radical changes in the Czech setting. The divergence in solutions proposed for the imminent crisis may well have constituted one of the causes behind the discord between the ruling Duke Wenceslas and his younger but vigorous brother Boleslav. This discord climaxed in a tragedy: Wenceslas was murdered at Stará Boleslav on 28 September 935. On the one hand, this deed of political terrorism opened the way to a radical transformation of Czech society. On the other hand, it built the memory of Wenceslas as a saint and martyr and, later on, elevated the murdered duke to the status of patron saint of Bohemia. Also, it became clear that the territory of Bohemia could not be efficiently defended merely by the combined forces of the small warrior guards of individual members of the Přemyslide lineage and other semi-independent Czech *duces*. This purpose would have been best served by a more numerous retinue ('great guard') of several thousand warriors commanded solely by the ruling member of the Přemyslide dynasty.[10] Of course, such a design represented an economic problem, first and foremost, since the resources of the Přemyslide domain in central Bohemia could not bear such a burden. In the tenth-century context, such an undertaking required the economic resources of the whole land of Bohemia. Ultimately, the prerequisite was the dismantling of the rest of the semi-independent *duces*, up to that time co-existing with the Přemyslides, and the creation of a unified Přemyslide administration for the entire territory of Bohemia.

And all this actually came to pass in the course of the exceptionally long reign of Duke Boleslav I (935–972). It required both considerable determination and a great deal of political insight. On the basis of archaeological evidence, around 950 the hillforts in the territory of Bohemia (up to that time not governed by the Přemyslides directly) were being deserted and new sites, the foundation of the Přemyslide administration, were being established in their vicinity. This change connects with Boleslav's military operations against the individual Czech *duces*. Let us note that this is the last major event in the history of Bohemia which is evidenced primarily by archaeology, as no unequivocal information turns up in written sources.

That Duke Boleslav managed to assemble a 'great guard', is attested, for instance, by the participation of 1,000 Czech horsemen in the battle on the River Lech where the Magyars were defeated (955). This fact notwithstanding, the duke, a seasoned politician, always weighed up the situation before embarking on military action. The beginnings of Boleslav's foreign policy were dominated by his armed resistance to the successor of Emperor Henry, Otto I. After a war of fourteen years, Boleslav terminated the hostilities and formally recognized Otto's suzerainty in 950. This was clearly based on a reasoned estimate of the situation as Duke Boleslav considered it more prudent not to waste his warriors but to preserve them for then planned campaigns against Moravia, Silesia and Little Poland. While this Přemyslide duke and his successors in office formally acknowledged supremacy of the Empire, in actual fact they carved for themselves an entirely independent position within it. From the eleventh century, this is cogently demonstrated by the fact that, alongside the German kings or emperors, they were the only ones to bear the royal title. The Přemyslide rulers erected an effective barrier to German expansion into Bohemia, and thus saved the Czech population from the fate of both the Elbe and the Baltic Slavs who, losing their political independence at first, were subsequently fully Germanized.

The emergence of the Přemyslide administrative organization on the whole territory of Bohemia under Boleslav I constituted the foundation of a true early medieval state. In this connection, it is not without interest that the name of this Přemyslide ruler is the first to turn up frequently in contemporary non-hagiographical written evidence, while the lives of the earlier members of the Přemyslide lineage are illuminated almost exclusively by legends. Boleslav may also be credited with minting the first denarius coins of Bohemia in Prague in the later 950s; here, economic needs, as well as political reasons, were obviously playing their part. The growing number of churches built in the newly erected fortified seats of Přemyslide regional administration induced Boleslav I to seek the independence of Bohemia from the ecclesiastical jurisdiction of the Regensburg bishops, and to establish the independent bishopric of Prague. This ducal design, realized only after Boleslav's death, was brought about by his son, Duke Boleslav II (972–999). In the sphere of ecclesiastical life, Boleslav I is connected with the foundation of the very first Christian monastery of Bohemia for Benedictine nuns at the Prague Castle. His reign also saw the beginnings of a vigorous expansion eastwards which won for the Czech state, at least for a time, extensive territories reaching as far as the frontier of Kievan Russia.

Čechy ('Czechia')

Written sources of foreign origin which record events in the territory of Bohemia from the beginning of the ninth century refer both to the land and to its population by various names. The names, which include Beheim, Bohemia, Beheimi, Boemani, and Beheimare, are all derived from the ethnonym of the Celtic Boii who lived here at the close of the pre-Christian era. Of course, all knowledge of the pre-Slavic settlement of Bohemia was lost in the course of the early Middle Ages. For this reason Cosmas, the first chronicler of Bohemia writing at the beginning of the twelfth century, and taking inspiration from contemporary literary models, had to invent a 'heros eponymos' named Bohemus who had conferred his name on Bohemia. A similar process in the vernacular is pursued by an unknown chronicle writer at the beginning of the fourteenth century, commonly referred to by the erroneous name of Dalimil, who introduces the 'forefather' Čech from whom the land was supposed to obtain its name, 'Čechy' (approximately 'Czechia' in English). The etymology of the ethnonym 'Čech' presents a hitherto unresolved problem to both historians and philologists. The very first instance in which it may be quite safely identified is the first Old Slavic Legend of St Wenceslas which is likely to have been written between the thirties and seventies of the tenth century. This legend contains a single reference to the 'česki muži' (literally Czech men), the members of the ducal guard and retinue. Thus the term might have originally denoted members of the ducal retinue on whom, according to the words ascribed by the chronicler Cosmas to the Duke Jaromír, 'the land of Bohemia has always stood, stands and will stand for ever'. In Boleslav's time and later, the retinue played a major role in building and defending the state of the Přemyslide dynasty and, in fact, conferred its name 'Čechy' on it, though this became widely used only after several centuries.[11]

Notes

1 For the most detailed survey of Bohemian prehistory, see R. Pleiner and A. Rybová (eds.), *Pravěké dějiny Čech* [Prehistory of Bohemia] (Prague, 1978).

2 Among Czech specialists, the most detailed treatment of the Celtic problems and history of the Boii is by J. Filip, *Celtic Civilization and Its Heritage* (Prague, 1976).

3 The most detailed analysis of all Classical sources of this geographical term by

Czech specialists appears in J. Dobiáš, *Dějiny československého území před vystoupením Slovanů* [The history of the Czechoslovak territory before the appearance of the Slavs] (Prague, 1964). Basic reference works on this problem have been summarized by R. Wenskus, 'Boiohaemum' in *Reallexikon der Germanischen Altertumskunde* (Berlin-New York, 1978) III, pp. 207–8.

4   Dobiáš, *Dějiny československého území*, pp. 89–148.

5   For the most recent treatment of the origins of Slavic settlement of Bohemia, see J. Zeman, 'Nejstarší slovanské osídlení Čech [Summary in German: 'Die älteste slawische Besiedlung Böhmens', *Památky archeologické*, 67 (1976), 115–235. For a discussion of the assimilation of considerable numbers of the population by Slavic newcomers, see M. Stloukal, 'Die Ethnogenese der Westslawen aus der Sicht der Anthropologie', in *Ethnogenese europäischer Völker* (Stuttgart-New York, 1986), pp. 323–30.

6   W. Pohl, *Die Awaren, Ein Steppenvolk in Mitteleuropa 567–822 n. Chr.* (Munich, 1988); on Samo's realm, see pp. 256–61.

7   All historical documents regarding *duces* in ninth-century Bohemia have been summarized by F. Graus, *Die Nationenbildung der Westslawen im Mittlelalter* (Sigmaringen, 1980), pp. 194–6.

8   A new historical assessment of the importance of Duke Bořivoj has been put forward by D. Třeštík, 'Bořivoj und Svatopluk, Die Entstehung des böhmischen Staates und Grossmähren', in J. Poulík and B. Chropovský (eds.), *Grossmähren und die Anfänge der tschechoslowakischen Staatlichkeit* (Prague, 1986), pp. 311–44.

9   For a detailed treatment of the development of the Přemyslide domain in central Bohemia and of its transformation into an early medieval state with reference both to historical sources and to specialized literature, see J. Sláma, *Střední Čechy v raném středověku III. Archaeologie o počátcích přemyslovského státu* [Central Bohemia in the early Middle Ages III. Archaeology and the beginnings of the Přemyslide state] (Prague, 1988).

10 For the most detailed assessment of the development of the ducal retinue and its significance, see F. Graus, 'Raně středověké družiny a jejich význam při vzniku států ve střední Evropě' [Summary in German: 'Die frühmittelalterlichen Gefolgschaften und ihre Rolle bei der Entstehung der Staaten in Mitteleuropa'], *Československý časopis historický*, 13 (1995), 1–18.

11 All the designations in early medieval sources for Bohemia as a land are cited in F. Graus, *Die Nationenbildung*, pp. 162–81. The most important specialized works on the etymology and meaning of the word 'Čech' have been summarized by L. Hosák and R. Šrámek, *Místní jména na Moravě a ve Slezsku, I, A-L* (The toponyms of Moravia and Silesia I, A-L) (Prague, 1970), p. 154.

2

The making of the Czech state: Bohemia and Moravia
from the tenth to the fourteenth centuries

ZDENĚK MĚŘÍNSKÝ AND JAROSLAV MEZNÍK

I

The history of the Czech state, from the development of the centralized
governing powers of the Přemyslide dukes in the tenth century until the first
half of the fourteenth century, together with the succession of the
Luxemburg dynasty to the Crown of Bohemia presents a picture of out-
standingly dynamic development in political as well as in social and economic terms. But this development was neither continuous nor stable:
typically, a period of upsurge, expansion and stabilization was followed by
a crisis, sometimes even a struggle for the very survival of the state, and its
subsequent renewal, consolidation and reconstruction. Such patterns recur
repeatedly from the early Middle Ages up to the beginning of the thirteenth
century. They were caused by a number of factors, which varied over time
and in relation to the structure and development of economic and social
conditions. One factor remained constant: Bohemia's geographical position
at the centre of Europe, both literally and metaphorically, at a cross-roads
of competing political forces. Such a position had a formative influence on
the attitudes and orientation of the Přemyslide dynasty as it struggled first
to build the state and then to ensure its survival.[1]

Above all, the position of the German Empire within Europe, and its
influence on the balance of power, had a significant impact in Bohemia.
The Empire's concerns always impinged on a number of European countries and in Central Europe they were of particular importance, because the
German court had a number of interests at stake on its eastern margins, and
usually addressed them by using force. Whenever the German
King/Roman Emperor had to attend to urgent matters in the south or west

of his territory, or to intervene in internal affairs, he would have to safeguard his 'eastern interests' too, and perhaps take the opportunity to expand them as well. These concerns were always reflected in the political developments of Přemyslide Bohemia, Piast Poland, Árpád Hungary, and also the Babenberg Eastern March (Ostmark), the future Austrian duchy, as well as in relations between these countries. Besides pursuing its eastern interests by military force, not always a successful procedure, the Empire could make use of internal convulsions in each country and exploit mutual animosities.[2]

The expansion to the east began in Charlemagne's reign (742–814): Bavaria was brought under control (788), and the power of the Avars, settled in the Carpathian basin, was broken (798), so opening the way to further eastward expansion along the Danube. At the same time, these changes in the balance of power created an opportunity for Slavonic tribes north of the middle Danube to begin the process of state formation. When Charlemagne, building on the defunct Roman Empire to found a European political organization, was proclaimed Emperor in 800, a system of border marches was emerging at the eastern boundary of the Empire. These were territories with a particular military function which also served as the base for further expansion. At the same time, a complex system of subordination and dependency in relation to the surrounding newly emergent states was developing.

The efforts at influencing and subordinating Slavonic leaders can be traced to the beginning of the ninth century. They concern both the Bohemian basin and the emerging Great Moravian state, whose position, military power and territorial extent in the last third of the ninth century enabled its ruler, King Svatopluk (871–894), to negotiate with representatives of the Franconian Empire not as a subordinate but as a sovereign ruler. In 890, the East Franconian King and future Emperor Arnulf (887–899) formally ceded Bohemia to him as a fief since that territory, traditionally claimed by the Franconian Empire, had previously been annexed by Svatopluk.[3]

The decay of Great Moravia at the beginning of the tenth century, besides being typical of crises usually overtaking such ambitious states in this period due to expansion and other factors, was also hastened by a continuing change in the balance of power in the Carpathian basin, with nomadic Magyars penetrating from the east. The centre of gravity for new developments therefore shifted to the Bohemian basin. The basin, surrounded as it was by a wreath of mountain ranges and frontier forests, afforded a more propitious site in turbulent times for growth and consolidation. Apparently with the support of Svatopluk, the Přemyslide dynasty came to the fore, gradually establishing an hegemony over other tribal dukes, and unifying individual subjects under their rule. The superiority of

the Prague tribal duke over other chieftains was evident by the time of
Boleslav I (935–972), who began the process of constituting a central governing power.

II

By the latter half of the tenth century, new trends were apparent in the
construction and administration of the state. The same period was marked
by Bohemia's growing importance within Central Europe and its territorial
expansion in the reign of Boleslav I and Boleslav II (972–999) in a manner
reminiscent of Great Moravia. Here Bohemia had the advantage over the
competing powers of Poland and Hungary when it was able to benefit from
the recurrent changing balance of power on the middle Danube. In 950,
after a long struggle, Boleslav I was forced to recognize the superiority of
the Empire but in 955 under the Emperor Otto I (936–973) Czech forces
participated in the decisive victory on the River Lech near Augsburg against
the Magyars. Otto's victory stopped the Magyars raiding Southern,
Western, and Central Europe, and they quickly adapted to their new circumstances, constituting themselves into a new state under King Stephen I
(997–1038, King from 1000), who was canonized as St Stephen.

The new situation also opened up possibilities for the Přemyslides, who
until now were confined to the Bohemian basin, even though the task of
unification there was still incomplete. Eastern, southeastern and southern
Bohemia at the time came under sovereignty of the Slavník dynasty with its
centre at Libice. Although it is thought that from the time of Duke Václav
(Wenceslas) the Saint (after 922–935) the Slavníks had recognized the
suzerainty of the Přemyslide dukes, increasingly by the latter half of the
tenth century they were attempting to achieve autonomy or even independence. In Moravia, after the collapse of Great Moravia, the remains of
a state were preserved probably on a limited scale, in the first half of the
tenth century, dependent on Hungary. The beginning of the eleventh
century saw the growing influence of the Polish King Bolesław I the Brave
(992–1025). Some church organization remained intact, as evidenced by the
presence of the Moravian bishop at the synod of Mainz in 976.

Boleslav I began by building a new castle organization, introduced the
peace tax as the first state tax, and from the 960s coined the first denarii
based on Bavarian models. Prague at this time was situated on a major trade
route leading from the Cordoban Caliphate in the west, via Regensburg to
Prague and Cracow, and thence to Kievan Russia and further east. The
mint was a symbol of state sovereignty and, above all, a demonstration of
the prestige of the ruling dynasty.

Changes also occurred in the ecclesiastical organization which hitherto had lent support to outside powers. From the ninth century, with the possible exception of the period when Bohemia was part of Svatopluk's Great Moravia, Prague had come under the supervision of the Regensburg diocese. Apart from strengthening the position of the ruler, the new trends served the internal development of the state by building a unified church structure which reached all levels of the population. At the beginning of the 970s, the first Benedictine nunnery was founded beside the church of St George at Prague Castle. Some time around 973, most probably after the death of Boleslav I (972) but certainly due to his efforts, the first Prague bishopric was established under the authority of the primatial see of Mainz. Prague was thus freed from the direct influence of German clergy, even though the first bishop was the Saxon Thietmar (?973–982), and for a long time afterwards, even at the lower grades of the church hierarchy, there were foreigners.

The establishment of the episcopate in Prague and the building of an independent church organization was also important for the further diffusion of Latin culture in Bohemia. A Latin school had already been founded there. The political, cultural and ecclesiastical heritage of Great Moravia, and the influence of Old Church Slavonic liturgy and literature persisted for a while, but this phase came to an end after the martyrdom of Duke Wenceslas (28 September 935). The establishment of the episcopate meant a definite orientation to the Latin West, with all the consequent advantages and disadvantages for a relatively small political unit at the eastern margin of the Empire.

In the second half of the tenth century, the efforts of the Emperor Otto I to renew the Empire following Charlemagne's example forced Boleslav to look for an effective counterbalance, which he found in the form of an understanding with the emerging Polish state. This took expression in the marriage of his daughter Doubravka with the Polish Prince Mieszko I (962–992) and in his role in mediating Mieszko's baptism in 966. Boleslav II and Mieszko were to participate in the succession disputes following the death of Otto I in 973 and Otto II ten years later.

This relatively favourable concentration of forces contributed to the territorial expansion of the Czech Přemyslide state in the latter half of the tenth century. For a time Boleslav annexed Meissen, and occupied Silesia and the Cracow region; expansion was only halted at the border of Kievan Russia. This excessive growth provoked conflict with Poland and led to the loss of Silesia in the war between Boleslav II and Mieszko I in 990. For several decades the mutual hostility of the two neighbouring Slav countries affected the political attitude of the Přemyslide dukes and to some extent facilitated the intervention of the Empire into the internal affairs of Přemyslide Bohemia.

In the last years of Boleslav II's reign, the Czech state still represented an imposing territorial unit, stretching from its core in the Bohemian basin up to Little Poland. The internal unification process was completed in 995 with the murdering of the Slavník dynasty. The latter had signified their ambition by minting their own coins and by maintaining close relations with the Saxon imperial dynasty, thereby becoming a serious threat to the unity of the Czech state. Their efforts were helped by the fact that since 982 the second bishop of Prague, Vojtěch (Adalbert), was from the Slavník dynasty. In the 980s he left Bohemia as a result of conflicts regarding church practice and administration, as well as unpopularity due to his strict assertion of religious ideals. After a brief attempt at compromise with Boleslav II during 992–3 (in 993 they jointly founded the monastery Břevnov near Prague), Adalbert left the country for good in 994, and found a martyr's death in 997 among the pagan Prussians, becoming the second patron saint in Bohemia (after St Wenceslas) and the first Polish one.[4]

If the Czech state had already lost some territory in the last decade of Boleslav II's rule, a deep crisis was to occur after his death (999). Between 999 and 1003, three rulers occupied the Bohemian throne, one of whom, Boleslav III, lost the Cracow region. Vladivoj was the first ruler of Bohemia to accept the land as a fief from the Roman (German) king while Jaromír was expelled by the Polish ruler Bolesław the Brave, who now acquired Bohemia. The cause of this crisis was both internal and external. Internally, political, social and economic structures were still rudimentary and undeveloped, state formation was weak, and well into the eleventh century its stability was questionable. Externally, Bohemia was partly isolated, but also figured in the plans of Emperor Otto III (983–1002) who wished to renew the Empire and needed Bohemia to help challenge Bolesław I the Brave and his expanding Polish state.

But the crisis of Bohemia at the turn of the millennium, typical of a stage reached by early feudal states when, after the territorial expansion necessary to their existence and to provide for a sufficient ducal retinue, their stability is called into question, did not result in total disintegration and the enduring weakness of the ruler. After Jaromír's expulsion he was enthroned again as Duke in Prague with the help of Henry II, whose politics he closely supported, participating in campaigns against Bolesław the Brave in 1004, 1005 and 1010; Henry for his part needed the Czech state (under his control) as a counter-weight to Poland. The Czech state was further stabilized by Oldřich I (1012–1034), usurper of his brother's throne, and more particularly by his son, Břetislav I (1035–1055), who annexed Moravia and followed an expansionist policy against Poland and Hungary, sometimes in accord with imperial interests and sometimes in defiance of them.[5] This is illustrated by his campaign against Poland in 1039, when Sile.ia was occupied and the relics of St Adalbert transferred to Prague as pai t of the attempt by Břetislav I to have the Prague episcopate raised to an archiepiscopate.

Bohemia's strengthened position met with opposition from Henry III (1039–1056), who prevented the establishment of the Prague archbishopric. After an unsuccessful campaign against Břetislav I in 1040, he succeeded in reaching as far as Prague with his army in 1041, assisted by domestic leaders and Bishop Šebíř (1030–1067). The ruler had to capitulate and accept Bohemia as a fief of the Empire: that is, to recognize its dependency on the Empire. Silesia was also eventually lost; the treaty of 1054 with King Casimir I of Poland (1034–1059) established that tribute from Silesia should be paid, and freed Břetislav's forces for a campaign against Hungary. Attacks on Hungary had already featured as early as 1030 or 1031, and again in 1042, 1044, and 1051, following imperial policy. But on the threshold of the new expedition prepared for the year 1055, Břetislav I died at the castle of Chrudim.

The annexatioi of Moravia was thus the only territorial gain made by the Přemyslides ai 1 their expansive policy in the first half of the eleventh century, essential for the state's existence by virtue of the gains made which could be used to reward members of the duke's retinue and grant positions to its leaders. Oldřich I may be considered the first ruler of Bohemia to inaugurate the new trends which led to the gradual reshaping of the Czech state, the stability of its government and the strengthening of its position in the balance of power – developments consolidated more markedly during the reign of his son Břetislav I.

III

Prior to his accession, Břetislav became administrator of conquered Moravia: the land was an independent demesne (*úděl*) within the Czech state, a sort of frontier march with a military orientation reminiscent of the imperial frontier marches rather than an apanage granted to an unprovided-for member of the ruling dynasty. This role continued until the end of the eleventh century with the accession of Břetislav's sons, Spytihněv II and Vratislav II to the Prague throne. Břetislav had three other sons, of whom Konrád I of Brno (1092) ruled briefly in Prague, while Jaromír-Gebhart (1068–1090) became Bishop of Prague, and Otto (1061–1087) held the demesne of Olomouc.

Numerous progeny required the establishment of succession rules in the state. The so-called Seniority Law provided that the eldest son would succeed to Prague, while others would be based in demesnes in Moravia, and possibly also in Bohemian castles such as Žatec or Hradec Králové. This law of succession was observed more or less until the end of the twelfth century even though it became the occasion for repeated conflict between individual Přemyslides, and a source of various crises from which imperial policy profited. (Most of the Prague dukes, following Jaromír, also accepted Bohemia as a fief from the German ruler.)

This was the case particularly with the system of Moravian demesnes, introduced first by Břetislav I and fully constituted only after his death into three independent units, Olomouc, Brno and Znojmo. Cadet branches of the Přemyslides ruled for several generations, and the units became a source of centrifugal trends due to their rulers' ambition to achieve autonomy, offset at the same time by the possibility of them obtaining the throne in Prague.

The Prague dukes, on the other hand, made strong efforts to guarantee the succession of their sons. Already Spytihněv II had to intervene fiercely against the separatist trends of his brothers Vratislav, Konrád and Otto, at that time Moravian demesne rulers, who were none the less opposed by the Moravians themselves supporting Břetislav's political testament.[6]

The latter half of the eleventh century saw significant changes in the overall European balance of power. The climax of the investiture struggle, opposing secular control to the claims of the papal court over ecclesiastical appointments, left the imperial government under Henry IV in a weakened position. This created new possibilities for manoeuvre between ecclesiastical and secular powers, between the Empire and the Roman papal court. The weakened power of the German rulers was also reflected in political relations between the Empire and all three Central European powers, all of whom now saw strong leaders emerging, such as Bolesław II the Fearless (1058–1079) and Ladislaus I (St Ladislaus) (1077–1095) in Poland, and Koloman (1095–1116) in Hungary. All tried to strengthen the position of their states and to free them from dependence on the Empire, and additionally in the case of Hungary, to carry out further expansion, such as the personal union of the Kingdom of Magyars and Croats in 1102. The results of these policies only became evident at the end of the eleventh century, and the methods and strategies used in attaining these aims differed.

Spytihněv II tried to utilize the papal court to obtain the title of king during 1059–60, but succeeded only in getting the right to wear the mitre, in return for an annual vassal fee. His successor, Vratislav II (1061–1092), altered the direction of Czech state policy. He brought back the Moravian demesne system, placing his brother Otto at Olomouc and Konrád at

Znojmo and Brno, and at the same time restored the Moravian episcopate at Olomouc as a political outpost of the Prague Přemyslides. This simultaneously weakened the ambitions of his younger brother Jaromír-Gebhart who, as expected, became Bishop of Prague in 1068.

His opposition to Jaromír, together with the traditional anti-Polish attitude of the Přemyslides, underlined by the support of Bolesław II the Fearless for the papal court, facilitated Vratislav's going over to Henry IV's camp. He remained Henry's supporter through thick and thin, giving him military support from 1075 almost every year in all his struggles in Italy and Germany until the Imperial coronation in Rome in 1084. This help secured him the personal title of King of Bohemia in 1085, but gave no territorial gain (with the possible exception of Bautzen and Görlitz) while his attempt to secure Meissen met with Henry's resistance. Further growth in the power of the first King of Bohemia was also prevented by internal dissension which came fully into the open after his death (1092). This dynastic crisis, which continued into the beginning of the twelfth century, facilitated the intervention of German rulers into internal affairs, allowed the growth of power of domestic principals, weakened Bohemia's external standing.

In the double reign of Vladislav I (1110–1118, 1120–1225), internal conditions calmed down and there was a search to guarantee the continued succession of the Prague lineage, which bore fruit after his death. Against the wishes of the Roman (German) King Lothar (1125–1137) and the claims of Otto II the Black (1107–1110, 1113–1125) who resided in Olomouc, Vladislav's younger brother Soběslav I (1125–1140) ascended the ducal throne in Prague. Lothar's support of Otto resulted in the invasion of Bohemia, but Soběslav was victorious near Chlumec in 1126, where Otto the Black met his death. After this victory Soběslav did not press his claims too far, accepting a compromise with King Lothar whereby he held Bohemia as a fief from him.

Soběslav I succeeded in suppressing a grandees' conspiracy and stabilizing his government in the country. But changing social conditions, economic growth and the increasing role of the nobles on the one hand, coupled with the growing power of the Empire on the other, became apparent after his death when the nobility elected Vladislav II (1140–1172) as Duke of Bohemia. Vladislav spent several years securing his position with substantial help from the Roman (German) King Konrad III (1138–1152) as well as Jindřich Zdík (1126–1150), Bishop of Olomouc. This meant Bohemia giving unambiguous support to the Empire which, after the accession of Frederick I Barbarossa (1152–1190), was in the process of restoration with all the consequences for Central Europe this entailed.[7]

IV

In the twelfth century gradual changes made themselves felt both in the political sphere, including the relative power of the ruler; and in social structure and the economy, including types of colonization. They also showed up in cultural development, art and education where, as in previous centuries, the Church had a central role. The indigenous Church also became more powerful as an institution and lent its support to the ruler. As early as 1146–7 (or 1148) privileges exercised by King Konrád III and Duke Vladislav II, enabled Jindřich Zdík to obtain a number of immunities, which amounted to stealing a march on the Prague diocese for approximately three quarters of a century. These ecclesiastical changes were linked to economic and social changes evident by the latter half of the eleventh century.

The most obvious achievement was in Romanesque architecture and sacral objects, but painting, sculpture and literature must be included. Natives of Bohemia who had received education at leading cathedral schools in France and the Empire became more numerous. They began to resent the prevalence of foreigners among the church hierarchy in Bohemia. The sentiments of the new group of educated Czechs and their awakened national feeling found clearest expression in the work of the Prague chronicler, Canon Cosmas (*c.* 1045–1125). Starting in the mid-eleventh century and developing intensively in the twelfth, the cult of St Wenceslas became the chief ideological expression of the state: St Wenceslas symbolised the eternal ruler, the ruling duke his representative on earth, and his followers his subjects.[8]

Throughout this entire time, starting with the tenth century, agricultural production increased only modestly. Technical innovations began to percolate into the system only in the thirteenth century. Similarly, handicrafts for the market developed only gradually and within the confines of traditional technology, chiefly under the patronage of the ruler and the Church. Once the home market had emerged and stabilized, it stimulated the demand for handicraft goods, including the mintage of Czech denarii, but these developments lagged behind Western Europe, both qualitatively and quantitatively.

All of these processes – the development of culture, the rise of indigenous educated people, the emergence of a land-owning nobility and the corresponding decline of the feudal retinue, gradual economic growth, and the emancipation of the Church – laid the groundwork for far-reaching developments in the Czech Lands. The twelfth century was a period of dynamic growth, based on earlier trends and also linked to the beginning of internal colonization from older bases of settlement into previously uncolonized upland positions, in areas located along main communication routes and upstream of major rivers.[9]

Political development of the Czech state in the latter half of the twelfth century took place under the strong political pressure created by the rising prestige of the Empire of Frederick I Barbarossa (1152–1190), in whose military and political projects Vladislav II was closely involved. In 1158 Vladislav II obtained the royal title for himself and his descendants, and his participation in Barbarossa's expedition against Milan yielded further gains: the securing of Bautzen, and tribute from Silesia. Yet this was at the expense of increasing dependence on the Emperor and loss of personal reputation. Then he fell out of favour with the Emperor – a fatal hazard of being dependent on the will of the German ruler. Only abdication in 1172 in favour of his son Bedřich might have enabled Vladislav II to ensure that the royal title was hereditary. However, Barbarossa did not acknowledge Bedřich's claims and granted the Czech state as a fief to Oldřich (1173) and, after the latter's abdication, to his elder brother Soběslav II (1173–1178), son of Soběslav I. For the first time, power was gained by members of the Přemyslide dynasty, who were installed by the German ruler and not elected.

The political crisis consequent on King Vladislav's death (1174) persisted with the twelve changes of ruler on the Bohemian throne between 1172 and 1197. The last quarter of the twelfth century saw the power and prestige of the Czech state and Přemyslide dukes at its nadir, with the authority of the state as well as its ruling dynasty on the wane, and an unprecedented series of imperial interventions into the internal affairs of Bohemia and Moravia. The individual members of the dynasty figured only in relation to the Emperor's interests and were dependent on him. Přemyslide old-style dynastic policy had grown from the retinue type of early feudal absolutism. By the twelfth century, ignoring the differentiated inner structures of the state, the dynasty was clearly reaching a point of crisis.

A serious rival to the Prague Přemyslide dukes now emerged in the person of Konrád II Ota from the Znojmo cadet branch of the dynasty who tipped the balance of power in his own favour. From his accession to the Znojmo demesne, during 1161–68, he strove hard to extend his rule over all Moravia. By 1174 at the latest he had obtained the Brno demesne, but his attempt at annexing Olomouc was strongly resisted by the Prague dukes. In the end, foreign and domestic difficulties caused Soběslav's fall. Frederick I Barbarossa placed the previously unrecognized Bedřich on the throne (1179–1182) but the Czech nobility, who had opposed the installation of Soběslav II as duke, now supported Konrád II Ota's attempt to claim the throne in 1182. The Emperor abandoned his earlier support for Bedřich who was forced to flee the country.

This dispute between the expelled Bedřich and his supplanter on the Prague ducal throne, Konrád II Ota, the demesne ruler of Znojmo, was resolved by the decision of Frederick I Barbarossa at the Diet of Regensburg (1182) to declare Moravia an independent margravate and grant it to Konrád I Ota as a fief, while Duke Bedřich was to reign in Bohemia (1182–1189). In 1187 the integrity of the state was weakened again with the elevation (1187) of the Prague Archbishop Jindřich Břetislav, a Přemyslide, to the rank of an Imperial Duke. If the Olomouc bishopric and its extensive estates with their immunities are also taken into consideration, the Czech state was divided into three to four units, making it much easier for the Emperor to make it submit to his policies.

The Prague duke was well aware of the implications of the Regensburg pronouncements, especially from the point of view of the international balance of power, and he tried to counterbalance the 1182 decision by diplomatic and political means. In 1186, negotiations began between the chief protagonists at Starý Knín, which were of significance for restoring the unity of the state. After Duke Bedřich's death (1189) and Konrád II Ota's renewed ducal enthronement, this capable representative of the Znojmo cadet branch of the dynasty revived the idea of the unification of Bohemia and Moravia (1189–1191). But the crisis continued to reverberate during most of the 1190s and only the royal enthronement of Přemysl Otakar I (on this, more below) brought it to an end, as well as reversing the position, so that the result was to enhance the power of the Czech state and ensure its continuing development under the last Přemyslides during the thirteenth century.[10]

In the thirteenth and fourteenth centuries the medieval Czech state reached the apogee of its power. Its core remained Bohemia and Moravia, but under the last Přemyslides and the first Luxemburg rulers there began a process of territorial expansion. Its influence extended beyond Central Europe and it became one of the important powers in Europe.

V

There were several reasons for this upsurge.[11] In the thirteenth to fourteenth centuries the Czech Lands experienced fundamental economic and social changes. Agricultural productivity increased thanks due to better techniques, better equipment and greater peasant motivation. The spread of *emphyteusis* ('German law') led to loosening relations between feudal authority and villein (subject peasant). Previously uncultivated areas were colonized, agricultural land increased at the expense of forests, and many new villages were founded. Medieval towns developed as centres of crafts and trade and in them emerged a new class of inhabitants: the burghers. The position of the nobility also changed. As early as the end of the twelfth century it already held a considerable part of its property through hereditary possession, making it more independent of the ruler. The transition to money economy together with more colonization enriched part of the nobility, establishing the basis for the estate of lords (magnates, barons) later on. The Church was also gradually liberated from subservience to the secular power, making the clergy another estate of the realm. Both clergy and burghers obeyed their own jurisdiction.

These processes were manifest throughout Western and Central Europe. Although evident earlier in the West, there were some specific features and consequences in the Czech Lands. It was here that in the thirteenth century silver mining developed. The discovery of silver ores and the commencement of mining at Jihlava in the 1230s and 1240s, and near Kutná Hora in the 1280s, has been compared with the gold rush in the nineteenth-century Alaska. Silver became the chief article of export from the Czech Lands, and its ruler enjoyed an enormous income from the mines.[12]

Rural, urban and mining colonization was not implemented solely by domestic man-power. German-speakers moved into the Czech Lands, making them bilingual, which they remained until the twentieth century. The significant participation of foreigners at the Czech court of the last Přemyslides, and the fact that most burghers were German, provoked a spread of Czech national consciousness, especially among a section of nobility, which in some respects anticipated modern nationalism. This early Czech nationalism stimulated the development of Czech written literature, which circulated among Czech-speaking burghers who by the second half of the fourteenth century had become a majority in many towns.[13]

All these changes combined to make the Czech Lands in the thirteenth century markedly wealthy, and a wealthy land makes a wealthy ruler. Despite the growing independence of the barons and the Church hierarchy, a political system and social structure based on estates of the realm were not yet in existence. The ruler acquired additional income, above all from mining, and new support from the royal towns and new castles. Succession disputes also disappeared: Přemyslide cadet branches died out between the end of the twelfth and the beginning of the thirteenth century, and in the main branch, after King Wenceslas I (1230–1253), there was always only one surviving male heir. In the first half of the thirteenth century the brothers or sons of King of Bohemia were rulers in Moravia, but from 1253 until 1334 the King of Bohemia was also Margrave of Moravia. In a divided Central Europe, the Czech state thus constituted an entity which surpassed its neighbours in riches and territorial extent.[14] At the same time, the weakness of the Roman Empire enabled the Kings of Bohemia to free themselves from the dependence of the Emperor.

Přemysl Otakar I (1197–1230) made good use of the crisis in the Empire at the turn of the twelfth and thirteenth centuries. In 1212 the Roman King (later Emperor) Frederick II issued the Golden Bull of Sicily, confirming the ruler of Bohemia as an hereditary king and defining his duties in relation to the Empire.[15] These were not onerous but conferred prestige on the Czech state within it. During the thirteenth century the King of Bohemia became one of the seven Electors who elected the King of the Romans.

During the interregnum (1254–1273), when the Roman Empire had no generally acknowledged ruler, the King of Bohemia, Přemysl Otakar II (1253–1278) emerged as the most powerful ruler in Central Europe.[16] When still Margrave of Moravia during the reign of his father Wenceslas I, he was elected ruler of Austria (1251) after the extinction of the native Babenberg dynasty. His efforts to secure the entire Babenberg inheritance brought Přemysl Otakar II into conflict with King Béla IV of Hungary whom he defeated at the battle of Kressenbrunn (1260). He further acquired Styria and neighbouring Carinthia and Carniola during the 1260s, extending his realm to the Adriatic. Tenure of these Alpine lands in Otakar's possession was confirmed by one of the two elected Roman kings, Richard of Cornwall (brother of the English King Henry III), who also gave him the imperial town Cheb and its environs as security. Otakar also went on crusade to the pagan Prussians but his grand design for the establishment of Olomouc as an archdiocese for his close collaborator Bruno of Schaumburg – as a centre for the Christianization of Prussia and Lithuania – did not come to fruition.

Otakar was twice candidate for King of the Romans, but was too powerful a figure for the German princes to elect him. In 1273 Rudolf of Habsburg was elected king. Otakar did not acknowledge him but in this he overestimated his power. He had aroused the resistance not only of the Pope, but of most of the Austrian and even some of the Czech nobility, who disliked his strong rule. In 1278 he was killed in Austria at the battle of Marchfeld. Despite this defeat, Otakar II is considered to be one of the great rulers of Bohemia. He contributed to the spread of the Gothic style in the Czech Lands and in Austria, and implemented some internal reforms. He is mentioned appreciatively in Dante's *Divine Comedy*.[17]

VI

The Czech state found itself in a difficult situation. Otto, Margrave of Brandenburg, was on the throne in Bohemia and Rudolf of Habsburg was

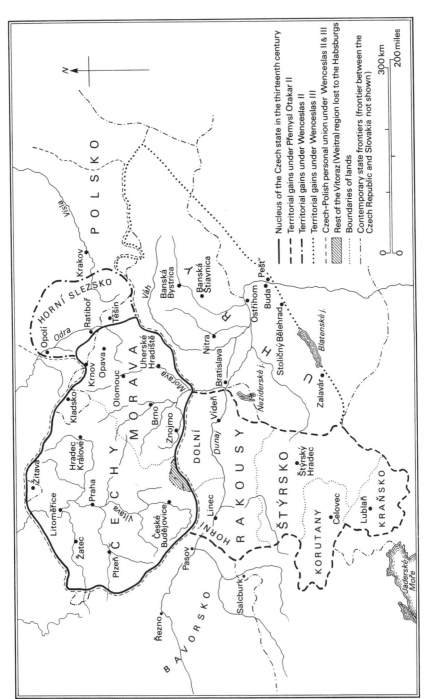

2. The Czech state in the thirteenth century.

Margrave of Moravia. But sensitive to the role they could play furthering the state, the barons promoted the restoration of indigenous administration and the enthronement of the rightful heir. Wenceslas II (1283–1305) had to face internal obstacles in the first years of his rule but the wealth of the Czech Lands soon enabled him to embark on an expansionist policy.[18] As early as the 1290s he gained territories north-west of Bohemia, some Silesian dukes acknowledged his suzerainty, and he acquired Little Poland. In 1300 he became King of Poland and in 1301 his son, another Wenceslas, was elected King of Hungary. Wenceslas II implemented extensive internal reforms. During his reign the *groš* was minted, a stable silver currency throughout Central Europe. He aspired to the introduction of legal codes valid throughout Bohemia, and the founding of a university in Prague, but in both instances was thwarted by the resistance of his barons.

The enlargement of the Kingdom of Bohemia was short-lived. In Hungary and Poland there was soon resentment at Czech hegemony, and the Roman King, Albrecht of Habsburg, as well as Pope Boniface VIII, became opponents of Wenceslas II. Even though Albrecht's campaign against Bohemia in 1304 was unsuccessful, it was evident that the King of Bohemia would have to surrender some of his gains. His ambitious foreign policy was very costly and despite his vast income he found himself in financial difficulties. He died in 1305 and his son, Wenceslas III (1305–1306), surrendered the Hungarian Crown and negotiated peace with Albrecht of Habsburg. Wenceslas III was murdered at Olomouc in 1306 *en route* to a military campaign in Poland; the motive and identity of the murderer has never been satisfactorily accounted for.

With the death of Wenceslas III the Přemyslide dynasty, which had ruled the Czech state since its beginnings, came to an end. The extinction of a dynasty in the Middle Ages always produced a political crisis. In Bohemia this had to be resolved by the barons, the Church, and the most influential burghers from the large towns. Part of this elite supported the candidature of Henry, Duke of Carinthia, and part that of the Habsburg Rudolf, son of Albrecht, King of the Romans. With his father's support Albrecht was at first successful, but died in less than a year. Henry of Carinthia became the ruler, but soon antagonized most of the political elite. In 1309, the abbots of the Cistercian monasteries at Zbraslav and Sedlec began negotiations with the new King of the Romans, Henry VII of Luxemburg. In 1310 Henry of Carinthia was expelled from the land while John of Luxemburg, son of Henry VII, became King of Bohemia aged only fourteen. A condition of his coronation was his marriage to Elizabeth, the second daughter of Wenceslas II.[19]

The history of the Czech state under the rule of the Luxemburg dynasty introduced some new features. By the thirteenth century Bohemia was one of the more important European countries, but its influence was limited to Central Europe. English and French chronicles only make sporadic mention of Bohemia and Moravia. This changes in the fourteenth century. Rulers of Bohemia made alliances with French and English kings, and relations were strengthened by marriage alliances: the French Kings Charles IV and John II, and England's Richard II, married respectively the sister, daughter, and grand-daughter of John of Luxemburg, while his second wife, and the first wife of his son Charles, came from the French royal family. This rapprochement, also found in spheres of culture and education, had several causes.[20] It reflected pan-European trends: even though there were political divisions within fourteenth-century Catholic Europe, there were also extensive contacts between countries. The importance of the Czech state increased in relation to its power, and the Pope's residing in Avignon was also significant. But of import was the role played by the Luxemburg dynasty itself, which originated from the French–German borderland. Both John of Luxemburg and his eldest son, the future Emperor Charles IV, spent part of their childhood in France.

The accession of John of Luxemburg (1310–1346) did not put a stop to the crisis of the Czech state.[21] In the first years of his reign the young king depended on foreign advisers and relied upon his father's authority. But when Henry VII died in 1313 and John failed to succeed him as King of the Romans, the Czech barons issued a demand that he expel foreign advisers from the royal court. But the barons were not united; personality clashes and intervention from Prague patricians added to the controversy. An outbreak of fighting threatened John's tenure of the Crown of Bohemia. Only in 1318 under the auspices of Ludwig of Bavaria as King of the Romans was an agreement reached between the king and the barons, and the following year a definitive solution was found when John of Luxemburg parted from his wife and left the country, allowing the barons to rule. The remainder of his life was then spent abroad, largely at the French court, but his rank and royal title were no longer in dispute.

The barons administered the country in their own interests, of course, but not irresponsibly. Internal feuding came to an end and the Czech Lands continued to benefit economically: agricultural colonization was still going on, the towns prospered and continued to grow, and the mines at Kutná Hora and elsewhere still produced plenty of silver. However, Bohemia and Moravia suffered from having an absentee monarch. King John needed much money to finance his expensive way of life abroad. He burdened his lands with taxes, pawned most of the royal castles together with their contents, and even sold some regal rights to raise money. When his son Charles came to Bohemia in 1333, taking the title Margrave of Moravia after 1334 and beginning to participate in the government, there was much damage to redress. Cultural life also suffered from the absence of a centre in the royal court. Other centres took over, notably monasteries, noble seats, and some towns, with the help of patronage from outstanding individuals, such as John of Dražice, Bishop of Prague, and Elizabeth, widow of Wenceslas II.

None the less, despite his instability and inconsistency, this knightly and intelligent king succeeded in expanding the state. When John of Luxemburg came to the throne, the state comprised only Bohemia and Moravia, with the newly inherited Luxemburg; John was also the titular King of Poland until 1335, but never tried to conquer Poland. During his alliance with Ludwig of Bavaria, King of the Romans, he gained as forfeit the Cheb region and some possessions in Germany. He gradually managed to acquire Upper Lusatia and part of Silesia, where several dukes accepted their lands in fief from him. His further attempts to expand Luxemburg rule to other territories failed. He became a legendary figure in Bohemia's history with his heroic death in the Battle of Crécy in 1346 where, already blind, he fought in the French army against Edward III.

Despite various critical setbacks, the development of the Czech state from the beginning of the thirteenth century was characterized by expansion, political growth, and cultural development. These trends were to culminate in the reign of Charles I/Charles IV as King of Bohemia and Roman Emperor respectively.

VII

The fundamental features of development of the Czech state in the tenth to fourteenth centuries can be summarized into four basic points:

1. At the beginning of the period, the Czech Lands became a part of Western European (Latin, Catholic) civilization, the matrix of their political, economic, social and cultural development.
2. Economic and social development was delayed in comparison with more advanced countries in Western and Southern Europe, due to the peripheral position of the Czech Lands, particularly up to the thirteenth century. In Hungary, Poland and the Czech Lands in the eleventh and twelfth centuries there were still some features of the economy and society peculiar to the region, but after the twelfth century the West European pattern began to predominate.
3. From the tenth to thirteenth centuries, the cultural impetus came from

the west and south. Only in the fourteenth century did the Czech Lands become a centre of education and culture, radiating through Central Europe; this only really comes to fruition in the reign of Charles IV.

4. The Czech state came into being in the tenth century. It was unified internally and expanded into Poland and Silesia. The bishopric of Prague was established and the first three Czech saints (St Ludmilla, wife of Duke Bořivoj, St Wenceslas, and St Vojtěch (Adalbert) date from this century. The second stage of the Czech medieval state began with the crisis at the turn of the tenth century. Territories acquired in the preceding years were lost but about 1019 Duke Oldřich conquered Moravia, which then became a permanent part of the Czech state. The bond to the Roman (German) Empire was strengthened even though the Czech state kept its special position. The third stage, from the thirteenth century to the early fourteenth, can be characterized as a period of marked growth, which gradually generated one of the important stages within Central Europe and then Europe as a whole.

Notes

1 See R. Nový, *Die Anfänge des böhmischen Staates* (Prague, 1968), I; and *Přemyslovský stát 11. a 12. století* [The Přemyslide state of the eleventh and twelfth centuries] (Prague, 1978); R. Turek, *Böhmen im Morgengrauen der Geschichte* (O. Harrassowitz, 1974).

2 See Z. Fiala, 'Vztah českého státu k německé říši do počátku 13 století' [The relation of the Czech state to the German Empire up to the beginning of the thirteenth century], *Sborník historický*, 6 (1969), 23–95.

3 J. Dekan, *Moravia Magna The Great Moravian Empire Its Art and Times* (Bratislava, 1980); B. Chropovský, *The Slavs Their Significance, Political and Cultural History* (Prague, 1989), pp. 73–149.

4 Nový, *Die Anfänge*; D. Třeštík, *Počátky Přemyslovců* [The beginnings of the Přemyslides] (Prague, 1981); R. Turek, *Slavníkovci a jejich panství* [The Slavníks and their domain] (Hradec Králové, 1982); on the Moravian development, see Z. Měřínský, 'Morava v 10.století ve světle archeologických nálezů' [Moravia in the tenth century in the light of archaeological finds], *Památky archeologické*, 77 (1986), 18–80.

5 B. Krzemieńska, 'Krize českého státu na přelomu tisíciletí' [The crisis of the Czech state at the turn of the millennium], *Československý časopis historický*, 18 (1970), 497–532; 'Politický vzestup českého státu za knížete Oldřicha (1012–1034)' [The political rise of the Czech state under Duke Oldřich (1012–1034)], *ibid.*, 25 (1977), 246–71; and 'Wann erfolgte der Anschluß Mährens an den böhmischen Staat,' *Historica*, 19 (1980), 195–243.

6   B. Krzemieńska, *Břetislav I.* (Prague, 1986); and on the Moravian development and demesnes, 'Die Rotunde in Znojmo und die Stellung Mährens im böhmischen Přemyslidenstaat', *Historica*, 27 (1987), 5–59.

7   On the political development, see Nový, *Přemyslovský stát*, pp. 14–23.

8   D. Třeštík, *Kosmas* (Prague, 1972); and *Kosmova kronika. Studie k počátkum českého dějepisectví a politického myšlení* [The Cosmas chronicle. A study on the beginnings of Czech historiography and political thinking] (Prague, 1968); A. Merhautová and D. Třeštík, *Románské umění v Čechách a na Moravě* [Romanesque art in Bohemia and Moravia] (Prague, 1983); and *Ideové proudy v českém umění 12. století* [Currents in Czech art of the twelfth century], *Studie ČSAV*, 2 (Prague, 1985).

9   D. Třeštík, 'K sociální struktuře přemyslovských Čech [Social structure of Přemyslide Bohemia], *Československý časopis historický*, 19 (1971), 557–87; B. Krzemieńska and D. Třeštík, 'Hospodářské základy raně středověkého státu ve střední Evropě (Čechy, Polsko, Uhry v 10. - 11. století' [Economic foundations of the early medieval state in Central Europe (Bohemia, Poland, Hungary in the tenth to eleventh centuries)], *Hospodářské dějiny*, 1 (1978), 149–230; J. Žemlička, 'K charakteristice středověké kolonizace v Čechách' [On the characteristic of medieval colonisation in Bohemia], *Československý časopis historický*, 26 (1978), 58–81.

10 Nový, *Přemyslovský stát*, pp. 23–6; J. Žemlička, *Přemysl Otakar I. Panovník, stát a česká společnost na prahu vrcholného feudalismu* [Přemysl Otakar I. The ruler, the state and Czech society at the threshold of high feudalism] (Prague, 1990), pp. 32–85.

11 For a general overview of Czech history in the thirteenth century, see J. Žemlička, *Století posledních Přemyslovců* [The century of the last Přemyslides] (Prague, 1986).

12 J. Janáček, 'Stříbro a ekonomika českých zemí ve 13. století' [Silver and the economy of the Czech Lands in the thirteenth century], *Československý časopis historický*, 20 (1972), 875–906.

13 F. Graus, 'Die Bildung eines Nationalbewußtseins im mittelalterlichen Böhmen', *Historica*, 13 (1966), 5–49; the same; *Die Nationenbildung der Westslaven im Mittelalter* (Sigmaringen, 1980).

14 Whereas in the fourteenth century Poland was split, the powerful Kingdoms of Bohemia and Hungary balanced each other. Less strong were Austria and Bavaria.

15 Žemlička, *Přemysl Otakar I.*

16 J. K. Hoensch, *Přemysl Otakar II. von Böhmen. Der goldene König* (Graz-Vienna-Cologne, 1989).

17 J. Kuthan, *Zakladatelské dílo Přemysla Otakara II. v Rakousku a ve Štýrsku.* [The founding deeds of Přemysl Otakar II in Austria and in Styria] (Prague, 1991).

18 There is no monograph on Wenceslas II. In spite of its age, J. Šusta's *Soumrak Přemyslovců a jejích dědictví* [The twilight of the Přemyslides and their heritage] (Prague, 1935) provides a good background. It appeared in the series *České dějiny* (Czech history), II, 1. See also works in notes 9 and 11.

19 For a detailed treatment of the Luxemburg ascendancy, see J. Šusta, *Dvě knihy*

českých dějin [Two books of Czech history], 2nd edn (Prague, 1926, 1935), 2 vols in 1.

20 See the stimulating reflections in F. Seibt, *Karl IV. Ein Kaiser in Europa 1346 bis 1378* (Munich, 1978), pp. 9–15.

21 R. Cazelles: *Jean l'Aveugle* (Paris, 1947); J. Spěváček: *Král diplomat (Jan Lucemburský 1296–1346)* [The king-diplomat (John of Luxemburg 1296–1346)] (Prague, 1982).

3

Politics and culture under Charles IV

FRANTIŠEK KAVKA

Homo politicus

We know considerably more about Charles IV than about any other monarchs at the time.[1] We are familiar with his appearance from pictures and statues; we can deduce a lot about his acts and demeanour from written records. Most of the contemporary observers were attracted by the sharpness of his intellect and the almost 'too cool' realism that helped Charles IV to see the limits of his possibilities in time. Nor did his aptitude for judging human nature, which proved almost infallible in the choice of his advisors and collaborators, remain unnoticed. A great advantage was his ability to communicate with people in the vernacular. 'We could speak, write and read not only Czech, but also French, Italian, German and Latin', he said in his autobiography, 'so there was no difference in using any one of them.'[2] Hardly any other medieval monarch could have said the same. Charles's calculating nature and interest in economics, especially in commerce, were the cause of his being called 'a tradesman on the throne' by some historians. He had a quality that transforms political activity into art: he was able to estimate reliably when it was necessary to act immediately, and when it was better to wait. Even his contemporaries were astounded by his pragmatism, at times verging on cynicism. In the times when political considerations and actions were often influenced by chance, especially with royal palaces not immune to recurrent plague and death, he was in fact lucky and enjoyed favourable outside circumstances.

He was born in Prague in 1316. His father, King John of Bohemia, was a Luxemburg; his mother Eliška (Elizabeth) was a Přemyslide. He was brought up in Paris, at the court of his uncle Charles IV (in French reckoning), from whom he had got the name at confirmation which he used ever since (instead of Václav [Wenceslas] with which he was christened). In the years 1331–1333 he represented his father in the north Italian signory which, as with Bohemia, was to provide backing to the Luxemburgs; similarly with Carinthia and Tyrol, where his younger brother John Henry married. Both of these attempts failed, though. In 1333 Charles returned to Bohemia, and until 1346 he shared rule with his father. Shortly before he inherited the Kingdom of Bohemia, he was elected to the imperial throne as an anti-king to Ludwig the Bavarian. After the latter's accidental death in 1347, Charles was able to ascend the throne himself. After the imperial coronation in Rome in 1355, he referred to himself as 'Fourth'. The previously little known family of counts from the French-German border had entered the European political stage as early as 1308, with the election of Count Henry (d. 1313) to the Roman throne. He was soon to be crowned Emperor. Only when Henry's son John became King of Bohemia in 1310, succeeding the extinct Přemyslides, did the Luxemburgs rise in status alongside the European royal families. Striving to consolidate their position on the imperial throne, they leaned on the popes of Avignon, and the traditional alliance with the French kings, reinforced by family relations. Charles's first wife Blanche (d. 1348), was of the Valois family. Charles fought against the English side by side with his father, who died in the battle of Crécy (1346). It was the last expression of Charles's active support of France in the Hundred Years War, as he then took a neutral stand.

Charles IV was aware of the fact that he had to base his imperial power on a hereditary kingdom. He duly stressed its importance and, unlike his predecessors, listed King of Bohemia among his other titles, even after he had been elected Emperor, displaying the Czech lion beside the imperial eagle emblem on his seals. Prague was his official residence. According to John's testament, Charles's half-brother Wenceslas (d. 1383) ruled in the family County of Luxemburg (from 1354 a dukedom). The strengthening of the power of the Kingdom of Bohemia by territorial expansion, constitutionally supported by its primary position in the Golden Bulls of 1355 and 1356 approved at the imperial Diet in Nuremberg and Metz respectively, was a basis for achieving a broader aim: building the Luxemburg empire in extensive areas of Central and East-Central Europe. Even though Charles IV preferred using the power of money and skilful diplomacy rooted in a clever marriage policy to waging wars, the bad consequence of this expansionist strategy was an increase in taxes in the hereditary lands, especially towards the end of his reign.

The Crown of Bohemia and its expansion

The reign of Charles IV (1346–1378) is the culmination of a medieval Bohemia which even then was showing signs of decline. In many aspects it was this very period that reaped the fruits of previous development in the time of the last Přemyslide kings. After falling nearly a century behind Western Europe, Bohemia now made it up through the so-called agrarian and urban revolution. The Kingdom of Bohemia had quickly been incorporated into the system of traditional cultural institutions of Latin Christendom. On this matter, the period of Charles IV in many ways represented the end point.

The Kingdom of Bohemia belonged to that part of Europe where the fief system played a secondary role. The lands owned by the nobility were their free property, and from them the nobles also derived their claim to participation in government. As in other countries of Central and Northern Europe, a typical power dualism existed. Whereas in Poland and Hungary it led to the disintegration of the central monarchical government, in Bohemia the balance of power was restored. It was achieved through the remarkable state acts of the last Přemyslides, especially of Přemysl Otakar II (d. 1278) and Wenceslas II (d. 1305).[3] Bohemia followed England and France in asserting the principle of primogeniture, and as a consequence the nobility became excluded from decisions about royal succession. The right of election was admitted only in case the dynasty died out, which happened in 1306. As compensation, a writ issued in 1310 confirmed the nobles' claim to the highest posts, the exclusion of foreigners from them, tax allowances, and the right to refuse to participate in military campaigns abroad. It was a concession of the new Luxemburg dynasty by which they bought an acceptable *modus vivendi* in what were uncharted waters.

It was for these reasons that the power of the monarchy remained unshaken even then. The period of Wenceslas II saw the establishment of the independent economic basis of the ruler's power, the 'dominium speciale'. It was the joint income of the royal revenues from mining, minting, customs, and others; from towns and monasteries founded by the ruler, and from royal estates. Towns and monasteries had become sources of a special tax that was not liable to nobles' approval. A dense network of recently built royal castles and fortified towns created a defensive potential for the nobility. Moreover, the rulers of Bohemia, thanks to the lucky discovery of profitable silver ore deposits at the end of the thirteenth century, became very rich indeed. It was in these prerequisites that Charles IV rooted his power, developing it even further. The chain of not mortgageable castles that he created was reminiscent of the French kings' domain.[4] Still, not even he could reverse the dualistic principle of governmental power. Despite some success, the attempt to enlarge areas of enfeoffment in the country, and thus reinforce his own influence, did not bring a change in the relationship between the king and the nobles. Also unsuccessful was the effort to push through a new code ('Maiestas Carolina') that would have weighted the balance in the king's favour. Such was the nobles' resistance that Charles IV was obliged to withdraw the code (1355).[5] Yet the counter efforts of the nobility (the rebellion of the most powerful Rožmberk family in 1356) led only to the resumption of the status quo. This was a valuable royal success that did not vanish even later. The nobles did not refuse to support Charles, especially in the two Italian campaigns of 1355 and 1368/9, in which the contingents from Bohemia were the most important ones. Nobility also had a decisive share in the executive bodies of the royal power – in the court posts dependent on the ruler himself, the jurisdiction of which extended to the imperial government as well.[6]

Since the time of Wenceslas II, the rulers of Bohemia like those of England and France, had sought the endorsement of the home Church for themselves. The clergy had a large share not only in the administration of the country, especially in the Royal Chancery, but provided an ideological support to the rule that in turn protected them against the nobles, who watched the increasing wealth of the Church with resentment. Wenceslas II had the support of the Cistercian monasteries. Their abbots also smoothed the way for the Luxemburgs to the Prague throne. Charles IV took full advantage of the establishment of the archbishopric in Prague (1344), which he and his father had helped to found (through links to the Avignon papacy), and of the opportunities provided by this completed act of church organization. The first two archbishops of Prague, Arnošt of Pardubice (d. 1364) and Jan Očko of Vlašim (d. 1380), were heads of the Royal Council and in the ruler's absence they became vice-regents. In this position they also influenced the imperial government. Charles's wary attitude to the nobility can also be seen in the fact that neither of them belonged to any of the powerful noble families: Archbishop Arnošt was from a moderately well-off noble family in royal service, his successor was in fact of burgher origin. And the third most powerful man of the government, Charles's chancellor Jan of Středa (Neumarkt) (d. 1380), was of similar descent.[7]

The importance of the Kingdom of Bohemia at the turn of the thirteenth century was also one of the fruits whose harvest remained for Charles IV to reap. After the decline of the ruling power in the Empire in the course of the thirteenth century, the Kings of Bohemia became influential actors and, in fact, gained an independent position, despite remaining therein.

Soon they became permanent members of the College of (four lay and three spiritual) Electors and, owing to their royal status, they took precedence over the other lay Electors.

It was just a matter of time before the ruling dynasty in Bohemia would put forward the election of its candidate to the imperial throne.[8] This is what the Luxemburgs calculated as soon as they had become Kings of Bohemia through the election of Charles IV, and later of both his sons. The Přemyslide rulers had likewise made use of the unstable governments in neighbouring countries: Přemysl Otakar II temporarily seized the Alpine lands; in 1300 Wenceslas II was elected King of Poland. And in the chaos resulting from the extinction of of the Árpád dynasty, he acquired the Crown of Hungary for his son of the same name. It was the first union of the three Central European kingdoms, anticipating the future typical form of multinational monarchies in this region. Hungary was soon lost to the Anjous of Naples, who competed with the Luxemburgs in the eastern part of Central Europe but the claim to Poland was successfully defended by King John for a number of years, and when he later resigned, there was a good financial compensation. By that time he had already extended the Kingdom of Bohemia, hitherto formed by Bohemia and Moravia, to include Upper Lusatia (the Bautzen and Görlitz regions). Moreover, he had secured his claim, from the Polish King Casimir III, to most Silesian dukedoms which were through the fief in lord–vassal relationship with the powerful king (1335).[9] Thus the area of the kingdom was almost doubled. This development culminated under Charles IV when the geographical picture of the hereditary dominions was stabilized for another 250 years.

Soon after the death of the Emperor Ludwig the Bavarian, Charles IV was able to come to an agreement with the Wittelsbachs, even though they had been under the papal ban, and he even became related to them through his second marriage to Anna (d. 1353), daughter of the Count Palatine Rudolf. He thus acquired a considerable part of the Upper Palatinate as far as Nuremberg. It was incorporated into the Crown of Bohemia, which was the name given to the countries newly adjoined to the Kingdom of Bohemia. His third marriage, to Anna of Schweidnitz (d. 1362), heiress to the only still independent Silesian dukedom, had the same purpose. The young bride was to fulfil yet another expectation. Neither of the previous marriages brought the most important thing – a son who would ensure the continuity of rule. Charles's successor was still his brother John Henry, the Margrave of Moravia, and his offspring. The expected heir was born as late as 1361 and was christened by the name of the patron saint of Bohemia (later Wenceslas IV). In making an agreement of inheritance with Ludwig the Roman and Margrave Otto of Brandenburg in 1363, Charles IV revealed his intention to gain this margravate. After the death of Anna, he quickly married Elizabeth of Pomerania (d. 1393), granddaughter of the Polish King Casimir, and his possible heiress. As he himself had not yet had a son, Casimir had promised the succession to his nephew, Louis the Great of Hungary, who too was without a son at the time. Elizabeth, on the contrary, bore Charles two more sons: Sigismund (1368) and John (1370) – a valuable asset in the marriage game for inheritance of the dynasties which were dying out.[10]

To carry out these plans which, in fact, were changing the balance of power in Europe, closer links for the House of Luxemburg with the papacy were necessary. An opportunity arose in the increasingly frequent criticism of the Avignon popes in connection with the moral disruption, affecting both 'the head and the limbs' of the Church, for which the desertion of Peter's see was blamed. To return the papacy to Rome was seen as the starting point for reform. Charles IV supported this demand. He knew that if the seat of the Curia was moved back to unquiet Italy, and severed from French influence, it would be bound to accept his help, and therefore forced to comply with his plans. To hasten this development he undertook two trips: to Avignon in 1365, and to Italy in support of Pope Urban V in 1368–9. Elizabeth was crowned Roman Empress in Rome. Pope Urban V promised not to give any bishopric within the Empire, or in the Kingdom of Bohemia, to anybody without Charles's prior approval.[11] However, this agreement only confirmed the practices which the Emperor had carried out even earlier on and which belonged to the effective mechanism of his rule: any services to himself were paid for by the Church. His councillors and notaries of the Chancery lived on canonical benefices and those of particular merit were rewarded with vacant bishoprics.

In 1370, having returned from Italy, Charles IV bought Lower Lusatia, another imperial territory, and incorporated it into the Crown of Bohemia. When Margrave Otto of Brandenburg, now his next neighbour in the north, began going back on the agreement of inheritance, Charles IV held him to it by the threat of military force (1373). Brandenburg was not annexed, as spoils of war, to the Crown of Bohemia, a wise move since it provided one lay Elector.

This vast territory was bought for the Emperor's sons, Sigismund and John, at the enormous sum of 400,000 florins, and joined to the Crown of Bohemia only loosely: basically through a dynastic union. Most of the purchase-money was not raised through the hereditary dominions, already exhausted by the purchase of Lower Lusatia, but from levies imposed by Charles on numerous imperial German towns.[12] In 1376, likewise at considerable financial cost, Charles IV carried through the election of his son

Wenceslas as King of Rome (he was crowned King of Bohemia as a child in 1363).[13] Thus, the rule of the Luxemburgs in the Empire was secured and he could start extending it in the East of Europe.

Other steps taken by Charles IV concerned the fate of the Piast–Anjou inheritance.[14] The King of Hungary, Louis the Great, who had ascended the Polish throne after Casimir's death, was no longer childless – but his only children were daughters. A diplomatic fight broke out about who would marry them, and thus acquire the claim to the inheritance, in which Charles IV's interests clashed with those of his nephew Charles V of France. Towards the end of 1377, the Emperor, afflicted with gout, resolved to undertake a stressful journey to Paris to reach an agreement through personal negotiations. He conceded the administration of the French part of the Empire – the Kingdom of Arles – to the dauphin Charles. Charles V then promised not to dispute the claim of Charles IV's son Sigismund, engaged to Louis's daughter Mary, to the Kingdom of Poland. As is known, Sigismund acquired Hungary after his father's death. When in 1419 he inherited the Kingdom of Bohemia from his childless brother Wenceslas IV, Bohemia and Hungary became unified under the one sovereign, a union which, with the exception of the years 1458–1490, was to become an enduring component of Central European history.

Society and the economy

In the social area, as well, the period of Charles IV saw the culmination of certain developments. Society of the high Middle Ages in Bohemia resulted from impulses and developments analogous to those in West European countries and northern Italy[15] – especially in terms of advanced urbanization. In this, Bohemia differed considerably from neighbouring Poland and Hungary. The important process of rural and municipal colonization had been completed by the mid fourteenth century. All social constituencies – nobles, burghers, clergy and peasants – in their respective ways enjoyed the fruits of economic prosperity of the preceding years. The dynamic development of socio-political relations had not stopped though, and was reflected in growing material, social and national differentiation. With rare exception, the nobility was Czech-speaking – we must not be misled by the fashionable German names of their castles, attributable to the age of thirteenth-century chivalry and its culture. It had remained the politically privileged component of society, the 'body politic'. The smaller group of the high nobility (*domini, barones*) became increasingly remote from the more numerous lower nobility (*milites*), although these groups were not yet mutually exclusive. The execution of political power in the Land Diets, law courts and in the Land administration offices became almost entirely a domain of the high nobility. The attempt of the Prague patriciate, in the early four-teenth century, to penetrate into the Land Diet did not succeed and was not repeated. The actual influence of the burghers was asserted all the more in unconstitutional ways, as it were, the burghers (primarily as clerics) served variously at the court of Charles, mostly in the Chancery and in the finan-cial administration. The reason for this kind of influence was, besides nec-essary educational qualifications, an ability to arrange both public and private loans for the ruler. This in turn was rewarded by a court or church career mediated by Charles IV, or by a rank of provincial nobility.[16] A remarkable feature of Charles's times was the shift in the national composi-tion of burgherdom in favour of Czech ethnicity. Only the border regions of rural areas were solidly settled by German peasantry. By contrast, towns even in the interior of the country had been German. Now, however, the towns were gradually becoming Czechized, a process quickened by epidem-ics of the plague that stopped the influx of German population from the Empire. But in larger Moravian towns the Germans still predominated. Nonetheless, cases of nationalistic encounter were rare not only within the kingdom, but also in other Lands of the Crown of Bohemia, in both Lusatias and in Silesia, where most inhabitants were Germans. In towns clashes tended to surface in connection with the ethnic make-up of town councils. Charles IV tried to assuage the differences and strike the balance even in this sphere.[17] More important was the material and social differentiation in the population of towns, but rising social tension did not go beyond the framework of conflicts between artisan guilds, journeymen and the patriciate, usual in West European towns, or those of northern Italy. Since the 1360s tumults periodically afflicted mainly the Upper Lusatian towns. New findings have corrected the image of earlier literature that Charles IV was an enemy of artisans and always stood on the patriciate's side. His main concern was the maintenance of peace in towns, and if the patriciate was the cause of a breach of the peace he was capable of inter-vening. But he was not partial to guilds, which were regarded as the source of disturbances.[18]

Some time towards the end of Charles's rule the social conditions changed for the worse. The reasons for the reversal have not yet been reli-ably and completely clarified.[19] It possibly originated in a certain monetary and economic crisis. The export of silver – the most important exported article – went down, apparently due to a temporary decline in mining. The inferior quality of coin and the lowering of its value was more palpable than usual. One of Charles's last government acts was the introduction of a 'mintage ordinance', intended to restore sound coin but we do not know the

results. Thus a chain reaction was started with well-known social consequences. The decrease in the value of coin lowered the revenues of landed
feudal authorities, consisting of rents in money form from the dependent
peasants. Apparently the first to suffer were members of lesser nobility, who
increasingly sought service at royal castles or with prominent magnates.
Prices of craft products rose, creating in turn a sales crisis. Regarding international trade, it was not helpful that Prague was situated inland and away
from the main long-distance trading arteries. Therefore, commercially
speaking, the most important town of the Crown of Bohemia was Breslau
at that time. During all his reign, Charles IV tried to support the trading
route Nuremberg – Prague – Breslau – Cracow. Further, by buying the
castle Donaustauf near Regensburg, he attempted to improve conditions on
the Danubian route which, until then, had been utilized mostly by
Moravian towns. Despite a certain success he could not reverse the decline.
From the 1360s, in connection with his expansion to the north, Charles IV
tried to incorporate Prague in a trade link between Venice and the
Hanseatic cities, using the Elbe river. The grand plan failed due to unfavourable natural conditions (the difficulty of crossing the Bohemian mountains),
and due to the resistance of German towns, especially Magdeburg. The
stagnation of Bohemia's long-distance trade had thus not been overcome
by him either.[20] The wealth of the country was also diminished. Gold
reserves had to be used to pay the papal Curia as a part of the traffic in
prelates' benefices. Moreover, in the last decades of the fourteenth century,
the population of Bohemia and Moravia decreased as, unlike Western
Europe, it was only then that Charles's domains were afflicted with plague
epidemics – mostly in towns – which provoked another wave of rising costs.

All these developments created prerequisites for the political crisis that
occurred during the reign of Wenceslas IV, Charles's successor.

Church

Clear symptoms of a crisis in the Church were discernible in this period,
and the situation in Bohemia was to attract attention of all Europe in the
next half-century. Efforts at renovating the secularized Church of the
Avignon papacy period had been widespread in a large part of Western
Christendom. Reform was supported by high ecclesiastical dignitaries,
famous canonists, mendicant preachers, including some rulers, and in this
respect the reforming zeal displayed in the Kingdom of Bohemia was no
exception. Great reforming effort was exerted by Arnošt of Pardubice, the
first Archbishop of Prague, authoritatively supported by Charles IV. Even
though Charles himself as ruler shared in the simony system of the Curia

– one of the causes of the demoralization of the clergy – he was simultaneously aware of the dangerous features that discredited the Church in the
eyes of the lay public. From Vienna he called to Prague the Augustinian
Konrad Waldhauser (d. 1369) and provided protection for him. In his
sermons in Prague churches, Waldhauser mercilessly criticized the moral
offences not only of the clergy but also of society as such, and of the court.
According to contemporary testimonies, his German sermons had no less
effect than those of Savonarola in Florence a century later.[21]

Not so widespread was another movement of the time, not involved in
the reform of the Church but concerned with the development of individual Christian life. It undoubtedly related to contemporary society's existential anxiety: fear of death. Was the minimum spirituality required by the
Church sufficient to prepare the individual to face the last things? Attempts
to reform religious life also came from within the Church itself, that is, from
the Augustinian monasteries, soon finding response in the more educated
lay strata of the population in a movement called 'devotio moderna'. Apart
from the Netherlands, it was Prague that became the second centre of this
movement.[22] Individual religious experience was to be attained by prayer
and contemplation of suitable texts. There were influential supporters of
this movement at Charles IV's court, even in the immediate environment of
the monarch, especially Chancellor Jan of Středa (Neumarkt) and
Archbishop Arnošt. German and Czech translations of various contempla-
tive pieces of literature materialized, such as the Chancellor's German
translation of the so-called Pseudoaugustine. Under Charles's protectorship
in Prague the translation (otherwise banned by the Church) of the whole
Scripture into Czech was carried out and soon afterwards into German, following the versions into French and Italian.[23] When later Charles's daughter Anna, who married the English King Richard II, brought the Czech and
German versions of the Scripture to London, it may have spurred the local
reformists to complete the English translation of the Bible.[24] To enhance
religious life it was not sufficient do away with the obstacle in the shape of
the Latin language, it was also necessary to fill a gap in the rather poor
knowledge of the Christian doctrine. This was to be achieved only by
proper religious educational literature. In this the Czech milieu surpassed
the analogous efforts of indigenous Germans, for example, by the extensive
writings of literary value by Tomáš of Štítné (1311–d. before 1409), who
came from lesser nobility in south Bohemia but lived in Prague.

'Devotio moderna' was a current circulating among court circles and
well-to-do Prague burghers. It was not providing a viable opening to
broader social groups and strata also longing to escape the unease caused
by questions about salvation. For them the sermons delivered from the

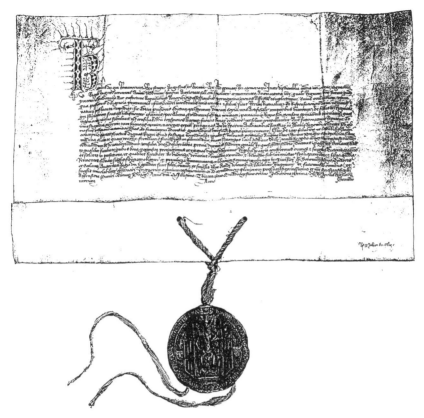

3. Founding Charter of Charles University, 1348.

pulpit were much more important, and if these were to attract, they had to respond to topical problems of the present, and yet provide more conclusive answers than those provided by Waldhauser. Such living words became trumpets of the Czech Reformation. Its 'father' is rightly said to have been the former member of the Chancery Jan Milíč of Kroměříž (d. 1374), who left a courtier's career to dedicate himself to preaching as Waldhauser's successor. His sermons had a wider response for he preached in Czech, and thus addressed more people, but also the contents of his sermons surpassed those of Waldhauser. Theologically they were formulated by Milíč's contemporary, the learned university Master Matěj of Janov (d. 1393), in his work called *Regulae veteris et novi Testamenti*. Both men turned attention to the approaching period of the 'end of ages'. They recognized its various signs and found Christendom unprepared for the arrival of Christ's kingdom. This eschatological incorporation of the Church into the context of the future necessarily showed the relativity of its historical existence, revealed its insufficiency as an institution of salvation, and urged the need for other salvational means: for the reform of the Church by going back to apostolic origins, to consistent observation of 'Scripture rules', and to discarding all that is not supported thereby. Milíč's and Janov's biblicism, interfered with by their belief in the continued revelation of the Holy Spirit, did not yet lead to the reformational principle 'Sola Scriptura'.[25] Milíč's views were condemned by the Church, he was called to Avignon and imprisoned but, probably through Charles's influence, shortly before he died he was acquitted of the accusation of heresy.

Foundation of Prague University: Language and literature

The rule of Charles IV was a golden age of education in the Czech Lands. Education spread through numerous Church and town schools attended even by children of villeins – Master Jan Hus himself is a proof. The ability to read, 100 years earlier a privilege of clergy, disseminated among lay people. The epochal act of Charles IV in 1348 was the foundation of Prague University with all faculties (including the rarely authorized theological one) that was to observe the customs of the universities of Paris and Bologna. It was the first *studium generale* in the Germanic-Slav world, bearing the picture of St Wenceslas on its seal, and provided for financially by the Kingdom of Bohemia whose Chancellor was the Archbishop of Prague.[26] Prague University also pioneered a new type of university institution soon to be widespread: the system of professorial colleges (students' colleges had been the norm).[27] the first two colleges were founded by the ruler in 1360; one called 'Carolina' gave the name still used by the University of Prague at the present time. In 1372 the faculty of law, with Charles's consent, changed into a juridical university.[28] The Prague theological faculty, which became also *studium generale* for some religious orders, was soon competing with the sister faculties of Paris and Oxford. Even after several secessions, Prague University served for decades not only as a nursery of indigenous Czech and German intellectuals but of all Central Europe. Its radius of action reached south-east to Hungary, and also far east and north to Poland, Prussia and Scandinavia.

Apart from members of the court society, a few monasteries and solitary nobles, it was burghers who participated significantly in cultural activities, especially in both Czech and German literature. Czech as a stable literary language, uniform for both Bohemia and Moravia, was finding ways into other Lands of the Crown of Bohemia, especially into Upper Silesia because of the closeness of Polish and Czech. Czech was used in town offices before it found use in the court Chancery, which still conducted its business solely in Latin and German.[29] The first document written in Czech dates from 1370. Theological writings, legends and chronicles, to which Charles IV contributed by his autobiography (*Vita Caroli*), were still dominated by Latin, but soon legends and chronicles were being translated into Czech and German. The need was felt for more translations of scholarly literature into the vernacular languages. The headway made by Czech is well evidenced by several Latin–Czech dictionaries which were compiled in connection with the translation of the Bible. The best known is the Latin–Czech encyclopaedia assembled by Master Klaret, a name adopted probably by Master Bartoloměj of Chlumec, the physician of Archbishop Arnošt. This collective work contains entries by Charles IV himself, for example, on religious holidays. Original scholarly works in Czech also appeared, the most important of which were the already mentioned writings by Tomáš of Štítné. Czech original literature, such as the legend of St Catharine (Charles's favourite female saint) which still affected readers by its expressiveness, or the meditative *Tkadleček* (Tiny Weaver), had to compete with indigenous German literature. Towards the end of the fourteenth century the town scribe of Žatec in northern Bohemia, Jan of Šitboř (Sitbor), composed the poem 'Ackerman aus Beheim', a jewel of German medieval literature.[30] In the court of Charles IV, whose Chancery contributed to making German a literary language, poetry made its appearance in the form of *Meistersang*.[31] Perceived as an early practitioner of this art, the court poet Heinrich von Mügeln (d. c. 1372), dedicated the allegorical poem 'Der meide kranz' to the ruler soon after Charles's imperial coronation. However, the Prague court entered European literary history primarily through correspondence and personal links of Charles and his closest courtiers with Cola di Rienzi, Petrarch and other humanists which, in fact, opened the door for Italian cultural influence to the whole of Central Europe. This was aided by Charles's intimate knowledge of Italy where he had spent almost five years. To Italy is traceable the inspiration to collect extensively not only holy relics and other objects, but also ancient and medieval manuscripts. Also in Italy originated his preference for theological doctrines of St Augustine, which became the basis of his spirituality. The animated environment of Charles's court induced Petrarch – who visited Prague and who, indeed, was invited to stay permanently – to compare it to Athens.[32]

Fine arts. Town planning, building and architecture

Charles's court also entered the history of European fine arts.[33] In the tradition of the last Přemyslide kings, his grandfather and great-grandfa-

ther, the Emperor was undoubtedly one of the greatest patrons of art of
his time. The courts of Přemysl Otakar II and Wenceslas II successfully
competed with those of Paris, London and Naples in the development of
a remarkable court culture. Charles's mother Eliška continued in the same
spirit, and so did her relative Jan Volek, the Bishop of Olomouc and one
of Charles's first Chancellors. Also his father John, stimulated as he was by
the court art in Paris and Avignon, did not lack the inclination of a patron.
Inspiration flowed also from the general development of cultural life in the
country, where the Gothic had already been firmly rooted in the secular
architecture of castles, town halls and wall towers, and also in the sacral
architecture of monasteries, capitular and parish churches. Important
works of wall paintings, book illumination and sculpture appeared, linked
mostly to monasteries, occasionally to aristocratic settings and only gradually taken up in the burgher millieu. Court painters, illuminators and
panelists depended largely on commissions from prominent members of
the court circle. Around 1350 Protonotary Velislav commissioned one of
the most extensive medieval codices known as the 'Velislav Bible' that contains about 750 coloured pen-drawings. Reminiscent of illuminated manuscripts from the eleventh to twelfth centuries, it was the work of two
unknown artists echoing programmatic historicism, typical for Caroline
art and in accordance with most progressive contemporary trends in
Italian and French-Flemish art. This was approximately the period when
a great donation was made by two Rožmberks, Petr I and Jošt, who in turn
held the post of High Chamberlain. It consisted of a cycle of pictures from
the life of Christ (out of which nine have been preserved) by an artist
known as the Master of Vyšší Brod ('Hohenfurter Meister'). Following up
impulses from contemporary Italian painting, he laid the foundations of a
notable chapter in the history of art in Bohemia, that is, panel painting of
the fourteenth and fifteenth centuries.[34] Book painting also drew on Italian
art. Its major patron was Chancellor Jan of Středa (Neumarkt) whose
scriptorium contained a magnificent travel breviary ('Liber viaticus'),
dated *c.* 1360. Historically, the unknown illuminator occupies a similar
position in his genre (which was to reach European significance at the court
of Wenceslas IV) as the Master of Vyšší Brod achieved with his *Altarpiece*
in panel painting.

At the beginning of his reign, Charles's interest focused on large building and urban planning projects. He changed the appearance of Prague in
many ways: by the foundation of the New Town of Prague (1348), one of
the last medieval urban developments on a large scale; by founding (*c.* 1350)
the castle town Hradčany (*hrad* = castle); and by enclosing all the Prague
towns within uniform walls with seven gates, linked inside by a stone bridge

('Charles Bridge') with the Old Town Bridge Tower in the form of a triumphal arch. Thus Charles IV reconstructed Prague into a residence, which in its design was to be a kind of 'second Rome',[35] and Prague still bears visible traces of his reign. The resumption of the construction of the Gothic cathedral (St Vitus Cathedral) at Prague Castle, and the creation of a number of new monasteries in the New Town transformed Prague into one large building site where, in addition to the court building works under the Swabian Peter Parler (d. 1399), others were active. Among the monasteries the most important were the Augustinian foundation at Karlov and the Benedictine foundation known as Emauzy, which practised the Slavonic rite.

Charles was not very interested in book painting, but he was remarkably knowledgeable about gold articles and pieces of jewellery which he not only collected but also commissioned from court and Prague artisans. Although only a fraction is extant, an idea of their quality can be deduced from the Royal Crown of St Wenceslas in Prague and the imperial one in Aachen, the crown of Charles's daughter Anne the English in Munich, and especially the highly valuable reliquaries donated by the monarch to the treasures of St Vitus and Aachen respectively.

In the latter half of his rule, Charles IV concentrated on monumental art, most suitable for the purpose of glorification. He turned to wall painting as a form capable of rendering the religious and political programmes more convincingly than panel painting. Only towards the close of his rule did sculpture, the art preferred by the Paris court, come to the fore. Glorification of the ruler and his family was realized through portraits of himself, picture cycles of ancestors and predecessors, and extensive iconographies at St Vitus Cathedral and Karlštejn Castle.[36]

Like his Paris nephew, Charles IV helped decisively to ensure the position of portrait painting in court art first through wall paintings at Karlštejn Castle which depict himself and the dauphin Charles, his third wife Anna of Schweidnitz and an unknown monarch (probably Peter I of Cyprus). The last word of Prague portrait art was said by sculpture, represented in a cycle of twenty-one busts in the inner triforium of St Vitus Cathedral, the work of Peter Parler and his workshop, which immortalizes Charles's parents, his brothers, four wives and son Wenceslas IV, together with Prague archbishops and canons supervising the construction of the Cathedral. Located as they were in the sacred space above the chancel, the portrait busts played an important part in mythologizing Charles's reign. The bust of the Emperor, well-known from many reproductions, does not take into account his age, and while drawing on earlier realistic renderings, it represents a stylized, idealized, official portrait.

By means of monumental art Charles IV was to be glorified as the ruler through whom the power of his family, and achievements of his predecessors on the throne came into their own. This had been the function of French court art since the thirteenth century, and the idea had not been unknown in Prague. The two traditions were then followed in picture cycles serving as the main decoration of the stately halls in the palaces at Prague Castle and Vyšehrad and Karlštejn Castles. As in Paris, they were not preserved but, except for the Vyšehrad ones, we at least know their themes. In Prague there were about 100 panel paintings of Charles's predecessors on the imperial throne, while the mural paintings at Karlštejn depicted the genealogy of the Luxemburg House. Paris court art combined glorification of the kings and their families with sanctification of their rule as 'Christ's deputies on the earth'; symbolic language thus placed them in semantic relations to the celestial sphere. It became typical of Prague court art that various allegorical and symbolic elements were incorporated in extensive iconographic cycles adorning Karlštejn, and culminating in the St Vitus Cathedral.[36]

The castle at Karlštejn, founded in 1348 in the middle of the old royal forest, half day's ride from Prague, may have had a purpose similar to that of royal castles near Paris. Since the imperial coronation it had become the place where Charles kept his most valuable relics – the main relics of Christ's Passion, deposited in the imperial coronation insignia, and in the Czech relic cross. The glorification of Charles as keeper of this treasure, an equivalent, as it were, to the keeping of Christ's crown of thorns by the French kings in Sainte-Chapelle in Paris, became the programme of the mural paintings at Karlštejn Castle. Among the artists involved were Nicholas Wurmser of Strasbourg and Master Theodoric. The latter was the author of panel paintings in the central space of the castle – the chapel of the Holy Cross – shaping it into an enormous reliquary of stunning splendour reminiscent of Byzantium, or the Orient. The apotheosis of the Luxemburg empire at Karlštejn was accessible only to members of the court and distinguished guests.

Different as well as more public was the glorification theme in St Vitus Cathedral. In this, the principal church of the Kingdom of Bohemia, the theme had to be adapted both to domestic tradition and Charles's state – dynastic ideology. The monarch found a brilliant interpreter of his intentions in the second architect of the Cathedral, Peter Parler, a creative anticipator of further developments in Gothic architecture. The central place of the Cathedral was taken up by the grave of St Wenceslas and the expanse above it, the chapel of St Wenceslas (finished in 1366), was conceived as an independent sacral space of the kingdom. The staircase here was the only access to a chamber containing the Czech coronation jewels. In its immediate vicinity was a ceremonial portal through which the Cathedral was accessible from the royal palace. It was called the Golden Gate and towards the end of Charles's life, it was decorated by a mosaic of the Last Judgement. A picture of the worshipping Emperor and his wife Elizabeth placed above the altar of this sanctuary symbolized the connection of Charles's reign with the indigenous cult of St Wenceslas, and the Přemyslide dynasty. Tombs of its most important members, created by Peter Parler and his workshop, were placed in the ambulatory chapels of the choir. A tall choir with a lofty vault by the same master was assigned to the Luxemburg present and future, protected by the heavenly patrons: Christ, the Virgin Mary and the saints of Bohemia. The placement of their busts in the outer triforium correlated with the arrangements of the busts of the Emperor and his family in the inner triforium. Corresponding to Christ's position, Charles's bust occupied the place of honour.

A work thus came into existence that both in its programmatic and artistic aspects had no predecessors or successors in Europe. Remarkable also is the fact that depicted with busts were not only members of the royal family and ecclesiastical dignitaries, involved in the construction of the Cathedral, but also two court, lay, artists: the first architect Matthias of Arras and the second architect Peter Parler. To preserve the appearance of artists in suitable places of cathedrals which they had created, was an existing tradition. But the manner in which they are immortalized in the Prague Cathedral is quite unique. The homage of Charles to the majesty of art had already gone beyond the horizons of the Middle Ages.

Notes

1 The well-regarded work in English by B. Jarret, *The Emperor Charles IV* (London, 1935) has been superseded. B. Frey's *Pater Bohemiae – Vitricus imperii, Böhmens Vater, Stiefvater des Reichs. Kaiser Karl IV. in der Geschichtsschreibung* (Bern, 1978) contains a useful historiography. There are extensive monographs by F. Seibt, *Karl IV. Ein Kaiser in Europa bis 1378* (Munich, 1978); J. Spěváček, *Karl IV. Sein Leben und seine staatsmännische Leistung* (Prague, 1979); H. Stoob, *Karl IV. und seine Zeit* (Graz-Vienna-Cologne, 1990).

2 *Vita Karoli IV imperatoris*, ch. 8, in J. Jireček, J. Emler and F. Tadra (eds.), *Fontes rerum Bohemicarum* (Prague, 1882), III. For the German version, see A. Blaschka (ed.) *Vita Karoli Quarti – Karl IV. Selbstbiographie*; trans. L. Ölsner (Prague, 1979).

3 On power dualism, see F. Seibt, 'Land und Herrschaft in Böhmen', *Historische Zeitschrift*, 200 (1965), 284–315.

4 For more detail, see F. Kavka, 'Královská doména Karla IV a její osudy' [The royal domain of Charles IV and its development], *Numismatické listy*, 33 (1978),

129–50.

5 The code has recently been dealt with by J. Kejř, 'Die sogennante Maiestas Carolina. Forschungsergebnisse und Streitfragen', in *Stu'ia Luxemburgensia. Festschrift Heinz Stoob zum 70. Geburtstag* (Warendorf, 1989), pp. 79–122.

6 Cf. F. Kavka, 'Správci financí Karla IV. Příspěvek k dějinám české královské komory' [The administrators of Charles's IV finances. A contribution to the history of the Czech Royal Chamber], *Numismatické listy*, 46 (1991), 138–50.

7 G. Losher, *Königtum und Kirche zur Zeit Karls IV* (Munich, 1985) is the classic account on the church policy of Charles IV.

8 For a judicious survey, see F. Seibt, *Zur Entwicklung der böhmischen Staatlichkeit (1212 bis 1471) Der deutsche Territorialstaat im 14. Jahrhundert I* (Vorträge und Forschungen 14, Lindau and Konstanz, 1971), pp. 463–83.

9 On the annexation of Silesia in more detail, see O. Pustejovsky, *Schlesiens Übergang an die Böhmische Krone. Machtpolitik Böhmens im Zeichen von Herrschaft und Frieden* (Cologne and Vienna, 1975).

10 A detailed analysis of Charles's marriages policy is provided by D. Veldtrup, *Zwischen Eherecht und Familienpolitik. Studien zu den dynastischen Heiratsprojekten Karls IV* (Warendorf, 1988).

11 On Charles's relations to Papacy, see W. Hölscher, *Kirchenschutz als Herrschaftsinstrument. Personelle und funktionelle Aspekte der Bistumspolitik Karls IV.* (Warendorf, 1985). On Charles's negotiations with Pope Urban V in Rome, see G. Pirchan, *Italien und Kaiser Karl IV. in der Zeit seiner zweiten Romfahrt I* (Prague, 1930), pp. 313–38.

12 Cf. H. Thomas, *Deutsche Geschichte des Spätmittelalters 1250–1500* (Stuttgart-Berlin-Cologne-Mainz, 1983), p. 293.

13 The negotiations concerning the election of Wenceslas IV were recently elucidated in W. Klare, *Die Wahl Wenzels von Luxemburg zum Römischen König 1376* (Münster, 1989).

14 F. Kavka surveys controversial issues in 'Zum Plan der luxemburgischen Thronfolge in Polen (1368–1382). Strittige Forschungsfragen', *Zeitschrift für historische Forschung*, 13 (1986), 257–83.

15 See F. Šmahel, 'Die böhmischen Länder im Hoch-und Spätmittelalter', in Th. Schieder (ed.), *Handbuch der europäischen Geschichte* (Stuttgart, 1987), II, pp. 507–32.

16 The importance of the burgher element within the court of Charles IV was underlined by P. Moraw, 'Monarchie und Bürgertum, Kaiser Karl IV. Staatsmann und Mäzen', in F. Seibt (ed.), *Kaiser Karl IV. Staatsmann und Mäzen* (Munich, 1978), pp. 51–62.

17 Cf. F. Graus, 'Die Bildung eines Nationalbewusstseins im mittelalterlichen Böhmen', *Historica*, 13 (1966), 4–50.

18 On the situation in the Lusatian towns, see F. Kavka, 'Karl IV. und die Oberlausitz', *Letopis – Jahresschrift des Instituts für sorbische Volksforschung, Reihe B-Geschichte*, 25 (1978), 141–60.

19 On disputed questions, see F. Šmahel, 'Krise und Revolution: Die Sozialfrage

im vorhussitischen Böhmen', in F. Seibt und W. Eberhard (eds.), *Europa um 1400, Die Krise des Spätmittelalters* (Stuttgart, 1984), pp. 65–81.

20 On the economic importance of Prague, see J. Mezník, 'Der ökonomische Charakter Prags im 14. Jahrhundert', *Historica*, 17 (1969), 43–92.

21 On the reform efforts of Archbishop Arnošt of Pardubice, see E. Winter, *Frühhumanismus. Seine Entwicklung in Böhmen und deren europäischen Bedeutung für die Kirchenreformbestrebungen im 14. Jahrhundert* (Berlin, 1964), p. 64; on Waldhauser, *ibid.*, p. 79.

22 On 'devotio moderna' in Prague, *ibid.*, p. 79.

23 V. Kyas, *První český překlad bible* [The first Czech translation of the Bible] (Prague, 1971) is fundamental.

24 Queen Anne's evangelistaries are mentioned in J. Wyclif's *De triplici vinculo veritatis*. At the time of her arrival in England in 1381, the English translation of the Bible under his supervision was approaching completion. That the Czech and German translations offered protection is more than probable.

25 On the beginnings of the Czech Reformation in the times of Charles IV, see R. Říčan, *Das Reich Gottes in den böhmischen Ländern. Geschichte des tschechischen Protestantismus* (Stuttgart, 1957), p. 21; A. Molnár, 'Die eschatologische Hoffnung der böhmischen Reformation', in *Von Reformation zum Morgen* (Leipzig, 1959), p. 59.

26 For the known facts, see F. Kavka, *The Caroline University of Prague* (Prague, 1962).

27 Cf. P. Moraw, *Die Universtät Prag im Mittelalter. Grundzüge ihrer Geschichte im europäischen Zusammenhang. Schriften der sudetendeutschen Akademie*, 7 (Munich, 1986).

28 P. Moraw, *Die Juristenuniversität in Prag (1372–1419) verfassungs- und sozialgeschichtlich betrachtet, Schulen und Studium im sozialen Wandel des hohen und späten Mittelalters* (Vorträge und Forschungen, 30) (Sigmaringen, 1986), pp. 439–86.

29 For the personal composition of the court Chancery, see P. Moraw, 'Grundzüge der Kanzleigeschichte Kaiser Karls IV.', *Zeitschrift für historische Forschung*, 12 (1985), 11–42.

30 Though factually obsolete, still stimulating is H. Friedjung, *Kaiser Karl IV. und sein Anteil am geistigen Leben seiner Zeit* (Vienna, 1876).

31 Cf. P. Wiesinger, 'Das Verhältnis des Prager Kreises um Karl IV. zur neuhochdeutschen Schriftsprache', in H. Patze (ed.), *Kaiser Karl IV. (1316–1378). Forschungen über Kaiser und Reich* (Göttingen, 1978), pp. 847–64.

32 See *Petrarcas Briefwechsel mit den deutschen Zeitgenossen*, in K. Burdach and P. Puir (eds.), *Vom Mittelalter zur Reformation*, VII (Berlin, 1933); J. Klapper, *Johann von Neumarkt, Bischof und Hochkanzler* (Leipzig, 1964); and Klapper, *Schriften Johannes von Neumarkt* in *Vom Mittelalter zur Reformation*, VI (Berlin, 1930–1939); letters were published in P. Piur (ed.), *Briefe Johannes von Neumarkt*, in *Vom Mittelalter zur Reformation*, VIII (Berlin, 1938).

33 On the atmosphere at Charles's court, see F. Kavka, *Am Hofe Karls IV.* (Leipzig, 1989): on his importance for art and culture of the period, see K. Stejskal and K. Neubert, *Karl IV. und die Kultur und Kunst seiner Zeit* (Prague, 1978) and A. Legner (ed.), *Die Parler und der schöne Stil 1350–1400* (Cologne, 1978–1980), I–IV.

34 J. Pešina, *Der Meister des Hohenfurter Zyklus* (Prague, 1983), is fundamental.
35 For a pioneering study of the foundation of the New Town of Prague, see V. Lorenc, *Das Prag Karls IV. Die Prager Neustadt* (Stuttgart, 1982).
36 On the iconographical programmes of the court art, see the article by J. Homolka, 'Zu den ikonographischen Programmen Karls IV.', in Legner (ed.), II. pp. 607–18.

4

The Hussite movement: an anomaly of European history?

FRANTIŠEK ŠMAHEL

Introduction

It does not always pay to be the first or to refuse to toe the line. History displays a host of cautionary examples of both these cases. Bohemia did not pay for non-conformity in 1968 alone. An anomaly *sui generis* was constituted by the Hussite movement, this Reformation before the Reformations and revolution before the revolutions.

If we disregard the Cathar movement in southern France for the moment, it was only England's 'Premature Reformation' that infringed on the universality of Roman Catholic doctrine.[1] The reform campaign, however, was preceded there by the major social revolt of 1381, so that in spite of all its partial success, Lollardism remained a marginal phenomenon bereft of hope for legalization by either domestic or foreign Church authorities; and support extended to Wyclifism and Lollardism by the higher aristocracy was negligible. This constituted one of the major differences from the reform movement in Bohemia where Hus's active group of followers enjoyed the protection of influential officers of the court and the land. It is a historical paradox that only this far-off continental kingdom managed to put into practice, at least partially, John Wyclif's strategic concept of reform-from-above through intervention by the secular power. When the current of reform overflowed the banks of its carefully planned riverbed three years after the Constance martyrdom of Jan (John) Hus (6 July 1415), the protectors from the high aristocracy sounded the retreat, but it was already too late.[2]

At the beginning of 1420, the chiliast wave shattered the foundations of the old order and attempted a practical realization of the ideals of consumer equality, religious brotherhood and liberty of faith with the establishment of the model Tábor community. Sigismund, the King of Rome and Hungary, mounted two unsuccessful military campaigns, under the banner of the Cross, to secure the throne of Bohemia, vacated by the death of his brother Wenceslas IV (1378–1419). The same fate awaited two other massive invading crusades during 1427–1431, which were defeated by the Hussite 'warriors of God' deploying skilfully fortified waggons in defensive as well as offensive actions. By carrying the 'holy' war to neighbouring countries, the radical Hussite army units compelled King Sigismund and the representatives of a new council of the Church, meeting at Basle, to open negotiations on the Hussite confession of faith, laid down in the so-called Four Articles of Prague (1420) and deemed to be heretical. The pace of negotiations for a compromise was quickened by the defeat of the permanent military units of radical Hussite brotherhoods in May of 1434, removing the armed pillar of the revolutionary forces from the scene.

Unity of action between the leaders of the Hussite Right and the royalist Catholic party crumbled instantly: the confessional split into two parallel blocks affecting the whole spectrum of the estate societal order – a legacy of the revolution. An approximate balance of power in the interregnum period (1439–1452) resulted in toleration out of necessity, and this approach became a feasible concept of the Czech state in the reign of the Utraquist King Jiří (George) of Poděbrady (1458–1471) as well. Of course, the concessions ('Compactata') in religious matters by the Council of Basle (1436–7) were a thorn in the side of the consolidated papacy. In March of 1462, Pope Pius II cancelled the agreements legitimating in the Czech Lands, among others, Holy Communion in two kinds (*sub utraque specie*) – holy bread and wine – (hence Utraquism), but this was not enough to eradicate the Hussite heresy. A new crusading army led by Matthias Corvinus, King of Hungary, clashed with Jiří of Poděbrady's troops.

The deadlocked situation in which neither of the parties was able to tip the balance in its favour had to lead to a truce and agreement sooner or later. The religious reconciliation at Kutná Hora (1485), overcoming the religious split, flowed from the common estate interests of both Catholic and Utraquist aristocracy. Though the concessions in the Compactata (as the Basle agreement is called) were never officially renewed, their validity both in Bohemia and its vicinity was tacitly acknowledged. Not even Ferdinand I, who succeeded King Louis II of the Jagiellon dynasty on the throne of Bohemia, in 1526, dared to do away with the *de facto* legality of Utraquism. On the other hand, changes were certainly wrought in the Czech Lands by the coming of the Lutheran Reformation which, among others, exposed the decay of the native reform heritage. Even afterwards, however, the Czech Reformation did not lose its distinctive features. This distinctness can be credited to the Unity of Brethren (*Unitas Fratrum*), the first reformed Church in the history of Western European Christianity. In contrast with this, most school textbooks separate the Czech Reformation from the Reformations of the sixteenth century, in as far as they mention Hussitism at all, representing it more or less as a defeated heretical movement.

The similarity between historical trends in the First and Second Reformation is truly striking.[3] Hus's repudiation of indulgences in 1412 was no less a dramatic prelude to religious upheaval than Martin Luther's Ninety-five Theses, nailed to the door of the castle church at Wittenberg 150 years later. Luther did not repeat the mistake committed by Hus in accepting the invitation to the Church Council in Constance. By failing to appear before the papal court, he was able to carry further the torch ignited by John Wyclif. At first, Luther had no notion of the radicalism of Hus's teachings about the Church, or of Czech Utraquism, which became a component of early Protestant liturgy. For the success of German religious protest, the invention of book-printing was of momentous import. It may be unnecessary to enumerate other similarities as well as other differences, the weight of which should not be under-estimated. Let it suffice here to point to a certain continuity of religiously inspired regeneration of society in a long-term perspective, from the doctrinal non-conformism of John Wyclif via Hussitism in Bohemia to latter-day Reformations.

To its contemporaries, Hussitism appeared as a holy war between the Cross and the Chalice. This notion lived on until the first half of the nineteenth century when the growing strength of the Czech national movement marked research into Hussitism with clear manifestations of militant Czech and German nationalism. At a time when the destructive impact of religious conflicts belonged to a distant past, the national idea was perceived to have been the primary drawing force that pushed the Czechs of bygone days to struggle not only for moral regeneration, but also for hegemony within their own country. Last to enter historical scholarship dealing with the Hussite movement were social aspects. Though this approach was already in evidence at the close of the nineteenth century, it came into its own after the Second World War when Marxist historiography subordinated religious and national impulses to the determinant factors of class and social nature.

Social dimension

The seemingly convincing notions about the dramatic deterioration of conditions of life of those who provided for society's livelihood, leading inexorably to revolutionary conflict in 1419–1420, could gradually be shown to have been quite unfounded. This should not be interpreted as if socially disquieting phenomena had not existed in pre-Hussite Bohemia. On the contrary, crisis deeply affected the whole social body, including the all-too-worldly Church and all sections of the aristocracy. The dead hand of economic determinism simply refused to take into account the explanatory possibilities of different developmental trajectories: the role of short-term stimuli, the impact of irrational components of collective religious emotions, and, last but not least, also the role of leading individuals. Wishful thinking made Marxist historians bridge the gap between the testimony of the sources and their own conjectures with speculative hypotheses. Nevertheless, the *a priori* theses induced, already some time ago, thorough systemic analysis of the pre-revolutionary situation of the Czech Lands. This is far from being completed; among other questions, more attention will have to be paid to comparisons with neighbouring countries. For this reason, the following reflections cannot be expected to cover all subtleties of the Czech anomaly.[4]

The considerable diminution of royal power under King Wenceslas IV resulted in a crisis of the state finances. The introduction of an annual 'special' tax placed a heavy strain especially on towns and monasteries under direct royal control. A plague worse than taxation, however, was the constant decline in the real value of the Prague silver *groš* and smaller denominations. This systematically devalued the revenues of secular as well as ecclesiastical feudal authorities as it was exceptional for the nominal value of rents, interest and various payments of villeins (subject peasants) to change under Wenceslas IV. The quest for arable land came to a halt in consequence of epidemic plagues which, belatedly and repeatedly, afflicted vast rural areas. Thus it was in the interest of feudal authorities to hold on to their own villeins and give them no excuse to leave for deserted grounds owned by other feudal authorities.

A number of impoverished nobles embarked fully on a professional military career. As small-scale warfare continued in the country and its vicinity, both belligerent parties during the period of Hussite wars were able to draw on a host of seasoned professional warriors. Almost all representatives of old baronial families – some gaining and others losing property and influence – felt threatened by the style of government of Wenceslas IV, who surrounded himself with a small group of courtiers and upstarts of altogether low social origins. Pressing with two revolts and exploiting skilfully conflicts between factions of the ruling Luxemburg family, the high nobility substantially curtailed the sovereign's powers and thus laid the foundations of the future monarchy of the estates.

Internal strife and continuous small-scale warfare endangered the possessions of ecclesiastical institutions in particular. Although the Church in Bohemia held about one-third of all arable land, it was a colossus with feet of clay.[5] Many ecclesiastical domains, including the landed property of the Prague archbishopric, were in economic decline. Persistent efforts of the Archbishop Jan of Jenštejn to transform the Prague province into a centralized state within a state were wrecked by the determined resistance of Wenceslas IV and, in their consequences, contributed to the erosion of power of the Church, the emergence of schismatic divisions within it, including its moral decay. The excessive riches of the Church together with its misconduct could plainly be seen by all. Even before the revolutionary secularization of ecclesiastical properties, the Catholic nobility took over a part of major monastic holdings, ostensibly to protect them from Hussite usurpers. In reality this was another secularization procedure, albeit under a different ideological pretext.

In spite of a considerable degree of social division both in towns and country, the conditions of life of 'the common people' (*obecní lid*) did not deteriorate sufficiently to ignite a social explosion. It is significant that minor social revolts tended to erupt in towns with German majorities but there is no evidence for their existence in the three decades preceding the Hussite revolution. In other towns, ethnic and linguistic kinship was blunting the impact of social differentiation within the Czech and German communities. Most likely the opposite obtained so that the struggle for decisive influence in representative organs did not involve any violence. In contrast to the situation in Bohemia, the population of major towns in Moravia both overall and in terms of town-hall representation was German-dominated. All the same, even here, belonging to the German 'language' did not constitute the sole reason for the turning away from the 'Czech' heresy. A factor to be taken into account were the conflicts between Moravian towns and robber barons and knights, not a few of whom joined the Hussite brotherhoods later on.

There is a good deal of evidence that the impulse behind concurrent social movements in some rural regions, especially in southern Bohemia, grew out of the mental climate of increasing collective and individual uncertainties of an existential character, reflecting, as they did, economic and other consequences of small-scale warfare, power clashes and devastating epidemics.[6] The immediate feudal authority was usually not to be blamed directly for all the misery; peasant rebels gathered under the banner of the Chalice because their lord belonged not to the wrong class but the wrong faith. Even the most radical Hussite groups voiced social demands only in a general religious-biblical guise. Things did not differ even in the revolutionary commune established on Mt. Tábor, the peasant programme of which failed within a year under merciless pressure of wartime requisitions.

National dimension

During the whole Hussite period, there were daily manifestations of national hatred, and it is tempting to exaggerate their significance. Investigations of ethnic composition of sixty-four towns and townships in Bohemia, before and after 1420, have confirmed beyond doubt that Hussitism neither Czechized at one go all formerly German or half-German towns, nor wholly prevented the return of ousted Germans, including partial shifts in the linguistic border. Nine of the towns under review had been Czech from the beginning and remained so. In twenty-one towns the German-speaking majority had been replaced by a Czech-speaking one already before 1420. Sixteen previously German towns became Czech in the course of, or owing to, the revolution. It should be borne in mind that in a number of towns the overall position of the Czech-speaking population was consolidated and that in the interior of the country German-speaking enclaves disappeared.

In addition to widespread bilingualism, the territorial co-existence of the two ethnic groups brought about a peculiar asynchrony of manifestations of religious character. Among the German colonists there was a large number of Waldensians who, fleeing the Inquisition, settled in the Czech Lands where they found work as capable craftsmen. But from the 1320s onwards the Inquisition caught up with them even here and quickly made up for lost time. Even on the basis of fragmentary inquisitional records, it is reasonable to assume that heresy in the German setting was extensive and resulted in the premature exhaustion of reforming zeal. Apprehension and fear, difficult to overcome, continued to perturb the minds of generations of afflicted families. With respect to the relations between heretical groupings, it is symptomatic that the spokesmen for the Czech Wyclifists were referring to the German origin of all heretics condemned in Bohemia.

In contrast to spontaneous xenophobia and unreflective ethnic sentiment, the ideologically inspired notion of a national community appealed only to a narrow circle of university intellectuals. Out of this environment grew two most important theoretical impulses by which early Hussitism anticipated modern concepts of a nation. In an address in January 1409, Master Jeroným (Jerome) of Prague included in the Czech nation all its members, starting with the King and ending with the least day-labourer. According to Jeroným, the essential features of a nation were: a native homeland, a common language, ethnic descent from both parents and, last but not least, immaculate faith. Only together as a whole did these features define a 'true' Czech in a country in which even indigenous Germans spoke Czech as a matter of course. At the same time, Jan of Jesenice, a jurist, brought forth arguments – based on natural law and historical reasoning – for giving the community of 'pure' Czechs special privileges in the kingdom's administration. Illusions concerning the 'sacrosanct' Czech nation and the purity of its faith disappeared soon after it became evident that by no means every Czech embraced the cause of John Wyclif and Utraquism. The belligerent confessional factions regarded only the followers of their own 'true' faith, either Hussite or Catholic, as true Czechs. For a long time, the Czech nation split into two confessionally different communities whereby religion acquired primacy over the interests of the nation and homeland.[7]

The initial interlinking of the national emancipation process with the struggle for Wyclif's truths was to have fateful consequence for the size and linguistic contours of the reform movement in the Czech Lands. Initially, the main opponents of both the reform and national currents, the German university masters, managed to win over the reluctant German minority of the Prague towns. As a consequence, only the Czech public responded favourably to the words of the Czech reformers. Even before Hussitism entered its revolutionary stage, the indigenous Germans overwhelmingly came to oppose the Chalice. When the Hussites realized the limitations of a propaganda expressed in Czech, they began to send out manifestos in German and Latin to all places. But it was too late – their reform ideas remained marked by a national Czech tone. A similar asynchrony was to reappear a century later when the Czech-speaking community, worn out by the preceding religious strife and war, viewed with mistrust the rise of the Lutheran Reformation whereas the German speakers in Bohemia and Moravia embraced it *en masse*.

Hussitism and Prague University

It would appear that in the period of the Great Schism doctrinal deviations reflected decomposition of Church power. This was true only in part because the institutionalized mechanism of ecclesiastical supervision in individual provinces and dioceses did not cease to function over the whole period of about forty years. Though the first reactions to the heretical theses of the Oxford reformer in Prague University circles date to the end of the 1370s, the oldest copies of John Wyclif's philosophical treatises are here documented in 1397. A year later a recent Master of Arts, Jan Hus (*c.* 1370–1415), managed to obtain a more complete set. Some twenty marginal glosses by his own hand indicate that he foresaw irritated reaction of the German professors to the Oxford realist who was undermining the foundations of their nominalist beliefs. However, the expounding and defending of Wyclif's writings in the university was not initiated by Jan Hus but by his older colleagues, Stanislav of Znojmo and Štěpán Páleč. Everything points to the conclusion that the reception of Wyclif's philosophical categories offered the Masters of the *natio Bohemorum* an opportunity to separate doctrinally from most German nominalists. Since in this domestic academic corporation a vigorous group of young Masters of Czech origin gradually gained decisive influence, the struggle for Wyclif merged with the nationally linguistic emancipation movement in both the University and Towns of Prague.[8]

The nominalists at the university lost no time in responding. Though forceful philosophical disputes were not a novelty in Prague, they by no means transgressed the limits of permitted '*more scholastico*' discussions at the arts faculty. Only after the arrival of Wyclif's doctrinal writings, brought from Oxford by the Master of four universities, Jeroným of Prague, did connections rapidly emerge between realist concepts and their theological consequences, especially in relation to the Eucharist. The role of spokesman for the anti-Wyclif opposition fell to the doctor of theology Johannes Hübner, who in the spring of 1403 added twenty-one articles to the twenty-four denounced by the synod of London, thereby demarcating unequivocally lastingly the heretical core of John Wyclif's teachings.

Although the vehement dvelopment of events cannot be followed here in detail, what merits attention is the resolute action of Jan Hus. He was head of the university Wyclifists who were angered by the effect of the growing numbers of students who came from abroad after 1405. These students were buttressing the position of the anti-reform university group and lowering, at the same time, the hopes of representatives of the *natio Bohemorum* to obtain a decisive voice in the highest educational institution of the land. Their fears and desires were shared by the reform-minded members of the court aristocracy as well as Czech councillors of the Old Town of Prague who became the majority group in the town council for the first time in 1408. Of no less importance for the future was the fact that Jan Hus's group started to win favour with the younger members of high nobility who had previously taken arms in their opposition to King Wenceslas.

The Czech Wyclifists desired to be 'the head and not the tail' of Prague University. They managed to attain their goal in January 1409 with effective support from their well-born partisans at the royal court. The international and national consequences of the mass secession of some 800 professors and students, following the change in the university constitution, were far-reaching not only for the faculty but also for the reform movement.[9] Prague University acquired the character of most 'national' universities, thus losing for good its leading position in the 'new' Europe. The temporary predominance in the arts faculty, numerically the largest faculty, opened a legal way to extend the missionary campaign by Hus's reform party. In this aspect, the decisive role was played by student pressure groups whose demonstrations during 1409–1412 contributed to the radicalization of the movement both in the capital and in the country.

The teachings of Jan Hus

'When thou speakest the truth, they break thy head'. Though the prosecution files against Jan Hus, who pronounced these words, are far from offering a reliable idea of his teachings, they do give clear hints as to what was regarded as the core of his heresy. First and foremost, they show Jan Hus as a student and follower of John Wyclif. No major impulses, going beyond Wyclif, are imputed to Jan Hus by his accusers. Apparently, all his erroneous formulations did was to substantiate and propagate among people the ideas of the English archheretic. The other feature characteristic of the accusations are numerous testimonies to his disobeying of superior Church offices by which he was setting a bad example to the faithful. The prosecution files refer much less to the thoughts or deeds of Jan Hus by which he could have endangered existing social conditions.

With John Wyclif's vision of the Church, as the sum total of those who were elected, was connected the eschatological trajectory, linking the past and present with future expectations of the purifying renewal under the direct rule of Christ the King. No less was Hus affected by the logic of metaphysical mechanism which Wyclif used to separate the 'Church of the sheep' from the 'Church of the goats': the community of the predestined for salvation from false Christians, heading for eternal doom. This weakened the official doctrine of a temporal militant Church constituted as a hierarchical corporation of all baptised Christians and headed by the Pope as the representative of Christ. Regardless of all fatalism inherent in Wyclif's teaching about predestination, Hus was far from neglecting the merit of observing in everyday life the commandments of divine law; on the contrary, he was constantly bringing such observance to the fore. But even Hus was unable to exclude the possibility that Christ predestined for salvation a prelate or a lord, who remained for a certain period of time in the state of mortal sin, while for someone else doing good deeds Christ foreordained another destiny. Hus attempted, especially in his sermons, to make the predestination principle, so difficult to understand, more transparent, by leaving to the faithful the decision how to separate the corn from the chaff, good from evil. Simoniacs, usurers, adulterers and robber barons indicated by their deeds that they were 'goats' in a Church to which they, most likely, did not even belong.

Nevertheless, there were certain consequences of Wyclif's teachings about the Church and its offices which Hus was hesitant to accept unequivocally. Here he was inhibited less by fears of possible repercussions than by purely practical considerations of the reform pastoral care. Though he sided with the Oxford teacher in arguing that a priest may preach the Word of God without prior consent of a bishop or a pope, he nevertheless acknowledged a distinction between clergy and laity, the sacrament of the priestly office and hierarchical structure of the Church organization. Basically, Hus also believed spiritual power to be more perfect than temporal power, both generally and specifically. All these ideas, needless to say, were operating on an ideal level. All this should have been the ideal and highly desirable state of affairs. In reality, in its wordly dominion, practising simony and transgressing divine law in other ways, the Roman Church, headed by the Pope, was turning on its back the theocratic ideal. According to an informer's report, Hus said in the Bethlehem Chapel that 'indeed, may it come to pass that we girth ourselves with swords and defend the divine law, as Moses ordered in the Old Testament'.

Jan Hus was not an advocate of violence but he recognized its inevitability in many forms, including capital punishment. In his view, the Old Testament maxim of 'an eye for an eye, a tooth for a tooth' constituted a more justifiable retribution than money payments, whose level was socially determined by belonging to one or the other estate. 'Wherefrom does the doctrine come', he criticized contemporary judges, 'that a burgher is worth ten or five threescore [*groš*] more than a peasant and a knight is worth forty threescore more than burgher?' Hus had a positive answer to the question of whether the lords temporal are entitled to bring by force obvious sinners, including unworthy priests, to the spiritual Lord's Supper. The answer followed naturally out of Wyclif's teachings. Specifically, Hus bestowed on the king not only the right but also the obligation to punish unworthy priests, take away from them their worldly goods, and suspend scoundrelly or shameless bishops, and at the same time to defend against them priests heeding the commandments of divine law. Thus, Hus's teaching already provided higher ideological sanction and theoretical support for potential use of force against a secularized Roman Church.

Even if Hus was gaining support for the reform programme from nobility at large (not confined to the court), he harboured no great illusions about higher or lesser 'lords'. In a manner more consequent than Wyclif, he exposed the social evil of simony, usury and excessive demands on the poor by means of dues, taxation or fines. He did not aim his criticisms at the estate of the feudal landlord and the property embedded in it as such, but at acts of exploitation which contradicted divine law. Hus reasoned that when a lord retains his office even though he has lost the moral right to do so, a pauper in the state of grace, who steals out of sheer necessity, cannot be considered a thief. Hus's social teachings oscillated between differentiated categories of good and evil, albeit marked by subtleties which interpreters, under the influence of preconceived ideas, not seldom overlooked.

It was Hus's teaching about obedience which became *via facti* the keystone of both his reform programme and public activity. In principle Hus granted to all subordinates, dependent and subject followers of God's law (but not to the estate of burghers and subjects as such) the right to disobey and resist those ecclesiastical and lay feudals who lived in flagrant contradiction with the above mentioned norm – but again, not to ecclesiastical and lay feudality as a whole. Thus, not even at the height of his intellectual development did Jan Hus go so far as to relativize the whole feudal system by putting the principle of divine law above the feudal institutions. He was only after changing them for the better, especially by radically reforming a secularized Roman Church. It might be argued that no secular power could meet divine law in this categorically demanding form, and that, as his opponents claimed, Hus's teaching was potentially subversive. It should be added, therefore, that the Wyclifian–Hussite norm of divine law required, at the same time, the proper performance from subordinates and subjects of their duties and obligations towards all 'good', that is, god-fearing feudal authorities. It is only through this double obligation, upwards and downwards (by which also the socially universal profile of the Hussite reform front may be explained) that the divine law was attaining the integral character of a constitutional norm. The unattainable ideal of social harmony and a just social order based on three estates ('tripartite people') was behind Hus's admonition, addressed to all his faithful rich and poor Czechs from Constance before his death: 'I also entreat you to love each other, not to let the good be oppressed by force and to let everyone find the truth.'

Revolutionary dimension

There is no revolution without dictatorship and violence. Regardless of whether Hussite Bohemia became the scene of the first European revolution or not, the mechanism of this long-term all-embracing social process did contain the classical elements of a revolution. Significantly, repression and violence were initially not part of the programme of the Hussite reformers who, only after considerable hesitation gave their consent to the 'holy war' imposed on them. When in 1420 internal conflicts and intervention disrupted the whole country, the revolutionaries ceased to lead the revolution. It was the revolution that pushed them on.

Full-scale warfare brought to prominence a group of professional fighters from the ranks of lower aristocracy, who had earlier embraced the reform programme and occasionally clashed both with patronizing preachers and the unleashed religious fanaticism of the 'warriors of God'. During the first year of the revolution, when activities of the popular crowds, preachers and military commanders converged in a common direction, non-Utraquists became the exclusive target of repression. However, when in the spring of 1421 the sacramental nihilism of the Táborite sectarians (Pikharts) subverted the Eucharistic mystery of the Chalice, factional struggle in the form of a heresy emerged.[10]

The university Masters of Prague (to whom the theologians from the south Bohemian town of Tábor turned for advice) immediately sounded the alarm against the new heretics. The Táborite 'party of order' (following H. Kaminsky) did not lag behind. It ousted the sectarians from the community and assigned them a place for habitation at a safe distance from the fortress proper. The Pikhart group soon became notorious by indulging in new spiritual and physical excesses.

Because the group continued to cause agitation among the troops and elsewhere, a confrontation with fire and sword was inevitable. Provisional inquisition tribunals acted resolutely. The sectarians who refused to renounce their errors went to the stake. The cleansing was completed by punitive expeditions in the woods of southern Bohemia in the autumn of 1421. The violent annihilation of Táborite freethinkers brought about the first major shift in the balance of power within the Hussite cluster whose Left was now represented by moderate Táborites together with the Orebites in east Bohemia and the Prague tribune Jan Želivský.

The assassination of Jan Želivský, in March 1422, marked the end of the dictatorship of radicalized craftsmen in Prague. The new ruling group headed by Sigismund Korybut, a Lithuanian duke, attempted to establish closer connections with both the Hussite and Catholic aristocracy. Restoration was prevented by Hussite troops, which were not numerous, under the command of the undefeated blind Captain Jan Žižka. After Žižka's death in October 1424, the Táborite and Orebite brotherhoods merged temporarily but even after renewing their independence, they retained a close active alliance; and, after exercising restraint, they took the

4. Blind Jan Žižka leading Hussite troops.

offensive during 1427–1428. In the following period, the mobile troops of the radical brotherhoods, commanded by Prokop Holý, held sway not only over the Czech Lands but also over adjacent regions. Their crushing defeat, at Lipany in May 1434, by the military forces of a coalition of the Utraquist and Catholic nobility and of the Prague burghers brought about the second shift in the balance of power within the Hussite community. Now the Council of Basle took the moderate Prague centre, to which a good many who fought at Lipany on the side of the victorious coalition belonged, to be the chief defender of the Czech heresy. This was fully corroborated in the course of continuing negotiations by representatives of Hussite Bohemia with the Council, which ended in the Compactata agreement, thanks to which Sigismund of Luxemburg was ultimately able to ascend to the throne of Bohemia in August of 1436.

Spiritual and cultural dimension

Though the Muses were not entirely silenced by the clamour of the Hussite arms, some went into hiding. Listening triumphed over looking, words won over images. The domination of the spoken word in reform agitation matched both contemporary conditions and the needs of missionary agitation. The spoken word conveyed the message of the renewed ideal of early Christianity together with the commandments of divine law. Passing from mouth to ear, it weakened and invigorated at every turn; changing frequently, it sounded hopeful as well as threatening. Rhythmic verse, rhyme and tune helped the listeners to memorize the contents of the message. As vehicles of ideological dissemination, rhymed compositions and songs thus greatly expanded the scope of their genre. On the other hand, the written word remained confined to a narrow circle of the educated. Transportable painted boards were a rare sight in demonstrations and processions, while church frescoes could have been employed by the reform preachers only exceptionally for the purpose of basic religious instruction. Not only the decoration of the Prague churches, but also that of the monastery and of town churches offered visitors a multifold cultural experience. The reform currents took an apposite direction, condemning the exaggerated iconolatry of the Church. Aesthetic puritanism was one or two steps away from verbal negation and, later on, from physical destruction of those works of art deemed to have harmful sacral functions. In the vision of the reformers, form negated contents so far as it was not considered altogether redundant in its multiform and provocative appeal to the senses. Needless to say, the heralds of religious purification and of internalized faith were far from unanimous in their attitudes towards the cultural heritage. Most of the university reformers remained in a halfway position, while radical theologians went to extremes. It is also significant that one of the Tábor captains, who had participated in the destruction of holy tabernacles, commissioned an exquisitely illuminated Bible manuscript for himself in a later period.

Not things old, but things *new* had to be pulled down so that Christianity could revert to its ideal, primary, sources. The historicism of the reform vanguard has been confusing the seekers after Hussite modernity up to now. Of course, systematic purging of all additions to the doctrine and practice of the earliest Church remained a utopian wish. Skipping centuries of development, the world simply could not revert to the self-sufficient, money-free, agrarian community visualized by the demolisher of the doctrine of the 'tripartite people', Petr Chelčický (d. *c.* 1450). Nor could it advance its dream of free spirit and body, conforming to the ideas of the freethinkers from the commune sprung up in the fortress on Mt. Tábor.

Sooner or later, retrospective ideals were grounded in the shallow waters of conservative Hussite orthodox teaching and practice. Tried norms and values subsequently became a shield which helped the cloistered ruling elite of the Utraquist reform community ward off domestic malcontents, intellectual non-conformists, and the external influences of early Humanism. On the other hand, the exhortations of Utraquist moralists, who saw the decline in religiosity all round them, were to be listened to. 'Lo, they blew their noses, their ardour is extinguished' were words uttered from the pulpit by Jan Rokycana, the elected Hussite Archbishop of Prague (never acknowledged as such by the Roman Church), when he addressed Utraquists in Prague and elsewhere. He saw very few good Christians around him, there were more who mocked the preacher, took him by his word or even informed against him. Burghers stopped falling on their knees in order not to soil them when bells rang; once-pious peasants argued with priests who had the courage to tell the plain truth. Moreover, even an official of an Utraquist king wrote a pamphlet inveighing against the attempts of the clergy to intervene in political life. Nor did the Czech Reformation succeed in the fight with magic and popular superstitions. Other bad habits and major sins which had been thrown out of the door, at the onset of the revolution by Hussite puritans, came back by the window.[11]

Superficially, post-revolutionary Bohemia could indeed appear as a spiritually barren land which managed to preserve only the communion Chalice out of its whole reform programme. Though in accord with the aims of the Council of Basle, it was not in accord with the treaty concluded with representatives of the Hussite parties in 1433–1436.[12] In addition to this, the elderly Emperor Sigismund of Luxemburg, in his wish to accede to the throne of Bohemia as soon as possible, made a number of concessions which went far beyond the exceptions allowed by the Council.

To some extent, the marginalization of the Compactata agreement followed on from the sidelining the central Hussite programme, the Four Articles of Prague. The extremist radicals of Tábor in particular viewed the commonly acknowledged Articles of spring of 1420 as an insufficient expression of reform desires and aims. However, when the Hussite community started to swing to the Right after the fall of the Táborite sects and of the Prague dictatorship of Jan Želivský, the Four Articles steadily gained in significance until they attained the status of a maximal Hussite programme not only at home, but *vis-à-vis* the Roman Catholic world in the first half of the 1430s. The transformation of the ideological function of the Four Articles of Prague through time thus reflected to a considerable extent the main phases of the revolutionary cycle. Three of the four reform demands formulated in the Articles were more or less put into practice: free preaching of the Word of God; the right of lay Christians to the communion in both kinds, i.e., in bread and wine; return of the Church to the simple way of life led by Christ and Apostles. The last, fourth, article demands immediate punishment of 'mortal' sins, especially those that are public. It mirrored all the illusions, twists and turns of the cleansing process but those who defended it and tried to put it into practice, soon lost control and it gradually vanished into thin air as utterly impracticable.

After the defeat of the Hussite brotherhoods at Lipany, Bohemia became a kingdom of twopartite people, of two legal faiths.[13] Tolerance out of necessity was practised even before the religious compromise itemized in the Four Articles. The two confessional communities began to diverge, not only over Holy Communion. In time the Utraquist milieu created special customs, feasts, rituals, norms of behaviour and attitudes, thus consolidating group cohesion. Two codes of religious doctrine and life style were, in part, disturbing the cultural domain, hitherto unified in the territorial and ethnic sense. There is no need to conceal the cultural losses and forfeitures suffered by the Czech Lands in consequence of their premature Reformation. Similar losses were incurred, a century or more later, by other European lands or regions, which seceded from the community of the Roman Catholic Church.

Consequences

In many respects, the Hussite revolution may be regarded as a fateful intervention in the late medieval history of Bohemia. All the preceding order, institutions and values seemed to have collapsed and fallen into ruins on which then the new historical epoch began to grow. In the opinion of a number of historians, the re-structuring of the order of the land and estates received its decisive impetus from this revolutionary upheaval. But a perspective which encompasses the periods before and after the Hussite era makes it possible to discern contours of longer term processes, either temporarily weakened or obscured by Hussitism, which began to re-emerge in its end-phase. This was not merely a question of trends which were momentarily interrupted; the revolution left permanent consequences in a deep-reaching transformation of property and societal structure.[14]

Up to the beginning of the fifteenth century there were only two fully established estates: clergy and high aristocracy (lords, barons). The highest dignitaries of the Church did not form an independent 'curia' in the Diets and intervened in practical politics either by their own influence or by means of their court functions. Against this, the barons, as representatives of the commune of free landowners, possessed an institutional base in the Land Court and the Land Register Office from the end of the thirteenth century. Their persistent efforts at gaining greater influence in the political administration of the country came to a climax in two rebellions (1394–1405) against King Wenceslas IV. Before the barons succeeded in curtailing the sovereign's power, their estate community and other strata of the social pyramid split into two parallel segments divided by their attitudes to the reform teachings of Jan Hus.

In the years of Hussite wars (1419–1436), the societal order of estates adapted and expanded, but did not unequivocally influence decisively the revolutionary process. The ideological differences between the two leading towns of the rival Hussite factions, Prague and Tábor, were so deep that despite close factional cooperation in the fields of battle, common municipal interests were pushed into background. On the other hand, because of the revolution not only Hussite burghers but also warriors from the ranks of lower aristocracy were admitted to prominent roles in the political life of the country, thus accelerating their transition from the estate *an sich* to the estate *für sich*. The time of solidarity, self-awareness and political activity on the part of the lower aristocracy came only after the accession of Emperor Sigismund to the royal throne of Bohemia in August 1436.

The lower aristocracy's claims for places on the benches of the Land Court were resolutely rejected by Utraquist and Catholic barons who aimed at the restoration of the pre-revolutionary status quo. The confessional split of the high aristocracy temporarily deepened in the second half of the 1360s when Matthias Corvinus, King of Hungary, led a crusade against Jiří of Poděbrady, King of Bohemia. The Peace of Olomouc, in 1478, enabled Catholic barons to become reintegrated into the Czech Land commonalty (*česká zemská obec*). An attempt by King Vladislav II Jagiellon (1471–1516) to restore Catholicism was wrecked by the insurgence of Utraquist Prague in September of 1483. The lords belonging to both confessions came to realize that a balance of power existed, and agreed upon a religious truce in 1485.

Two years later, the barons concluded compromise agreements with representatives of the lower warrior aristocracy, which gave them a free hand to attack revolutionary privileges of the royal towns, in particular, the right to participate fully in the work of the Diets. In 1490, the emergence of the barons into positions of power in the land facilitated the election of Vladislav II to the royal throne of Hungary and the establishment of his residence in Buda. The legal codification of the so-called Vladislav Land Ordinance (1500) deprived the royal towns, among others, of the right of participation in the Diets. Only then did the towns, with Prague in the lead, become aware of missed opportunities. Moreover, the towns in separate conventions speedily overcame the confessional disunion, formed a country-wide union and, for the first time in the history of Bohemia, formulated a programme which voiced the will of the towns as an 'estate' in the full sense of the word. Common political and military action bore fruit in 1517 when an amendment of the Land Ordinance entitled the towns to representation in the Diet. In this way the long-term maturation of the Czech state into a developed monarchy of the estates was completed.

Notes

1 In this context, see the penetrating work by A. Hudson, *The Premature Reformation. Wycliffe Texts and Lollard History* (Oxford, 1988).

2 The literature on the Hussite movement is vast. K. Zeman's *The Hussite Movement and the Reformation in Bohemia, Moravia and Slovakia* (Ann Arbor, 1977) is a bibliographical study guide with particular references to resources in North America.

3 On the concept of the First and Second Reformation, see mainly A. Molnár, 'Elementi ecclesiologici della prima reforma', *Protestantesimo*, 19 (1964), 65–77.

4 See F. Šmahel, *La révolution hussite, une anomalie historique* (Paris, 1985). My *Husitská revoluce* [Hussite revolution], vols. I–IV (Prague, 1993) contains a fuller treatment of the subject.

5 The Church in late medieval Bohemia is examined in essays by F. G. Heymann, Zdeňka Hledíková, Zdeněk Kalista, Franz Machilek und Rostislav Nový in F. Seibt (ed.), *Bohemia sacra. 1000 Jahre Christentum in Böhmen* (Düsseldorf, 1974).

6 On the social crisis in general, see F. Graus, *Das Spätmittelalter als Krisenzeit. Ein Literaturbericht als Zwischenbilanz* (Mediaevalia Bohemica, Supplementum 1) (Prague, 1969); F. Seibt and W. Eberhard (eds.), *Europa 1400. Die Krise des Spätmittelalters*, (Stuttgart, 1984).

7 Cf. F. Šmahel, 'The idea of the "nation" in Hussite Bohemia', *Historica*, 16 (1969), 143–247; 17 (1969), 93–197.

8 See F. Šmahel, 'Wyclif's fortune in Hussite Bohemia', *Bulletin of the Institute of Historical Research*, 43 (1970), 16–34.

9 F. Šmahel, 'The Kuttenberg decree and the withdrawal of the German students from Prague in 1409: a discussion', *History of Universities*, 4 (1984), 153–66.

10 A recent examination of the history of Tábor is contained in F. Šmahel, *Dějiny Tábora*, I, 1–2 (České Budějovice, 1988–1990).

11 Cf. F. Šmahel, 'Stärker als der Glaube: Magie, Aberglaube und Zauber in der Epoche des Hussitismus', *Bohemia*, 32 (1991), 316–37.

12 On this, see e.g., E. F. Jacob, 'The Bohemians at the Council of Basel, 1433', in R. W. Seton-Watson (ed.), *Prague Essays* (Oxford, 1949), 81–123.

13 For the long-term context, see F. G. Heymann, *George of Bohemia. King of Heretics* (Princeton, 1965).

14 On the subject of the estates, see my paper 'Das böhmische Ständewesen im hussitischen Zeitalter', in H. Boockmann (ed.), *Die Anfänge der Stände in Preussen und seinen Nachbarländern* (Munich, 1992), 219–46.

5

The monarchy of the estates

(+) JOSEF MACEK

One of the most remarkable Late Gothic works of art in Bohemia is the Vladislav Hall of Prague Castle; 62 metres long, 16 metres wide and 13 metres high, this vast hall with its magnificent lierne vaulting was accessible to mounted noblemen via the Horse Steps.[1] The hall is one of the most monumental examples of Gothic architecture in Central and Eastern Europe.[2] It took its name from the King of Bohemia and Hungary, Vladislav Jagiellon (1471–1516). This period of Czech history was interpreted by earlier historians as a time of anarchy and turmoil (1471–1526), and both King Vladislav and his son Ludvík (Louis) who reigned 1516–1526, were stigmatized as weak and incompetent rulers who failed to bring prosperity to the country. Art historians, however, fundamentally disagree with this view and conclusively show that this was a glorious period of Late Gothic art.[3] The result is a dilemma: how can one explain the emergence of this illustrious art at a time of declining royal power? Whence did this art spring? What made it possible to produce the idea of the Vladislav Hall, a concept quite out of keeping with the modest hopes of a weak and hopelessly insolvent king? Who was behind this and other great works of Late Gothic art? Who was the patron?

The estates

These questions can be understood if we consider the significance of the estates monarchy in the Jagiellon era. Until recently the contribution of the estates to Czech statehood and culture has been played down. From the time of František Palacký onwards the estates were regarded as a destructive, anarchic element which weakened the power of the Czech monarchy.[4] Yet if we turn aside from the glorification of centralized power, we find many positive features in the rise of the estates at the end of the fifteenth century. This development drew on earlier traditions and contributed to both social and cultural advance.

In the Kingdom of Bohemia the nobles had been trying to get a share of power ever since the end of the thirteenth century.[5] As the fourteenth century drew to a close, King Wenceslas IV was forced to hand over considerable power to the higher and lower aristocracy, lords and knights. They played a notable role during the Hussite revolution of 1419–1437. The burghers then began to play an active part in politics, and by the end of the fifteenth century they were recognized as the third estate, an independent entity. Under Jagiellon rule the three estates, three political forces, were the most significant factors in the Czech state, the Kingdom of Bohemia. The part played by the third estate during the Hussite revolution earned that phenomenon the designation of a 'revolution of the estates'.[6] The renowned German historian Karl Bosl declared that in the fifteenth century Bohemia was a model for the evolution of the estates, the country which saw their most mature form.[7]

Detailed study of the structure of the estates in Bohemia reveals that conditions here differed greatly from those elsewhere in Europe. The Hussite revolution had broken the secular power of the Church; the prelates had no place in political life and were no longer powerful in the estates, where the lords had acquired greater influence.[8] In Moravia the burghers did not achieve political influence until the end of the Jagiellon era, and even then had far less power than their neighbours in Bohemia.

The situation of the estates in Bohemia, where there were no church dignitaries and the third estate (the burghers) enjoyed considerable power, differed from conditions not only in Moravia but in particular in Poland and Hungary, where the burghers had not yet achieved independent political identity and where, on the contrary, the prelates were among the principal supporters and partners of the ruler, along with the high aristocracy.[9] The structure of the estates in Saxony, Bavaria,[10] and the Austrian territories followed the traditional model, with the Church hierarchy well to the fore, again very different from their structure in Bohemia. Bearing in mind that England was only just recovering from the Hundred Years War, and that from the time of Louis XI the French kings had consistently pushed Parliament into the background, it is possible to compare the political influence of the estates in Bohemia only with some regions of Renaissance Italy, or with the Netherlands.[11] Even there, however, the Church was omnipresent in the apparatus of power. At the end of the fifteenth century the estates in Bohemia were indeed a unique and unusual phenomenon.[12]

It was the Czech Reformation that created the unusual conditions of political life in the country. During the long interregnum from 1437 to 1453 the thirty-two towns with a Royal Charter became powerful enough to withstand pressure from both the higher and the lower aristocracy.[13] While the Hussite King Jiří of Poděbrady (1458–1471) reduced the power of the burghers and the third estate,[14] they came into their own again during the reign of Vladislav. To the amazement of foreign observers, those who assembled at Kutná Hora in May 1471 to call the fifteen-year-old Vladislav, son of the Polish King Casimir, to ascend the throne of Bohemia, included simple tradesmen and craftsmen as well as nobles. Elected king, Vladislav II Jagiellon (1471–1516) had to take the oath that he would rule over 'twopartite people', i.e. the Utraquists and the Catholics, according to the terms of the Compactata agreement between the Czech Hussites and the Council of Basle.[15]

Vladislav's reign began in violence. The King of Hungary, Matthias Corvinus, instigated by radical elements in the Church, had declared himself King of Bohemia (1469); his armies controlled Moravia, Silesia and Lusatia, and were attacking Bohemia.[16] Vladislav was a Catholic, too, but the Roman Curia did not want to recognize him as king because he stood by the Compactata which successive popes had repudiated. The Prague king was not one of those virulent heretic-hunters. Instead, he preferred to seek an understanding with the Czech Utraquists who were already well organized in Bohemia. During the war with Corvinus, Vladislav continually made concessions to him and the estates of Bohemia, trying to find a compromise, a way to peace. In 1479 he made his peace with Corvinus in Olomouc, but his rule covered only Bohemia; Corvinus kept his title of King of Bohemia, and retained control over the lesser Czech Lands, Moravia, Silesia and Lusatia.

As King Vladislav came to the throne, it was necessary to define quite clearly the power mechanism controlled by the estates of Bohemia. Following the Peace of Olomouc in 1479, the Royal Council became a powerful entity; consisting of about thirty members, this body lived at the court and was governed not only by the king, but also by a committee of the estates. The Diet even agreed that each region was to send successively noblemen to be members of the Royal Council, without the king's knowledge.[17] This institution became the supreme governing body, regularly meeting to discuss all urgent questions be they political, ecclesiastical, military, diplomatic or financial. With the King's consent they ordered the Royal Chancellery to issue the relevant documents, decrees and ordinances. The Royal Council even expressed its views on royal marriages, and prevented the King from marrying the daughter of the Margrave of

Brandenburg Achilles Count Albrecht. The bride, Barbara Hlohovská [of Glogau], was robbed of her Silesian homeland by King Matthias Corvinus. The estates refused to allow a dowryless princess to ascend the throne of Bohemia. And so, although Vladislav had been officially married, the wedding ceremony never took place, and although Barbara Hlohovská called herself Queen of Bohemia, she never met her royal husband, and never crossed into Bohemia.[18] Such was the power of the Royal Council, the executive organ of the estates in Bohemia.

The regular mechanism of executive power in Bohemia became the Diet.[19] Officially convoked only with the King's consent, this body often met without his knowledge, and informed him of its activities only afterwards – especially after 1490 when Vladislav was elected to the Hungarian throne and made Buda his residence. There were three divisions ('curias'): the nobles, the knights and the burghers; they met separately, and then met together to pass common resolutions. Thus at least four times a year between 150 to 200 men met to decide on such matters as taxes, defence of the kingdom, dealings with the Emperor, with neighbouring rulers, the currency, and all questions that had to be decided by law. There were 190 meetings of the Diet between 1471 and 1526, convoking thousands of nobles and burghers, active participants in the political life of the kingdom – in effect, legislators. The resolutions of the Diet had the character of law, and were inscribed in special books, the so-called Land Register.[20]

It was not rare for the assembly meetings to be chaotic, never-ending, and members to be criticized for their empty speeches and useless discussions. Thus the weaknesses of later democratic parliaments may be perceived. Nevertheless, the fact that the lesser nobility and the burghers took an active part in the meetings of the Diet showed the growing participation of broader elements of the population in political decision-making. If one assumes democratization to mean the gradual awakening to political and public activity of these sections of the population previously partially or completely excluded from it, then the meetings of the Diet in Bohemia were doubtless a form of a process of democratization. The years from 1471 to 1526 saw the most active period of the Diet, equalled perhaps only by the second half of the nineteenth century, when it met frequently and civil society was developing under very different conditions.[21]

The growing importance of offices of the Land formally bound by royal consent but in fact by the estates, was characteristic of the times. The highest office, that of the Burgrave of Prague invested with supreme military power, was one such instance.[22] Then there was the High Judge, the holder of the highest juridical office and another was the Chamberlain, in charge of the finances of the Land, and the Chancellor as the head of the

Royal Chancellery.[23] Taken together, these officers could be regarded as the government of the Land. They were aristocrats, drawn from the most powerful families, who did not always distinguish clearly between private and public interest; often they ruled the country from their castles. A bureaucracy of lawyers and scribes was slowly coming into existence under the Jagiellons, but for the most part these were employees of the individual aristocrats – officers of the Land. It was only at the Land Court that the so-called orators, i.e. lawyers, schooled advocates, began to insist on written legal norms.

At times, especially when the kings (Vladislav and Louis) were out of the country (at their Buda residence), the highest officers of the Land were in fact the rulers; although their decisions were to be confirmed by the royal seal, in the course of time the seal was left in the care of the Chancellor who with his fellow officers came to take vital decisions for the country. Royal power was further undermined when the Master of the Mint became an officer of the Land subject to appointment by the Diet.[24]

Thus the estates controlled the Land Court, which was concerned with suits involving aristocratic property, as well as the Chamber Court, which settled cases between aristocrats and burghers.[25] The Chamber Court, in particular when it was headed by the magnate Vilém of Pernštejn (who was in charge of the royal household), became the supreme court of justice, and the king was by no means rarely one of the parties in disputes. The kings respected the jurisdiction of these courts.

The royal towns, however, did not recognize the Land Court which they considered an aristocratic institution. They looked to Roman law and German codes of law (such as that of Magdeburg) for models, thus creating a separate political power sphere, independent of the nobility. This is also why the burghers did not identify with the nobles in their efforts to codify a Land constitution. In 1500, when the lords and the knights tried to codify customary law in a statutory constitution, the so-called Land Ordinance, the royal towns refused to accept it.[26] The Land Court, for example, called in vain upon the burghers to account for their actions. The royal towns not only refused to obey but they formed an armed Union of Towns, and not even the king himself could persuade them to concessions.

A striking feature of the monarchy of the estates in Bohemia was the decentralization of executive powers. Historically, in Bohemia there were fourteen regional political and judiciary centres located in towns. Regional government was in the hands of the Regional Captain, usually an aristocrat, aided by a council of burghers and the lesser nobility.[27] The principal agenda was to keep the peace in the region, and to dispense justice in local disputes. The regions had the right to elect their representatives to the Diet, and to see to it that laws of the Land and regulations adopted by the Diet were carried out. In Moravia the regional administration system developed and the principal centres were Brno and Olomouc.

The powers enjoyed by the estates of Moravia are clear evidence of the degree of governmental decentralization.[28] It is possible to say that Moravia was only loosely linked with the other Lands of the Crown of Bohemia through the person of the king. The separate political and cultural development of Moravia, from 1471 to 1526, was strengthened by the fact that from 1469 it was ruled by King Matthias of Hungary. Matthias was recognized as King of Bohemia by Rome and, in 1479, by King Vladislav as well. Matthias left wide-spread powers in the hands of the Moravian nobility, and did not intervene in the proceedings of the Diets and courts. He gave considerable power to the towns, too, particularly in matters of foreign trade. Thus the structure of the estates in Moravia – the Church was represented by the Bishop of Olomouc and other prelates – differed from the structure of those in Bohemia. Even Matthias's death in 1490, when the lesser crownlands of Bohemia, that is Moravia, Lusatia and Silesia again came under the rule of Vladislav, the estates in Moravia retained their political independence. The close contacts Moravia maintained with Vienna, in particularly with Buda, led to early interest in Italian Renaissance culture, which came to Bohemia only later.

Urban democracy

As suggested, all these activities by the estates were signs of a process of democratization. Until this time the lesser nobility and the burghers had been excluded from government, from the judiciary and the legislature. Following the Hussite revolution and during the Czech Reformation thousands of those belonging to these groups gradually became active for the common weal and created appropriate institutions and machinery for their political activity.[29] Under Jagiellon rule, the burghers, in particular, increasingly wielded more power in political life in the Kingdom of Bohemia. The number of free royal towns rose to forty; these towns were independent of the nobility, formally under the rule of the king himself who, with the aid of the Deputy Chamberlain and the Court Sheriff (*hofrychtíř*) was to appoint the town council and supervise the town judiciary. The king also appointed town sheriffs (usually an aristocrat) but from the middle of the fifteenth century first Prague and then other royal towns were successful in having the royal sheriff abolished.[30] The Catholic towns, including those of Moravia, followed by the Utraquist towns, freed themselves of this royal officer. After 1500, when Prague and then other towns, acquired the privilege of electing their town council and burgomaster without interference from the king's officers the powers of the town councils increased.

As the power of the royal towns increased, so did that of the 'Great Commune' – the town parliament.[31] In royal towns it had existed even before the Hussite revolution as an association of well-off town inhabitants with full rights for the purpose of looking after the town's finances. During the Hussite revolution the Great Communes extended their jurisdiction both into military-political and ecclesiastical-religious spheres. They intervened, for instance, in the work of preachers and church institutions and also played a part when international agreements were drawn up.

The Great Communes held on to all these powers under the Jagiellon rule, and strengthened them. While the town councils were appointed from above, by the king and his officers, the town parliaments were elected from below, in individual town districts. The Great Communes elected delegates to Diets, where they represented the towns; they participated in decisions regarding the composition of delegations to the king and were involved in shaping price and commercial policies. Every important measure passed by the town council had to be agreed with and ratified by the Great Commune which established special commissions and committees in individual town districts. In the course of a year hundreds of burghers would play an active political role in these town institutions.

Wherever the nobility tried to contain or even abolish the Great Communes, social and political unrest broke out, often culminating in revolutionary uprisings. This happened, for instance, in Prague in 1483, and it looked as though the Hussite revolution was about to be repeated.[32] The patricians who did not wish to accede to the demands of the Great Communes were massacred; the victorious craftsmen and shopkeepers also succeeded in facing the departure of monks and prelates from the capital of the kingdom. Then even the royal court left Prague, and it was a year before Vladislav made his peace with the burghers. There were similar encounters in other towns of Bohemia: Nymburk, Žatec, Hradec Králové, and later in Moravia as well (Brno, 1520–1525).[33]

The Great Communes became an important political instrument in the democratization process of Czech society. At first it was in the Towns of Prague that the parliaments became very active (Old Town, New Town, Little Side) followed by all Utraquist towns. The Catholic towns soon perceived the revolutionary character of this new form of power and, from the middle of the fifteenth century, they also organized Great Communes (Plzeň, towns in Moravia). Even in some towns under the jurisdiction of Utraquist feudals or members of the Czech biblicist Church of the *Unitas fratrum* (Mladá Boleslav), burghers could become active in the organs of the

Great Commune. It was significant that after the Habsburg Ferdinand I (1526–1564) came to the royal throne of Bohemia, he at once tried to subdue the estates and to lay foundations of a centralized monarchy; the Great Communes were abolished and it was forbidden to convene them (1528). This was the deathblow to democratization in the townships of Bohemia. When the royal towns were defeated in the so-called War of Schmalkalden (1546–7), the political power of the burghers was completely annihilated and the third estate virtually ceased to exist in the Kingdom of Bohemia.

While I view the increasing power of the Great Communes in the towns of Bohemia and Moravia during the Jagiellon era as part of society's democratization, I do not wish to hide the fact that this active participation of the broader burgher strata in politics had its dark sides. Relatively broad groups of the townspeople came to the fore, with their virtues as well as their vices. These outsiders brought into politics not only their radicalism but also their hatreds, their desires for power, their illusions and their passions. It was not rare for these so-called commoners (*obecní lidê*), that is, members of the Great Communes, to burst into fiercely radical attacks not only against their real opponents but against their own leaders. This pseudo-radicalism of the new elite came to the fore in Prague in the stormy years of 1523–1524 when the demagogue Pašek of Vrat, as head of the Great Commune, joined forces with the nobility to instal a dictatorship in Prague, and took bloody retribution from the Czech and German followers of the Reformation.[34] Influenced by popular nationalistic slogans, the crowd attacked decent honest men who were representing the interests of the towns. These disturbances indicated that clever demagogues could manipulate crowds.

Under the rule of the Jagiellons, however, the burghers ensured their position both as regards the king and the nobles. It was a hard struggle. In 1500 the third estate did not give way to the lords and knights, and did not recognize the codification of the Land Ordinance. In the years that followed, the royal towns formed a political and military union to defend the rights of the third estate by force of arms. In vain the lords and knights came to Buda to persuade King Vladislav that he should condemn the armed opposition of his burghers. King Jiří's grandson, Prince Bartoloměj of Minstrberk, and some of the lesser nobility (Albrecht Rendl of Ušava, Procek of Cetná, and others) managed to convince the king that the burghers were not rebels but loyal allies against pressures brought to bear on him by Czech and Hungarian magnates. Prince Bartoloměj became the political and military leader of the towns in Bohemia, and successfully defended their rights. After his sudden death in 1515 the union did not retreat from its position and obtained the confirmation of all the rights of the third estate in the St Wenceslas Agreement of 1517.[35] Then the towns were led by the burgomaster of Litoměřice, Václav of Řepnice, whose miniature portrait can be seen in the Litoměřice gradual, kneeling by the stake where Hus was burned, as a pious donor.[36]

The Czech Reformation

This gradual, a magnificent relic of Utraquist burgher art, provides a suitable introduction to the study of another characteristic feature of the monarchy of the estates (1471–1526) – the Czech Reformation.[37] The second half of the fourteenth century saw the emergence of a movement that was closely connected with Wyclifism and Waldensianism and that culminated in the writings and activities of Jan Hus. His death at the stake in Constance (1415) led to the Hussite revolution in Bohemia (1419–1437). The Compactata of Basle meant that the Roman Church acknowledged the Chalice as the symbol of Hussite reforms but Popes Pius II and Paul II abolished the communion in two kinds and tried to re-establish the secular power of the Church in Bohemia and Moravia. Under the Utraquist King Jiří of Poděbrady, the rift between the supporters of the Czech Reformation and the Roman Church widened to a breach. In the Jagiellon era most of the higher and some of the lesser nobility proclaimed obedience to Rome, as did some of the towns in Bohemia (České Budějovice, Plzeň, Cheb, Chomutov, Most and Ústí nad Labem) as well as in Moravia (Brno, Olomouc, Jihlava, Znojmo). Silesia and Lusatia remained within the fold of the Catholic Church.

Thus by the end of the fifteenth century a complicated ecclesiastical organization gradually came into being in Bohemia and Moravia.[38] In Bohemia the Romans (as they were called) had two administrators residing in Prague, while in Moravia the Church was headed by the Bishop of Olomouc. The Utraquist Church – to which most of the population belonged was headed by Jan Rokycana up to his death in 1471; elected Archbishop of Prague, he was not acknowledged by the pope and ignored by the Roman Church. The Utraquist Church was administered by a consistory located in the university in the Old Town of Prague. For both Catholics and Utraquists, rebuilding the ecclesiastical administration broken up during the revolution and the long years of anarchy that followed (1437–1457) proved a difficult task. Only in Moravia had the Roman Church retained some of its landed property and managed to maintain a few monasteries. In Bohemia the property of the Church had been secularized and almost all the monasteries abolished; a few lingered on in regions where the Catholics were strong.

Alongside these two ecclesiastical organizations another radical Reformation Church became very strong, especially after the end of the fifteenth century: the Unity of Brethren (*Unitas Fratrum*).[39] At first only commone s could be members of this church but after 1500 nobles were also admitted. While the Utraquist Church considered itself Catholic, that is, part of the universal Church, the Unity of Brethren rejected the pope and the Catholic Church in principle, and elected laymen and preachers to administer their affairs; they identified with the evangelical church of Christ. This radical wing of the Reformation in Bohemia endeavoured to find its place in the Christian world, entering into contact with the Armenian Church and, after 1517, seeking common ground with the German and Swiss Reformation. After 1500 it was principally Lukáš Pražský (Luke of Prague) who shaped the theology of the Brethren. He was a graduate of Prague University and laid stress upon the principal importance of faith, thus coming close to the views of Luther.[40] King Jiří and with him many Utraquist ideologists condemned the Unity of Brethren as heretics. King Vladislav, pressed by Rome and by the Hungarian prelates, attempted to persecute the Unity of Brethren, especially in decrees issued after 1508. But the heretics found protectors among the Utraquist nobles and burghers; the estates ignored royal decrees, and the Unity of Brethren flourished both in Bohemia and Moravia.

These complex religious patterns made everyday life very difficult in Bohemia, for it must not be forgotten that the Church organized and administered the passage of time. Since the Utraquists as well as the Unity of Brethren refused to acknowledge and worship many of the saints, including the Virgin Mary and the founders of monastic orders (St Francis and St Dominic), the calendar of the Czech Reformation differed from that of the Catholic Church.[41] The latter kept fifteen to twenty or more saint's days on which no work was done. They were not included in the Utraquist calendar which often led to confusing and troublesome situations. In Prague, for instance, work was allowed on Marian feast days, while in the Catholic towns those non-Catholics who worked in workshops or fields on those days were punished as sinners who desecrated the holy day. Religious tolerance, a spirit of conciliation and compromise, was urgently needed.

In the Kingdom of Bohemia estates were the basis and motivating force of bringing about religious tolerance. After long years of war and conflicts both Catholics and Utraquists were getting together to achieve peaceful conditions for everyday life. Particularly important on the Utraquist side were two noblemen, the brothers Tovačov of Cimburk, and the burghers of the royal towns. On the Catholic side, besides the administrator of the Prague archbishopric, Pavel Pouček, there were two noblemen, Vilém of

Pernštejn and Jan of Šelmberk, and the sons of King Jiří of Poděbrady, Jindřich and Hynek, who had joined the Catholic Church after 1479. King Vladislav himself urgently sought a compromise solution and pressed the opposing sides to make truce, which was finally achieved at the Diet in Kutná Hora in 1485 where agreement on religious freedoms was reached.[42] As a law of the land it guaranteed freedom of confession not only to Utraquist and Catholic nobility and burghers but to the villeins as well. Every inhabitant of the Kingdom of Bohemia was free to decide between the Church of Rome and that of the Utraquists; it was explicitly stated that a non-Catholic villein on the estate of a Catholic lord was free to worship according to the Utraquist rite, while a Catholic villein on a Utraquist estate could attend services in the Catholic church and obey its priest. Though the religious peace of 1485 was not helped by lengthy theoretical discussions of tolerance, it was the first practical attempt at real tolerance in the history of Europe. Moreover, it went beyond the later Religious Peace of Augsburg (1555) in that the common people, villeins, were also given the right to worship according to their conscience. (The Unity of Brethren was not granted this right at Kutná Hora in 1485 – indeed it was only just coming into existence.) Thanks to the stand taken by the estates, an atmosphere of tolerance reigned in Bohemia and Moravia, and religious bodies of different views existed side by side for a period of thirty-one years.

While democratizing movement affected the political sphere, it also made itself felt in religious matters. Alongside the secularization of church property, there also was a tendency to laicize religious life. Thus, when the Kutná Hora agreement was being drawn up, the principal actors were laymen, nobles and burghers; there is no mention of church dignitaries being present. In the ecclesiastical organization of both the Catholic and Utraquist Churches, as in the Unity of Brethren, laymen were the prime movers, while priests and preachers were pushed into the background. In the Utraquist Church the collective of laymen, called *osada* (settlement), enjoyed complete autonomy from the end of the fifteenth century.[43] The collective administered parish property (altar vessels, vestments, missals and prayerbooks) and many parishes had the right to appoint and dismiss priests, pastors and preachers. These laymen determined what the clergy should be paid and what emoluments they should enjoy.

Education, vernacular culture and the arts

The University of Prague, reduced as it was to the Faculty of Arts, also came under the rule of the Utraquist Church.[44] The so-called Lower Consistory had a say in the election of Rectors and Deans. Moreover, the estates too put forward their own candidates for the top offices. By and large these interventions did not improve the educational standard of the university; men of average or little ability were often placed in office. The University of Prague also doggedly resisted attempts to introduce the study of commentaries on Greek and Latin authors into the syllabus. A stern and narrow religious outlook repudiated Classical authors, regarded by some Utraquists as abominable pagans. Nor did young Catholics from the towns enter the Prague Faculty, for an essential qualification was recognition of the Compactata of Basle, and taking Holy Communion in both kinds. Czech Catholic students went to Leipzig University while Moravian Catholics studied in Vienna or Cracow. Students from noble Catholic families usually went to Italy, particularly to the Universities of Padua and Bologna. It was these young men studying abroad who mediated Renaissance humanist ideas of education, art and scholarship to Bohemia and Moravia.

As early as the Hussite revolution, the use of Czech instead of Latin had been accentuated not only in political life but also in church ritual.[45] The estates took up this practice and Czech became the language of the proceedings in the Diet and law courts. Laws were drawn up in Czech first in Moravia in 1494, followed later by Bohemia. It was stressed that proceedings in the law courts and Diets had to be comprehensible to broad sections of the population. Moreover, the radical Utraquists insisted that religious services be held in Czech, and that Czech should be the language of the Mass as well as of the sermons. The Compactata of Basle had not granted the Czechs this right, but in practice Czech became the language of religion in the Utraquist Church, which was becoming more and more negative in its attitude to the Papal Curia. The Unity of Brethren, too, rejected the use of Latin, and employed Czech in sermons, hymns and prayers.[46] Of course, this intensified the specific character of the Czech Reformation while, at the same time, it brought the lay people more actively into religious life.

Czech had been the language of literature and of official municipal documents since the end of the fourteenth century. During the Reformation it became the language of theology and scholarship as well. The original thinker and critic of feudal society, Petr Chelčický, wrote his tracts in Czech as did the Utraquist humanists.[47] Alongside Latin humanism, cultivated by such Catholic scholars as Bohuslav Hasištejnský of Lobkovice, an Utraquist humanism flourished, enriching cultural life in Bohemia by translations from Latin and Greek into Czech.[48] Among those who followed these lines were the outstanding jurist Viktorin Kornel of Všehrdy and Řehoř Hrubý of Jelení, who was the first European scholar to translate into vernacular Erasmus of Rotterdam's famous *Encomium moriae* (1512).[49] In addition to a translation of Plato's *Republic* into Czech, which has not survived, other Greek writers were translated by Václav Písecký, one of the bright hopes of Czech humanism who unfortunately died young.

The poets and scholars who wrote in Czech constantly stressed their commitment to spreading Czech culture among the broadest sections of the population throughout the kingdom. Leading humanists praised Czech as a language adequate to express the most involved theological and philosophical concepts. By the end of the fifteenth century humanism, reaching Bohemia from Italy, was represented by two trends. On the one hand, there were poets and scholars who remained in the Catholic Church and wrote in Latin; the greatest among them, the aristocratic Bohuslav Hasištejnský of Lobkovice, refused to write in Czech, sharing the Italian humanists' lack of respect for the vernacular. On the other hand, a group of Utraquist humanists opposed Latin humanism and wrote in Czech, claiming Petrarch and Boccaccio as their models in the use of the vernacular. Prominent in this context was Viktorin Kornel of Všehrdy, mentioned above, the author of an exhaustive treatise on the laws and courts of the Kingdom of Bohemia.[50] Řehoř Hrubý of Jelení devoted himself primarily to translating Latin authors into Czech, with the explicit aim of serving Czech national culture. He was a determined fighter for the rights of the 'third estate', and set before the burghers of Prague the ideal of the heroes of the Roman republic.

In Bohemia and Moravia the humanists welcomed the invention of printing as a God-given means of raising the intellectual level of the broadest possible strata of the population.[51] Parchment manuscripts were exorbitantly expensive, and the lesser nobility and the burghers could not afford them. Praising printing, Augustinus Olomoucensis, a Moravian humanist, noted that '[w]orks for which evil booksellers would ask inordinately high prices can now be purchased for an insignificant sum'. A book which formerly would be owned only by a king or a prince 'even a poor man can have as his own possession today'.[52] Printing too helped the democratization of culture in Bohemia. The date of the first publication printed in Bohemia is a matter of debate, but it is certain that the first printing presses were in operation after the year 1472. The first were established in Plzeň by printers who came from Germany; although this was a Catholic town, it is significant that Czech books predominated among incunabula. In Moravia (Brno and Olomouc) Latin and German texts were printed. Regarding incunabula they contain a considerable number of Czech Bibles for printing met the needs of the Czech Reformation which laid so much stress on knowledge of the Bible. The radical wing in the Reformation movement used the press to defend its position. The Unity of Brethren, polemically engaged in argument against the attacks of the Roman Inquisition, published the *Apology for the Teachings of the Unity of Brethren* in Nuremberg (1512). In this town, which maintained close trade relations with Prague and Kutná Hora, the first map of Bohemia was printed in 1517. It was commissioned by Mikuláš Klaudyán of Mladá Boleslav, a physician and printer for the Unity of Brethren. This was the first realistic map of any part of Central Europe – maps of Hungary and Poland appeared much later.

Although the printing presses could not satisfy the demand, and were supplemented by books printed in Bavaria, Franconia and Saxony, several Czech printers were well known abroad. The first Portuguese book was printed by Valentin of Moravia, who learned his trade in Nuremberg. One of the first printers to achieve fame in Genoa was Matyáš of Olomouc, who was actively engaged in printing in Naples after 1500. After 1513 the first Jewish printing press in Central Europe was set up in Prague – the Jewish minority in Bohemia enjoyed special protection by the estates. The first Russian Bible was printed in Prague in 1517–1519 by the Belorussian physician F. Skorina. Other Orthodox liturgical texts were also printed in Prague to be sent to Russia.

Looking at the work of Czech printing presses from 1471 to 1526, we find that the vast majority of the 250 books were printed in Czech. In the main, they were editions of the Bible or selected biblical texts, and then religious tracts and polemical writings on the subject of communion in both kinds. In printed books, in this first land of the Reformation, secular themes remained in the background. The estates were decidedly in favour of printing, and by the end of the fifteenth century had ensured that certain important resolutions were issued in print.[53] Even so, ecclesiastical and religious themes accounted for more than two thirds of all texts printed. A similar trend can be seen in literature and the fine arts. In poetry and prose medieval forms and medieval themes persisted in Czech literature; poets succumbed to the moral intransigence of the Reformation and achieved highest proficiency in creating religious hymns. The strict Reformation line can be clearly seen in translations of Boccaccio's tales into Czech. Tales containing erotic incidents were excluded, the naked female body was either chastely covered or the love scene was altogether omitted in the Czech translation. There is a parallel to this pictorial art, in the representations of the Virgin Mary suckling the infant Jesus; unlike in Italian or Netherlands representations, Czech Madonnas always have the breast veiled.

Those paintings of the Jagiellon era which have survived in Bohemia and Moravia clearly show the difference between Italian Renaissance art and that of the Late Gothic in Bohemia.[54] While Italian Renaissance painting reveals up to 20 per cent secular themes between 1400 and 1550, in Bohemia and Moravia they barely reach 6 per cent. The choice of subject of Jagiellon painting shows a significant preference for the life and crucifixion of Jesus Christ. This confirms the Christological orientation of the Czech Reformation, and its profound influence on Czech art, restraining the penetration of Renaissance secular elements.[55]

In architecture of the Jagiellon period, the Late Gothic style also prevailed. Geographically, the sources of inspiration lay along the trade routes that brought the Czech Lands into contact with the rest of Europe. Besides Renaissance Italy, the regions of southern Germany, the Rhine and Danube basins brought outstanding architects to Bohemia and Moravia. Renaissance elements merged into Late Gothic architecture from Italy and (in the reign of Matthias Corvinus) from Hungary, first in Moravia (e.g. Tovačov Castle) and then in Bohemia (the windows of the Vladislav Hall, dating from 1493). The strongest impulses, however, came from southern Germany, whence came the architect and stonemason Benedikt Ried who gradually changed his national allegiance and became known under the Czech name of Rejt. He was responsible for adapting the fortifications of Prague Castle and the magnificent church of St Barbara in Kutná Hora. At first Rejt worked for King Vladislav, but later he also served burghers, noblemen and the estates as his patrons. It was for the meetings of the Diet and sitting of the Land Court that he built the Vladislav Hall of Prague Castle from 1481 to 1500. It is quite clear that this vast hall in Late Gothic style was not intended for the king and his council – the halls used by the Emperor Charles IV would have more than sufficed. The Vladislav Hall is several times larger than the throne room of Charles IV. Knowing the wealth and power of the estates in Bohemia, and aware that in the absence of King Vladislav (after 1490) they had supreme power, controlled the Mint and all political life, we realize that the Vladislav Hall became a permanent monument commemorating the power and the glory of the monarchy of the estates in Bohemia. There is a deeper link between the democratizing traditions of the estates in the Jagiellon era and the fact that to this day the presidents of the Republic are elected in the Vladislav Hall of Prague Castle.

Notes

1 This essay is based on my seven-part synthesis of the Jagiellon era in Bohemia and Moravia (1471–1526) which is still in manuscript, since the censorship did not permit its publication after 1968. [Editorial note: Since this was written, the following work appeared posthumously: J. Macek, *Jagellonský věk v českých zemích (1471–1526)* [The Jagiellon era in the Czech Lands (1471–1526)], pt. 1:

Hospodářská základna a královská moc [Economic basis and royal power]; Pt. 2: *Šlechta* [Nobility] (Prague, 1992, 1994)].

2 For a concise summary see, J. Hořejší, *Vladislavský sál Pražského hradu* [The Vladislav Hall of Prague Castle] (Prague, 1973).

3 The volume *Pozdně gotické umění v Čechách (1471–1526)* [Late Gothic art in Bohemia] (Prague, 1978), edited by J. Homolka, J. Krása, V. Mencl, J. Pešina and J. Petráň is the authoritative work.

4 F. Palacký, *Dějiny národu českého v Čechách a v Moravě* [History of the Czech nation in Bohemia and Moravia] 5 vols., 2nd edn (Prague, 1878), I–II.

5 W. Eberhard provides an overview in 'The political system and the intellectual tradition of the Bohemian Ständestaat from the thirteenth to the sixteenth century', in R. J. W. Evans and T. V. Thomas (eds.), *Crown, Church and Estates* (London, 1991), pp. 23–47.

6 E.g. F. Seibt, *Mittelalter und Gegenwart Ausgewählte Aufsätze* (Sigmaringen, 1987), p. 257.

7 K. Bosl, 'Böhmen als Paradefeld ständischer Representation vom 14. bis zum 17. Jahrhundert' in K. Bosl, *Böhmen und seine Nachbarn* (Munich-Vienna, 1976), pp. 188–200.

8 J. Válka, *Přehled dějin Moravy* (Survey of Moravian history), 2 vols. (Prague, 1987), II; and, 'Stavovství a krize českého státu v druhé polovině 15. století' [The estates and the crisis of the Czech state in mid-fifteenth century], *Folia historica bohemica*, 6 (1984), 80–7.

9 J. M. Balk, *Königtum und Stände in Ungarn im 14.–16. Jahrhundert* (Wiesbaden, 1973); G. Rhode, 'Stände und Königtum in Polen/Litauen und Böhmen/Mähren', in H. Rausch (ed.), *Die geschichtlichen Grundlagen der modernen Volksvertretung*, 2 vols. (Darmstadt, 1980), I, pp. 467–506; and, *Histoire de Pologne* (Warsaw, 1971), pp. 159, 193.

10 M. Spindler (ed.), *Handbuch der bayerischen Geschichte* (Munich 1966), II, p. 298.

11 W. Blockmans, 'A typology of representative institutions in late medieval Europe', *Journal of Medieval History*, 4 (1978), 189–215.

12 J. Béranger wrongly compares the estates in Bohemia with those in Hungary and Poland in his *Histoire de l'Empire des Hapsbourgs 1273–1918* (Paris, 1990), pp. 89, 96. *The New Cambridge Modern History*, I, 'The Renaissance (1493–1520)' (Cambridge, 1957), ch. XIII, equally wrongly identifies the Czech estates with those in Poland and Hungary.

13 J. Macek, 'El husitismo en campos y cindades', in J. LeGoff (ed.), *Herejías y sociedades en la Europa preindustrial siglos XI–XVIII* (Madrid, 1987), pp. 185–95.

14 O. Odložilek, *The Hussite King. Bohemia in European Affairs, 1440–1471* (New Brunswick, NJ, 1965); J. Macek, *Jiří z Poděbrad* [George of Poděbrady] (Prague, 1967), pp. 172–3.

15 J. Macek, *Osudy basilejských kompaktát v jagellonském věku* [The fate of the Basle Compactata in the Jagiellon era] (in press).

16 K. Nehring, *Matthias Corvinus, Kaiser Friedrich III und das Reich. Zum hunyadisch-habsburgischen Gegensatz im Donauraum* (Munich, 1975), pp. 46–52; a broad

summary of Matthias and his reign can be found in the volume *Hunyadi Mátyás. Emlékkönyv Mátyás Kiraly halálának 500. évfordulójára* [Matthias Hunyadi. Collection commemorating the 500th anniversary of King Matthias's death] (Budapest, 1990) where my article on the relations between King Jiří and King Matthias is also printed (pp. 201–44).

17 *Archiv český*, 4 (1846), 500, 508–11.

18 J. Macek, *Tři ženy krále Vladislava* [Three wives of King Vladislav] (Prague, 1991).

19 J. Pelant, 'České zemské sněmy v letech 1471–1500' [The Czech Diets 1471–1500] in *Sborník archivních prací*, 31 (1981), 340–417.

20 J. Čelakovský, *O deskách krajských a zemských v zemích českých* [Regional and Land Registers in the Czech Lands] (Prague, 1893).

21 J. Macek, *Histoire de la Bohême* (Paris, 1984), pp. 308–424.

22 V. Kosinová, 'Nejvyšší úřad purkrabský v zřízeních zemských století XVI' [The highest burgraviate in the Land Ordinances of the sixteenth century], *Pekařův sborník* (Pekař-Festschrift), 2 vols. (Prague, 1930), I, pp. 353–7.

23 V. Vojtíšek, 'Vývoj královské české kanceláře' [Evolution of the Royal Bohemian Chancellery] in *Idea státu československého* [The idea of the Czechoslovak state] (Prague, 1936), pp. 253–4; J. Heřman, 'Kancelář Ludvíka Jagellovce(1516–1526)' [The chancellery of Louis Jagiellon], *Zápisky československých dějin* 7 (1963), 91–3.

24 V. Lukáš, 'Počátky úřadu nejvyššího mincmistra království českého' [The beginnings of the office of the Master of the Mint in the Kingdom of Bohemia] *Numismatický sborník*, 6 (1960), 169–205.

25 J. Čelakovský, *Soud komorní za krále Vladislava II* [The Chamberlain Court under Vladislav II] (Prague, 1895).

26 J. Martinovský, 'Okolnosti vzniku Vladislavského zřízení zemského' [The origin of Vladislav's Land Ordinance], *Ústecký historický sborník* (1979), pp. 125–30.

27 B. Rieger, *Zřízení krajské v Čechách* [Regional administration in Bohemia], 2 vols. (in 1 vol. continuously paginated) (Prague, 1889), especially pp. 96–148.

28 K. Kadlec, *Přehled ústavních dějin Moravy* [Survey of the constitutional history of Moravia] (Prague, 1926); see also J. Válka, *Přehled dějin Moravy* [Survey of the history of Moravia] (Prague, 1987), II; and, 'Die Stellung Mährens im Wandel des böhmischen Lehenstaates', in F. Seibt and W. Eberhard (eds.), *Europa 1500* (Stuttgart, 1987), pp. 292–312.

29 J. Macek, '"Bonum commune" et la Réforme en Bohême', *Histoire sociale, sensibilités collectives et mentalités. Mélanges R. Mandrou* (Paris, 1985), pp. 517–26.

30 Z. Winter, *Kulturní obraz českých měst. Život veřejný v XV. a XVI. věku*, [The cultural scene in Czech towns. Public life in the fifteenth and sixteenth century], 2 vols. (Prague, 1890–2), I, pp. 622–5.

31 I pointed out the principal significance of the Great Commune in a study published under J. Pečírková *et al.* 'Pojem a pojmenování městské obce ve středověkých Čechách' [The concept and the name of the town commune in medieval Bohemia], *Listy filologické*, 98 (1975), 79–87.

32 F. Šmahel, 'Epilog husitské revoluce. Pražské povstání 1483' [Epilogue to the

Hussite revolution. The Prague Uprising of 1483], A. Molnár (ed.), *Acta reformationem bohemicam illustrantia* (Prague, 1978), pp. 45–127.

33 J. Dřímal, 'Sociální boje v moravských královských městech ve dvacátých letech 16. století [Social struggles in the royal towns of Moravia in the twenties of the sixteenth century], *Brno v minulosti a dnes* [Brno in the past and today], 5 (1963), 114–67. See also *Dějiny města Brna* [History of the town of Brno], (Brno, 1969), pp. I, pp. 125–7.

34 W. Eberhard, *Konfessionsbildung und Stände in Böhmen (1478–1530)* (Munich-Vienna, 1981), pp. 125–7.

35 K. Malý, 'Svatováclavská smlouva, třídní kompromis mezi šlechtou a městy' [The St Wenceslas Agreement, a class compromise between the aristocracy and the towns in 1517], *Acta Universitatis Carolinae*, 1/2 (1955), 195–222.

36 See e.g. illustrations in *Pozdně gotická malba* [Late Gothic Painting] (Prague, 1978), p. 444.

37 J. Macek, *Jan Hus et les traditions hussites (XVᵉ–XIXᵉ siècles)* (Paris, 1973), pp. 204–325.

38 W. Eberhard, *Konfessionsbildung*, pp. 41–73.

39 B. Říčan and A. Molnár, *Die böhmischen Brüder* (Berlin, 1961).

40 A. Molnár, *Bratr Lukáš, bohoslovec Jednoty* [Brother Luke, the theologian of the Unitas] (Prague, 1947).

41 J. Macek, 'Pojem času v jagellonském věku' [The concept of time in the Jagiellon era] in Z. Beneš, E. Maur and J. Pánek (eds.), *Pocta J. Petráňovi* (Petráň-Festschrift) (Prague, 1991), pp. 137–60.

42 W. Eberhard, 'Entstehungsbedingungen für öffentliche Toleranz am Beispiel des Kuttenberger Religionsfriedens 1485', *Communio viatorum*, 29 (1986), 129–354.

43 J. Macek, 'Osada. Z terminologii sredniowiecznego osadnictwa', *Kwartalnik historii kultury materialnej* (1977), 359–73.

44 F. Šmahel and M. Truc, 'Studie ke dějinám University Karlovy v letech 1433–1622' [Studies in the history of Charles University], *Acta Universitatis Carolinae, Historia*, 2 (1963), 3–60.

45 F. Šmahel, 'The idea of the "nation" in Hussite Bohemia', *Historica*, 16 (1969), 143–247; 17 (1969), 93–197.

46 A. Molnár, *Českobratrská výchova před Komenským* [Education and the Czech Brethren before Comenius] (Prague, 1956).

47 Macek, *Jean Hus*, pp. 270–80.

48 J. Heinic and J. Martínek (eds.), *Rukověť humanistického básnictví v Čechách a na Moravě* [Handbook of humanist poetry in Bohemia and Moravia] (Prague, 1969), III, pp. 170–203.

49 E. Pražák, *Řehoř Hrubý z Jelení* (Prague, 1964); A. Molnár, 'Erasmus und das Hussitentum', *Communio viatorum*, 30 (1987), 185–97.

50 H. Jireček (ed.), *Viktorin Kornel ze Všehrd o praviech, o súdiech i o dskách země České Knihy devatery* [Nine books on the laws, courts and Land Registers of Bohemia] (Prague, 1874).

51 *Knihtisk a kniha v českých zemích od husitství do Bílé hory* [Printing and the book in the

Czech Lands from the Hussites to the Battle of the White Mountain], *Sborník prací k 500. výročí českého knihtisku* [Collection marking 500 years of Czech printing] (Prague 1970).

52 D. Martínková, *Poselství ducha* [The message of the spirit] (Prague, 1975), pp. 116–17.

53 W. W. Tomek, *Dějiny města Prahy* [History of Prague], 10 vols. (Prague, 1902), X, p. 133.

54 J. Pěšina, *Česká malba pozdní gotiky a renesance. Deskové malířství 1450–1550* [Late Gothic and Renaissance painting in Bohemia. Panel painting] (Prague, 1950); P. Burke, *Die Renaissance in Italien. Sozialgeschichte einer Kultur zwischen Tradition und Erfindung* (Berlin, 1984), pp. 152–3.

55 J. Macek, 'Bohemia and Moravia', in R. Porter and M. Teich (eds.), *The Renaissance in National Context* (Cambridge, 1992), pp. 197–220.

6

—

Rudolfine culture

JOSEF VÁLKA

I

Around 1600 – after two centuries – Prague regained its significance as an important political and cultural centre in Europe. The cultural explosion which took place around both 1400 and 1600 resulted in Prague becoming the imperial residence; it came to be not only the capital of the Crown of Bohemia but also of the Holy Roman Empire, that is of West–Central Europe.[1] While the Luxemburgs had been intent on making Prague the centre of their dynastic Czech state as well as of the Roman Empire, the Habsburgs in the sixteenth century were deciding whether Prague or Vienna should become this centre. Connected with Vienna through their ancestral political tradition, the Habsburgs were also hereditary rulers of the Austrian domains. Since the fifteenth century the estates of Bohemia have always demanded that the King of Bohemia should reside in Prague. For Czechs, this would provide easier access to court offices and would enable them to influence not only the Crown but also the Empire; for Prague itself this would remove the danger of provincialism. The Czechs could support their wish for the ruler to reside in Prague by the ancient residential tradition of this town, and by the existence of a stately royal and imperial seat in the shape of the Prague Castle.

The catastrophes of the fifteenth century had already been overcome and at the beginning of the sixteenth century Prague had again become a lively metropolis where the Jagiellons were transforming the castle and the town into a magnificent Late Gothic residence. By the end of the sixteenth century, Prague already numbered 60,000 inhabitants. Vienna could perhaps equal Prague only by the fact that it also was an imperial town conveniently situated on the Danube. However, since the Turkish occupation of the Hungarian lowlands, including the establishment of the Buda pashalik in the mid sixteenth century, Vienna had got into immediate reach of Ottoman power and was developed as a frontier fortress. The Habsburgs' struggle against the Turks legitimized their claim to establish an absolute and centralized state. From this point of view the question of the seat of the sovereign's court was of paramount importance.

Both Ferdinand I (1526–1564) and Maximilian II (1564–1576) preferred Vienna and laid the foundations for its later significance. Vienna's case was further strengthened by the unsuccessful uprising by Protestant Czechs in 1547–8. After the suppression of the revolt, Ferdinand I entrusted the government of Bohemia to his son Ferdinand of Tyrol (in Bohemia from 1547 to 1567). It was he who laid the foundations of Renaissance and Mannerist courtly life in hitherto Late Gothic Bohemia and taught the aristocracy in Bohemia a new life style.

In 1583 the Emperor and King of Bohemia Rudolf II (1576–1612) moved his court to Prague and stayed there until his eventful end in 1611–12.[2] At last the royal and imperial seat was in Prague again. Although the Emperor did not give any reasons for his decision, they can be guessed. Prague was safer than Vienna, it was the capital of the most important state entity of the Habsburg monarchy – the Crown of Bohemia. Also the presence of the Catholic court, the papal nuncio and the Spanish ambassador could support the recatholicization of the largely Protestant kingdom. However, Rudolf II obviously preferred Prague to Vienna for personal reasons as well. From its security not only could he conduct the imperial policy of the Habsburgs in Central Europe but he could ideally realize his cultural and artistic interests which, in his life, played an equally important role as his political endeavours. During his rule in Prague the traditional Habsburg patronage of culture was to reach its peak.

The Prague Castle towered in safe distance above the restless Towns of Prague but formed with them one residential organism.[3] Even the unfinished cathedral added to its monumentality and the Vladislav Hall, built under the Jagiellons, was the largest Late Gothic stateroom in Europe. In the Castle there was sufficient room for the Bohemian and the Court Chancellory as well as for the reconstructions and extensions which the Emperor, after his arrival, initiated with the support of the estates of Bohemia. A bridge over the deep moat joined the Castle with the gardens leading to Queen Anne's summer-house, the first Renaissance building in Prague, erected during Ferdinand I's reign. There was enough room here for a menagerie, botanical gardens, riding schools, ball game halls and parks. The Castle (*Hrad*) located in 'Hradčany' ('Castle Town') was surrounded by great noblemen's palaces, rebuilt in the Renaissance style. The

Emperor had his abode joined with the areas of the Castle's complex by passages from where he could, unobserved, watch the to-ing and fro-ing in his court. The complicated structure of both the Castle and the settlements around it became, in his time, not only the centre of social life and great politics but also of great art and remarkable culture influenced by the taste of Rudolf II, the imperial Hermes Trismegistus.

II

At his arrival, Rudolf II was confronted with a situation in Bohemia and in Prague which can be characterized as a frail balance of deep contradictions.[4] The least tension emanated from the national question. From the thirteenth century the Crown of Bohemia had been, ethnically and linguistically, a mixed state where Czechs, Moravians and Germans had learnt to live in national co-existence. The medieval nationalism of the Czech nobility directed against 'foreigners' and other 'languages' surrounding the sovereign had already been overcome; moreover, the Reformational messianism of the Czech Hussites had long come to an end. The German Reformation had, through Luther, acknowledged the legacy of Hus and thus removed the isolation of the Czechs in Protestant Europe; furthermore, the Catholics had good relations with the Catholic world. Territorial patriotism of the humanist type based on the law, liberties and autonomy of the Czech Lands – particularly strong in Moravia – became the fundamental political 'us-feeling' of the estates. Territorial patriotism complicated the creation of state consciousness pertaining to the Crown of Bohemia. We find this 'Crown-consciousness' only within the estates of Bohemia, that is, in the Kingdom of Bohemia. The Habsburgs were not considered a 'foreign' dynasty and they were adroit in adapting to Central European circumstances. Until the Battle of the White Mountain (1620) they respected essentially the Lands' autonomy and laws which included the obligation, in Bohemia and Moravia, to use Czech as the official language. However, this was not adhered to and the defence of the language was taken up by Czech intellectuals rather than politicians.

In the second half of the sixteenth century the cosmopolitanism of the aristocracy in the Czech Lands contributed to the weakening of ethnolinguistic antagonisms. The beginning of this tendency is marked by an event with symbolic resonance: the journey of a large group of Czech and Moravian aristocrats to Northern Italy in 1551.[5] They were to await the arrival by boat from Spain of the Infanta Maria, wife of Maximilian II, and to escort her to Vienna. The journey took several months and proved costly, but the Czech and Moravian noblemen became thoroughly acquainted with the Italian Renaissance milieu. The middle of the sixteenth century saw the end of the era of Gothic castles in Bohemia and the beginning of the building of chateaus designed by Italian architects and artists. While the style of the Renaissance was respected, the size of the buildings exceeded the Italian models. What was tantamount to the invasion of Italian architects and artists followed during the next two centuries. A large colony of several hundred Italians developed in Prague and individuals also settled in other towns. Czech aristocrats began to study abroad and as part of their travels they visited European courts. They adopted not only 'foreign' dress but also 'foreign customs' and with increasing frequency entered into marriages with foreigners. Court society thus became entirely cosmopolitan with, however, Czechs still playing a decisive role in it.[6]

III

Far more sensitive than the national question was the religious problem in the Czech Lands. For more than a century the Czech Lands were the only area in Europe where two legitimate religious confessions lived side by side: Utraquism (Hussitism) and Catholicism. The term 'Utraquism' covered non-Catholics of all kinds of confessions who had achieved almost true 'liberty of faith'. The century-old co-existence had changed into tolerance; the Czech Lands had become a great place of religious freedom and the refuge of persecuted sects, as for instance the 'Anabaptists'. Czech Protestants conceived the Czech Confession as an attempt to combine the heritage of the Czech Reformation (Hussitism) with that of the European Reformation. Maximilian II had promised to legalize this Confession before the election of Rudolf II as King of Bohemia (1575). Neither he nor Rudolf II fulfilled this promise because of influential Catholic opposition. Rudolf II had received a strictly Catholic education at the court of Philip II in Madrid and was expected to attempt the Catholic reconquest of the Czech Lands in the spirit of the principle *cuius regio, eius religio*. This effort met with strong resistance from the Protestant estates. Soon Rudolf II recognized that a sudden reversal of the religious situation in the Lands of the Crown of Bohemia would not be possible without a war which he wished to avoid. Thus, until the turn of the sixteenth century, he continued to pursue the traditional Habsburg religious policy essentially respecting 'liberties', yet supporting the local Counter-Reformation. The majority of the members of the aristocracy in Bohemia believed in a 'supradenominational Christianity' which guaranteed the subjects on their estates confessional freedom.[7]

The spirit of intolerance arrived in the Czech Lands from a Europe, both Catholic and Protestant, which had decided to solve religious conflict by war. The arrival of Rudolf II's court in Prague deepened religious conflicts by establishing a strong centre of Catholic power directed from Rome and Madrid in the spirit of harsh Counter-Reformation. Protestant aristocrats, especially members of the *Unitas Fratrum*, kept close links with the ideological and political centres of the Reformation.[8] As they had no university or academy of their own at home – the attempt at creating a Protestant academy in Moravia failed – young Protestant noblemen went to study in Wittenberg, in Strasbourg and especially in Basle and Geneva. The intellectual and political paths of the aristocracy in Bohemia, united until now in their defence of their territorial interests and liberties, diverged and became irreconcilable. A few aristocrats from Bohemia accompanied the Habsburgs on their visits to the court of Madrid and returned home with Spanish wives.[9] One of them, Maria Manriquez de Lara, came as the wife of the High Chancellor of the Kingdom of Bohemia, Vratislav of Pernštejn. The powerful and religiously tolerant Pernštejns became Catholic and Spanish in the course of merely one generation similarly as several other important Czech noble families. They formed the 'Spanish Party' in the Crown of Bohemia, whose interests were connected with Absolutism and Counter-Reformation. On the other hand, Karel the Elder of Žerotín, a Moravian nobleman who embodied the hopes of the *Unitas Fratrum*, during his studies in Switzerland became friends not only with the professors of the Calvinist academies but also with Henry of Navarre, who represented the hopes of the Protestants. Karel the Elder of Žerotín supported Henry of Navarre's struggle for the French Crown with loans and a small army unit which he personally led into the battle of Rouen.[10] The palaces of the papal nuncio and the Spanish Ambassador as well as the Catholic salons became the headquarters of the 'Spanish Party'. At the turn of the sixteenth century, the 'Spanish Party' tried to gain control of the state and territorial administration in Bohemia and Moravia. Their members were installed in high offices. Zdeněk Vojtěch Popel of Lobkovice, for example, became Chancellor of Bohemia, while in Moravia the title of Cardinal and Bishop of Olomouc was conferred on Franz Dietrichstein, member of an influential family and favourite of Pope Clement VIII (Ippolito Aldobrandini). Traditional religious tolerance in Bohemia was being displaced by irreconcilable conflict of ideologized confessions and everything was pointing in the direction of war. Here the upswing in spiritual Gothicism had led to the Hussite revolution, now the overturning of the frail balance of tolerant and sceptical Mannerism ended in the uprising of the estates of Bohemia and the Thirty Years War.

IV

Social conflicts were dominated and complicated by religious tensions and religious 'parties'. While the aristocratic estates and the Church in the Czech Lands developed economic enterprise in the second half of the sixteenth century, the royal towns continued to stagnate.[11] In Moravia, their inhabitants were not even considered to belong to a free estate but to one which was part of the Royal Chamber. The large feudal estates represented economic wholes located around flourishing subject (villein) towns – they endeavoured to monopolize commerce on their territories. The aristocracy played a leading role in the financial and credit economy both as debtor and creditor. The legal interest rate amounted to 6–10 per cent which indicates intensive market relations. Furthermore, the subject peasants (villeins), burdened with feudal rents and debts, became involved in market relations. They appealed against increasing feudal duties and against the monopolies of the feudal lords, especially the beer monopoly, claiming their 'old rights' and expecting help from the sovereign. But, on the whole, social peace reigned in the countryside and the aristocracy was more afraid of the sovereign exploiting the trust of the peasants in order to strengthen Absolutism. Therefore, the Land Courts of the estates provided some protection for the subject peasants.

As soon as they ascended to the Czech throne the Habsburgs began systematically strengthening the power of sovereign and court according to the Spanish model.[12] As in Spain and in the Netherlands, they curtailed property, communal and political liberties, as well as the autonomy of royal towns. After the defeated uprising of 1547–8, the towns in Bohemia lost their jurisdictional autonomy, part of their property and their political influence. The Habsburgs laid the financial foundations of a modern state by exacting regular taxes. While carrying out this highly unpopular policy, they skilfully used the 'Turkish card'. Under the threat of the Turkish menace, they permitted meetings of provincial diets and they themselves collected taxes for the defence of their state and Christianity against the enemy, the Turks, who were pushing into Central Europe. However, in the sixteenth century the Habsburgs had not yet built a centralized system of taxation and state administration, nor a state structure parallel to the feudal and provincial administrative bodies. They had, however, tried to recruit the most influential noblemen into their 'services'. Aristocrats, preferably of the younger generation, were invited to the court where service, together with the offices increasingly dependent upon it, paved the way to great careers and large amounts of property for them. By the end of the sixteenth century, the nobility in Bohemia and Moravia, hitherto united in its territorial patriotism, split into a court and a territorial aristocracy. The ideological aim of the territorial nobility, whose core consisted of Protestants of various confessions, was to defend the liberties and autonomy of their Lands. In Catholic circles the greatest virtue and value was soon the service to the sovereign and the Church. Several major trials involving leading representatives of the territorial aristocracy were staged under the pretext of *criminis laesae majestatis*. At the turn of the century, one of the victims of such trials was Karel the Elder of Žerotín, the leader of the estates of Moravia. The Catholic party in Moravia and at the royal court in Prague intended to take revenge for his French adventure and to remove this personage of European vision and innumerable political contacts with the Protestant world from the political scene. Paradoxically, with the formation of the centralized and absolutist state the role of the Crown of Bohemia was revived, especially when the ambitious, intelligent and efficient Zdeněk Vojtěch Popel of Lobkovice became its Chancellor. Out of the Bohemian Chancellery he created the first regularly functioning bureaucratic office of the Czech state, but his efforts to extend his powers from Bohemia into the 'lesser Lands of the Crown', Moravia and Silesia, met with resistance.

V

Rudolf II was not expected directly to interfere with the colourful chaos of his Crown and domains. His mission was to be 'great politics', that is diplomacy, war and the representation of sovereign power. In his era great politics were practised in Prague, and Prague became the seat representing the Central European part of the Habsburg monarchy as well as partly of the Roman Empire. Reports of ambassadors of different European powers which had established their embassies in Prague are the most valuable source for Rudolf's activities in this as well as the imperial area; they make up for the lack of memoirs of Rudolfine Prague.

Great politics turned out to be a series of defeats and ignominious failures for Rudolf II. All his attempts to marry a bride worthy of an Emperor failed. Thus Rudolf II lived in Prague with his concubines, and his court lacked an Empress and her entourage. The only great war Rudolf II led against the Turks, between 1593 and 1606, ended in failure and in a degrading peace. The attempts of his portraitists and historians to represent him as a great 'Turk-beater' was merely an expression of his wish. However, the greatest difficulties were in store for Rudolf from within his own family, especially when his ambitious younger brother Matthias (1612–1619) launched his claim for the succession. The 'brotherly dispute' undermined his power and temporarily split the Crown of Bohemia when Moravia and

Silesia went over to Matthias. Both Protestants and Catholics brought about the fall of his officials in Moravia. Political and personal failures deepened the Emperor's inclination to 'melancholy' and diverted him from his governing tasks to the magic world of his scholars and artists.

VI

In Rudolf's times the word 'melancholia' referred to various mental diseases, deviations, abnormal moods, depressive states of mind and madness.[13] Numerous studies about the Emperor's psyche show that periods of normality alternated with maniac-depressive states. These changes became more frequent until, at the turn of the century, they resulted in permanent schizophrenia and paranoia. The Emperor's advancing illness complicated the work of the court and delayed the discharge of matters of state. Frequent rises and falls of the Emperor's all-powerful confidants and high dignitaries allowed persons of dubious reputation to worm their way into the court. The latter was becoming a closed and impenetrable net of intrigues and the Emperor's life produced wild and dark rumours in which reality and fabrication were intermingled.

These rumours and the longing for sensation have continued to colour the image of Rudolf in historical novels, films and historiography. It is the world of Prague Rudolfine culture which has resisted an objective analysis the longest. Lack of understanding of this culture is connected with the scientistic concept of esoterism and the concept of artistic Mannerism as denoting the decadent phase of High Renaissance and as a mere overture to the great Baroque that flourished in Bohemia. No wonder that the most valuable impulses to acknowledging Rudolf as a great cultural benefactor and intellectual came from abroad – from modern cultural and intellectual history.[14]

The three decades of Rudolf II's court in Prague mark a period of continuous intensive artistic and intellectual activity centred around the sovereign's personality and his Castle. What Rudolf II lacked to become a successful ruler – a persistent will directed towards a definite aim and, above all, a favourable outcome – was amply compensated for by his successful patronage of culture. Today there can be no doubt that Rudolf II created another, parallel, world where he took refuge from his failures and troubles of political and family life. His cultural universe is magical, symbolic, mythological and arcane, but it also has its very empirical and rational aspects. Rudolf belongs to those initiators of modern culture who, at its beginnings, attempt to master the secrets of the cosmos, matter and terrestrial as well as posthumous life by all possible means: from ancient hermetic practices, spiritualism, all forms of magic and cabala to purest empiricism, mechanics and mathematical rationality. This link of traditional analogy-based learned culture with the emerging 'new science' of mathematical and physical laws is characteristic of Rudolfine culture. His court, on the one hand, became the Mecca of alchemists, astrologers, magicians, cabalists and spiritualists; here, on the other hand, in the service of the Emperor Tycho Brahe (1546–1601) was completing precise observations of the movement of celestial bodies on which Johannes Kepler (1571–1630) based those exact calculations which opened paths to the Scientific Revolution. Anatomical dissections were carried out in Prague and a host of geologists, land-surveyors, mechanicians, zoologists and botanists worked in Bohemia. All this 'double-world' finds its expression in Rudolfine art: canvases with complicated mythological compositions full of symbolic meaning and emblems, on the one hand, and exact portrait studies, paintings and drawings of landscapes, fauna and flora, on the other. The origin of everything is the longing for beauty, for knowledge and, above all, for pansophic harmony.

VII

In his sponsorship of the arts Rudolf II followed the tradition of his family: of his father in Prague and his uncle, Ferdinand of Tyrol, who was still living in the Ambras castle in Tyrol. From Vienna Rudolf brought a number of artists to Prague; but first he had to rebuild the Prague Castle to represent his imperial power as well as to serve his personal predelictions.[15] Italian architects and builders Ulrich Avostalis de Sala (Aostalli), Giovanni Gargioli and Giovanni Maria Filippi directed the continuous activities of the imperial building workshop, mainly financed from the resources of Bohemia's Royal Chamber. To the Late Gothic complex of the Jagiellonian Castle, they added the new 'Spanish' wing above the vast stables on the ground floor. The court society met regularly in the Vladislav Hall, the activities of which are documented in Aegidius Sadeler's engraving where the painter and engraver had placed his own easel into the first sketch. The Emperor pursued his building plans not only at the Castle and in its environs but also on his estates in Bohemia where, during the first years of his rule, he used to go hunting.

The beginning of his reign and ceremonial entrance into the residential town was promising that Prague would become a place of great festivals, which Czech aristocrats admired and described on their travels visiting courts of sovereigns in Europe.[16] This was evident from the coronation in Prague or the festival in 1585 at which Ferdinand of Tyrol, as the family senior, conferred the Order of the Golden Fleece on Rudolf II and his brother Ernest. Bohemia's high aristocracy as well as the public watched the ceremony of conferring the Order, the feast of the participating princes and the tournaments and games which accompanied the festivities. Court 'state' festivals demonstrated the sovereign's power as well as the social hierarchy and order, but Rudolf II rarely used this instrument of propaganda and shut himself away into the rooms housing his collections. Although he did not isolate himself completely from social life, he preferred observing it to acting his role as a ruler.

Rudolf II's lasting favourite component of festive culture was music, to which he paid particular attention.[17] His court orchestra, consisting of about sixty Italian, Dutch and Czech musicians, was one of the largest in Europe. In addition to the long-time conductor de Monte, many excellent instrumentalists and singers performed with it and many composers wrote for it, including Charles Luyton, Jaques Regnart, Jakobus Gallus-Handl and Kryštof Harant of Polžice, the Czech aristocrat, traveller and unfortunate politician.[18] Apart from their duties at the court and church services, the members of the orchestra participated in the musical life of the aristocratic palaces in Prague. It served also as an example for other aristocratic courts where smaller orchestras were formed, as for instance, at the court of the south Bohemian Rožmberks.

Central to the Emperor's artistic interest and collections were painting, sculpture and miniatures.[19] In purchasing works of art and attracting artists to his court, Rudolf II had extraordinary good taste and luck. Artists flocked to Prague not only from the Empire and Italy but also particularly from the Low Countries with which, being a Habsburg province, Bohemia had many contacts. From the court of Maximilian II came the versatile Giuseppe Arcimboldi(o) who excelled not only as a painter but also as inventor of various machines, organizer of games and festivals, and architect. He became famous, above all, through his allegories and portraits, composed very cleverly and with uncommon inventiveness of fruit, animals and plants. He used this method of composition to portray the Emperor as Vertumnus (the god of changing seasons), thus posing the question whether this portrait is a caricature showing the Emperor's sense of humour, or a commemorative symbol.

The 'Prague School' reached its peak in the work of the three famous painters – Bartholomaeus Spranger, Hans von Aachen and Josef Heintz. Adriaen de Vries became the congenial Rudolfine sculptor. The leading figure was Spranger, originally from Antwerp, who after years of apprenticeship in the Low Countries went through schooling in Italy, where he became renowned among cardinals and at the papal court. From 1580 he lived permanently in Prague working not only for the court but also for Prague churches and for the aristocracy in Bohemia. Also von Aachen had been trained in the Low Countries and in Italy where he became famous as a portrait painter. In 1592 he came to Prague having been in the service of the Bavarian dukes. After Heintz had returned to Germany from Italy and could not enter the service of the court of Saxony, von Aachen helped him to get a place in the Emperor's service. During the 1590s Rudolf II sent Heintz to Italy to portray Roman monuments.

These three leading Rudolfine painters are linked by the same artistic view, the same experience of painting of the Italian and Dutch High Renaissance and Mannerism, an emphasis upon technical virtuosity and the use of common models: for instance, the Parmigianino faces and figures. These artists came to Prague when their creative power was at its height. Having obtained fame, they reached positions of privileged court artists. They found open doors not only to patrician but also to aristocratic houses as well as to the Prague brotherhood of painters; they were ennobled and acquired considerable wealth. They were masters of secular and religious painting and excellent portraitists. They passed onto us self-portraits as well as the first likenesses of members of Bohemia's high nobility who began installing their family galleries. Above all, they were virtuoso masters of mythological and biblical themes. The elegance and intellectuality of their works for the Emperor suited his tastes which, as evidence shows, also included erotica and a certain lasciviousness. Mutual influences emanating from their co-operation and friendly relationship, so clearly visible in their works and their style, also affected other less famous Rudolfine painters.

In sculpture the parallel to these artists is Adriaen de Vries, born in The Hague, another Rudolfine artist of European significance. He was a pupil of Giovanni Bologna, and after returning from Italy to Augsburg where he produced a number of great works of art, he permanently settled in Prague at the beginning of the seventeenth century. There he created a unique gallery of monumental sculptures. His art represents the peak of Mannerism in sculpture by its perfect technical mastery of gesture and posi-tion of the body, full of inner tension. He created mythological groups of statues and, in co-operation with painters, an allegory of the Emperor's virtues. He is the author of several portraits of the Emperor doubtlessly con-veying successfully his imperial status along with features of his face and character.

Alongside the mainstream of figural, mythological, allegorical and symbolical painting and sculpture, landscape and genre drawing and paint-ing flourished in Prague. These activities were also pursued in the service and through commissions of Rudolf II, mainly by the Netherlanders Peeter

Stevens, Roelant Savery, Paulus van Vianen and others. They effectively worked for the Emperor as documentary artists producing interesting landscapes, flora and fauna. They left us unique views of the Castle and of Prague of the Rudolfine era. Documentation was, above all, a matter for graphic art. Representative of this genre was Aegidius Sadeler, born in Antwerp, an able landscape painter and brilliant engraver. From his workshop in Prague poured thousands of technically perfect, wide-ranging engravings, including prints after drawings and paintings of other Rudolfine artists. It was thanks to him that their themes and styles of Rudolfine artists became popular and spread far and wide. It was no accident that Sadeler placed his shop into the Vladislav Hall, the centre of social activity which he captured in a remarkable print. His engravings have all the marks of Mannerist elegance and perfection of Rudolfine art.

These great stars attracted to their circle further artists, especially unique artistic craftsmen. The Emperor purchased works in gold, enamel, glass, wood, tin; artefacts of book-binding, clock- and toolmaking. The rooms of the Kunsthistorisches Museum in Vienna house the most representative collection, displaying superb taste, inventiveness, refinement and a combination of exquisite materials, all characteristic of the artistic heights reached during the Rudolfine era. The most minute details are subordinated to the symbolic order and artistic taste of the Rudolfine universe. The Emperor's jewellers' workshops created new imperial crown jewels comparable with those of Charles IV.

Collections of paintings and sculptures, together with products of artistic handicrafts, manuscripts, books, antiques and even rare minerals were placed in the precincts of the Castle. Imperial agents endeavoured to purchase great works of art of the past in accordance with the Emperor's taste and views. Paintings by Albrecht Dürer and Pieter Breughel the Elder found their way to Prague to be installed in Rudolf's gallery next to contemporary artists and other treasures; their price, estimated to be millions of florins, made Prague into a magnet for collectors and robbers.

The few remaining catalogues of the collections, from the life time of the Emperor and the period shortly after his death, give us a meagre idea of their contents. It is part of the tragedy of Prague that Rudolf's collections were transferred, sold or stolen. Shortly after the Emperor's death the liquidation of his collections and their transfer to Vienna began. In the last year of the Thirty Years War, the Swedes occupied the Castle and got hold of its collections. As it happened, the art-loving Queen Christina was still on the throne and provided this great robbery with organization, thus saving many objects at least for Europe. Today only very little of what was created or purchased during Rudolf's reign remains in the Castle.

VIII

An important part of Rudolf's magical universe was the world of knowledge. Rudolfine art was admired for its beauty and perfection; its complicated symbolic meanings were comprehended and gradually elucidated. Quite different, however, was the attitude of contemporaries and, for a considerable time, also of historians towards intellectual, investigative, scholarly and scientific activities carried out at Rudolf's court. Unlike the museums and galleries, Rudolf's library and laboratory long remained misunderstood. Not a single literary work of this library would find its way into European literary heritage as a widely read work of lasting value. There was no parallel in Prague to the great Mannerist literature and drama of Elizabethan England, Catholic Spain or Italy. For literature written in Czech, the court remained closed and no impulses came from there. The literary public was changing; the aristocracy (feeding on literature in the languages of great nations) was abandoning it and it was burgherdom which became the consumer of literary works written in Czech. Under the influence of humanism, Latin was revived as the language of poetry and, naturally, as the language of science as well. In the libraries of mansions and monasteries of this period, or in their catalogues, one finds literary works side by side with standard books of contemporary learning. Baldassare Castiglione, and later Baltasar Gracián and their text-books of courtly manners were especially popular. Moreover, in the towns Czech and German humanism evolved alongside Latin Humanism, and Czech was promoted as the official language and the language of Protestant theology. Grammars and dictionaries were published and, at the end of the sixteenth century, the humanist Czech language reached its peak in meticulous prints of the Prague publishing houses, Jiří Melantrich of Aventýn and Daniel Adam of Veleslavín, and of the printing press of the *Unitas Fratrum* in Moravian Kralice, above all the *Bible of Kralice* (1579–1588), which established the code of literary Czech.

In Bohemia, therefore, books of learning were of far greater interest than humanist verses and dramtic endeavours. At the beginning of modern Czech culture, their common characteristic feature is their European dimension. Translations into Czech abounded both in literature and, especially, in the field of science. There were Czech translations of the primary works of the European Reformation, such as Calvin's *Institutio Christianae Religionis*, as well as books on history, geography, cosmology and natural history. News about the New World also caused excitement in this entirely land-locked nation, forging a popular tradition in travel books which continues to the present. Literary and cultural endeavours (in which aristocracy as well as burgherdom participated) were concentrated in informal communities of educated persons rather than in schools. They were well informed about what was going on in court circles and in learned Europe. Rudolfine scholars also entered into lively relations with the Prague intellectual milieu.

The Emperor's interest in learning and knowledge was just as keen as in the arts, and between both areas of culture there is an obvious connection relating to the world of science and symbols. Rudolf II tried to attract scholars of the period to his Prague court and place them in his employ. His interest in learning concentrated mainly on the cosmos and nature, and on their mysteries, which excited his desire for knowledge as well as his fancy. For scholars the attraction of the cosmos and nature lay in the traditional reasons for learned pursuits: knowledge of God and knowledge of the forces and phenomena between Him and the world. A dangerous tension existed between the two. Nature was seen as a perfect and unspoilt product of creation where God's order of things and their original purpose undamaged by man were preserved; it represented the world of perfect harmony and models. Hitherto nature was conceived as a world of signs and symbols of original harmony but, in the sixteenth century, this was becoming problematic and science endeavoured to understand the forces dominating life and nature. Two ways were open to this knowledge: exact observation, including precise description, and magic practices, hidden in bookish culture and in the learning of initiates. The latter approach had its epistomological foundations in the drawing of analogies, emanating from the idea of the unity of a world dominated by forces released from a single source and composed of simple elements. The knowledge of one thing promised to lead to the knowledge of a parallel or similar thing. At the court of Rudolf II, this old mode of thinking was meeting with the beginnings of empirical and rational science, often combined in the learning of one and the same scientist.[20]

In the circle of Rudolf's scholars his personal physicians occupied a privileged position. Among them an important place was held by Tadeáš Hájek of Hájek (Thaddeus Hagecius) (1525–1600), a man of wide theoretical and practical interests: botany, surveying, brewing, alchemy, astrology, astronomy. It was due to Hájek that the Emperor invited Tycho Brahe to Prague when he was losing favour with the King of Denmark.

Tycho Brahe arrived in Prague at the end of 1599; having achieved renown in the world of learning on account of the astronomical observations he carried out from his observatory on the island of Hven. In Prague he received a high salary, and the Emperor's castle at Benátky nad Jizerou near Prague was made available (for his family and collaborators. Tycho Brahe brought to Bohemia his unique astronomical instruments for exact observations of celestial bodies. The task of calculating horoscopes on the basis of observing the exact course of celestial bodies was left to Johannes Kepler, the mathematician and astronomer in the service of the Upper Austrian estates, who found himself in difficulties not only financially but on account of his Protestant faith. For these reasons he accepted the offer to move to Prague and around the turn of the sixteenth century, two of the most famous astronomers met to collaborate. After Tycho's death in 1601, Kepler took over his position at a slightly reduced salary. In spite of various difficulties he was able to spend more than a decade studying and working on his astrological tables in Prague to which the observatory had been transferred. The result of this work, the *Tabullae Rudolphinae* appeared in print as late as 1627, long after the Emperor's death, but the path to this work is marked by a number of great discoveries published in Prague. In 1605 Kepler proved the elliptic course of planets around the sun, thus not only correcting an error of contemporary astronomy but shattering belief in the circle as the universal principle underlying the structure of the universe. In 1609 Kepler's *Astonomia nova*, one of the pioneering works of modern science, was published in Prague.

Tycho Brahe and Kepler had not created an oasis of modern knowledge in a desert of backwardness. Modern science grew out of an empirical basis and practical technological skills in most varied fields of production. After the catastrophic fifteenth century, the Czech Lands enjoyed a very long period of peace which led to economic revival in traditional and new branches. The new wave of activity occurred mainly in mining of silver and iron ores and metallurgy which, at that time, was under the management of feudal authorities. In Jáchymov (Joachimsthal) silver *thalers* were minted and, based on Czech and German experience, Agricola wrote one of the most accomplished treatises on mining and metallurgy. On their Moravian estate, Janovice, the Austrian aristocratic family Hoffmann, originally from Styria, introduced highly advanced methods of iron production. The Hoffmans, like the Rožmberks or Cardinal Dietrichštein, belonged to Rudolf's courtly world and their libraries were treasuries of traditional and contemporary learning. An important field of technical and technological experience in the Czech Lands became the breeding of fish in large fishponds, the building of which required excellent knowledge of the landscape as well as of surveying. The technology of breeding the Czech carp reached a very high standard.

Prague and other towns saw strong growth in the manufacture of instruments, especially clocks and astronomical clocks – symbolic mechanisms of the Rudolfine era. The Emperor was intrigued by mechanics and commissioned a variety of machines. However, his main interest, like that of aristocrats and intellectuals in Bohemia, was in alchemy and occultism.

Thanks to recent scholarship we are well informed about occultism of the Rudolfine era, especially about the alchemy either practised in or channelled through Prague. Alchemy represented an intricate corpus of practices and theories, a mixture of chemical and biological empiricism but also, perhaps chiefly, continual meditation about nature, man and the order of the cosmos. It was linked with the technology of chemical experiments and metallurgy, and strongly influenced medicine. Alchemists were typical intellectuals of their time; the best of them combined learning and the study of occult tradition with freedom and spiritual independence; nevertheless, their way of thinking is anchored in what Foucault terms 'preclassical' epistemology, in the use of analogy and symbolism. Society viewed occultists with suspicion, they were disliked by the Church and their arcane experiments provoked hopes as well as fears. Even their contacts with the Emperor were not nearly as easy as those of the artists. Often they fell into disfavour with their masters and had to lead a nomadic life. Prague and the courts of some magnates in Bohemia attracted them and a number of great alchemists and occultists at least came on visits and some published their writings there.

Among the most important alchemists connected with Rudolfine Prague for part of their lives was the Emperor's court physician Michael Maier, a Paracelsan, alchemist and reformer. After the Emperor's death, he left Prague and visited England several times where his friends were Robert Fludd and Sir William Paddy. Maier's books *Symbola aureae Mensae* (1617) and *Atalanta fugiens* (1619) were very well received in the world of learning. The Paracelsan Oswald Croll whose work *Basilica chymica* (1608) was illustrated by Sadeler made periodical appearances in Prague. One of the most interesting personalities of the alchemistic and occult world, the Pole Michael Sendivogius, was helped by the Emperor to get out of prison. Apart from Hájek of Hájek (Hagecius) among the Czechs moving in medical-alchemistic circles was Doctor Borbonius, a physician much in demand by aristocrats who in his notebooks described not only their illnesses but all sorts of interesting events from their lives.

Two Englishmen, John Dee and his assistant Edward Kelley, belong to the most remarkable figures of the occultist world. Travelling from Poland, they arrived 1584 in Prague where Dee stayed to 1589 and Kelley until his death (1597?). Czech historiography has long considered them typical charlatans who succeeded in taking advantage of the occultist fancies of the Emperor and the Czech aristocracy. Evans's treatment, however, provides a more balanced description of their activities. Dee was one of the most learned men of his time who had built up perhaps the best contemporary scholarly library; he had served for a time as court astrologer to Queen

Elizabeth. He was well versed in occultist literature, believed in hidden forces behind the visible world and in cosmic harmony. The spiritual world he considered a reality which could be made accessible by means of media. Kelley served him as a medium at spiritualist séances and through his ventriloquist skills reproduced the voices of the archangels Gabriel and Uriel. The Englishmen's spiritual séances not only caused a sensation but also aroused suspicion in Prague high society. Dee, however, had influential protectors in Vilém of Rožmberk and the Spanish ambassador San Clemente. He stayed for some time at the court of the Rožmberks to the chagrin of their chronicler Václav Březan, a member of the *Unitas Fratrum*. In the end he had to leave Prague although his learning was appreciated there. More dramatic was the end of Kelley who was unable to escape imprisonment.

Under the Emperor's protection, the Prague Jewish community flourished economically and culturally. The community included financiers of great calibre and fabulous wealth, for example, the richest man in Prague Mordechai Meisl, and Jacob Bassevi. The Emperor, and later the renowned military man Albrecht of Valdštejn (Wallenstein) (1583–1634), used the services of such men and granted them protection. The overcrowded ghetto saw the emergence of new synagogues in the Renaissance style, and Rudolf's Prague attracted Jewish as well as Christian scholars. The cultural life of Prague's Jewry, for a long time shrouded in misunderstanding and mystery, contributed both to Prague's history and to its mythology. In the Jewish Town lived and worked Jehuda Liva ben Bacalel, known as Rabbi Loew (1512–1609) – a scholar, cabalist and remarkable thinker who, like his Christian contemporaries, strove to reform life in the sense of harmony. He occupies a place in the cultural history of Prague as the inventor of the mythical Golem, a 'robot' paralleling the homunculus of the alchemists.

IX

At the turn of the sixteenth century tensions in the Czech Lands came to a head: Mannerism demanded catharsis. As Rudolfine culture reached its peak, rifts deepened between the religious parties, between the domains of the Habsburg monarchy and, particularly, between the ageing, melancholic, Emperor and his ambitious brother Matthias. Finally, the council of the Habsburg family allowed Matthias to depose the Emperor and to assume his place. Both the opposition within the estates dissatisfied with the newly installed Catholic governments at the turn of the century, and careerists calculating upon his accession, were coming over to his side. In 1606 Matthias joined forces with the estates of Austria, Moravia and Hungary to defend the peace agreement with the Turks which the Emperor had rejected as

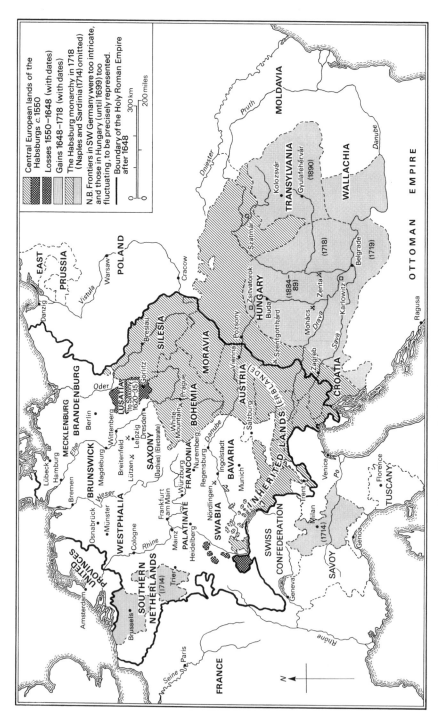

Central European lands of the
Habsburgs c. 1550

Losses 1550–1648 (with dates)

Gains 1648–1718 (with dates)

The Habsburg monarchy in 1718
(Naples and Sardinia (1714) omitted)

N.B. Frontiers in SW Germany were too intricate,
and those in Hungary (until 1699) too
fluctuating, to be precisely represented.

Boundary of the Holy Roman Empire
after 1648

0   200 miles

0   300 km

5. Central Europe in the sixteenth and seventeenth centuries.

shameful and had refused to sign. At this time, the allied estates put forward the concept of a confederate monarchy which was expected to overcome the contradiction between central government and territorial autonomy. However, the march of the confederates on Prague in 1608 did not succeed in dethroning the Emperor because the estates of Bohemia rallied to his defence. Their loyalty was rewarded by Rudolf's Letter of Majesty in 1609 promising religious liberties; at the same time, Matthias's succession and his rule over Moravia were acknowledged. Thus the Crown of Bohemia was, once again, divided between two sovereigns. Rudolf II tried once more to prevent Matthias's accession to the imperial and royal throne of Bohemia but the abortive invasion of Prague in 1611 by an army which his nephew Bishop Leopold of Passau had recruited to give support to the ailing Emperor accelerated his abdication. He died the following year. Matthias and his court stayed in Vienna, and Prague finally lost its position as the capital of the Habsburg monarchy and the seat of the Empire. Events sped towards the uprising of the estates of Bohemia in 1618 which set off the Thirty Years War with all its political, religious and cultural upheaval. Did the war also ruin the entire magical and cultural universe of Rudolf II?

X

Although the Emperor's court had moved to Vienna, many Rudolfine artists and scholars had settled in Prague, as did part of Rudolf's collections. The war that Central Europe witnessed from the middle of the 1620s to the middle of the 1630s coincided with a steep rise in the military and political fortunes of Albrecht of Wallenstein.[21] He grew up in the Rudolfine milieu and by character and fate he appears as a product of the Mannerist age. He created a representative court worthy of the most powerful men in the Czech Lands and Central Europe. It is Wallenstein's active interest in the building of monumental architecture that stamps his position in Bohemian Mannerist culture. In the 1620s he built the first of the large Prague Mannerist palaces, under the royal Castle in the Little Side on the bank of the River Vltava. Prague and Wallenstein's estates in northern Bohemia provided great opportunities for Italian architects and artists as well as for artists of the Rudolfine court. Not undeservedly, Wallenstein the victorious military leader had himself portrayed in full armour in a fresco on the ceiling of his palace as the god of war Mars. Perhaps the greatest artistic chance was given to Adriaen de Vries whose statues embellished the garden of Wallenstein's palace in Prague. Queen Christina had them removed to Sweden in 1648. Like Rudolf II, Wallenstein was interested in the occult, had frequent bouts of melancholy and believed fervently in astrological prophecies. Sometime earlier he had had his horoscope prepared by Kepler himself whose competence he valued highly. He tried to win Kepler as his own mathematician and astronomer offering him protection and attractive conditions of service at his court as well as a post at the university he was intending to found. But Kepler died in 1630 and did not live long enough to see the Habsburgs' last reward for Wallenstein's services – he was murdered by Ferdinand II's colonels in Cheb in 1634.

After the Battle of the White Mountain Wallenstein's contemporary and rival at the imperial court, Cardinal Dietrichstein, became the rising star.[22] He belongs to the gallery of great cardinals of the sixteenth and seventeenth centuries who assisted in establishing Absolutism based on orthodox Catholic faith. Of Austrian descent, Dietrichstein's father had, in the Emperor's service, been rewarded with the rich Moravian estate of Mikulov on the Austrian border where he built a new chateau on the site of the old castle. During the uprising of the estates the Cardinal was threatened with defenestration and confiscation of his property, however, after the White Mountain he became governor and sovereign ruler of Moravia until his death in 1636. His preoccupation with the defence and administration of Moravia and with the Counter-Reformation, which he carried out with missionary zeal, did not prevent him from pursuing his wide-ranging cultural interests. Life at the Mikulov chateau, where he had transferred the seat of the Land's administration, began to resemble that of a princely court. Cardinal Dietrichstein was interested not only in religious affairs but also in main contemporary intellectual currents. Embracing as he did Franciscan and Capuchin *pietas*, Dietrichstein established one of the largest libraries of his age containing books on most varied fields. It seems that he was interested in modern science rather than occultism. He belonged to the followers of Galileo Galilei and contemplated publishing his works in Moravia.

The second half of the Thirty Years War brought ruin to the Czech Lands. In some areas the population had been depleted to half of its pre-war size.[23] Promising social developments of the sixteenth-century Central European 'Low Countries' came to a halt and the outcome of the war brought about a parasitic economy of the large estates based on forced labour (*robota*) and monopolies. The aristocracy, reduced to a few tens of magnates and insignificant numbers of lesser nobility, was absorbed entirely into service of the absolutist state and became Catholic. Punishment for participation in the uprising was so severe and rewards to loyal servants of the Habsburgs so generous that in the Czech Lands of the seventeenth century, as perhaps nowhere in Europe, there was no aristocratic resistance to absolutism left. Moreover, territorial patriotism and Czech culture lost their aristocratic component. Pure Catholic Baroque reflects the new situation in the Czech Lands.

All this has usually been regarded as a complete cultural upheaval, a radical change of the cultural situation and, by Czech national historiography, as a tragedy before the incorporation of the Baroque into national culture. Only recent studies have put emphasis on continuity, particularly in the cultural sphere.[24] A change of religion in itself need not necessarily mean a change of *mentalité* or faith. Religious dogma and ceremonial changed, as did certain cultural inflections, influenced by theology. The Baroque in Bohemia found its expression in architecture, sculpture and painting and its theme was the representation of the sacred. The changes were also manifest in Catholic sermons; hymns and pastoral texts which predominated in Czech literature were still written in a pure Czech nursed mainly by Jesuits. Thanks to them, awareness of state and national continuity were preserved. Fine arts lost their aura of Mannerist exclusivity and embraced a new audience, the masses of believers. At the same time the Baroque is also indebted to certain values and concepts of Rudolfine Mannerism. Although the work of the first great Czech Baroque painter Karel Škréta is firmly rooted in the Rudolfine tradition, it also assimilates important elements of the Czech High Baroque. After the end of the war a new building boom began; the style of churches and, particularly, of chateaus of the second third of the seventeenth century is, according to some scholars, more Mannerist than Baroque. A good example is the monumental Černín palace in Prague which overshadowed the Castle, or the Liechtenstein Plumlov in Moravia, a typical Mannerist nonsense the design of which was also influenced by Václav Eusebius of Liechtenstein, a dilettante who numbered architecture among his interests.

Neither did the learned component of Rudolfine Mannerism, especially occultism, disappear with Rudolf II and Wallenstein. Evans points out that the aristocratic and ecclesiatic milieu retained a lively interest in alchemy and astrology and that alchemistic endeavours were further pursued at the courts of nobles in Bohemia and Moravia, and even penetrated the monasteries. 'Catholic learning', still humanistic, began to develop scientific as well as historical research. Nevertheless Bohemia and Moravia, indebted as they were to late scholasticism in philosophy and education, remained clearly outside the epistemological turnaround of the mid seventeenth century symbolized by Descartes.

Czech thinking had not yet abandoned the aim to reach, through knowledge, pansophy as well as harmony and reform of life. Here the culminating endeavour is represented by the greatest figure in Czech culture of the seventeenth century, Jan Amos Komenský (Comenius) (1592–1670).[25]

XI

This persecuted scholar grew up in the milieu of Rudolfine, pre-White Mountain society and culture. His benefactors and the protectors of his church, *Unitas Fratrum*, whose priest and eventually bishop he became, were the Žerotíns. He dedicated his treatise *The Labyrinth of the World and the Paradise of the Heart* to Karel the Elder of Žerotín on whose estate he experienced the post-White Mountain catastrophe of his Church. Benefactors of the *Unitas Fratrum* supported his studies in Germany. He was interested not only in theology but in all old and new knowledge; he familiarized himself with the Rosicrucians and pansophists, with the teaching of Copernicus and with mysticism. He wanted to devote himself to the advancement of culture and education of his native Moravia, whose language and history he studied and whose schools he aimed to improve. The defeat of the uprising of the estates of Bohemia and the Counter-Reformation forced him to emigrate, first to Polish Leszno. After its destruction during the Swedish invasion in 1656 and after his wanderings through Central and Northern Europe, he found protection and peace for writing his last works in Amsterdam where, in this city in the most liberal country of Europe, he died.

Comenius was acclaimed throughout Europe for his language textbook *Janua linguarum reserata* (1631) which, as the most popular textbook on languages of that time, was translated into most European tongues. His pioneering method of language teaching was based on the content and meaning of words. He paid continuous attention to paedagogical-didactical questions and his efforts in this area represents the peak of humanist paedagogics. As organizer of education, he was invited not only to Protestant countries but was also well known in France and in America.

For all that, Comenius believed that the fame of his educational and didactic work diverted him from his main task of elaborating pansophism, systematically cultivating all learning and from reforming society on the basis of faith and knowledge. He planned to summarize his work in *De rerum humanarum emendatione consultatio catholica* (1645–1670).[26] Through personal meetings and correspondence he maintained contact with many important contemporary scholars in Germany, Central Europe, the Netherlands, Sweden and, above all, in England. He sought ways to influence the powerful of this world from whom he hoped to get assistance in realizing 'universal reform'. Before that it was, according to his conviction, indispensable to conquer the 'Antichrist' embodied in the papacy and the Empire against whom he fought with the help of contemporary 'prophets' and their pugnacious challenges. He believed that he might invent the 'machine' (*perpetuum mobile*) and, for the purpose of realizing his pansophist and universal reform plans he called upon all scholars of the time to found a world academy. *De rerum humanarum* remained unfinished, especially its pansophic part, and was published uncompleted. However, the modern edition of its preserved parts have shown that it belongs to one of the most interesting intellectual works of the seventeenth century.

On his pilgrimage through Europe Comenius met Descartes in the Netherlands in 1642 where, in a conversation lasting four hours, they discussed 'the secrets of their sciences'. It was a meeting of two worlds which, for all their mutual respect, did not draw these two scholars any closer together. Indeed, it was a meeting of two 'epistémé' which Foucault called 'preclassical' and 'classical' respectively. Comenius' repudiation of Cartesianism constituted a trauma for his interpreters and admirers. Modern cultural history, however, rejects the linear progressivist theory of the history of knowledge in which every new level censures preceeding achievements as mistakes which had been overcome, or condemns them to the world of oblivion, where Comenius was cast by Pierre Bayle at the beginning of the Enlightenment. Comenius did not accept the Cartesian method which rejected old learning and which erected a new system of knowledge on the basis of the subject's evidence to establish truth or falsehood and the inductive method. He neither parted with traditional knowledge nor with the culture of his time but saw its consummation in a pansophic and pan-reformist system. He believed in the divine substantialness of man and his ability of self-improvement not only through deep faith – in the spirit of the Czech Reformation – but also through knowledge. He was firmly rooted in the 'preclassical' era which, in the Czech Lands, culminated in Rudolfine Prague. Comenius represents the attempt at reaching its intellectual peak by great synthesis of knowledge and Christian morality. This is how he was understood in the past by the great figures of Czech culture, František Palacký and Tomáš Garrigue Masaryk, and this is how he is also understood at the present time. He belongs to the eminent defenders of Christianity at the beginning of the modern era. Unlike Pascal, he rejected its Cartesian starting point.

Notes

1 The literature on the Rudolfine era and its culture is massive. Here I only refer to recent works of synthesis with bibliography, and to collections. On the historical concept of Central Europe, Central-West and Central-East Europe, see the studies in W. Eberhard (ed.), *Westmitteleuropa – Ostmitteleuropa, Vergleiche und Beziehungen. Festschrift für Ferdinand Seibt zum 65. Geburtstag* (Munich, 1992).

2 For a recent overview, by a Czech author, of Rudolf's times and his personality,
   including commented bibliography of sources and literature, see J. Janáček,
   Rudolf II a jeho doba [Rudolf II and his era] (Prague, 1987). Further K. Vocelka,
   Rudolf II und seine Zeit (Cologne and Vienna, 1984). For Rudolfine culture of prin-
   cipal significance is the work by R. J. W. Evans, *Rudolf II and his World. A Study in
   Intellectual History 1576–1612* (Oxford, 1973); I have used its German version *Rudolf
   II. Ohnmacht und Einsamkeit* (Graz-Vienna-Cologne, 1980). There is also the two-
   volume catalogue, with accompanying studies, of the exhibition at the
   Kunsthistorisches Museum in Vienna (24 Nov. 1988–22 Feb. 1989): *Prag um 1600
   Kunst und Kultur am Hofe Rudolfs II*, vols. I, II (Freren, 1988). See also E. Fučíková
   et al. (eds.), *Rudolf II and Prague. The Imperial Court and Residential City as the Cultural
   and Spiritual Heart of Central Europe* (Prague-London-Milan, 1997).

3 J. Hausenblasová and Zd. Hojda, 'Pražský rudolfinský dvůr mezi Hradem a
   městem' [The Prague Rudolfine court between the Castle and the town], *Opera
   Historica Editio Universitatis Bohemiae Meridionalis*, 3 (1993), 115–36.

4 For an attempt to look at society and culture of the time as a whole, see J. Válka,
   *Česká společnost v 15.–16. století II. Bělohorská doba. Společnost a kultura manýrismu
   (Skriptum)* [Czech society in the 15th–16th centuries. The era of the White
   Mountain. Society and culture of Mannerism] (Teaching text), (Prague, 1983).
   On Moravia, see J. Válka, *Dějiny Moravy II. Morava reformace, renesance a baroka*
   [History of Moravia II. Moravia of the Reformation, Renaissance and
   Baroque] in *Vlastivěda moravská, země a lid* [History and geography of Moravia,
   country and people], ns, vol. 6 (Brno, 1996).

5 J. Pánek, 'The expedition of the Czech noblemen to Italy, 1551–1552, A
   contribution to history of international relations in the field of culture, politics
   and finances in the 16th century', *Historica*, 30 (1990), 29–95.

6 About the life style of the Czech aristocracy in the Rudfolfine era see collection
   Život na dvoře a v residenčních městech posledních Rožmberků [Life at the court and in
   the residential towns of the last Rožmberks], *Opera historica*, 3 (1993); J. Pánek,
   Poslední Rožmberkové Velmoži české renesance [The last Rožmberks Grandees of the
   Czech Renaissance] (Prague, 1989); *Adel im Wandel. Politik-Kultur-Konfession
   1500–1700* (Vienna, 1990); this is the catalogue of the exhibition of
   Niederösterreichisches Landesmuseum held at Rosenburg (12 May–28 Oct
   1990), ns, vol. 251, ed. H. Knittler, G. Strangler and R. Zedinger. Interesting
   cultural-political aspects of the Rudolfine era, especially about life in the salons
   of the aristocracy, see H. Janáček, *Ženy české renesance* [Women of the Czech
   Renaissance] (Prague, 1977).

7 J. Válka, 'Politika a nadkonfesijní křesťanství Viléma a Jana z Pernštejna' [The
   policy of supradenominational Christianity of Vilém and Jan of Pernštejn], in
   P. Vorel (ed.), *Pernštejnové v českých dějinách* [The Pernštejns in Czech history],
   (Pardubice, 1995), pp. 173–86.

8 The correspondence of Czech and Moravian Protestants who studied in
   Switzerland was collected by Fr. Hrubý and published by L. Urbánková-Hrubá,
   *Etudiantes Tchèques aux écoles protestantes de l'Europe occidentale à la fin du XVIe et au début
   du XVIIIe siècle* (Brno, 1970).

9 B. Chudoba, *Španělé na Bílé hoře* [The Spanish at the White Mountain] (Prague, 1945).

10 P. Chlumecky, *Carl von Zierotin und seine Zeit* (Brno, 1962); O. Odložilík, *Karel starší ze Žerotína* [Karel the Elder of Žerotín] (Prague, 1934).

11 Numerous studies on the economy of the Czech Lands in the sixteenth and seventeenth centuries are summarized in J. Válka, '*Česká společnost* [Czech society], and A. Míka, 'Sociálně ekonomická struktura českých zemí před třicetiletou válkou' [Socioeconomic structure of the Czech Lands before the Thirty Years War], *Sborník historický*, 21 (1974), 41–7; *Sborník historický*, 24 (1976), 37–80; J. Válka, 'Le grand domaine féodale en Bohême et en Moravie du 16ᵉ au 18ᵉ siècle. Un type d'économie parasitaire', *Economic History* 10 (1982), 141–79.

12 An entirely novel analysis of the political system of the Habsburg monarchy is presented by R. J. W. Evans, *The Making of the Habsburg Monarchy 1550–1700 An Interpretation* (Oxford, 1979), the German version *Das Werden der Habsburgermonarchie 1550–1770. Gesellschaft, Kultur, Institutionen* (Vienna-Cologne-Graz, 1986). J. Pánek summarizes his studies in 'Das politische System des böhmischen Staates im ersten Jahrhundert der habsburgischen Herrschaft (1526–1620)', *Mitteilungen des Österreichischen Instituts für Geschichtsforschung*, 97 (1989), 53–82. See also J. Bahlcke, *Regionalismus und Staatsintegration im Widerstreit. Die Länder der Böhmischen Krone im ersten Jahrhundert der Habsburgerherrschaft (1526–1619)* (Freiburg i.B., 1993).

13 Literature about Rudolf II's illness is listed and commented upon by Janáček, *Rudolf II*, pp. 536–7.

14 Evans, *Rudolf II Ohnmacht* is a pioneering work; studies by M. Foucault, *Les mots et les choses, une archéologie des sciences humaines* (Paris, 1966) and *L'archéologie du savoir* (Paris, 1969) have been influential.

15 Cf. Janáček, *Rudolf II*, pp. 529–30.

16 K. Vocelka, *Die politische Propaganda Kaiser Rudolfs II (1576–1612)* (Vienna, 1981), pp. 140–6. The experience of court festivals are described in *Příběhy Jindřicha Hýzrla z Chodů* [Adventures of Jindřich Hýzrl of Chody] (Prague, 1979), the most interesting travel diary of an aristocrat of the Rudolfine era.

17 J. Racek, *Kryštof Harant z Polžic a jeho doba* [Kryštof Harant of Polžice and his times], I *Opera Universitatis Purkynianae Brunensis*, Fac. Fil., No. 149, (Brno, 1970); R. Lindell, 'Das Musikleben am Hofe Rudolfs II' in *Prag um 1600*, I (Prague, I), pp. 75–84; P. Daněk, 'Die Rudolfinische Musikkapelle und die böhmische Musikkultur' in *Prag um 1600*, II, pp. 39–45.

18 In 1621 he was among the executed twenty-seven leaders of the anti-Habsburg Rebellion, instigated by the estates (1618) and defeated in the Battle of the White Mountain (1620).

19 J. Dvorský (ed.), *Dějiny českého výtvarného umění. Od počátku renesance do závěru baroka* [History of Czech fine arts. From the beginning of the Renaissance to the end of Baroque] (Prague, 1989), II/1; J. Neumann, 'Rudolfinské umění' [Rudolfine art], *Umění*, 25 (1977), 400–48; and *Umění*, 26 (1978), 343–7; E. Fučíková, *Rudolfinská kresba* [Rudolfine drawings] (Prague, 1986); T. DaCosta Kaufmann, *The School of Prague. Painting at the Court of Rudolph II* (Chicago and London, 1986).

20 For an excellent account of these matters see Evans, *Rudolf II. Ohnmacht*, ch. 6. Readers may find useful J. Smolka, 'The Scientific Revolution in Bohemia', in R. Porter and M. Teich (eds.), *The Scientific Revolution in National Context* (Cambridge, 1992), pp. 210–39.

21 J. Janáček, *Valdštejn a jeho doba* [Wallenstein and his era] (Prague, 1978); G. Mann, *Wallenstein* (Frankfurt/Main, 1971); J. Polišenský and J. Kollmann, *Valdštejn. Ani císař ani král* [Wallenstein. Neither emperor nor king] (Prague, 1995).

22 P. Balcárek, *Kardinál z Dietrichštejna (1570–1636)* [Cardinal Dietrichstein] (Kroměříž, 1990).

23 J. V. Polišenský, *War and Society in Europe 1618–1648* (London–New York–Melbourne, 1978); Fr. Matějek, *Morava za třicetileté války* [Moravia during the Thirty Years War] (Prague, 1992).

24 *Dějiny českého výtvarného umění* [History of Czech fine arts], II/2 (Prague, 1989); J. Neumann, *Český barok* (The Czech Baroque) (Prague, 1969, 2nd edn 1974); Z. Kudělka, I. Krsek, M. Stehlík, J. Válka, *Barok na Moravě* (Baroque in Moravia), forthcoming; Zd. Kalista, *Česká barokní gotika a její žďárské ohnisko* [Czech Baroque Gothic and its centre in Žďár] (Brno, 1970); P. Preiss, *Boje s dvouhlavou saní, František Antonín Špork a barokní kultura v Čechách* [Struggle with the doubleheaded dragon, Franz Anton Sporck and Baroque culture in Bohemia] (Prague, 1981); P. Preiss, *Italští umělci v Praze. Renesance, manýrismus a baroko* [Italian artists in Prague. Renaissance, Mannerism and Baroque] (Prague, 1986); J. Válka, 'Manýrismus a baroko v české kultuře 17. a 1. pol. 18. století' [Mannerism and the Baroque in Czech culture of the 17th and first half of the 18th centuries], *Studia comeniana et historica*, 8, 19 (1978), 155–213.

25 Basic biographies and literature: M. Blekastad, *Comenius. Versuch eines Umrisses von Leben, Werk und Schicksal des Jan Amos Komenský* (Oslo and Prague, 1969); D. Čapková, *Myslitelsko-vychovatelský odkaz Jana Amose Komenského* [Jan Amos Komenský's intellectual and educational heritage] (Prague, 1987); J. Pánek, *Jan Amos Komenský-Comenius* (Prague, 1990), published in various languages; J. Polišenský, *Jan Amos Komenský* (Prague, 1963); P. Floss, *Jan Amos Komenský. Od divadla věcí k dramatu člověka* [Jan Amos Komenský. From the theatre of things to the drama of man] (Ostrava, 1970); J. Kumpera, *Jan Amos Komenský* (Ostrava, 1992); K. Schaller, *Comenius* (Darmstadt, 1973); R. Kalivoda, *Husitská epocha a J.A. Komenský* [The Hussite epoch and J. A. Komenský] (Prague 1992).

26 *De rerum humanarum emendatione consultatio catholica*, vols. I, II (Prague, 1966). In Czech annotated translation: Jan Amos Komenský, *Obecná porada o nápravě věcí lidských*, vols. I–II (Prague, 1992).

7

The White Mountain as a symbol in modern Czech history

JOSEF PETRÁŇ AND LYDIA PETRÁŇOVÁ

I

Ask anyone Czech about the White Mountain and even if only a tiny fragment of school history remains in his memory, the question will conjure up the vision of an historic national defeat. From the nineteenth century the White Mountain has been one of the symbols whose function it is to promote the cohesion of the community which adopts them, then encourages a particular emotional relationship to the community itself.[1] One witness, a defender of the method which requires historians to explain rather than to judge historical events, can speak for many. The positivist historian Jaroslav Goll wrote in 1875 that he could not imagine a Czech of any religious denomination or political party 'who when speaking about the consequences of the White Mountain could remain entirely calm and cool and could content himself simply with an explanation of how these events came to pass . . .'.

The name of the plateau that once lay just beyond Prague's western margin and is now included within the city limits apparently comes from the colour of slate – a white stone which from time immemorial was taken from the hill for the building of the metropolis and its environs. For several generations of the modern Czech nation, however, the significance of the name lies in the fact that here, in a battle on 8 November 1620, the armies of the King of Bohemia and Roman Emperor Ferdinand II (1617 [1619]–1637), together with divisions of the League of the Catholic states, defeated the forces of the rebellious estates of Bohemia and their allies from the Protestant Union.[2] In a conflict which later developed pan-European dimensions and became known as the Thirty Years War, there was no dearth of battles and bloodier defeats. In the sort of humane overview which is possible only with the passing of time, this mass slaughter of hired (mercenary) soldiers might be regarded as an astonishing example of the strangeness of human behaviour.

Considered historically, however, 1618 and the years following saw the culmination of the long-term struggle concerning the nature of the monarchy of the estates, a struggle identified with the specific character of Habsburg rule in the Czech state.[3] The estates of Bohemia in opposition recognized the ascendancy of the reformed faith (identifying partly with the long-established domestic Hussite-Utraquist tradition and partly with the new currents of European Reformation). The Habsburgs, meanwhile, who had ruled the Czech state since 1526 held to the Catholic faith and all this linked the religious with the political issue. The dispute over the character of the monarchy (symptomatic for European political life at this period) in which the representative public – the estates – defended the principle of the 'division of power' (*imperium mixtum*) against the centralizing tendencies of the princely court, then naturally found an external, international response and stimulated alliances. Regarded in this way, the increasingly tense political-confessional situation was closely related on the one hand to the Habsburg programme for political dominance in Europe and on the other to the formation of an anti-Habsburg Protestant political bloc. The Czech Lands, then, became one of the focal points of the conflict where a programme of freedom of religion and the maintenance of liberties of the estates represented a defence against centralization and, at the same time, linked the domestic and foreign 'representative' public. By this we mean a certain select elite, social strata, which represented their own socio-political (estate) standing and addressed themselves to a public made up of those of the same rank. The Habsburg great-power complex in Central Europe was, of course, a union of states each having their own form of administration and linked by no strong economic, political or cultural interests. The estates as the representative public organ then filled the role of defender of distinctive Czech statehood and, at the same time, of the *vlast*. This is Czech for 'homeland' but with connotations of ownership (*vlastnictví*), absent in the English term, in its original sense of the appropriated space, which it wished to control.

II

Through a combination of circumstances which it is not our task to explain here, the estates suffered a weakening of the will and strength to continue the fight. These circumstances made the White Mountain a certain watershed in the war. As a result the happy victor, Ferdinand II, turned to his court counsellors a month after the battle with specific questions arising

from the uncertain international situation and the unforeseeable development of internal politics. How was he to use the political dominance that
he had gained in the interests of rehabilitating the Catholic faith, and especially the religious orders that the estate regime had previously suppressed
(Jesuits and others)? How was he justly to punish those responsible for the
rebellion and what was he to do to strengthen his military forces with a view
to the continuance of international conflict? This last question was closely
connected with the further question of how to improve the financial situation (by confiscating rebels' property). Ferdinand's court counsellors, who
felt themselves bound by their offices to support a programme of central
power in every possible way, gave answers that were legally based and
framed with a view to constitutional change. They recommended that the
Emperor make aggressive use of the situation in which defeat had dealt a
heavy blow to the estates' self-confidence and had disarmed them in their
preparations for the defence of their liberties. The imperial counsellors
wanted to declare the throne to be hereditary as against a matter of free
election by the estates, and to weaken the power of the state offices held by
the estates; they suggested that the privileges of the estates be revised and
that several Protestant denominations be expelled from the country in order
to uproot the intellectual seedbed of political 'rebellion'.

Further repressive political decisions and acts followed in the spirit of
these recommendations and of these some were to become 'historic' events
with the force of symbols signifying a 'break'. They had in themselves an
emblematic function: for example the execution of twenty-seven leading
figures of the rebellion in Prague's Old Town Square on 21 June 1621, the
confiscation of the rebels' property, the driving into exile a part of the
opposing estates together with the non-Catholic intelligentsia (which led to
sharp change in the composition of the estates), and the proclamation of
the so-called Renewed Land Ordinance (*Vernewerte Landesordnung*) in the
Czech Lands (1627), which removed the legislative initiative from the estates.

In considerations of constitutional doctrines the problem of the defeat or
the victory of the 'just' principle rapidly came to the fore. Subsequent historiography changed the theme of the debate into a question of the relative
progressiveness of the constitutional systems (estates and centralism) which
clashed in the rebellion of the estates of Bohemia.

The Viennese strategists of Habsburg dominance in Europe regarded the
uprising in Bohemia, at the time and immediately after the defeat, as
'heinous rebellion' which it was necessary to suppress not only in the interest of the monarch, whose 'majesty' had been betrayed by the estates, but
also on principle as a matter of overall social order. This could be maintained only by a central administration ('royal power') set above imperfect
territorial governments (estates, princes of Empire), whose destabilizing

tendencies it was capable of resisting. The claims of the doctrine of state Absolutism clashed with the theoretical principle of the division of state power which included the election of the king as a self-evident liberty of the estates. For the supporters of the constitutional principle of the estates, the *imperium mixtum* was guaranteed by a Land Ordinance, which was based on the country's earlier historical development and a tradition which royal power was bound to respect. It was with historical arguments that Pavel Stránský defended the State Rights of Bohemia in his *Res publica Bohemiae*, published in 1634, as did Pavel Skála of Zhoře and others among the writers of the defeated camp living in exile.

The representative public at home, especially politicians who had sided with the victors from the beginning or had adjusted more easily to the status quo, found themselves in quite a curious position. They could not simply shake off the estates tradition which had formed their mentality, but reminders of that tradition carried the stain of 'rebellion'. Vilém Slavata, the High Judge and President of the Royal Chamber, who had been thrown from the window of Prague Castle by the decision of the estates rebels in May 1618, saw the two pillars of the future development of the Czech state in a strong central power based on Catholic political commitment.[4] In contrast the other state official to have suffered defenestration, Jaroslav Bořita of Martinice, identified with the self-interested opinion of the majority of the estates community (regardless of religious affiliation) that it was necessary to maintain the estates' share of power and give it support. The 'rebellion' should not be linked to constitutional rights and the liberties of the estates, as the adherents of the theory of absolute power insisted. Even before the White Mountain he had expressed fears about the influence of foreign politicians who could not have sufficient feeling for the good of the 'homeland' in decision-making about the constitution of the Czech Lands. If in Slavata's case and under the influence of his personal experience, the dominance of the estates power was ineradically linked with uncontrolled licence and a deviation from a right order which could be guaranteed only by strong central power, this did not mean that he lacked awareness of belonging to the community of the 'Land' as 'homeland'. His wide-ranging memoirs are permeated by historicisms beholden to the estates and territorial patriotism, which betrays a mentality other than that of the court counsellors with their disciplined way of adhering to the ideology of new symbols and emblems – the utopia of the absolutist state.

It is not all surprising that the defeated should rapidly have asked themselves who or what was to blame for the defeat, while the victor could indulge in the simpler ritual of thanksgiving. The notion of the 'true Christian' acting in a 'good cause' played a major role in the politicized religious consciousness. None of those to whom victory had been denied had the smallest doubt of the justice of their cause in the defence of their religious and political rights and liberties. While on the other hand the methods by which the 'cause' was conducted, the degree of commitment and will to sacrifice, the political insight and capability of the leadership, whether military or political, the excessive self-confidence of the protagonists and their inadequate evaluation of their domestic and international support and of the reliability of their allies, together with a number of other issues, were not simply considered, but were made the subject of concrete and general accusations. The opinion was advanced that the estates had allowed themselves to be lured into a political trap prepared by post-Tridentine Catholicism, of which the Viennese court was the tool. From here it was only a short step to the messianism which became the lasting accompaniment of the myth of the White Mountain.

Much of what was said can be found in the writings of Jan Amos Komenský (Comenius) (1592–1670).[5] In the complex development of his opinions, however, we can find something which raises him above his contemporaries: reflection on ideologized and politicized religion as a deformation of true Christianity. With the passage of time we can fully appreciate his meditation on the unfortunate consequences of the politicization of the struggle for 'truth', a politicization which he blames for the catastrophe. Any elevation of confessional or patriotic feeling over the humble self-creation of the world under God's governance Comenius regards as selfishly perverse and dangerous, even if 'humanly' explicable in terms of the feeling of solidarity and tradition. The image of the 'divine comedy' which he uses in his account of history does not justify 'revenge' – it leads to positive solutions: conflicts and war, and stuff of human history, however unjustifiable, act as accelerators of change. And in this sense the author of the posthumous treatise on the general reform of human things (*De rerum humanarum emendatione consultatio catholica*) tries to perceive, alongside the ravings of a world sliding towards a fall, its renewal through the workings of God, in which the community should realize its true identity.

Comenius' critical appraisal of patriotism in no way weakened his sense of belonging to his homeland and its traditions. The symbols of 'Land' and 'commune' had been for a long time a part of state ideology which by tradition was inherited by the estates – the representative public, and that without regard to religious and political orientation. This makes it the more natural that such a language of emblems should be strongly invoked at a time when the estates found themselves under threat. The generations which succeeded those who could remember the uprising in Bohemia, and which were brought up in a far from 'rebellious' spirit, noticed the pressure of the court administration which, with a rather simple-minded view to the needs of a centrally organized state and its great power ambition, pushed aside the inconvenient and at the time admittedly poorly functioning estates system. A part of the country's spiritual and political elite, by this time already Catholic, emphasized in its defensive attitude the emblem of the *vlast/patria*, as an 'enclosed space' in which their rights and liberties as estates should be guaranteed. They protected their share in power. We can find their arguments in the Latin account of the 'once happy but now grievous state of the Kingdom of Bohemia' written at the beginning of the 1670s by the Jesuit Bohuslav Balbín (1621–1688).[6]

The defence of the enclosed space of the *vlast/patria* against foreign interference from without is formulated as the defence of the 'home', the stability and order, the sacred ground resisting destructive outside forces.[7] In this sense the concept *vlast/patria* has always been readily understood and the manipulation of its symbols has always been effective. The 'alien' powers, which the *vlast* – 'home' has to resist, are here partly foreigners who have settled in the country (this we find already in the work of the medieval chronicler so-called Dalimil) but who will not integrate with the home environment (primarily aristocrats who gained great landed estates), but mainly the court bureaucrats at the central state administration in Vienna. According to Balbín the imperial counsellors, often for selfish personal reasons and to advance their careers, constantly stirred up suspicion of conspiracies against the ruler by bringing up one-time 'rebellion'. Such unfounded accusations were a mere pretext for disrupting the bond between the king and the 'nation' of the Land ('people'), allowing the ministers to flaunt their loyalty and achievements and to improve their prospects by promoting empty suspicion of their fellows.[8] In defence of the rights of the estates Balbín rejected the doctrine of state absolutism which raises the central power above the laws of the Lands. 'They' – the court counsellors – imposed fiscal and other burdens on Balbín's homeland, shielding themselves with the royal emblem, which they put above the law. They claimed that the 'king' did not exist for the sake of the 'people', the inhabitants of the land who are protected by the Land Ordinance, but that the 'people' existed for the 'king'.

It is difficult to discern in individual interactions to what extent and for how long the emblem of 'rebellion' bound together the functions and mutual relations of the two power groups – the central court elites and the Land elites (estates). The essential point is the fact that the lasting semiotic sign for the estates as the representative public became the image of the *vlast/patria* with its 'people', the home which must defend itself against 'foreign innovations and injuries emanating from "Vienna"'. Later this was to remain the basic building block of the myth of the White Mountain.

III

Into this image, in the re-Catholicized Czech Lands, there was integrated the developing protective cult of saints who were 'Land patrons' – especially of St Wenceslas who in Balbín's work, as it were, cursed and condemned to defeat those foreigners who disturbed the enclosed space of the *vlast/patria* ('the Lands of St Wenceslas'), and who were unable to become as one with its inhabitants. The protective symbol of the *vlast/patria* was already and traditionally the Czech language, as an age-old, obvious sign of 'home' and 'tradition', clear in its contrast to the 'foreign'. (In Old Czech the terms 'nation' and 'language' coalesced.) The ideology of the estates employed this idea as a shield even before the uprising, without regard to political or religious groupings, as is evident from the 'language' resolution of the Diet in 1615. The symbol of 'language' in the proclamation of the demands of the 'indigenous' members of the political community for the right to decide on matters concerning the patria can be found in the works of both Jaroslav Bořita of Martinice and Pavel Stránský. There is no evidence in either private or official written records that at the time when Balbín wrote his treatise the Czech language was subject to external encroachment or even proscription. Rather, the decision on the equality of Czech and German in the state offices incorporated into the Renewed Land Ordinance (the constitutional legal code for Bohemia from 1627, and for Moravia from 1628), legalized existing practice and apparently simply suited the central administration for which it was more convenient to communicate in German.

In the previous constitutional law of the monarchy of the estates the Czech language had had a decidedly emblematic significance. Although its official status was declared by law in 1615, it was far from being required, as a consequence, in official practice. This was especially the case at a time when the community of the estates of Bohemia was becoming more international and was enlarging its vision of the 'world' within a European frame. Moreover, economic interests and religious tolerance meant that the Czech Lands before the rebellion of the estates were attracting foreigners whose native language was German. This did not present a barrier to their involvement with the community of the estates, whether they were noblemen or burghers. For those who wished to share in the rights of the estates and to assume responsibility for public affairs, the Land was their *vlast/patria*, even if they spoke German. This applied to the estate elite in greater measure in the period after the White Mountain. Even patriotic interest-groups, proclaiming the emblematic language of the 'enclosed space', recognized their cultural, social and family ties and, with an eye to political advancement did not content themselves with Czech–German bilingualism and the language of the intellectuals – Latin. Members of the aristocratic elite in particular, according to their capabilities and ambitions, tried to add to their familiarity with the leading European courts a mastery of their diplomatic languages.

The emblematization of *vlast/patria* incorporating the symbol of the 'language of St Wenceslas' and the cult of the country's patron saints cannot – as is apparent – be understood in purely national terms. Restricted by signs of the 'enclosed space', the organizing centre of images of 'home', it transcended the interest of a particular political group and ethnicity and could easily be the subject of symbolic manipulation in the interactions between the elite representative public and the community of the 'people', which always placed a high value on the symbols of the protected, appropriated areas. The patriotic community was shaped by an interest group of estates politicians and intellectuals, the representative patriotic public of the seventeenth century, in the context of distrust of and even antagonism to 'Vienna' which coalesced with symbols of 'foreigners' and 'injurious' centralized power. In the works of Balbín and later generations of patriotic Catholic intellectuals the image of the 'injured *vlast*', thus created, neutralized the confessional attitude to the 'rebellion' of the estates and to the Reformation tradition. František Jan Beckovský, who belonged to the *Ordo militare Crucigerorum* (Crusaders), saw the cause of the uprising in the preference for giving the highest offices in the Czech state to members of the Catholic minority who in this way elevated themselves above the Protestant majority in the estates.[9] This chronicler of the late seventeenth century was, in his patriotic enthusiasm, offended that the odium of 'rebels' remained attached – unjustly, as he thought – only to the inhabitants of his *vlast/patria* while others, who also opposed the imperial majesty (the Austrian and Hungarian estates) obtained mercy and purged themselves by blackening the Czechs. It seems that the same injustice, together with a parallel emphasis on 'fidelity' to the dynasty, for a long time was shaping the language of patriotic emblems. A century after Beckovský, the philologist Josef Dobrovský (1753–1828), complemented his predecessor by stressing the fidelity of the 'Slavic nation' to the dynasty connected with the conception of Austroslavism of the national revival.[10]

IV

Given the number and character of the sources pertinent to establishing the attitude of 'the people' we may never be able to answer the question of how far the wider public accepted the outlined image of the *vlast/patria* and when precisely this occurred. We can first of all consider the conditions created by the progress of the Catholic reformation which laid great stress on the pastoral role, especially in preaching. In the period of the flowering of Baroque ritual festivals in the first third of the eighteenth century, a new public emerges, not only in quantitative terms but also qualitatively (socially and culturally). The image of the *vlast/patria*, symbolically moulded into the likeness of the archetype 'home', was spontaneously acceptable to the wide public. The more so because it was presented as a story, as a legend about saint protectors and permeated by tales from the history of the *vlast/patria*. Patriotically oriented preachers in their mode of presentation could evoke an emotionally reformational (Counter-Reformational) effect. We do not, of course wish to simplify the multifaceted reality of everyday events in any way, but the reaction of the patriotic public to the reform programme of the state in the second half of the eighteenth century is, in our view, eloquent testimony to a manipulation of symbols which could not have been possible if the ideological image of the *vlast/patria* had not previously entered the collective subconscious.

Enlightened absolutism introduced a mechanically centrally controlled 'state machine' into the administrative system and in this the decisive places were in all instances supposed to be filled by qualified bureaucrats indifferent to nationality. In this system the once socially prestigious functions of the aristocratic elite of the estates lost significance. Indeed, even commoners could assert their talents and there occurred a degree of social levelling. With the introduction of this system and even at lower levels of the administration from the end of the 1740s, Czech was replaced in written agendas by German, which then became the 'official' language. This was taken into account in educational reforms under Maria Theresa and Joseph II in the 1770s. The reaction to these changes led to the emergence of a defensive component in Czech patriotism, which laid stress on historical, constitutional and cultural traditions. This based itself on the traditional Land (estates) conception of the *vlast/patria* and included elements of Enlightened 'territorial' patriotism and especially elevated the emblematics of language. This is the reason why modern Czech consciousness somewhat suppressed the general European process of the rise of civil society, which became overshadowed by the problem of 'revival', itself concentrated on the language problem and the continuity of historical tradition.

In view of our present theme it is not our task to judge rationalist Josephinism for its failure to comprehend the trickiness of the past which surrounds the present and limits the future. It consciously ignored the threat to reforms when it underestimated 'obsolete' feelings and the persistence of a tradition linked with the emblems of *vlast/patria* (language); it single-mindedly enforced the 'rational' course of action which, on the whole, was genuinely paving the way for liberties of a civil society. The resistance which it encountered, however, did not emerge only from the interest groups of the estates, the conservative representative public organ, which had their own reasons for rejecting reforms. The strength and endurance of this resistance depended on the results of previous manipulations of symbols and the continuity of 'Baroque patriotism' as well as the self-assertive agitation of national 'awakeners' among the public comprising a wider social spectrum. The revivalist intellectuals of burgher origin, who accepted the historical constitutional tradition of a geographically defined *vlast/patria* (Land), nevertheless gradually enriched the set of symbols with a national, linguistically genetic and socially levelling standpoint. In the language of ideological emblems, the 'nation' ('the people') then acquired an equal place alongside *vlast/patria* (Land). 'Revivalism' as a specific creation of the socio-cultural organism occurring from below, gradually brought about a divorce with the socio-political past of estatism. In the later stages of national and civil emancipation, which its nineteenth-century supporters themselves called the 'revival' the myth of the White Mountain found its most valid context.

V

The view that the date of the Battle of the White Mountain was a turning point within a national Enlightened conception of history was put forward by Josef Dobrovský in his address of 1791.[11] In his opinion the outcome of the battle crippled and exhausted the Czech people both physically and spiritually, and the nation had still to recover from its effects. Dobrovský's theme was the history of the Czech language and literature and the Enlightened historian's approach to the cultural field was sober and matter of fact. He was not developing a philosophy of history by reflecting on its moving forced and metaphysical' meaning'. What stands out here is the definition of the boundaries and characteristics of the epoch, which indirectly involved a challenge 'to make amends' for the defeat but this of itself was still insufficient for the full development of the emblematics of the myth.

The Enlightenment brought yet another development: indifference to the confessional aspect of the conflict. This led historians to condemn the intolerance shown by the victors of the White Mountain toward the Protestants and to accuse the political elite of the estates of stirring up the religious and constitutional disorders that culminated in the uprising. Ferdinand II's advisers could not be absolved on the basis of their regard for the good of the state and the maintenance of order; similarly there was no excuse for the greed and blind folly of the instigators and leaders of the uprising who so rashly, and without weighing real possibilities and rational approaches, brought matters to a head with terrible consequences for the nation.

The generations inspired by the patriotic atmosphere of the era of the Napoleonic Wars expected national history in the ethnic sense to provide them, above all, with a glimpse of its own specific 'meaning'. After the years of Enlightened Classicism, the current of Romanticism released an imagination which could dwell on the mythological elements of culture. This period and its culture was identified in the Czech ethnic community as one of 'revival'. It was a construct which of itself logically implied that a nation which needed to be 'revived' or 'awoken' had experienced a mortal agony. It assumed that there was, besides the causes, course and symptoms of that agony, a specific point from which the national tragedy could be dated. This point was identified with the Battle of the White Mountain as a pivotal event for the consequences of which could be 'made amends' by the will to continue the tradition which it had interrupted. The way in which Czech civil society sought to rationalize and justify its beginning by almost exclusive appeal to its past (and not the Enlightenment and liberalism as we would have expected) can be considered as its specific trait. According to the meanings given to the 'making amends' for the White Mountain, we can categorize the developmental variants of national soul-searching, confessing and understanding of the responsibility arising from it. We can also follow the variants of the myth as it was invoked to confirm the social and political programme and ideology of its bearers. In myth, just as in legend, the basic historical fact is not examined but used, with the help of symbols, 'to unveil' the meaning of an event which the positivist historian can only record and elucidate.

At the beginning of the nineteenth century we still do not find the unified symbolism of the White Mountain engrained in the consciousness of Czech society as a whole. If this had been the case, we should certainly have found it in the songs, tales, chronicles and writings of 'the common people'. Apart from an echo which can be regarded as a result of the manipulation of symbols by educated patriots, we find little in this social environment.

VI

Pilgrimages to the White Mountain, which served as a reminder of the benefits of 'victory' for the subsequent fate of the nation, were already traditional. In the second decade of the nineteenth century, however, a contrary, that is, a tragic perception of this symbol as a 'grave' or 'graveyard' was gaining control in the consciousness of a certain group of young, patriotic intellectuals. Sporadic allusions giving indubitable testimony to the rooting of this symbolism in national consciousness were soon overtaken in the work of the poet, Karel Hynek Mácha (1810–1836), whose feelings for the tragedy of the grave were different and more topical.[12] For Mácha the White Mountain became a symbol by which the 'national character' of the past two centuries could be explained. The nation, desecrated and broken by the departure of its greatest spirits into exile, underwent moral collapse; its wounds remain unhealed, they still bleed, weakening the nation spiritually and morally. This symbolic line of interpretation, differing from the more usual generally revivalist (awakening) approach, runs through the judgement of national character to the present day.

When we follow the moulding of the myth of the White Mountain in this period, we cannot avoid the Romantic influence coming from outside in the form of Polish messianism, an influence which could scarcely be ignored by Mácha's generation. This was the time of the birth of the comparison between the martyred Polish nation and Christ with his redemptive mission. Karol Malisz, the Polish participant in the Slavic Congress in Prague in 1848, in a sonnet in the cycle, *Poems in Praise of the Czech Nation*, used a parallel between the White Mountain and Golgotha.[13] The late revivalist environment accepted this emblematic code in imitative domestic verses and adapted the account of the White Mountain to the symbolism of Golgotha/Calvary. In ever more open analogies the 'sacrificial' victim became the ethnically defined 'nation' and (in accordance with the conception of society generated when the revival was culminating that it had grown from below) semiotically transferable to the social level of the 'people'. The nation became the innocent victim, paying for the sins of those who, as the political elite, should have guided and protected it, but who gave preference to their own often purely personal aims and profit. Among other reproaches, the leaders of the estates were especially blamed for 'infidelity to the cause' and for failure to make contact with the people who embodied the mass of the 'nation'.

The myth containing the symbols of the grave, the sacrifice on Golgotha and the Resurrection was readily acceptable to the national society in the aroused atmosphere of the revolutionary events of 1848. It evoked an emotional relationship between the individual and community in support of a political programme. This was ensured by Czech publicists in their frequent allusions to the theme of the White Mountain. From a Romantic dream of Resurrection the political publicists now moved on to a programme for 'making amends' for the White Mountain. Thus the journalist Karel Havlíček (1821–1856) continually reminded the readers of his newspaper of the 'shame of the White Mountain' which they should keep in their hearts as an inspiration to consistent resistance to Vienna and everything German.[14] Due to the unusual strengthening of the influence of publicists at this time, and the expansion of their activities to address a wide social spectrum, the myth of the White Mountain penetrated as an ideological element into the consciousness of a large part of the community which claimed Czech national identity.

VII

In the latter part of the period we should consider not only journalism and belles-lettres but also school education. Especially from the 1860s when the myth of the White Mountain was revived in connection with a new stage in the national movement. In contrast to 1848, however, the form of the myth was not determined by belles-lettres, but was based on a closely argued historical conception of national history by the historian and politician František Palacký (1798–1876), whether or not the authors accepted or rejected it. Neither poetry nor the historical belles-lettres and drama flourishing at this time brought much in the way of novelty to enrich the symbolism. In the same way, and like many well-known authors from our literary history, neither publicists nor politicians up to the 1890s had developed further than Palacký in the interpretation of the symbol of the White Mountain – sometimes not even as far.

The attempt to graft nineteenth-century democratic ideas on to the feudal conditions of the estates regime became the lasting maxim of the symbol of the White Mountain. It appears in striking form in the historical philosophy of Palacký, where it permeates the polarity set up between Slavic democratism and the alien (German) feudalism foreign to its spirit. According to this concept it was in Hussitism that 'democratism' raised itself to magnificent heights and transcended national and temporal boundaries in its emphasis on the idea of personal, intellectual and social liberty (in line with the liberalism of the nineteenth century.) Hussitism owed its victories to its powerful impact to which the whole nation contributed. In the black and white picture presented by this national historical philosophy, the estates national elite, once strengthened by Hussitism, is depicted as 'betraying' the mass of the nation, the 'common people' after the Battle of Lipany (1434), and as reducing them to feudal bondage and 'serfdom'. The estates paid for this estrangement in their conflict with the central (sovereign) power which, in line with the general European trend, was gathering strength through the 'new levers and new forces in social relations', which were being created by modern civilization.[15] The national mass of the 'common people', who might have been a support to the estates elite after the defeat of the White Mountain had they not been betrayed, suffered as well. As a consequence the entire nation was nearly ruined.[16]

The comprehensive historico-philosophical scheme of Palacký (not surpassed by later historians whether or not they accepted it), shifted the emphasis in accordance with the ideology of culminating revival. It now stressed the social level in which the symbolism, derived from it, was more easily acceptable to the modern Czech national public. There were sources available to confirm the material and spiritual misery of the nation after the White Mountain, the confessional intolerance and consequent violence of the secular and church authorities, the enserfment of the mass of the 'common people' and the decline of Czech linguistic and literary culture. A narrow social and cultural focus, however, inhibited a view of the whole spectrum of processes in post-White Mountain society. The scheme of national subjugation took no account of the mature culture of the social strata to which was assigned the role of 'subjugators' of the national population. Little notice was taken of the new social, cultural and political elite which maintained and opened contacts with the European West, or of general civilizational, economic and technical trends and scientific and educational progressive elements. Nor, obviously, was attention directed to the consequences of all this for later development of the Czech Lands.

Concentration on this level of the ideology of the culminating revival, very simply presented in Palacký's historical conception in the second half of the nineteenth century, funnelled research into the White Mountain, whether in the development of individual aspects of the concept or in polemic against it. The issue of 'national decline' led to the question of 'guilt' and 'the victim' – the nation and the 'guilty ones' – while the feudal estates were not called in question. With regard to the contradictory assessments of Hussitism (the Reformation) and the period after the White Mountain, the religious orientation of the authors as well as their political convictions came into play as a matter of course. Historians expressed opinions critical of the leaders of the estates who were brought up to countenance anarchy and with a lax attitude towards order. These leaders, incited by German Lutheranism that prevailed at the period, set themselves against the legitimate central power which represented a more developed form of authority and guarantee of political order. As a result punishment fell on the nation which they had betrayed (historians W. W. Tomek, A. Rezek).

VIII

The myth, which had been shaped so effectively and dramatically, steadily resisted the rise of positivism in the humanities. At the end of the nineteenth century the historian, Jaroslav Goll (1846–1929) and his pupils rejected metaphysical speculation in historical work, and in the spirit of positivist empirical criticism expressed their disagreement with the historico-philosophical conception of late revival historiography. The positivistic approach to history brought with it new methods and concrete gains in knowledge but, at the same time, it turned its back on the historian's age-old socio-ideological function. It paid no attention to symbols as the bearers of meaning in the chaotic onrush of history. It gradually lost touch with the political reality of the national movement in which, on the contrary, the revivalist tradition played a major part in historical consciousness. The philosopher and sociologist Tomáš (Thomas) Garrigue Masaryk (1850–1937), who was interested above all in the problems of human existence, realized this gulf.[17] Although he did not identify himself with those who wanted to define contemporary society exclusively in terms of its past but, perhaps, especially because he was a realist and recognized the intensity of the tradition of late revivalist historicism, he could not and would not neglect the images of the past created by national culture. His starting point was the needs of the present and he tried to discover in traditional moral values and ideas which could inspire the future. In Palacký's comprehensive historical conception he found support for his own notion of 'humanity'; Palacký's historical dimension was supposed to authenticate the consciousness of the contemporary nation which had been 'reborn'. The protests of the Goll school against the dubious application of historical method stimulated controversy over the 'meaning of Czech history', which in its turn led the national cultural public to define itself preeminently in relation to the past. One can wonder whether so exclusively a retrospective view was not, in the context of the overall spiritual orientation of the modern age rather, a retarding force and an obstacle.[18]

While Masaryk emphasized the ideological connection between the 'revivalist programme' and Hussite-Reformation tradition, his opponent, the historian Josef Pekař (1870–1937), found striking continuity in patriotic and national feeling in the modern nation apart from the impulses of Enlightened liberal ideology. In the course of the controversy, the historians of the Goll school substantially enriched our knowledge of the problem of the White Mountain. One example is Kamil Krofta's account of the domestic Reformationary development in the period before the White Mountain.[19] Thus the historical focus widened, but the established traditional view did not fundamentally lose its structural elements and symbols. It was a view supported by the readers' reaction to the Czech translation of two works by Ernest Denis, *Fin de l'independence bohème* (1890) and *La Bohème depuis la Montagne-Blanche* (1901–3).[20] As a Frenchman he was not educated in the late revivalist tradition of Czech culture and approached the historical philosophy of Palacký from the outside. He was also a member of a society which was being validated by its own revolutionary myth. His work, written in the 1890s for a French readership, has a completely fresh angle, even though Denis found abundant inspiration in the writings of F. Palacký, W. W. Tomek, A. Rezek and A. Gindely and was entirely dependent on these for information. His contribution consists of a main thesis to which he subordinates his method in an impressively cultivated expository style and with copious use of symbols. The thesis was unusual enough to catch the attention of the Czech public (brought up in the revivalist myth of the White Mountain) to a much greater extent than that of the French public to whom it was addressed. It consisted of the idea that 'the lot of nations which anticipate the future and which break with tradition and open up new paths for humankind' tends to be a kind of fatal 'punishment', exhaustion of energy, fatigue and a gradual lagging behind other nations who make use of their historical contributions and push them out of their leading position. To point the way for others acquired the attribute of 'guilt' in history. Czech national history from the high point of Hussitism, moved further, 'dramatic entanglements' to the 'thickening of the plot' ending in the White Mountain which was, at the same time, 'the end of Czech independence' in the European framework.

Denis's work came to the attention of the Czech reader in 1893, at a time when views of the Czech past and of history in general were a matter of controversy for the domestic culture. This period saw the culmination of the dispute over the 'meaning of Czech history', finding a response in a rather small circle of the intellectual political public. The results of the research of historians who were seeking to raise the problems of the White Mountain above the established historical perspective did not altogether penetrate into the general consciousness. A wide reading and theatre-going public was for the most part satisfied with representations of the content of the myth in its late revivalist form, enriched by Denis. The former intellectual charges conditioned its historical context, petered out and in the contemporary situation it neither enriched the now fully constituted modern nation nor provided an opportunity to give events a new meaning. This was clear only to a small group of 'modern' intellectuals, who regarded the artificially created historical myth (tradition) as a paralysing ideology where the 'idiotic bleating' about the White Mountain was a poor substitute for necessary political action (the poet V. Dyk).[21]

During the dispute over the 'meaning of Czech history', historians realized the necessity of a deeper study of the conditions of pre- and post-White Mountain developments unencumbered by the notion of 'destiny' enshrined in the myth. Pekař tried to show that not everything blamed on the White Mountain was exclusively a consequence of that event.[22] In the light of current research we can add that Pekař was far from perceiving traits in the pre-White Mountain economic, social and civilizational making of Central Europe of a certain retardation which shifted the region to the periphery of developed countries of integrating modern Europe. Where Pekař above all struck a blow at the established scheme of the White Mountain myth was in his judgement of the dominant spiritual movements in European cultural typology. Here the Gothic period, whose culmination for the Czechs was Hussitism, was succeeded after its gradual decline by the Renaissance and later by the 'Romanesque' Baroque period (stemming from the Romanesque cultural milieu) with beginnings before the White Mountain. In the schematic pattern of this historian, whose fertile imagination created a panorama of the past according to an aprioristic design (in just the same way as Palacký, Denis and other masters of the word and intuition before him) we can see as a general principle the notion of the victory of the aristocratic ideal over an ideal that was democratically tinged. The Czechs could not have prevented this development (and many did not even wish to prevent it). Pekař explains the arrival of the Baroque and other socio-cultural changes without ignoring the dark shadows of the post-White Mountain period, the spiritual and material decline spread by 'the violence of an often narrow-minded authority'. This appraisal of the values of Baroque showed Pekař's opinions to have been far from those of some of his contemporaries who celebrated the White Mountain as the victory of Romanesque joy of life and order not from the confessional standpoint, but exclusively as sources of aesthetic qualities.

IX

The myth of the White Mountain was highly active and effective in the years of the First World War when emotions ran high throughout Czech society reflecting tragedies in many families, poverty and general social tension. In such historical situations the symbol's significance and mobility increase: there is a search for 'guilt' and for 'the guilty'. The myth incorporating the symbolism of Golgotha knew of old the 'guilty ones' who lived on in dynastic successors. Moreover Denis's addition to the myth found a wide response. This atmosphere was carried over into the social and political climate of the anniversary dates of the estates during the first months and years of the independent Czechoslovak state. The myth affected not only minds but also actions of the crowds.

It is worth noticing the way in which, as time went by, the symbolism of myth entered the language of history writers trained in the positivist school. They began to use expressive phrases taken from a vocabulary more usual for poets. Between 1918 and 1921 many professional historians took up writing journalistic essays for papers and magazines and even pamphlets for a wide public, and in these the engrained symbols of the White Mountain myth permeated accounts of current affairs.[23] The adaptive function of symbol in myth came to the forefront: a new reality was considered as a reality authenticated by national historical values.

The Czech dream which gave myth meaning was at this time and in the ideas of many, politically fulfilled. The rise or restoration – 'resurrection' – of the independent state was the 'making up' for the White Mountain, the 'sacrifice' had not been in vain (as already Palacký and some generations after him had believed), the 'guilty' – chiefly the Habsburgs – had been removed (admittedly at times anti-Catholic resentment remained); the author of *The Czech Question* (the future President) T. G. Masaryk, had become the 'avenger' who purged the 'national shame'. 'The meaning of Czech history' shifted to 'the idea of the Czechoslovak state' where the symbolism of the White Mountain found a new significance. Here the national catastrophe was recalled in order to stimulate the will to a new life; comparable symbols were sought elsewhere, in the 'resurrection' of Poland, Serbian Kosovo, French Sedan – in 'beatified defeats', symbols conducive to the inner regeneration of the nation.[24] Not only on the political, but also on the moral level, in the role of some kind of national conscience, the 'blessing' of the White Mountain was the symbol supposed to lead to the discernment of the legacy of history in the spiritual character of individuals and, indeed, the whole society. This of course presented an opportunity to attribute several bad traits simply to the 'bacillus' of the White Mountain.

The myth of the White Mountain, revived by the First World War and the beginning of independence, seemed likely to lose its edge and fade with the peaceful development of the Republic; perhaps with time it would even disappear, together with the trauma which gave it birth. This did not happen due to the resolution of 'the inheritors of the glorious national tradition' as historian and politician Zdeněk Nejedlý termed the Communists – the force of totalitarian power from 1948.[25] The late revivalist construction of the symbols of the White Mountain, in which the 'people' appeared as the 'victim', can already be found in a pamphlet by Nejedlý in 1920. Later, as one of the ideologues deciding on the selection of historical symbols which (even though of bourgeois origin) had to be accepted and mastered as a tool of propaganda, enforced in the schools and throughout cultural life, Nejedlý chose a variant of the White Mountain myth, which had already appeared in the rhetoric of the political Left before the Munich crisis.[26] Nejedlý was only one of those for whom the 'revival' became a 'meta-language' for the current cultural and also social and political situation. In one of the post-war speeches Nejedlý addressed the present: 'Let us make up for the White Mountain!' He had in mind the 'victory of the working people' over the former 'ruling class', which was not of course the aristocracy but the bourgeoisie. Through analogy with the revivalist text of the White Mountain myth, the new regime connected with its ideological interests eased itself into the role of 'saviour' with the will to 'redress' for the injuries inflicted on the 'people' – the nation. In addition to its normative function, the myth had a significant adaptive role: the 'people's democratic' system was here put forward as the authentic image, to a well-versed public, of tried and tested national values, painted in the black and white of the revivalist emblems: Hussitism – The White Mountain. This was the lesson imposed on present generations at the school bench.

A society which needs to define itself almost purely in terms of its past – either because it feels threatened or because it is uncertain of its own strength – seeks support in ideology or historical myth. The myth of the White Mountain and every other myth as a historical fact possessed in various historical situations and in different societies an adaptive function, whether in a positive or a negative sense.

Notes

1   For more detail on the myth of the White Mountain see J. Petráň, 'Na téma mýtu Bílé hory' [On the theme of the myth of the White Mountain], in Z. Hledíková (ed.) *Traditio et cultus. Miscellanea historica bohemica* (Prague, 1993), pp. 141–62; my essay draws on this article. Cf. also Z. Hojda, '"Idola" barokního bádání' in *Kultura baroka v Čechách a na Moravě* ['Idols' of research on the Baroque] in *Práce Historického ústavu ČSAV, Miscellanea C6* [Baroque culture in Bohemia and Moravia] (Prague, 1992), pp. 15–24. In this collection other articles can be found which to some extent allude to this theme. Cf. also R. J. Evans, 'Bílá hora a kultura českých zemí' [The White Mountain and the culture of the Czech Lands], *Československý časopis historický*, 17 (1969), 845–62 (with a summary in English).

2   The following works published in English are useful: T. K. Rabb, *The Thirty Years' War. Problems of Motive, Extent and Effect. Problems of European Civilization* (Boston, 1964); T. Aston (ed.), *Crisis in Europe 1550–1660* (London, 1965); J. Polišenský, 'The Thirty Years' War and the crisis and revolutions of seventeenth century Europe', *Past and Present*, 39 (1968), 34–43. Problems and literature are summarized by J. Polišenský, 'Der Krieg und die Gesellschaft in Europa 1618–1648', in J. Polišenský et al. (eds.), *Documenta bohemica bellum tricennale illustrantia*, 6 vols. (Prague, 1971–00), p. 1.

3 More recently on these problems see J. Pánek, 'Stavovství v době předbělohorské' [The estates in the pre-White Mountain era], *Folia historica bohemica*, 6 (1984), 163–219; by the same author, 'Republikánské tendence ve stavovských programech doby předbělohorské' [Republican tendencies in the programmes of the estates in the pre-White Mountain era), *Folia historica bohemica*, 8 (1985), 43–62. For a summary of the problems, see J. Janáček, 'České stavovské povstání 1618–1629' [The uprising of the estates of Bohemia 1618–1629], *Folia historica bohemica*, 8 (1985), 7–41; the same author deals in detail with particular problems in his commentary and conclusion to the edition *Pavel Skála ze Zhoře, Historie česká* [Pavel Skála of Zhoře, Czech history] (Prague, 1984).

4 See Petráň 'Na téma'.

5 N. Rejchrtová, 'Komenský a stavovské povstání' [Comenius and the uprising of the estates'], *Český časopis historický*, 88 (1990), 63–71.

6 Balbín's work, which could not be published during his life because of its political connotations, was published only in 1775 by František Martin Pelzel under the title *Dissertatio apologetica pro lingua Slavonica, praecipue Bohemica*. It was translated into Czech as *Obrana jazyka slovanského, zvláště českého* [Apologia for the Slavonic language, especially for the Czech language] and published by J. Dostál (Prague, 1923).

7 More recently about the symbolism of homeland, see E. Wimmer, 'Heimat. Ein Begriff und eine Sache im Wandel' in D. Harmaning and E. Wimmer (eds.), *Volkskultur und Heimat* (Königshausen, 1986), pp. 13–24.

8 Concerning the problematic of the relationship between 'lid' (people) and 'národ' (nation) in the post-White Mountain period, see J. Petráň, 'Lid a národ v pobělohorském labyrintu' [People and nation in the labyrinth of the post-White Mountain era) in F. Graus (ed.), *Naše živá a mrtvá minulost* [Our living and dead past] (Prague, 1968), pp. 72–106.

9 H. Opočenský, 'Bílá hora a česká historiografie' [The White Mountain and Czech historiography] *Pokroková revue*, 9 (1913), 184.

10 In the speech delivered in J. Dobrovský in the presence of King Leopold II in Prague – where he was crowned – in 1791; see J. Petráň, 'Učené zdroje obrození' [Learned sources of the national revival] in *Počátky českého národního obrození* (Beginnings of the Czech national revival) (Prague, 1990), pp. 314ff.; Z. Šimeček, 'Slavista J. Dobrovský a austroslavismus let 1791–1809' [The Slavist J. Dobrovský and the Austroslavism of the years 1791–1809], *Slovanský přehled*, 57 (1971), 177–90.

11 See J. Petráň, 'Ke genezi novodobé koncepce českých národních dějin' [On the genesis of the modern concept of Czech national history], *Acta Universitatis Carolinae, Philosophica et Historica*, 5 (1982), 67–89.

12 M. Hýsek, 'Bílá hora v české literatuře' [The White Mountain in Czech literature], in J. Teige, H. Kuffner, A. Hajn, M. Hýsek and Z. Wirth (eds.), *Na Bílé hoře* [On the White Mountain] (Prague, 1921), p. 109. The second edition appeared separately: M. Hýsek, *Bělohorské motivy* [The motifs of the White Mountain] (Prague, 1921). See also J. Werstadt (ed.), *Bělohorské motivy. Jubilejní anthologie z české poesie* [The motifs of the White Mountain. Jubilee anthology of Czech poetry] (Prague, 1920).

13 Hýsek, 'Bíla hora', p. 118.

14 *Ibid.*

15 B. Rieger (ed.), F. Palacký, 2 vols. *Spisy drobné* [Minor writings], I, p. 5.

16 F. Palacký, 5 vols., *Dějiny národu českého v Čechách a v Moravě* [History of the Czech nation in Bohemia and Moravia] (Prague, 1848), foreword to the 1st volume.

17 T. G. Masaryk, *Česká otázka* [The Czech question] (Prague, 1895).

18 See J. Marek, 'Ke sporu o "smysl českých dějin"' [Concerning the controversy about the 'meaning of Czech history'], in his *O historismu a dějepisectví* [On historism and historiography] (Prague, 1992).

19 K. Krofta, *Bílá hora* [The White Mountain] (Prague, 1913). Later two scholars returned to the White Mountain problematic: Robert Kalivoda in his attempt to rehabilitate the policies of the estates of Bohemia as an organic result of the 'democratic' development of the Czech Reformation, and Josef Válka in his defence of the Reformation movement in Moravia. Cf. R. Kalivoda, 'Husitství a jeho vyústění v době předbělohorské a pobělohorské' [Hussitism and its outcome in the period before and after the White Mountain], *Studia comeniana et historica*, 13 (1983), 3–44; J. Válka, 'K otázce úlohy Moravy v české reformaci' [On the role of Moravia in the Czech Reformation], *Studia comeniana et historica*, 15 (1985), 67–80. Both these concepts were subject to polemic by Petr Čornej in *Husitský Tábor*, 6–7 (1984, 514–16; *ibid.*, 9 (1987), 422–4.

20 The Czech versions, by Jindřich Vančura, *Konec samostatnosti české* and *Čechy po Bílé hoře* were published in Prague in 1893 and 1904 respectively. See also W. Eberhard, 'Ernest Denis' Konzeption der böhmischen Geschichte und ihre Funktion in der tschechischen Geschichtswissenschaft', in F. Seibt and M. Neumüller (eds.), *Frankreich und die böhmischen Länder* (Munich, 1990), pp. 49–60.

21 O. Urban deals with the general situation in his *Česká společnost 1848–1918* [Czech society 1848–1918] (Prague, 1982), p. 504f.; on the poet V. Dyk, see J. Med, *Viktor Dyk* (Prague, 1988), especially pp. 122f.

22 J. Pekař, *Bílá hora a její příčiny a následky* [The White Mountain, its causes and consequences] (Prague, 1921).

23 Petráň, 'Na téma'.

24 J. Werstadt, *Odkazy dějin a dějepisců* [The legacy of history and historians] (Prague, 1948), pp. 119–34.

25 An exhaustive comment is given by V. Macura in *Šťastný věk Symboly, emblemy a mýty 1948–1989* [The happy age Symbols, emblems and myths 1948–1989] (Prague, 1992), p. 61.

26 For examples and opinions, see the summary by F. Kavka, *Bílá hora a naše dějiny* [The White Mountain and our history] (Prague, 1962).

8

The alchemy of happiness: the Enlightenment in the Moravian context

---

JIŘÍ KROUPA

In 1784 young Count Johann Nepomuk von Mittrowský initiated, within the circle of his friends and acquaintances belonging to the Enlightened and Masonic milieu of Moravia's capital, Brno, a project to publish a new periodical. The new journal was called *Materialien für Österreichs Patrioten*, and its main objectives were to defend freedom of speech and debate and to propagate Enlightened patriotism:

> Although opinions may differ and one or the other party may or may not be right, yet the defence of differing, even political, opinions – provided they are based on arguments – is a sign of the fact that the public is beginning to think and to view subjects from various standpoints. Even those who may perceive a subject from a false standpoint are thinking nonetheless![1]

Thus the Enlightened count presented the ideas he had discussed in his Brno circle. He was a disciple and adherent of *Aufklärung* and his thinking embraced both Kant's motto *Sapere aude!* and the idea of the emancipation of the civic community through public opinion. Mittrowský, who always preferred the moral values of the Enlightenment to the aristocratic privileges of his birth, is a paradigmatic example of an Enlightened thinker in Moravia in the second half of the eighteenth century. His thought is cosmopolitan and encyclopedic, yet at the same time patriotic and historical. This patriotism was bound geographically to the heart of the Habsburg monarchy – Bohemia, Moravia and Austria – and temporally to the epoch of the Habsburg–Lorraine dynasty – from the 1740s to the end of the eighteenth century. In this period, a new community of the Enlightened in Moravia was being formed in which the utopia of happiness was interwoven with an ideal of moral and aesthetic education ('Bildung').[2]

Citizens of the Republic of Letters

The age of the Baroque is generally considered to have ended in the late 1740s, but in spite of its declining importance Baroque culture persisted as an aesthetic as well as intellectual style in its traditional centres, such as courts, monasteries and residence towns. Many of these centres saw the emergence and establishment of learned societies in which West and Central European notions of Enlightenment were cultivated and from which they were disseminated. The first such centre to emerge within the Habsburg monarchy was the *Societas incognitorum eruditorum in terris Austriacis*, founded in 1746 in the university and episcopal town of Olomouc (Moravia).[3] The Society was established through the initiative of two promi-nent aristocrats – Baron Joseph von Petrasch and Count Franz G. Giannini – and it propagated various streams of contemporary thought. Two of them were of particular importance: the philosophical rationalism of Christian Wolff, a practical approach to philosophy which in Moravia was combined with the Catholic reformism of Lodovico Muratori; and the school of crit-ical historiography stemming from Jean Mabillon. Neither of these two schools, to be sure, was more than a mere precursor of the fully-fledged Enlightenment; yet they offered the Central European scholarly community a foretaste of rationalism, tolerance and scientific criticism.[4] Among the members of the Society were aristocratic *curieux*, state officials (such as Theodor Anton Taulow von Rosenthal and Johann Chr. von Jordan), and clerical historians (Benedictines such as Oliver Legipont, Magnoald Ziegelbauer and Hieronymus Pez), including so-called corresponding members (Lodovico Muratori, Johann Chr. Gottsched, Matthias Bel and others). Here Baroque and Enlightenment strands were inextricably inter-woven, yet one can hardly fail to notice a certain connection with that phase of the European Enlightenment which R. van Dülmen has called learned-scientific.[5] The Society received state protection, but opposition from the Jesuit-dominated town, as well as disagreements from within the Society itself, led to its premature demise. Nevertheless, its periodical in particular represented a landmark: the first attempt within the Habsburg monarchy to unite the learned, the dilettanti and the *curieux* and to bring them into contact with the pan-European *République des lettres*.

   Although no other learned societies were established in Moravia in this period, similar interests gained a foothold in other institutions within it. Comparable efforts to found a new historical science, stimulated by Mabillon, and to establish a new practical philosophy, inspired by Wolff, can be found among the monastic orders in Moravia, especially among the Benedictines and the Piarists, and to some extent among the Premonstratensians as well.

The centre of this endeavour was the monastery of Rajhrad near Brno, which housed a number of important scholars in the eighteenth century and came to play an important part in the new attempt to include Moravia in the Republic of Letters.

Closer in nature to the *Societas incognitorum* was the *Committee of the Société patriotique de Hesse-Hombourg* established in 1780 by Count Maximilian von Lamberg in Brno. The *Société patriotique* itself had been founded five years earlier in Homburg by Landgrave Friedrich V von Hessen-Homburg and the French writer Nicolas H. Paradies, with the aim of promoting the exchange of academic and scientific projects and information.[6] The learned public did not fail to gather inspiration from the activity in Homburg – in Paris, for instance, *Le grand comité de France* was established. Yet it soon became apparent that the task would be difficult to accomplish, and the society gradually lost its initial vigour. In early 1780, however, an attempt was made to revitalize the society in the more manageable form of a correspondence society, with several regional committees. One such committee was established in Brno – a natural choice, given the recent foundation of a university there and its proximity to several important monasteries.[7] In particular the Benedictines of Rajhrad offered their cooperation, and Brno quickly emerged as the centre of Moravian intellectual life.

The Moravian chapter of the *Société patriotique* thus became to a large extent analogous to the previous *Societas incognitorum*. Even its social composition was similar: it was likewise established through the efforts of an aristocrat, and its members included university professors, regular clerics and even artists. The soul of the society was Count Maximilian von Lamberg (1729–1792), a proponent of French-oriented Enlightenment who was equally at home in the private studies of European scholars and in the salons of the aristocracy.[8] To the educated readership of his time he was well known for his numerous publications, above all for his *Mémorial d'un mondain* (1775, 2nd edn. 1776). This work might loosely be characterized as travel literature, but its subject was not so much foreign countries, buildings or sights, as people: men and women of extraordinary interest, conversation, learning and spirit whom Lamberg had met on his wide-ranging travels. The text is a labyrinth leading from one memory to the next: memories of people, of faces, of evanescent moments of happiness provoked by brilliant conversations. It also presents an implied analogy to the *Société patriotique*, whose patriotism was based on a cosmopolitan ethic and a civic-minded mentality. A patriot was one who strives for the general well-being, assists the advancement of science, aids his fellow-citizens with his counsel, and aspires to happiness. Lamberg himself wrote in introduction to his *Mémorial* that in his literary works he 'never laughs at people, but at their systems, their contradictions, and the prejudices to which they attach an air of indispensable importance' (in 2nd edn 1776). It was because of his efforts that an elitist, French-oriented salon culture was formed in Brno, and the personalities he succeeded in attracting were scarcely less original than himself.

The secretary of the *Committee of Société patriotique* for instance, was the learned Protestant Heinrich Friedrich Hopf from Balingen in Württemberg (1754–1825). He arrived in Brno as a *Hofmeister* (tutor) to children of aristocratic families. In Brno he wrote poetry, published a magazine, and made 'patriotic' suggestions for improving the economy.[9] In 1781 he became the head of Brno's Protestant community and in 1785 he founded a textile factory in Brno into which he eventually introduced the first wool spinning machine in the Habsburg monarchy. He was a member of a number of scientific and local history societies established in Moravia at the end of the eighteenth century, and he also played an important role in the order of Free and Accepted Masons (so called *System der strikten Observanz*). These impressive achievements combined with his literary skill and conversational flair to make him a key figure in the Moravian Enlightenment. He represents the desire to achieve in practice those goals so often discussed in the salons: practical usefulness, industrial growth and the advancement of the human spirit. Perhaps his persistent union of the moral and the practical should be viewed as a manifestation of a characteristically Enlightened mentality, as described, in a rather elevated manner, by a contemporary eulogy.[10]

Such a description could equally be applied to Josef Wratislav Monse (1733–1793), a university professor and one of the most agile correspondents of the Brno Committee.[11] Through his interest in both Moravian humanism and Benedictine historiography he linked the earlier *Societas incognitorum* in Olomouc with the *Société patriotique* in Brno. The record of his lectures reveals an increasing willingness to link the early Enlightenment claims made on behalf of natural law with an appreciation of the virtues of the historical law of Moravia, showing the influence of both a critical historical perception and the juridical theory of the renowned Joseph von Sonnenfels. He also saw the need for an ideological basis capable of uniting the new burgherdom with the Enlightened intelligentsia's interest in the arts and sciences. He found such a basis in critical historiography, and eventually created a platform for Moravian patriotism, enriched with historical Renaissance humanism.

A society less obviously related to the learned milieu of the Enlightenment was the *Agricultur-Sozietät* founded in 1770 with official patronage and state support under Maria Theresa. This agricultural society was principally designed as a political and economic instrument with which to promote the agriculture of Enlightened Absolutism. As elsewhere in the Monarchy, however, it was only during the initial years that the *Agricultur-Sozietät* succeeded in attracting the local landed aristocracy, who were primarily interested in technical innovations in agriculture.[12] The aristocracy often saw such initiatives as an opportunity to compensate for their lost prestige, but were never interested in any systematic changes. Nevertheless, the *Agricultur-Sozietät* contributed to the social elevation of the clerks and administrators who dealt with financial matters on Moravian estates.

Could such a society nevertheless be viewed as an early form of practical Enlightenment? How to explain that this agricultural society became the chief centre of scientific research in Moravia less than three decades later? That it initiated the establishment of the first museum in the Habsburg monarchy, encouraged and supported both scientific and scholarly endeavours as well as a new spirit in the humanities and sciences, and even became the place where early liberalism penetrated the Central European learned world? Where both the reforming rationalism and state-supported scientism failed, as did the tranquil, sombre reading rooms, nevertheless the quest for the key to human happiness emerges. Succeeding the alchemy of metals and occultism in the sixteenth and seventeenth centuries, the 'alchemy of happiness' and the search for a social ethic took their place. And on this new basis, paradoxically perhaps related to 'arcanum', mental attitudes gradually changed together with perceptions of scientific work and practical activity.

The secret of the Freemasons

The generation of Moravian proponents of the Enlightenment that entered social and public life in the early 1780s strove to comprehend both the 'macrocosm' and the 'microcosm'. There was something esoteric in the union of these spheres, which might explain why the bearers of knowledge during the Enlightenment formed secret societies. As L. Hammermayer has observed, the Enlightenment's paradoxical combination of rationalism and esoteric learning can be found at the origin of Academies, which often originated from small, private, 'secret' circles of scholars.[13] Indeed the Masonic brotherhood and its practice of 'secrets' provided the newly established Enlightened societies with an alluring model as well. The emphasis of esoteric societies and Masonic lodges was not primarily on intellectual wisdom but on 'experienced virtue' (*gelebte Tugend*), virtue experienced within the context of a community. This fact was given a precise expression by the famous adventurer and friend of Count of Lamberg, Giacomo Casanova. 'The Masonic secret', he wrote, 'is by nature impenetrable; if it is known to a Mason, it is because he has inferred it – he discovered it because he frequented the lodge, observed, reflected and deduced. He who has not been able to penetrate the secret by himself will not be able to benefit from it even when instructed by someone else.'[14] The secrecy of Masonic lodges created an exclusive atmosphere in which each member could search for 'happiness' and for a new pattern of thought and conduct which would improve his inner self. 'The Masons have all been decent, law-abiding citizens of the state to begin with', a document from the archives of the lodge in Brno proclaims, 'and by entering this regal order they are to become even better citizens'.

There were individual Masons in Moravia even in the middle of the century, but it was only after the end of the Seven Years War (1756–1763) that their number increased substantially. They did not yet have a consolidated organization, but some of them, followers of Templar-orientated 'strict observance' Masonery, were in the *Société patriotique* in Brno. As late as 1782, the Freemasons of Brno established the lodge which they named The Rising Sun in the Orient (*Zur aufgehenden Sonne im Orient*). The lodge was conceived as a 'knightly order' of Templar Masonry and thus included a number of aristocrats (Salm-Reifferscheidt, Monte l'Abbate, Mittrowský, Kaunitz). The main role of the lodge, however, was to provide an oasis, a refuge from the imperfections of the world.[15]

Although the lodge was anchored in the spirit of strict Catholicism, its activities contributed to the growth of religious tolerance in Brno. For example, a Catholic manufactory-owner, Johann Leopold von Köffiller, founded for his Lutheran employees a religious commune, school and a house of worship. An important role in the circle of the lodge was played by the salon of an educated Jewish woman merchant, Sara Dobrusca. Furthermore, the lodge assisted in the promotion of manufactories and commerce. Above all, it functioned as a salon cultivating learned conversation and patronage of culture.

The head of the lodge, Count (later Prince) Karl Joseph von Salm-Reifferscheidt (1750–1838), was undoubtedly one of the most interesting personalities of eighteenth-century Moravia. The remarkable breadth of his interests was borne out by his correspondence and above all by his library: it included not only books on law, history, philosophy, contemporary French literature, and history of arts, but also works dealing with magic, demonology, the Cabala, and magnetism. Salm was a 'philojansenist' and promoted late Jansenist culture both at the university and at the seminary in Brno.[16] While adhering to an elegant, early neo-classicist culture of strict Catholicism, he opposed not only Baroque theatrical splendour but had reservations about the radical Enlightenment as well. His inclination toward the esoteric led him to knightly Masonry (he took part in the convention in Wilhelmsbad in 1782), to the Lyonese mystical system of Jean Bapt.

Willermoz, and finally to the secret Order of Gold and Rosicrucians (*Orden der Gold- und Rosenkreutzer*), a circle of which he founded in his chateau. His correspondence and his interest bear witness to his support for 'conservative' currents growing out of the Enlightenment itself before 1800, and which reacted against it in the form of aesthetic-literary movements within the framework of a renewed Catholicism.

In 1783 a division of Brno Masons founded a new lodge, The True United Friends (*Zu wahren vereinigten Freunden*). The lodge became the refuge of the Secret Order of Illuminati (*Geheimorden der Illuminaten*). The association of the Illuminati with Freemasonry was in fact part of the expansion strategy of this secret society, which remains of great interest to historians, especially in Germany.[17] At the time of its greatest appeal within the Enlightened milieu, the circle of Brno Illuminati had about forty members and exerted authority over two smaller circles in Opava and Prague. We are best informed about the Brno Illuminati. Their circle organized a number of lectures and discussions dealing with such themes as education, popular Enlightenment, morality and virtue, academic institutions, and patriotism. Thus for a brief period they established a society 'in the manner of a learned Academy', concerned mainly with moral philosophy and with the individual, or rather with what in the milieu of the Illuminati was called 'character'. Through this secret union, Enlightenment and morality were introduced into the Masonic lodge. In his analysis of the function of the secret in esoteric societies, Norbert Schindler has accentuated the part it played in constituting a 'new subjectivity' for the neophyte.[18] The order also maintained an interest in the aesthetic aspects of humanities, which it nourished through contact with the professor of aesthetics at the Charles-Ferdinand University in Prague, the Illuminate and Protestant August Gottlieb Meissner.

The ideals of the Illuminati included above all 'diligence, thrift, a simple lifestyle, genuine religiosity, and love of education' as the means of attaining well-being and happiness.[19] Such definition begins to resemble the famous Protestant work ethic, and it is therefore not surprising to find that Enlightened Protestants took more than a passing interest in the activity of the Secret Order. In the Josephine period in Brno, the number of Protestants who owned manufactories and belonged to the *Bildungsbürgertum* grew steadily, mostly due to immigration (from Württemberg, the Rheinland and Saxony).[20] They were concentrated in the Protestant community of Brno, whose pastor Victor Heinrich Riecke (1759–1830) was a Freemason and a member of the Illuminati. Riecke had studied theology in Tübingen. In Brno, however, his ideas underwent a transformation and he became a keen supporter of the Enlightenment and Josephinism. He began to study Kant's philosophy, devoted considerable attention to the natural sciences and took up philanthropy.[21] He led the Protestant school in Brno in accordance with the principles of the philanthropists in northern Germany and he submitted a proposal for a private school ('Philanthropinum') to Countess Maria Truchsess-Waldburg-Zeil inKunín in northern Moravia (1787). He was an author as well and took part in the publishing of two Enlightenment periodicals. He focused his attention in particular on a reading club (*Lesegesellschaft*) which united a substantial number of educated worthies from smaller towns in Moravia. The aim of this society was to propagate a moderate form of Enlightenment and to spread mostly light literature. To some extent, however, these activities helped to constitute the Moravian 'public' and gradually to transform the traditional burgher mentality.

Most of the Brno Illuminati entered a newly reformed lodge which in 1786 replaced the two lodges previously not in accord with each other. The name of the lodge was The True United Friends at the Rising Sun in the Orient (*Zu wahren vereinigten Freunden bei aufgehender Sonne im Orient*), but was often simply called the Freemasons Society (*Freimaurer-Gesellschaft*), and its programme was essentially that of the Illuminati: to spread the ideas of Enlightenment and morality in the Moravian community. In the period from 1786 to 1790 it functioned as the organizer of the Late Enlightenment in Moravia. The importance of this initiative becomes apparent when we realize that this was the period in which the Josephinian reforms actually receded and the policy of 'Enlightened absolutism' was taking a different direction from that aimed at by the *Aufklärung*. At that time, the Brno lodge had created a large network of members throughout Moravia, had achieved changes in the system of education, especially in the elementary schools, had become interested in Moravian local history, in Moravian Renaissance humanism, in Enlightenment festivals, and in the education of the countryside in the spirit of the moderate (and comprehensible) Enlightenment. Along with the change of interests, the lodge had been changing its own character. The last remnants of esoteric learning were disappearing and, instead of being the haven of Masonic conversations, the lodge was increasingly developing into a private scientific society.[22] This evolution was influenced to a great degree by a young aristocrat of a novel and distinctive mind-set: Count Johann Nepomuk von Mittrowský (1757–1799).

From knowledge to modern science

In the time when it was fashionable to discuss the true meaning of *Aufklärung*, Count Johann Nepomuk von Mittrowský wrote in his diary:

'Enlightenment is a way of thinking in an independent, unprejudiced, and correct manner – thinking about law, nature, morality, religion and history'. Comparison of these reflections with the previously mentioned programme of his periodical demonstrates that Mittrowský's ideas developed in a consistent direction. Even the scope of his interests was truly 'Enlightened', ranging from mineralogy, vulcanology, medicine, and balneology to history, philanthropy, aesthetics, and the history of art. Shortly before he died, Mittrowský composed a ballet, which was performed by young aristocrats, and the earnings from which he gave to charities. It is hardly an exaggeration to say that Count Johann Nepomuk von Mittrowský came to personify the Enlightenment in Moravia.[23]

Viewed from a wider, European perspective, certain peculiar qualities of his Enlightenment thinking can be isolated, qualities which are also broadly characteristic of the Moravian Enlightenment as a whole. On the one hand, as R. Vierhaus has rightly observed, we have the 'anthropological inclination' of *Aufklärung*[24] and also of Mittrowský's Enlightenment: it envisions the personality of a 'moral man', an ideal individual in possession of virtue, education, culture, and inner freedom. The overriding goal of this Enlightened 'moral man' was education, creative activity and cultivation of a certain mentality and manner of life. The Central European milieu in particular accepted this focus upon education, and encouraged the full investigation of all 'moral' subjects from diverse perspectives. This original intention of the Enlightenment was transformed, however, into a search for the function: the use of Enlightenment notions and methods in civilization and culture.[25] The problem in essence, was the institutionalization of Enlightenment notions of science and culture.

The question of how scientific activity could best be institutionalized within the Habsburg monarchy generated much discussion until roughly the mid-1780s, and to this discussion Mittrowský (as shown by his correspondence and manuscript writings) contributed a characteristic solution which might be called 'the Moravian way'. At first, Mittrowský's curriculum vitae was hardly different from that of his aristocratic relatives: he joined the army, and maintained an interest in the Enlightened discussions in the salons.[26] Soon, however, he left the army, lived on his private income, travelled, and participated in scientific life. He became a member of a number of Enlightenment societies and became acquainted with north German Enlightenment during his two major journeys in 1785 and 1793. Through participation in the Berlin Academy of Sciences and other learned societies in the Prussian capital, he became conversant with the works of the French *idéologues*.[27] Thus the young aristocrat confronted with typical Late Enlightenment thinking. Here philanthropy and Masonry provided the basis on which to develop and cultivate the ideals of human progress and of universal cultural values and to realize these ideals through the agency of educational and scientific institutions. Mittrowský began to realize his ideas regarding scientific work in Moravia within the Masonic lodge, whose head he had become. Under his guidance, the Brno Masonic lodge was transformed into the Private Scientific and Patriotic Society in Moravia (1794).[28] He also linked its activities with those of the Royal Bohemian Society of Sciences in Prague, whose leading members were Masons or Illuminati and who thus could enter the Brno lodge as honorary members. His affinity for French *idéologie* explains why one of his preoccupations was Encyclopedism – Mittrowský himself wrote a manuscript called 'Supplements to the Real Encyclopedia'. The manuscript demonstrates that he was a keen follower of the philosophy of Immanuel Kant, which he derived from reading works, such as *Kritik der praktischen Vernunft, Kritik der Urteilskraft*, and *Religion innerhalb der Grenzen der blossen Vernunft*. Mittrowský published only a small proportion of his manuscripts. Yet reports from his contemporaries confirm that his unpublished texts circulated widely in the Enlightenment milieu and led to his remarkable renown.[29] Mittrowský himself was aware of this manner of conveying knowledge, which is reflected in the constitution he wrote for the Private Scientific Society. The constitution includes a practical section, describing precisely the rules of scientific work, the rules of observation, description, sorting, and classification. The constitution also urges all members to become familiar with these rules and to observe them in their scientific work.[30]

Mittrowský's pathway towards institutionalization through the Masonic milieu was naturally influenced by the state of affairs in the Moravian academic milieu. His was the pathway of private initiative. And in spite of the fact that in many respects its utopian design bears the unmistakable impact of its initiator, its parellel with other Late Enlightenment projects is certainly noteworthy. An inhibiting factor in Mittrowský's endeavour was in fact the uneven standard of work within the Moravian scientific milieu itself. The Private Scientific Society focused on mineralogy (Johann Nep. Mittrowský, Vinzent Petke, Felix Beck), medicine (mainly the reception of Howard's and Jenner's methods by Dr Gärtelgruber, Ernst Rincolini and Alois Carl), education (Ignaz Mehoffer, Johann Nep. Hausperský von Fanal), and topography (Franz J. Schwoy). The future of science in Moravia was affected by Mittrowský's correspondence with Rudolf Zacharias Becker from Gotha and particularly with Christian Karl André from Gotha and Eisenach, who, following Mittrowský's suggestion, eventually came to live in Moravia.

Years later in 1816, the Austrian historian Joseph von Hormayr wrote a proposal, commissioned by the Moravian estates, to establish a Moravian state museum. In the introduction he mentioned the aristocratic family of the Mittrowskýs, highlighting their contribution to Moravian cultural life.[31] He particularly emphasized the role of Johann Nepomuk von Mittrowský, one of whose original projects was in fact reborn in the founding of the new private museum. Due to Mittrowský's premature death, the realization of this and many other of Mittrowský's projects was to remain the task of his friends and followers. But his last years may serve as an example of a gradual transition from French encyclopedism to early English liberalism. At an earlier time, Ignaz von Born (1737–1791) who founded the Private Learned Society in Prague (1774?) and became a leading figure of the Enlightenment in the Monarchy, was accepted as a member by the Royal Society in London on account of his merits in the field of mineralogy.[32] Nor were Born and Mittrowský alone in establishing a reputation in the British Isles: Mittrowský's contemporary, a physician and economist, Count Leopold von Berchtold (1759–1809), was an acknowledged expert on England and his works received a wide reception there.[33]

Civilization and intellectual life

The Enlightenment in Moravia only gradually moved from its preoccupation with education and science towards politics. In fact, the only evidence of an engagement in the political sphere is a periodical written and published by Johann Nepomuk von Mittrowský (probably in cooperation with V. H. Riecke) during the French Revolution. The periodical, the *Patriotisches Tageblatt*, the aim of which was to defend freedom of speech and to propagate the Enlightenment, could be published only after Mittrowský's death and on a far less ambitious scale than he had envisaged.[34] By that point, the Age of the Enlightenment had come to an end, yet the pages of the periodical abound in topics related to the 'civilization' and 'mentalités' of the Moravian Enlightenment.

A noteworthy development in the Moravian Enlightenment was the development of a 'coalition' within the Enlightened community that included members of the 'new' aristocracy (promoted to the ranks of high nobility for their services either in the army or in the civil service), certain 'worthies' from larger towns (the so-called *Bildungsbürgertum*) and administrators of estates. These were not the only social groups involved, but they comprised the nucleus of the Enlightened community, which still remained an elite group whose self-identification was based on association with Masonic societies, the salon, and essentially private fora.[35] Another important element in the Moravian Enlightenment was religious tolerance. The expansion of the Protestant community in Brno after the proclamation of the Toleration Patent by Joseph II (1781) accelerated the spread of Enlightenment ideas in Brno.[36] Having found their 'second home' in Moravia, the Protestants also became proponents of Enlightened patriotism.

In the second half of the eighteenth century, Enlightened patriotism in Moravia had three primary facets, which naturally overlapped in many respects. First, patriotism was seen as the moral attitude of an Enlightened man who wants to serve others and promote the well-being and prosperity of his community and country. This would, in turn, advance the well-being and prosperity of the whole human community. Patriotism was also related to the state in which a patriot lives. In the Habsburg monarchy it was primarily oriented towards the Habsburg-Lorrain dynasty, rather than a supra-regional entity (Germany). In the most restricted sense patriotism applied to regional historicist patriotism bound to Moravia itself. As a result of this form of patriotism, a stimulus was imparted to historic and linguistic studies in Moravia. The difference between territorial patriotism (which developed from regional patriotism) and Enlightened patriotism was that the latter regarded as basic that the patriot always desires his own happiness, yet at the same time also the happiness and progress of all mankind.[37]

Progress in the second half of the eighteenth century was an intense and profound experience. Experiments were being carried out as a form of social entertainment;[38] new opportunities for social contacts were created in Brno, Opava and Olomouc (reading rooms, casinos, cafés),[39] and Enlightened Absolutism was still perceived as a form of progressive government which would eventually lead to the rule of the law.

Festivals were also of interest and importance to the Enlightenment patriots in Moravia. Franz Karl von Sonnenfels, counsellor at the court of Prince von Dietrichstein in Mikulov and the brother of Joseph von Sonnenfels, the renowned Viennese Josephinian, initiated a Feast of Roses (*Rosenfest*).[40] The feast combined a Rousseau-inspired concept of village festivals with the ideas of popular Enlightenment and reform-Catholicism. Each year, when the feast was held, town and country girls of education, diligence and virtue were crowned with a wreath of roses. Other places in Moravia were also interested in this kind of festival and the *Patriotisches Tageblatt* even published a reader's contest with this theme. The thinking of Jean Jacques Rousseau also inspired Joseph von Sonnenfels, and the cleric Franz Stephan Hanke wanted to create a society imbued with Rousseau's spirit.

Enlightened society focused on happiness as the new value of the eighteenth century. It attempted to base it on morality and virtue, on the harmony of a person with himself, and on friendship and community life. These were the terms in which Johann Nepomuk von Mittrowský contemplated the many-sided education of his daughter: 'she will enjoy the fact of being able to accept all people regardless of their rank, of being a good and moral person. And she will find happiness in her heart and her reason.'

At the end of the century, however, the obsession with happiness was supplanted by scepticism and hopelessness. To come to terms with the world required incorporating in one's starting point a sensitivity for the fragile, the human and the playful.[41] Thus Count von Mittrowský designed for his friends and for himself 'sentimental' gardens, which strove for a certain individuality. Adorned with small temples and monuments, they aroused the fantasy and imagination of their visitors.[42] These 'sentimental' or 'English' gardens have inspired a number of scholarly interpretations. They certainly did achieve a certain harmony, a balance between the optimistic utopia and the persistent grief of pre-Romantic sentiment, between the secret of the Freemasons and the playfulness of the Enlightenment. In the course of the nineteenth century, these gardens began to decay.

The ideal of the garden seems to have been the Enlightenment's utopia, manifested by esoteric and philosophical inspiration. Each of these gardens was created in a different manner, yet each of them included several characteristic features: (a) the feature and theme of the 'road of consecration', a road through the garden passing monuments and ruins; (b) the temple of Enlightenment (of friendship, love, sun etc.); (c) symbols of the new developments of sciences and technology; (d) another important symbol was that of the immortality of the soul and the vanity of the world (represented by inscriptions and monuments praising philosophers, friends of the master of the house etc.; arbours with broken pillars).

The builders of these gardens included important personalities of the Enlightenment in Moravia, building these gardens for themselves, or for the public in towns (Brno, Opava). For Moravia it is symptomatic that the owner-amateur cooperated with artists who provided him with drawings or even participated in the artistic decoration of the garden. That was also the case with Andreas Schweigl. He worked both on the so called 'Temple' in Dolní Rožínka (for Count Johann Nepomuk von Mittrowský) and on the 'Masonic road' on the slope of the castle Pernštejn (for Baron Schröffl von Mannsberg), where he carried out the sculptural decoration, including the family tomb, a memorial of the Enlightenment with individual sculptures.

At the end of the eighteenth century, there were quite a few such gardens in Moravia. In most cases, however, they did not last long. In the nineteenth century, some were rebuilt into large romantic parks. Nevertheless, a kind of cross-section has been preserved and others are known through drawings or graphic prints. Perhaps their remnants have become, in Colette's words, 'a poem on the portrait of an epoch'.[43] They certainly remain a reflection of an Enlightenment dream, which was transformed into the 'alchemy of happiness'.

Notes

1 The relevant documents are in Moravský zemský archiv, hereafter MZA, (Moravian Land Archives) Brno, Mittrowský Family archives, G 147, Box 46. Another signed copy is in Cerroni's collection in the same archives.

2 Rudolf Vierhaus, *Deutschland vor der Französischen Revolution, Untersuchungen zur deutschen Sozialgeschichte im Zeitalter der Aufklärung* (University Münster, manuscript, 1961), p. 311.

3 Eduard Wondrák, 'Die Olmützer "Societas incognitorum". Zum 225. Jubiläum ihrer Gründung und zum 200. Todestag ihres Gründers', in E. Lesky, D. K. Kostić, J. Matl und G. von Rauch (eds.), *Die Aufklärung in Ost- und Südosteuropa* (Cologne and Vienna, 1972), pp. 215–28; Rudolf Zuber, 'František Řehoř Giannini a jeho styky s L. A. Muratorim' [Francis Gregory Giannini and his relations with L. A. Muratori], *Okresní archiv v Olomouci 1984*, pp. 39–62; Antonín Kostlán, *Societas incognitorum. První učená společnost v českých zemích* [Societas incognitorum. The first Learned Society in the Czech Lands] (Prague, 1996). Although the Societas incognitorum has been mentioned in a number of publications dealing with Central European Enlightenment, a definitive and complete historical study of this society is yet to be written.

4 For the best treatment so far written on the Society's activities, see: Walter Schamschula, *Die Anfänge der tschechischen Erneuerung und das deutsche Geistesleben 1740–1800* (Munich, 1973), pp. 34–78.

5 Richard van Dülmen, 'Die Aufklärungsgesellschaften in Deutschland als Forschungsproblem', *Francia*, 5 (1977), 251–75; *ibid.*, *Die Gesellschaft der Aufklärer Zur bürgerlichen Emanzipation und aufklärerischen Kultur in Deutschland* (Frankfurt/Main, 1986). Societas incognitorum published a monthly *Monathliche Auszuege Alt, und neuer Gelehrten Sachen* in the years 1747–1750, which included reviews of 'learned' literature.

6 Jürgen Voss, 'Die Société patriotique de Hesse-Hombourg. Der erste Versuch einer europäischen Koordinationstelle für wissenschaftlichen Austausch', in R. Vierhaus (ed.), *Deutsche patriotische und gemeinnützige Gesellschaften* (Munich, 1980), pp. 195–221. Voss was primarily interested in German-French relations in the Société patriotique and his choice of the sources from the Darmstadt Archives was rather selective. Cf. Hessisches Staatsarchiv Darmstadt, Hausarchiv Hessen-Darmstadt, Abt. XI, Fasc. 1–16. For the statutes of the Committee, see: Wilhelm Schram, 'Die Statuten der Hessen-Homburgischen Gesellschaft in Brünn', *Mährisches Magazin für Biographie und Kulturgeschichte*, I (Brünn, 1908), 79–81.

7 Cf. Josef Wratislav Monse, *Versuch einer kurzgefassten politischen Landesgeschichte des Markgrafthums Mähren*, I (Brünn, 1785) see preface:

> The four years during which our university was situated in Brno (1778–1782) are in many respects, and especially in respect of patriotic literature, unforgettable. Respected patrons and benefactors of science in the town and country, literary contacts, supply of scientific materials, their easy availability, fruitful supervision, the possibility and wise effort to engage oneself in useful things – these were all at hand.

8 Josef Polišenský, 'Korespondence moravského osvícence Maxe Lamberga s J. F. Opitzem o francouzské revoluci' [Correspondence between the Moravian Enlightener Max Lamberg and J. F. Opitz about the French Revolution], *Časopis Matice moravské*, 71 (1952), pp. 140–8. Constant von Wurzbach, *Biographischer Lexikon des Kaisertums Oesterreichs*, vol. 14 (Vienna, 1865), pp. 42–6. Johann Georg Meusel, *Lexikon der von Jahr 1750 bis 1800 verstorbenen teutschen Schriftsteller* (Leipzig, 1808), VIII, pp. 14–15. A modern scholarly biography of Count Lamberg is desirable.

9 G. Ch. Hauberger- and J. G. Meusel, *Das gelehrte Teutschland oder Lexikon der jetzt lebenden teutscher Schriftsteller* (Lembo, 1796), III, pp. 375–7; Gustav Trautenberger, *Die Chronik der Landeshauptstadt Brünn* (Brünn, 1897), IV, *passim*.

10 Family correspondence of Johann Gottlieb Pressel (1789–1848) in private archives. I thank Dr Ralph Melville (Mainz) for having brought the correspondence to my attention.

11 Karel Žák, *PhDr. a JUDr. Josef Vratislav Monse, národní buditel* [Doctor of Philosophy and Doctor of Jurisprudence Josef Vratislav Monse, national awakener] (Nové Město na Moravě, 1933). In the Darmstadt Archives there is the list of his works, which Monse sent to Homburg (Hessisches Staatsarchiv Darmstadt, Hausarchiv Hessen-Darmstadt, Abt. XI).

12 Norbert Schindler and Wolfgang Bonss, 'Praktische Aufklärung: Ökonomische Sozietäten in Süddeutschland und Österreich im 18. Jahrhundert', in Vierhaus (ed.), *Deutsche Gesellschaften*, pp. 255–353.

13 Ludwig Hammermayer, *Geschichte der Bayerischen Akademie der Wissenschaften 1759–1807* (Munich, 1983), II, pp. 339–42, Michael W. Fischer, *Die Aufklärung und ihr Gegenteil. Die Rolle der Geheimbünde in Wissenschaft und Politik* (Berlin, 1982); Ulrich Im Hoff, 'Zur Rolle der Sozietäten im 18. Jahrhundert zwischen Utopie, Aufklärung und Reform', in Emil Erne (ed.), *Die Schweizerischen Sozietäten* (Zurich, 1988).

14 Giacomo Casanova, *Historie mého života* [History of my life] (Praha, 1968), p. 186.

15 Sources concerning the lodge's activities are in: MZA Brno, Family archives Salm-Reifferscheidt, the papers of Prince Karl von Salm (G 150, boxes 49, 50).

16 The best treatment dealing with late Jansenism in the Habsburg monarchy is Peter Hersche, *Der Spätjansenismus in Österreich* (Vienna, 1977) – on the Brno milieu, see especially pp. 274–305.

17 A large number of scholarly publications concerning the Illuminati includes: Richard van Dülmen, *Geheimbund der Illuminaten. Darstellung-Analyse-Dokumentation*

(Stuttgart and Bad Cannstatt, 1975), Manfred Agethen, *Geheimbund und Utopie [Illuminaten, Freimaurer und deutsche Spätaufklärung]* (Munich, 1987); Ernst-Otto Fehn, *Der Illuminatenorden und die Aufklärung. Kritik und Korrektur einer neuen Interpretation*, in H. Reinalter (ed.), *Aufklärung-Vormärz-Revolution* (Innsbruck, 1988), VII, pp. 6–30. Sources dealing with the Brno Illuminati will be published in a special study of mine.

18   Norbert Schindler, 'Aufklärung und Geheimnis im Illuminatenorden', in Peter Christian Ludz (ed.), *Geheime Gesellschaften* (Heidelberg, 1979), pp. 203–29.

19   Karl Schwartz, *Landgraf Friedrich V. von Hessen-Homburg und seine Familie* (Homburg von der Höhe, 1888), II, pp. 171–9 (Friedrich V, Gedanken über die Aufklärung).

20   Jan Janák, 'Počátky strojního předení vlny v brněnském soukenictví' [Beginnings of mechanized wool-spinning in the Brno clothing industry], *Sborník prací filosofické fakulty brněnské university* (1981), C 28, pp. 111–41. Hermann Freudenberger-Gerhard Mensch, *Von der Provinzstadt zur Industrieregion [Brünn-Studie]* (Göttingen, 1975).

21   *Allgemeine Deutsche Biographie*, vol. 28 (1889), pp. 508–12. Karl Riecke, *Meine Voreltern* (Stuttgart, 1896), *passim*. Obituary in *Hesperus* (1830), 253–5.

22   In 1788, the Brno lodge was linked with the Prague lodge Truth and Unity at the three Crowned Pillars (*Wahrheit und Einigkeit zu drei gekrönten Säulen*) as 'a sister lodge'. Each of the lodges was thus entitled to send a representative with a valid vote to the meetings of the other one. This kind of union was established through the efforts of former Illuminati from Brno (Peter Le Fort, Viktor H. Riecke, Hyacinth Arnold) and from Prague (Joseph Canal de Malabailla, Karl Raphael Ungar, Ignaz Cornova). Both lodges found inspiration in the Viennese lodge The True Accord (*Zu wahren Eintracht*), which probably was also a centre of the Illuminati.

23   Jiří Kroupa, *Alchymie štěstí. Pozdní osvícenství a moravská společnost 1770–1810* [Alchemy of happiness. The Late Enlightenment and Moravian society 1770–1810] (Brno and Kroměříž, 1987), *passim*.

24   Vierhaus, *Deutschland*, p. 313.

25   Horst Möller, *Fürstenstaat oder Bürgernation Deutschland 1763–1815* (Berlin, 1989), p. 323.

26   Count Josef von Mittrowský (1733–1808) was a general in the Habsburg army, a pen-friend of Prince Alexander Ypsilanti, the owner of a noticeable library and the author of no less remarkable observations and diaries. Count Johann Baptist von Mittrowský (1735–1811) was *Oberlandkämmerer* and the president of the High Appeals and Criminal Court in Moravia, one of the founders of the *Agricultur-Sozietät*, the president of the Private Scientific Society (founded by his nephew Johann Nepomuk von Mittrowský), a civil servant, an adherent of the reforms of Joseph II, a scholar interested in botany. Because of these facts, he is often mistaken for Count Johann Nepomuk. About the Mittrowský family, see Wurzbach, XVIII, pp. 384–98.

27   See Sergio Moravia, *Il tramonto dell'illuminismo. Filosofia e politica nella societa francese*

[1770–1810] (Bari, 1968); and *Beobachtende Vernunft. Philosophie und Anthropologie in der Aufklärung* (Frankfurt Main, 1989).

28 Christian d'Elvert, *Geschichte der k.k. mähr.-schles. Gesellschaft zur Beförderung des Ackerbaues, der Natur- und Landeskunde* (Brünn, 1870).

29 On his death, some of his manuscript writings were considered lost, having been lent to his friends. Sir Joseph Banks, the president of the Royal Society in London allegedly corresponded with Mittrowský and received from him materials concerning Moravian geography. See Joseph von Hormayr, 'Hugo Franz Altgraf zu Salm-Reifferscheidt', *Archiv für Geographie, Historie, Staats- und Kriegskunst* (1816), pp. 337–46.

30 The constitution is in MZA Brno, see papers of *K. k. mähr.-schles. Gesellschaft zur Beförderung des Ackerbaues etc.*

31 For a long time, this proposal was believed to have been the work of Christian Karl André. In actual fact, however, Count Hugo von Salm-Reifferscheidt assigned it to Baron Joseph von Hormayr, who was at that time the history tutor in the Salm family. I owe thanks for this information to Univ. Doz. Vladimir Nekuda [Moravské museum, Brno].

32 Mikuláš Teich, 'Ignaz von Born und die "Royal Society"', in Helmut Reinalter (ed.), *Die Aufklärung in Österreich Ignaz von Born und seine Zeit* (Frankfurt/Main-Bern-New York-Paris, 1991), pp. 93–7.

33 Correspondence with Royal Society and obituaries of Count Berchtold in English newspapers, see MZA Brno, Family archives – Count Berchtold, G 138, box 51.

34 It was published from 1799 to 1805 and then banned by the censors. It was followed, from 1809, by the journal *Hesperus*. In the 1820s, *Hesperus* was published by the publisher Cotta in Stuttgart, spreading the ideas of moderate liberalism until Cotta's death in 1831.

35 See Kroupa, *Alchymie štěstí, passim.*

36 Richard Pražák, *Maďarská reformovaná inteligence v českém obrození* [Magyar reformed inteligentsia in the Czech revival] (Prague, 1962); Eduard Winter, *Barock, Absolutismus und die Aufklärung in der Donaumonarchie* (Vienna, 1971).

37 For an interesting theory of the origin of national patriotism, see Robert J. W. Evans, 'Über die Ursprünge der Aufklärung in den habsburgischen Ländern', in Grete. Klingenstein (ed.), *Das achtzehnte Jahrhundert und Österreich* (Vienna-Cologne-Graz, 1985), II, pp. 9–31.

38 A former Premonstratensian Father Prokop Diviš (1698–1765) erected a lightning conductor in 1754. The first balloon ascent in Moravia was launched by Princess Maria Christine von Dietrichstein in 1784.

39 A reading room (*Lesekabinett*) was established by the bookseller Johann Georg Gastl. The 'casino' as the centre of social life was established within the Reduta theatre in Brno. Somewhat later, similar 'casinos' were founded in Opava and Prostějov.

40 Franz Kupetzky, *Josef und Franz von Sonnenfels. Das Leben und Wirken eines edlen Bruderpaares* (Vienna, 1882). Following the Feast of Roses in Mikulov, others were held in Vranov nad Dyjí, Hranice and elsewhere.

41 Cf. Růžena Grebeníčková in an undoubtedly interesting preface to the Czech edition of Diderot's selected works on aesthetics: Denis Diderot, *O umění* [On art] (Prague, 1983).

42 A. Braham, *The Architecture of French Enlightenment* (London, 1982).

43 Jutta Duhm-Heitzmann, 'Ein Garten verlorener Träume', *Zeitmagazin*, 18 (1992), 26–35.

9

Problems and paradoxes of the national revival

VLADIMÍR MACURA

I

During the first decades of the nineteenth century, an essential break in Czech history occurred. Most descriptions of this change have, to varying degrees, eschewed the sober tone usually considered suitable for accounts of historical events. The labels which have been applied to this process already suggest an unwillingness to submit this epoch to any kind of an objective, unsentimental evaluation: '*vzkříšení*' ('resurrection'), '*znovu-zrození národa*' ('national rebirth'), '*obrození*' ('revival'). And indeed, all of Czech national life seems to have sprung dynamically and quickly from the period of the first half of the last century. At this time, the foundations were laid for modern Czech literature – the first 'classic' works came to light. These were, for example, in poetry Jan Kollár's (1793–1852) *The Slávy dcera* (Daughter of Slavia 1824, 1833), a cycle of sonnets reflecting an intimate story of personal erotic disillusionment against the backdrop of the fate of the Slavic peoples, and the *Ohlas písní ruských* (Echo of Russian songs, 1829) by František Ladislav Čelakovský (1799–1852). Towards the end of his life Karel Hynek Mácha (1810–1836) published the poem *May* (Máj, 1836), a fully ripened fruit of European Romanticism. In fiction we can see that a unique poetic prose unexpectedly asserted its position. In this period the preconditions arose for the development of Czech theatre (Václav Kliment Klicpera (1792–1895), Josef Kajetán Tyl (1808–1856)).[1] Translation was established as an autonomous creative activity, and a number of excellent and challenging works of foreign literature were wrought into Czech (Milton's *Paradise Lost*, Chateaubriand's *Atala*, masterpieces of classical literatures). And conversely, Czech literature, contrary to all expectations, succeeded in reaching abroad: in London John Bowring published his *Cheskian Anthology* with

WÝBOR Z BÁSNICTWI ČESKÉHO.

CHESKIAN ANTHOLOGY:

BEING

A HISTORY OF THE

Poetical Literature of Bohemia,

WITH TRANSLATED SPECIMENS

BY

JOHN BOWRING.

Prawau wlast gen w srdci nosíme,
Tuto nebze bíti ani krásti.
                        KOLLAR.

Our heart—our country's casket and defence—
Our country, none shall steal—none tear it thence.

Hudbu a zpěwy Čech milug.

LONDON:
ROWLAND HUNTER, St. PAUL'S CHURCH-YARD.

1832

6. Title page of J. Bowring, *Cheskian Anthology* (1832).

'translated specimens' of Czech poetry and a brief comment on Czech literary history.[2]

The period of the national revival stands as the constitutive epoch of nearly all areas of national culture. This time marks the beginning not only of the arts – including the visual arts and music, but also of scholarship. In 1821, *Krok* – a scholarly review in Czech – was first published, followed in 1827 by *Časopis Českého muzea* (Journal of the Czech Museum) that still exists today (under the changed title *Časopis Národního Muzea* – Journal of the National Museum).

\/The process by which Czech culture appeared as a new feature on the cultural map of Europe is linked closely with the 'larger history' of the European continent and of the Habsburg monarchy. It grew out of the background of the reforms of Joseph II (Patent of Toleration, 1781; Abolition of Serfdom, 1781), and could be interpreted as a reaction specifically to the centralization of government and to the Germanization which was supposed to become a vehicle for the more efficient functioning of the empire. It is closely linked with similar emancipatory processes of other European nations under the influence of the French Revolution and its repercussions. However, a closer analysis of a seemingly normally functioning cultural system reveals a rather peculiar and very intimate 'micro-history' of mere personal, unofficial contacts, and thus a basis for cultural production which is quite different from the type that characterizes the larger and more prestigious nations of Europe. Although the physical evidence of Czech cultural artifacts indicates clearly that this cultural region, too, is a fully fledged part of the European context, something which gives us pause.

The notion of 'Czech culture' also presupposes a distinct temporal dimension. The present phase of culture is rooted in tradition and points towards the future.

II

At the beginning of the nineteenth century, the idea of 'Czech culture' was far from self-evident. The very notion of 'Czech culture' would then have seemed to be a *contradictio in adiecto*. The Czech milieu was for the educated European of this time something 'pre-cultural' or 'extra-cultural', a kind of naive Arcadia of pristine values, associated with childhood, Nature, or folklore. Any idea of a distinct, autonomous 'semiosphere', determined by the Czech language, a 'semiosphere' capable of completely surrounding the individual and satisfying all his/her social and cultural needs in the most general/abstract and in the most specific/concrete sense of the terms, was unthinkable. Contemporary scholarship, technology, the arts and literature – all of these were available in another sphere of communication, and in a different axiological and semantic context from the one that was usually the domain of the Czech language at the beginning of the nineteenth century. For its contemporary participant, the existence of Czech culture is self-evident. Czech culture surrounds him or her as an seemingly autonomous environment. It is a 'whole' which is differentiated both socially and territorially. Composed of distinct parts, it is at the same time more or less 'complete', representing a specifically 'Czech world'. Such a world is an example of what Juri Lotman calls a 'semiosphere'.[3] Lotman's semiotic approach usefully brings out aspects of how cultural domains are constituted and function, especially with regard to language. Any fact which penetrates the semiosphere is transformed according to the system's context, needs and potentials. In such a system, language plays an important part exchanging and preserving information. At once a means of distinguishing one national culture from another, it is also a membrane through which external information is processed, assimilated and hybridized.

These are normal processes which take place in any 'national' culture. They occur in time and they also incorporate ideas of time – of the present and the future but also, of course, of the past. The contemporary state of culture projects itself into the past; it tends to reevaluate history, to reconstruct it according to topical needs. And it is in this respect that an important aspect of the 'Czech world' emerges. The contemporary and seemingly unambiguous entity known as Czech culture – self-evident, autonomous, complete – is a projection into periods when something of this kind was entirely out of the question. Different intellectual and cultural activities of the earlier inchoate epochs are thus 'completed' in retrospect, adapted to the later order.

This fact does not mean that Bohemia and Moravia as regions of the Habsburg monarchy were somehow excommunicated from culture. Nor does it mean that these lands were deprived of any important cultural activity connected with the Czech-speaking population. Nevertheless, this cultural activity was not able to create any wholeness, any universality. It was strictly limited to partial manifestations of cultural life in the framework of a differently organized cultural structure.

In other words: 'Czech culture', or, more precisely, 'Czech culture *in spe*', was predestined to the role of a 'culture within a culture'. It could satisfy some strictly defined needs in this area. Other requirements could be satisfied only at other cultural levels – linked primarily of course with the German language.

For the time being hypothetical Czech culture found itself at a crossroads.

The first path open to it was to forego any kind of 'completeness', 'consistency', any attempt to become a whole, modern 'Czech world'. In the existing Czech state of limited completeness, wholeness as an essential aspect of any normally functioning 'national' culture must have appeared both unattainable and unnecessary. Strictly delineated modest partial functions looked more acceptable. This path led to a type of 'subculture' that could later be emancipated and only gradually developed in accordance with the growth of the aspirations of the Czech population. On the other hand, the alternative path led directly and immediately to the ideal of a complex, specific and, in all substantial aspects, self-sufficient cultural system.

All the historical transformations of the Czech culture in the first half of the nineteenth century can be viewed as a shift of its centre of gravity from the conception of Czech culture as a partial cultural area within a culture based on communication in German towards the conception of Czech culture as an autonomous and complex creation.

This shift was connected with an essential paradox. Though it represented an evolution towards the ideal of culture as a thoroughly organic social structure, at the beginning it had to produce quite the opposite effect. Namely, it had to rupture the existing social roots of the cultural production oriented toward the demands of the Czech-speaking population. The more explicit was the shift of the Czech cultural production towards the ideal of an autonomous culture, the more clearly Czech cultural production lost its social foothold. The formation of a fully developed, varied culture, up to European standards, preceded the formation of a modern, socially differentiated Czech society which could be its bearer and guarantor. This very issue defined all the basic features of the Czech national revival: the cultural project of the revival would have an inherently artificial nature.

Another specific characteristic was connected with that fact. A man is said to be born into culture, he is forced to accept it, before he is able to intervene in it. But for an intellectual taking part in the patriotic activities at the beginning of the last century the culture was less defined and much more an entity to be shaped than it could be nowadays. Czech culture was for a Czech intellectual much more his own creation than a milieu he entered from outside. This was possible because all the reality of the Czech world was deposited in cultural products and mostly directly in 'texts'. This fact provided for an extremely strong semiotization of any constitutive element of the Czech world.

The insufficient development of the social background forced the revivalist intellectuals to give priority to those fields of culture which were capable of presenting an illusion of a well-developed society with clear-cut national characteristics. The attention of the patriotic community was thus concentrated on all forms of verbal activity, above all on the language itself.

III

This process demanded the complete transformation of the functions of the Czech language. This fact can be easily demonstrated by a concrete example – a prominent normative manual of the Czech language from 1795, *Grundsätze der Böhmischen Grammatik*, by František Martin Pelcl (Pelzel) (1734–1801),[4] the Enlightenment historian and philologist. The conversational part of the book (*Gespräche*) presents the Czech language in at least three different communicative functions. Czech is presented as a medium of contacting speakers from a socially lower level (chapters on dressing, on a conversation between a noble and a tailor, on breakfast, on visiting a pub, and on writing). Pelcl reflects the Czech language also as a means of communication between socially equal educated persons or aristocrats (chapters on the morning visit, on the weather, on newspapers, and some containing general dialogues). Quite a specific type of communication is suggested by dialogues between a convinced Czech patriot and a nationally indifferent Czech (chapters on the Czech language and literature). Of all three levels of communication only the first one was really typical for the initial situation of Czech culture at the turn of the eighteenth century: the Czech language could serve an educated ('cultural') person as a means of communication with a member of the 'lower' classes of native speakers who did not know enough of the more prestigious German language. The Czech tongue represented a medium for conveying practical information, orders and inquiries. The possibilities of Czech being used as a language of communication by the middle and upper stratas were strictly limited, and as a means of communication among the nobility were quite remote. The examples of Czech conversations between aristocrats must have sounded highly improbable to contemporaries: 'Where were you yesterday?' – 'I was hunting at Měšice.' – 'Did you shoot many hares?' – 'We didn't shoot them, we had a chase.' – 'How many packs of greyhounds did you have?' – 'Fifteen hounds in all.'[5]

Pelcl's own preface nostalgically recalling the sixteenth century, 'when learned men were writing Czech in all areas of scholarship, when nobles of both genders used to speak to each other in Czech',[6] is symptomatic. It confirms that the different models of communication in Pelcl's grammar book serve to demonstrate the faculties of the Czech language rather than to reflect its true position, which was clearly less favourable. Yet as late as in the forties, Count Leo Thun-Hohenstein (1811–1888), the later Austrian

politician and statesman, wrote in his review of a book by an eminent
prose-writer and dramatist, Josef Kajetán Tyl: 'It is more than difficult to
write a Czech novella which takes place in the upper classes of the present
society, as every facet of life in these classes is in fact German, so that scenes
taken from it would sound false in Czech . . .'[7] František Palacký
(1798–1876), later a prominent historian, reviewing Turinský's tragedy
Angelína, also refers to the difficulties of writing high drama in Czech and
formulates the problem concisely: 'We were deprived of a public life!'[8]

Language provided a compensation for this 'deprivation of a public life';
through the mediation of signs it allowed a simulation of the non-existent
Czech 'public life'. Language helped to re-define the notion of the country,
the 'fatherland' as a community of Czech-speaking people and the land
they inhabit, the notion of the 'nation' which was then strictly limited to
users of the Czech tongue.[9] The universality of language compensated at
the beginning for the non-universality (fragmentary nature) of Czech
culture. A scholarly text written in Czech conveyed a message (false, for the
time being) about the existence of a Czech-speaking scholarly public; an
ode or a tragedy written in Czech indicated the existence of a cultivated
social strata which was receptive to such elevated genres.

The striving for the emancipation of Czech culture that gradually gained
ground from the eve of the nineteenth century was thus focused on language. In particular, it was oriented towards the cultivation of those levels
of verbal communication which, in Pelcl's book of grammar, had a rather
hypothetical or fictive character and presented the Czech language either
as an exquisite means of educated, sophisticated communication, or as a
medium of patriotic propaganda. Both functions helped to define a quite
different image of the Czech national identity than that suggested by Pelcl
on the level of practical conversation between an educated and a common
man or on the level of family communication (which was, however, totally
ignored by our scholar). This process of cultivation preserved a rather
archaic stage of the Czech language in grammar, but was linked with an
abundance of innovations in vocabulary.[10] By means of newly coined
words, of translations from German, Greek, and Latin, or with the help of
loans from other Slavic languages, the foundations were laid for the terminology of philosophy and aesthetics, of the theory of literature, linguistics,
physics, of chemistry, botany, zoology, medicine, psychology, logic, etc. (In
Estonia, in contrast, such far-reaching changes in the field of vocabulary did
not occur until the moment when the independent Estonian republic was
founded, and its government wanted to open schools.)

The extension of the capabilities of the Czech language at this time was
thus characterized by an extreme artificiality. The development of language

was not a mere by-product of the development of the culture as a whole. For the revivalist way of thinking rather, the converse logic was typical – the evolution of arts and sciences was regarded as a tool for developing the Czech language. Josef Jungmann (1773–1847), the unofficial head of the patriotic community, formulated this problem openly: 'The language is in need of cultivation, which is achieved by the cultivation of sciences . . .'[11] The representational character of scholarship, its orientations towards facts and new information as its essential quality, was overshadowed by the verbal form, by the 'Czech', 'national' garb of the scholarly discourse. The 'thematic' core (what is 'told' by a scientific text) was generally suppressed by the verbal form itself.[12] The motivation for scholarly activity did not lie in the thirst for knowledge. On the contrary, the very choice of a branch of study to pursue was regarded by the revivalist intellectuals as a quite unimportant, arbitrary act. Only the choice of language was essential and meaningful. The Czech language was accepted not only as a simple means of communication. With its communicative abilities considerably reduced, the 'mother tongue' tended to be sanctified. It was adored, considered 'the only commemoration of ancestors', 'their only legacy', 'the only device our ancestors can use to speak to us'.[13]

But the sanctification of the Czech language and the extremely reverent, pious attitude to it did not mean a scrupulous clinging to its older, archaic forms, inherited from past centuries. The same limitedness of Czech as an authentic means of communication throughout society, which stimulated sanctification of the language, also changed it into a field of a free creativity. This free verbal creativity helped the Czech intellectual of the first half of the nineteenth century to stand side by side with his ancestors and take part together with them in a common enterprise. The Czech patriot did not accept his mother tongue as a completed creation, but as material to be shaped. Václav Bolemír Nebeský, a Czech Romantic poet and critic, said later about the Czech language: 'it was deprived of its natural privileges; we did not live within it fully. Thus it became the object of our activity'.[14] That is why the coining of new words during the national revival did not serve only to complement the vocabulary, but turned, from later point of view, into a 'self-satisfied hunt for neologisms'[15] which exceeded 'any real demands'.[16] The result of this process was the creation of an artificial, exclusive language with an extremely high synonymity which was intended to demonstrate the variety of the mother tongue and to argue for its advantages over the German language. This fact had serious negative consequences for the social status of the Czech language – the artificial and exclusive 'high Czech' became scarcely comprehensible, even for active participants in the patriotic movement, and radically strayed from colloquial speech. This development further reduced the social base of patriotic activities. It is symptomatic that one of the characters of a later novella by Josef Kajetán Tyl regards Czech patriots as 'fellows who wish to help out the poor, old mother tongue, but at the same time speak or write in such a manner that not a living soul can make sense of it'.[17]

IV

The shift in emphasis from the 'thematic' to the 'verbal' element provided an exceptional opportunity for translation. At the beginning of the nineteenth century, the very use of the Czech language as a 'cultural' language was a strongly marked, ostentatious fact, and the stress put on the language encouraged the idea that the simplest way to create Czech culture was to do it with the help of translation. It is worth mentioning that the 'originality' of verbal form in a text was regarded as so decisive, that it was viewed as legitimate for a translator to suppress the name of the true author or even to substitute the translator's signature for the author's name. (In the sphere of scholarship this was the case with Antonín Marek's translation of Kiesewetter's *Logic* or *The Experimental Psychology* by Karel Ferdinand Hýna, both published without mentioning the names of their original authors on the title-pages.)[18] Furthermore, any mention of an author's name was not dictated by the normal respect for the etiquette of translating, as we understand it today. It could function instead as a means of referring to certain values associated with the original work and thus open the door to various ways of utilizing them further.

But the revivalist translation was unusual also with regard to other qualities. It was viewed as a device for cultural aggression, as a means of expropriating texts which were perceived as 'foreign', or 'in the possession' of other cultural spheres.[19] Translation was certainly not seen as a passive activity, or even as the result of a foreign culture's impact. Transposing foreign texts into Czech was often connected with a specific philosophy of revenge:

If – to the detriment of the Slavs – the Germans, Italians and Magyars try to denationalize both our common people and our upper classes, let us use a more noble form of retaliation. Let us take possession, for our nation, of anything excellent they have created in the realm of the mind.[20]

Translation could serve as a suitable device for the quick formation of a 'Czech world'. A foreign cultural value (a text) was, together with the whole context of the reality it evoked (the cultural 'donnée'), incorporated through translation into the 'Czech world'. This process was intensified by different techniques of adaptation popular in translations of that era. Names of characters in foreign works of literature were often 'Czechised,' foreign settings were displaced by domestic ones.[21] But even where such aggressive devices of adaptation were not applied, translation still represented an expropriation of the original cultural value, its usurpation for the Czech and Slavic context. Obviously, Jungmann's decision to translate *Paradise Lost* was occasioned by a similar motivation. The mixture of pagan, Christian and Jewish traditions, supplemented by Milton's obsession with exotic geographical names, make *Paradise Lost* into an epic of mankind as a whole. Simply by transferring the poem into Czech, Jungmann was able to 'usurp' this universe for the Czechs, to present it as a Slavic and Czech world. The initial, partial, non-universal nature of Czech culture simply cried out for works capable of evoking a vision of universality.

V

Formation of the 'Czech world' required the production not only of its present but also simultaneously of its past. Though the traditions of Czech culture before the White Mountain catastrophe[22] were usually highly appreciated and enthusiastically invoked, the revivalist generation found, that, as a whole, they were hardly appropriate to the framework of the prestigious, high Czech culture which they envisioned. In contradiction to the ideal of universality of the 'Czech world', the heritage of the past seemed to be too discontinuous and fragmentary. Furthermore, the literary values of the Middle Ages or of humanism had little to do with contemporary life and lacked the prestige to become the basis of a new culture. The peculiar situation of the revivalist cultural production, 'deprived of the public life' and thus predestined to artificiality, also helps us to re-evaluate the problem of mystifications and forgeries. The patriotic community, forced to produce both the present and the past of the culture at once, found in mystifications more than a kind of an aesthetic play. Czech patriots accepted forgeries as a device to complement the national past, to complete Czech cultural traditions with elements which could then be further developed and employed. From 1816 on, plenty of old Czech manuscripts were 'discovered', the most important of them (the Manuscript of Dvůr Králové 'found' in 1817 by Václav Hanka, later curator of the Czech Museum library, and the Manuscript of Zelená Hora, anonymously sent in 1818 to Count Kolovrat, then governor of Bohemia) entirely changed the picture of the Czech literary and cultural past. Mystifications became an ostentatious part of revivalist activities.[23] Jan Kollár, a poet, incorporated self-evident forgeries into his anthology of Slovak folk songs,[24] while another eminent poet, Ladislav

Čelakovský, was the initiator of many similar efforts (his literary hoax concerning a fictitious poetess, Žofie Jandová, worked its way into Bowring's *Cheskian Anthology*). In those times, the veracity criterion was rarely applied towards mystifications and forgeries. If the patriotic elite of the Jungmannian era felt compelled, along with its project of Czech culture, to be completely divorced from reality, and even in contention with it, they could hardly be bound by the strictures of truth and falsity. To stand outside of reality meant also to stand outside the dictates of the veracity of a fact. At the outset, revivalist culture as a whole engaged in a hoax – both through its original creative efforts, which produced the illusion of a normally functioning Czech society, fully developed and autonomous; and through the forgeries, which modified the picture of the past by direct falsification.

Such an artificially developed cultural system naturally presented quite clearly certain features of an archaic mythological system. The very striving for a sudden and immediate formation of the 'Czech world' could successfully employ the structures of mythological discourse. Czech culture was organized in analogies, as was typical for mythologizing thinking; Czech cultural phenomena were implanted into a network of relations towards cultural values borrowed from abroad ('our Petrarca', 'our Sappho', 'our Tasso'). Czech culture was in this regard 'translation-like' in the broadest sense of the word. A large part of it was generated as a set of values equivalent to the prestigious 'foreign' ones. Czech culture shared with mythology its interpretation of time as a cyclical motion. The ideology of the national revival characteristically strove to escape from history, to interpret history in terms of natural cycles. The increase of Czech cultural activities within the nationalist agenda was regarded more in terms of the mythological plots about the awakening of a hero in a myth, linked with the beginning of a natural cycle. This cultural boom represented much more a sacred 'rebirth' of the nation, than a result of an historical process: 'The Czech was aroused from his deep slumber for his celebratory work'.[25] In this sense, the world of Czech culture is 'passing from history to nature' in the terms of Roland Barthes.[26] Evolution is seen as a return to the past, to a 'former Czech glory'. Traces of this type of thinking can also be detected in the cases of figures who resisted the general ideological standards of their times:[27]

The freedom we are enjoying today, is not new and previously unknown in our nation, it is not something grafted onto us from abroad. It is a tree indigenous to our home soil, an original and direct legacy of our ancient fathers. The Old Slavs, equal to each other before the law and disinclined to rule over other tribes, understood this heritage much better than a good many of our neighbouring nations, which are nowadays glorified, but perhaps even now are not able to comprehend freedom without domination.

The idea of the 'rebirth', 'resurrection' of the nation was, despite the clearly prevailing secular character of the Czech national revival, linked with divine intervention: 'Oh Lord, give a new birth to the nation buried alive! We shall rise from the dead to your Word.'[28]

All the patriotic and national emblems became sacred: the native country was changed into a 'holy homeland', the patriotic community regarded itself as analogous to the Church, individual patriots were 'priests', apostles of the new 'patriotic belief', the task of building the Czech national culture was interpreted as 'the Lord's war'.[29] In addition, significant places of the native topography were sanctified – Prague (especially the Castle and the Vyšehrad hill), the Vltava river, the Krkonoše mountains, Blaník and Radhošť, the legendary mountains of Bohemia and Moravia, and the Tatry mountains in Slovakia. The everyday cultural and propagandistic activity of patriots was clothed in the ritual symbolism of sacrifice and made sacred together with the whole of Czech cultural production. Czech literature, language, theatre – all these were accepted as holy, sacral, and untouchable values.

VI

In summary, the striving for a quick and immediate formation of Czech culture as a complex and fully developed whole, occurred under circumstances in which a differentiated, developed and self-confident Czech society, sure of its national identity, did not yet exist. This problem led to an orientation towards language, towards the production of culture in the sphere of philology, and hence to the primacy of the verbal form over the content of a message, over originality in the realm of ideas. This trend resulted naturally in the artificiality of cultural production and, with it, a blurring of the boundaries between the true and the false, between illusion and reality. The deficiency of social structures, which could become guarantors of Czech cultural production, had to be compensated for by a much less official network of personal relations among participants in the patriotic movement. The revivalist elite created particular rituals of their own, which from the outside resembled the rituals of secret societies. 'Oh my goodness, what sort of thing is this patriotism? – a new fashion or a sport?, new manners?, new kind of speculation? a club or a casino? It must be something!'[30] says one of the characters of a Tyl novella, a young woman who does not belong to patriotic circles. Participants in the movement, viewed from the outside, indeed represented a mysterious, closed group that systematically underscored its exclusivity. Patriotic agitations for the national cause were developed as specific ceremonies of initiation into

'Czechness', where active patriots played the role of Teacher, Initiator, 'Awakener' and the unawakened assumed the role of Pupil, Initiate. Patriots often accepted ostentatious, unofficial Czech names that usually followed their first names and sometimes (informally) displaced them completely (Josef Ladislav Ziegler, Josef Myslimír Ludvík, Jan Milostín Vidimský, Josef Krasoslav Chmelenský, Jan Pravoslav Koubek and others.). Surnames also could be 'Czechised' (Antonie Reiss – Antonie Rajská).

At the beginning of the nineteenth century, Czech revivalist culture was (and had to be) extremely provisional precisely because of its striving for complexity. It was based on substitutes – what was deficient in reality, had to be supplied with the help of symbols. A work of literature was usually more a mere sign of literature than an autonomous value; it formally demonstrated the abilities of the nation and its language to write on the European level, but was hardly a natural result of this ability. The revivalist culture also conveyed the illusion of its solid background, but this background was in reality extremely weak. The absence of any political differentiation was then counterbalanced by differentiation in philological questions, in attitudes towards peripheral problems of orthography and grammar (the faction of advocates of 'v' versus advocates of 'w', supporters for 'au' against those preferring to write 'ou', 'iotists' against 'ypsilonists').

Yet the choice of this strategy made by Jungmann's generation through its refusal to accept a partial 'culture within a culture' as a necessity, and its decision to form immediately an autonomous and more or less complex whole, did not lead to a *cul-de-sac*. However, this historical deed at this moment did signify a choice of illusions, of mythicizing and sanctifying the national identity, a choice of a culture of a contentious nature (Czech culture as a call to arms against the German-speaking cultural sphere). This alternative necessarily resulted in an one-sided orientation toward language and led to an overestimation of the role of culture in representing the nation. These trends have proven able to regenerate themselves at later points, and from time to time they resurface even today as a powerful factor influencing current public attitudes (an extreme sensitivity regarding the mother tongue, the exaggerated social status of the writer, the inclination to prefer the discontinuous development of society, and a persistent starting from zero). There is no doubt that the negative aspects of the choice were anticipated. Furthermore, it was precisely this anticipation that became the motor of further evolution, despite the extreme scepticism sometimes associated with it. 'We play the piano which has no strings',[31] admits Jan Kollár in one of his epigrams; the topos of a sound produced by a non-existing string appears then in Mácha's verse, elevated to an ambiguous symbol: 'the note of a warped harp, sound of a broken string'.[32] In a private letter,

Čelakovský was apprehensive that Jungmann's monumental Czech–German Dictionary would become no more than the tombstone of a Czech culture, that was predestined to die out. In a poem, published at the same time, however, he welcomed Jungmann's work as evidence of the nation's vitality. Only the moments of scepticism, usually officially denied, and surrounded – if they came to light at all – by collective disagreement on the part of the patriotic elite (exemplified also in the rejection of Mácha's poetic imagery), represented a corrective to the strategy of an illusory creation of an exclusive Czech culture. This sceptism prepared a situation for an entirely different definition of Czech national identity, as a natural fact and a non-mythicized requirement (Karel Havlíček). This new self-confident national identity could be later manifested in a gesture attempting to question the very rationality of the former, Revivalist choice, as if only in putting questions like this could a sign of the maturity of a nation be found (H. G. Schauer). At the same time, the orientation towards an immediate and complex creation of Czech culture by means of, strictly speaking, artificial devices, did not eradicate other cultural activities, often still rooted in the tradition of the Enlightenment, and usually much better adapted to everyday life. The Revivalist strategy simply integrated them and gave them a new setting.

The evolution of Czech culture in the first half of the nineteenth century is thus not only a process of the creation of an artificial culture of the national revival type, but also a process of reflection on this artificiality and exclusivity, and, from the 1830s on, also of a growing controversy with revivalism as the dominant ideology. In this complex, paradoxical era at the intersection of opposite cultural trends, the path was provided to eventual 'normal' cultural and political life in Bohemia.

Notes

1 For more details, see Arne Novák, *Czech Literature* (Ann Arbor, 1986), pp. 113–60.
2 J. Bowring, *Cheskian Anthology being A History of the Poetical Literature of Bohemia, with Translated Specimens* (London, 1832).
3 See J. Lotman, 'O semiosfere' [On Semiosphere], in *Struktura dialoga kak princip raboty semiotičeskogo mechanizma, Tartu Riikliku Ülikooli toimetised*, No. 641. *Trudy po znakovym sistemam XVII (Tartu, 1984)*, pp. 5–23.
4 F. M. Pelzel, *Grundsätze der Böhmischen Grammatik*, 2nd enlarged edn. (Prague, 1792).
5 *Ibid.*, p. 232.
6 *Ibid.*, ('Vorrede'), unpaginated.
7 J. L. Turnovský, *Život a doba Josefa Kajetána Tyla* [The life and times of Josef Kajetán Tyl] (Prague, 1892), p. 143.

8 F. Palacký, *Radhost. Sbírka spisův drobných z oboru řeči a literatury české, krásovědy, historie a politiky I* [The Radhost Mountain. Collected Miscellanea from Czech philology and literature, aesthetics, history, and politics. Part I] (Prague, 1871), pp. 426–33.

9 J. Loužil, 'J. Jungmanns Begriff der Sprachnation und seine Gefahren', *Ost-West-Begegnung in Österreich* (Vienna-Cologne-Graz, 1976), p. 167.

10 R. Auty, 'The role of purism in the development of the Slavonic literary languages', *The Slavonic and East European Review*, 51 (1973), 335–43. V. Kolari, 'Notes on Jan Svatopluk Presl as terminologist', *Scandoslavica*, 19 (1973), 187–95. Wytrzens, 'Die Bedeutung der Etymologie für die slavische Wiedergeburt', *Wiener Slavistisches Jahrbuch*, 18 (1973), 99–110.

11 J. Jungmann, *Slovesnost* [Poetics] (Prague, 1846), p. 2.

12 A. Jedlička, *Josef Jungmann a obrozenská terminologie literárněvědná a lingvistická* [Josef Jungmann and the revivalist terminology in literary criticism and linguistics] (Prague, 1949), p. 23.

13 J. S. Presl in Jiří [Georges de] Cuvier, *Rozprava o převratech kůry zemní* [Discours sur les révolutions de la surface du globe] (Prague, 1834), p. v.

14 V. B. Nebeský, *O literatuře* [On literature] (Prague, 1953), p. 52.

15 Jedlička, *Josef Jungmann*, p. 23.

16 B. Havránek, 'Vývoj spisovného jazyka českého' [The evolution of the Czech literary language], in *Československá vlastivěda, řada II, Spisovný jazyk český a slovenský* (Prague, 1936), p. 92.

17 J. K. Tyl, *Kusy mého srdce I* [Pieces of my heart. Part I] (Prague, 1844), p. 281.

18 A. Marek, *Logika nebo Umnice* [Logic] (Prague, 1820). K. F. Hýna, *Dušesloví zkušebné* [Experimental psychology] (Prague, 1844).

19 V. Macura, 'Culture as Translation', in *Translation, History and Culture* (London–New York 1990), pp. 64–70.

20 J. E. Purkyně, *Opera omnia/Sebrané spisy XI, Básně a překlady* [Poems and translations] (Prague, 1968), p. 67.

21 For example, the names of Milton and Cromwell were removed from Jungmann's translation of *An Elegy Written in a Country Church Yard* by Thomas Gray and names taken from the Czech history were substituted: Jan Žižka and Jan Rokycana. The original text in a poem by F. L. Stolberg – 'ihr liebe deutsche Frauen' – was transformed into 'mladé dívky české' ('young Czech girls'). See J. Levý, *České teorie překladu* [Czech theories of translation] (Prague, 1957), pp. 96–8.

22 The Battle of the White Mountain (*Bílá hora*) was fought in 1620; it resulted in a defeat for the estates of Bohemia and a victory for the Habsburgs which for centuries, tied Bohemia to the Monarchy more closely than before. See Ch. VII.

23 See A. Lass, 'Romantic documents and political monuments: the meaning-fulfillment of history in 19th-century Czech nationalism', *American Ethnologist*, 15 (1988), 456–71, V. Otáhal, 'The manuscript controversy in the Czech national revival', *Cross Currents*, 5 (1986), 247–77.

24 E. Pauliny, 'Pramene Štúrovej kodifikácie' [The sources of Štúr's codification], in (no ed.) *Slovanské spisovné jazyky v době obrození Sborník věnovaný Univerzitou Karlovou k 200. výročí narození Josefa Jungmanna* [Slavonic literary tongues. Charles

University Collection marking the 200th anniversary of Josef Jungmann's birth], (Prague, 1976 [1974]), pp. 68.

25 J. Kamenický, 'První květen' [The first of May] *Čechoslav*, 6, 18 (1825), 137.

26 R. Barthes, *Mythologies* (New York, 1984), p. 143.

27 F. Palacký, *Radhost. Sbírka spisův drobných z oboru řeči a literatury české, krásovědy, historie a politiky III* [The Radhost mountain. Collected miscellanea from Czech philology and literature, aesthetics, history, and politics. Part III] (Prague, 1873), pp. 31–2.

28 F. J. Kamenický, *Lilie a růže* [The lily and the rose] (Prague, 1846), part II, LXXV (unpaginated).

29 K. A. Vinařický, *Korespondence a spisy pamětní*, 2. [Letters and memorials. Part II] (Prague, 1909), p. 637; J. B. Pichl, *Vlastenecké vzpomínky* [Patriotic reminiscences] (Prague, 1936), p. 25.

30 Tyl, *Kusy mého srdce I*, p. 149.

31 Jan Kollár, 'Básníř a národ' [The poet and the people] in his *Básně* [Poems] (edited by M. Otruba) (Prague, 1981), p. 273.

32 K. H. Mácha, *Máj* [May] (Prague, 1836), p. 67.

10

Czech society 1848–1918

(+) OTTO URBAN

1848 and 1918, seminal dates in the history of modern Europe, are likewise important turning points in the development of modern Czech society. The abolition of feudal subjection (villeinage), in 1848, was the basic step in the formation of a modern national society as a civil society; and pervasive changes of constitutional law in Central and Eastern Europe, in 1918, remade the conditions of co-existence between nations and states.

Czech society began this process with clearly expressed desires and a general national-emancipation programme, which it endeavoured to realize in the following decades. However, existing conditions and preconditions were inconsistent with this endeavour and caused difficulties.

I

The modernization of the Habsburg monarchy, which began with the Enlightenment reforms of the middle of the eighteenth century, changed its historical structure and tended towards the rationalization, unification and centralization of state power and the rules of public life. The unification of laws and regulations in the area of administration – economic, civil, criminal, canon etc. – was made hand in hand with a pragmatic programme of language unification. A unified state needed a unified and generally understandable means of communication, which became the German language. The state and its institutions stood above society as an administrative unit with special functions. National, ethnic and cultural differences were tolerated in the sphere of non-state life in the multinational Habsburg monarchy. Cultural and linguistic endeavours were also tolerated, unless they had obvious political content and interfered with the structure of state life.

The unitary policy of the Enlightened absolutist state, which included central control of cultural and educational policy created conditions for the formation of Czech society. Another, and no less important impulse was industrialization which began in the Czech Lands at the turn of the eighteenth century. This process affected not only the state but also strongly and intensively penetrated the whole of society – to a certain extent independently of the state. Novel scientific and technical knowledge, including new production and labour processes came in the main from Western Europe and, as a rule, were mediated via German-speaking regions. New terminology, new concepts and new language came with these innovations. The Czech language of that time, which had already lost the functions of a language of culture and science, did not have the vocabulary to express accurately novel terms and ideas. If a Czech workman did not want to work like his grandfather or great-grandfather, and thereby to succumb to the efficient competition of modern production, he had often to adapt and to assimilate, at least, partly linguistically.

The revival and renewal of the Czech language was the alternative to assimilation. Revived, it became possible to express new phenomena in grammatically and lexically relevant terms. A small but agile section of Czech burgher intelligentsia undertook this linguistic task. Its aim was the linguistic and cultural regeneration of the existing but considerably neglected Czech ethnicity. This process, which is called the 'national revival' by the older historiography, was a reaction to the progressive process of national assimilation. On closer examination we find that this process affected not only language and cultural affairs but had deeper social-psychological and social-cultural circumstances and dimensions.

Linguistic and cultural emancipation was, then, a wider social process and the first step toward complete national and political emancipation. The advocates of revival had different motives and relied on different sources as foundations for it. Besides the consciousness of a wider Slavonic community of interest, which played an important role in the first half of the nineteenth century, a basis of the revival was the very strong, strictly national-historical consciousness that developed. It was based on the real or putative past glory of the Czech nation. A further basis was the fact that in the Czech Lands there still lived numerous strata of Czech-speaking population and that it was insulated, particularly in rural areas, from assimilative influences. The national and emancipatory programme developed mainly from these three sources and was concretely formulated in 1848.

Before we look at political developments, I should mention the general social-cultural conditions as Czech society developed during this period.

In 1850 about 6.74 million inhabitants lived in the Czech Lands; of these about 4 million were Czechs and 2.7 million indigenous Germans. The Czech Lands, namely Bohemia, Moravia and Silesia, comprised an area of less than 80,000 square kilometres. In Bohemia the population was more than 60 per cent Czech and in Moravia it was more than 70 per cent, but in Silesia Czechs were less than 30 per cent of the population. In contrast to Bohemia and Moravia, which belonged to the typically bilingual lands of the Habsburg monarchy, Silesia belonged to the group of lands with three spoken languages: Czech, German and Polish. In spite of very positive demographic developments and the marked growth of population in the second half of the nineteenth century – in 1910 it reached 10.15 million – the population structure remained basically unchanged as Czechs still represented approximately two thirds and indigenous Germans one third of the whole population (in 1910 there were about 6.4 million Czechs and 3.5 million indigenous Germans in the Czech Lands). All the demographic data of both ethnicities are comparable and do not show marked differences. That is, the Czech-speaking and the German-speaking populations developed more or less in parallel and high growth rates continued despite the steady increases in emigration quotas. Increased migration within the Austrian or Western half of the Habsburg monarchy ('Cisleithania') was a special case. It strengthened especially towards the end of the nineteenth century in connection with growing economic prosperity and it intensified the diversity of the ethnic structure of the Monarchy. While in 1880 slightly more than 70,000 Czechs lived outside the territory of the Czech Lands, according to statistics of 1910 almost a quarter of a million Czechs lived in all parts of Cisleithania, particularly in Vienna and Lower Austria. To a certain extent Czech 'expansion' after 1880 was conditioned by the economic and social situation but, as we shall see, it had also its political components.

The Czech Lands belonged traditionally to the most populated territories of the Habsburg monarchy and they maintained their position in the second half of the nineteenth century. While the Czech Lands comprised only 26.4 per cent of the whole area of Cisleithania, they had 35 per cent of the population. A concomitant of population growth was population density – in 1854 there were approximately 84 inhabitants per square kilometre, in 1880 104, and in 1910 about 128 inhabitants, whereas the average for all Austria in 1910 amounted to only 95 inhabitants per square kilometre.

In density of settlement as well as population the Czech Lands exceeded the Austrian average and in this respect were similar to several European regions. Thus in 1910, 16,727 communes and settlements were recorded on the territory of the Czech Lands, that is 35 per cent of the Austrian part of

Table 10.1. *Sectoral changes in occupational structure (as a percentage of total number of persons employed*

	Agriculture		Industry and Crafts		Trade and Transport		Public Services and Professions	
	1890	1910	1890	1910	1890	1910	1890	1910
Bohemia	46.85	36.64	33.56	36.73	7.79	10.80	11.80	15.83
Moravia	56.21	45.80	26.52	30.13	6.18	8.68	11.09	15.39
Silesia	47.89	35.67	35.12	39.44	6.27	9.70	10.72	15.79
Austria (as a whole)	62.41	53.10	20.02	22.64	7.44	9.84	10.13	14.42

Source: Compiled from B. Bolognese-Leuchtenmüller, *Bevölkerungsentwicklung und Berufsstruktur, Gesundheits- und Fürsorgewesen in Österreich 1750–1918, Materialien zur Wirtschafts- und Sozialgeschichte*, vol. 1 (Vienna, 1978).

the Habsburg monarchy. The extraordinary density of settlements was connected with the fact that the countryside did not depopulate and the number of inhabitants in communes of up to 2,000 inhabitants increased moderately while the towns absorbed the greater part of the population surplus. In 1880 there were 38 towns with more than 10,000 inhabitants in the Czech Lands and, in total, these towns contained about 800,000 persons; but by 1910 there were 77 towns with a total population of 1.9 million.

The growth of urban population was a general European phenomenon of the nineteenth century, connected with the modernization of society as a whole. The urbanization of the Czech Lands was less directly connected with industrialization. Besides economic centres and agglomerations, such as Prague, Plzeň, Brno, Ostrava, industrial production developed widely in rural areas and small towns. Large inner migration did not occur and industrial potential was considerably dispersed. This also had consequences for the development of the social structure of both the Czech and Moravian countryside, where the combination and connection of agricultural and non-agricultural activity occurred at different levels.

In the process of modernization, the Czech Lands became economically the most important region of the Habsburg monarchy (see table 10.1).

There was a correspondance between the decline of the share of the population gainfully employed in agriculture and growth in the other three sectors. In this context it is necessary to mention two basic facts.

Above all, despite the decline in the number of persons employed in agriculture, the production of agricultural products continued to grow according to practically all indices. The Czech Lands were in fact agriculturally self-sufficient despite the rapid growth of population, and in areas such as sugar or beer they were significant exporters of food products. Due to this fact, the Czech Lands did not suffer from food shortages during the second half of the nineteenth century and the beginning of the twentieth century. Along with improved health services and general hygiene, this situation was reflected in the improvement of the average state of health, life expectancy and the standard of living in general.

Secondly, both Czech-speaking and German-speaking societies participated in these changes. From a demographic but also from the social point of view, the development of the Czech and German ethnicities was comparable, although there were differences. While the Czech-speaking population traditionally settled in the most fertile regions of the Czech and Moravian interior, the German-speaking population lived mostly in the craft and manufacturing 'piedmont' and uplands with less intensive and productive agriculture. Initially, industrialization occurred in German-speaking regions with their older tradition of crafts, and due to this and other reasons a stereotype grew up around the middle of the nineteenth century: the German as craftsman, industrialist, entrepreneur, workman; and the Czech as peasant, farmer or workman. This image changed profoundly during the second half of the nineteenth century due to the rapid development of the food industry, where Czechs predominated, and also due to the penetration of Czech capital into other branches of industry, including textiles, engineering, chemicals and leather goods (the famous Baťa boot and shoe factories were founded in south-east Moravia at the end of the nineteenth century). At the turn of the nineteenth and twentieth centuries, natural climatic and geographical differences facilitated that Czechs would have the edge over Germans in the agricultural sector. Thus in 1910, in Bohemia agriculture absorbed approximately 37 per cent of those employed, but in Czech-speaking regions this proportion amounted to about 43 per cent and in German-speaking regions to 31 per cent. On the other hand, there were 33 per cent persons employed in industry and crafts in Czech-speaking regions and 45 per cent in German-speaking regions. The share in the other two sectors was almost equal. However, the Czech share in the public services and professions was higher than the German one.

Positive demographic developments, a solid and efficient agrarian base and a reasonable pace of industrialization conditioned the generally favourable evolvement of Czech society and its further growth. The modernization and emancipation of the cultural and political spheres were rather more difficult.

II

The year 1848 not only signalled the decay of the old governmental and state system, but also foreshadowed the possibility of the disintegration of the Habsburg monarchy itself. The national principle, as an integral part of civic consciousness of the time, was coming clearly into conflict with the dynastic principle underlying the dynastic-territorial state. The growing influence of the 'third estate', represented by spokesmen in various constitutional bodies and assemblies, challenged the historical status quo and aspired to a new state-political structure of Central Europe.

Under these conditions in the spring of 1848, a Czech national programme was outlined in a general form for the first time. From the beginning, two different points of view existed. In harmony with the historical tradition, a section of the political public emphasized the political specificity and individuality of the Czech Lands and, in particular, the integrality of the Kingdom of Bohemia as an entity. Referring to natural rights and also to historical rights (both types of argumentation blended as regards Czech politics during the next decades), these politicians demanded the recognition of complete equality of both ethnicities and their languages. That is, they desired the status that had been formally guaranteed by the Renewed Land Ordinance of 1627, and reconfirmed after the Thirty Years War.

In addition to this restricted national programme, the historian František Palacký (1798–1876) proposed a wider Austrian programme binding the Czech and Austrian questions closely into a whole. Palacký was aware of broader European contexts and, with this in mind, he presented the principles of his programme in his well-known letter to the German *Vorparlament* in Frankfurt of 11 April 1848. Of course, he knew very well that for centuries the Czech Lands had been a part of the Holy Roman Empire, and that since 1815 they had been a part of the German Confederation (brought into being at the Vienna Congress); and therefore that the position of Czech society was conditioned by its belonging not only to the complex of the Habsburg monarchy, but also to the Confederation of German sovereigns. Palacký did not and could not ignore the existence of wider historical dynastic connections of the Czech Lands but he rejected the linking of Czech society with the process of German unification, based on the nationality principle. Although he applied the nationality principle to Czech society he, at the same time, believed that certain smaller Central European nations were immature and unfit to achieve an entirely separate political independence. The global process of centralization – it was in this sense that Palacký understood the integration processes of the nineteenth century – had gone so far that a truly independent policy could be pursued by no-one (later he conceded that perhaps only England and Russia were capable of acting on their own). Therefore he immediately combined his refusal to participate in the German unification process with a resolute plea for the creation of a big and powerful bloc of federated nations, situated between the rising Germany and the already existing Russian Empire.

For Palacký the Habsburg monarchy as it had historically developed – but of course as an internally reconstructed constitutional state – was the crystallizing nucleus of a possible Central European concentration. In this respect, his 'idea of the Austrian state' was a programme with far-reaching and, at that time, misunderstood perspective. The politician Palacký was to such an extent a realist that in his speeches in the Constituent Assembly in Vienna and Kroměříž (Moravia), and also in his published articles, he disavowed his being a historian and was clearly in favour of revising the existing historical borders. He envisaged the new non-German 'Central Europe' as a community of national states encompassed by new borders, respecting maximally real ethnic conditions. In this context, it must be stressed that Palacký's programme – contrary to its Austroslavistic interpretation by some Czechs – was basically Austrofederalist, and did not attend solely to specific interests of some national societies. In this regard, it constituted one of the most important programmatic political statements of the nineteenth century on a European-wide scale.

Formally in Central Europe the status quo ante was restored in the 1850s and all the reforming impulses of 1848/49 were kept down. But the neo-absolutist system differed in many respects from the former absolutism. Prince Klemens Metternich's (1772–1859) idea of a consolidated and conservative Austria was replaced by Prince Felix Schwarzenberg's (1800–1852) idea of an active and reformist Austria, in many ways reminiscent of and linked to Josephinian thinking at the end of the eighteenth century. The Habsburg monarchy was to become the powerful crystallizing nucleus of another Central European grouping – a new 70 million-strong empire, open culturally, politically, and above all economically to the German world. Never before had the pragmatic side of the unified state been stressed to such a degree, never before had the traditional structure of the Habsburg monarchy been encroached on so much. But also the real ethnic structure was obscured to an unprecedented degree. Under these circumstances Czech society disappeared, as it were for a while, not only as a political factor, but also as an active, cultural community. All the hopes of 1848 –

awakening public opinion, club activities, founding of higher Czech education, political journalism, participation in the work of the Diet and
Reichsrat (Imperial Parliament), etc. – were suppressed or reduced to a bare
minimum in accordance with the needs of the state.

The trend towards the combination of the Habsburg dynastic principle
and the German national principle might have had some chances under
certain conditions and in a historically long-term perspective. But this tendency was drastically called into question even before it could put down
deeper roots. The military defeat at Solferino in 1859 and its consequences
were of singular significance for the further development of the Habsburg
monarchy and of the whole of Central Europe. If development – fitful and
uneven – tended toward unification and centralization in the wake of the
Pragmatic Sanction decreasing the indivisibleness of the Habsburg realm
in 1713, an opposite tendency developed after 1860. It tended toward the
loosening up and eventually the complete break-up of this Central
European communality. From 1860, the Habsburg monarchy was forced to
forego ambitious Central European projects, and to find gradually a new
rationale for the Austrian state elsewhere.

III

A new cultural and political programme for Czech society was coming into
existence in the dynamic period of wars, conflicts, constitutional disputes
and experiments that led to the transformation of the state-political structure of the Habsburg monarchy in the 1860s. Unlike in 1848, the beginning
of this new stage of 'revival' was much more prosaic. The public was generally restrained and the representatives of Czech society were adopting a
careful, expectant stance. It was not clear when would be the right time to
come up with a concrete programme, and what the argumentation should
be. Those in power were carefully considering and weighing the state of
affairs and they presented the political public with a *fait accompli* by intro-
ducing key policies through the October Diploma of 1860, followed by the
February Constitution of 1861. As the political public's participation in
drafting them was practically nil, the reaction to them was either embar-
rassed, critical or directly negative – as in Hungary. Unlike the Diet of
Hungary, the Diet of Bohemia, including the Czech representation in it,
accepted the February Constitution as a possible starting point for further
changes.

Czech policy found itself in a very complex situation. Considering that
all changes were understood to be supplementary to existing conditions and
were not to affect the continuation of a certain evolutionary trend, the idea

of a possible ethnic federalism became totally unrealistic. Around 1860, also in the spirit of another continuity, the conception of so-called historical-political individuality was being promoted. Underlying it was the idea that the rights of historically constituted independent political entities, restricted by centralist measures, should be restored. The Hungarian political representation and the Diet of Hungary were advocating this policy in the most emphatic way. In 1863 the Czech representatives accepted this programme though interpreted in terms of State Rights federalism, again within a wide Austrian context.

After 1863 in the Diet of Bohemia was formed a rather strong coalition of Czech Liberals, headed by Palacký and his son-in-law František Ladislav Rieger (1818–1903), and the party of so-called 'historical aristocracy', in which some of the most influential noble families of Bohemia were represented. The coalition worked with greater or lesser emphasis for the restoration of the historical-political independence of Bohemia with all logical consequences, including the coronation. Unlike the more homogenous Diet of Hungary, there was a strong influential – about one third – German-speaking minority, which rejected the State Rights programme and looked at Bohemia and the Czech Lands respectively as 'German' provinces, either within the German Confederation or the Habsburg monarchy. Bohemian statehood in the supranational sense, that is, the conception of a unitary political Bohemian nation, was considered by the so-called constitutionalist German Liberals as a 'monstrous' unearthing of defunct historical documents – unacceptable both culturally and politically. The extent to which in fact demands, based on natural law, were hidden behind the historical State Rights argumentation, was not recognized by most contemporaries.

This was not so easy since the economic, cultural and political superiority of indigenous Germanhood was still strong at the time. In a way in the Czech milieu a new beginning had to be made, although it was possible to link up with the activities of the previous three or four generations. Czech newspapers, books and magazines continued to be published, and there were Czech theatrical productions, but everything seemed slightly amateurish and was carried out in the shadow of better developed German cultural activity. In 1860 there was neither a single Czech secondary school nor a Czech higher school in the Czech Lands. Practically, no institutional basis for Czech education was present and Czech intellectuals were actually amateurs and dissident products of German education. With the liberalization of public life after 1860, conditions changed very quickly and a number of educational, cultural and other associations were founded. The first secondary and higher schools were established but this was only just that 'new beginning'. Soon a far-reaching programme of cultural emancipation was formulated with the aim at creating proper Czech cultural institutions, such as the National Theatre, a school system, and aesthetically advanced literature, music and fine arts. The realization of this programme was made, of course, considerably difficult especially during 1866–67 and the following decade – owing to political concerns with State Rights.

The Austro-Prussian war of 1866 brought about principal changes in the state-political structure of Central Europe. The formation of a new Germany without the participation of Austria shocked the majority of the German-speaking population living in the Habsburg monarchy. The idea of a German Central Europe in Schwarzenberg's sense was forever buried, German national-political aspirations were 'split' and became limited. While under these conditions, the German Liberals in the Habsburg monarchy had to accept the dualist Austro-Hungarian Compromise (1867), they were even more strongly maintaining their positions in the Czech Lands. In 1866 Czech Liberals accepted with satisfaction the end of the German Confederation, which also meant, in dynastic terms, the end of the Czech Lands being a part of Germany. Initially, Czech politicians envisaged that the idea of historical-political individuality could be realized within an integral Austrian context. The shock of Dualism they experienced was all the greater since, from the Czech point of view, it did not contribute to a comprehensive but only a partial solution at the expense of others.

The Czech representatives manifested their dissatisfaction in a number of proclamations and declarations, and found strong support among the Czech public demonstrating its disagreement in numerous public meetings during 1868–70. In the critical years of 1870–71, when the process of German unification was completed, stubborn Czech defiance led to attempts to reach a special compromise. Negotiations about the so-called 'Fundamental Articles' in the autumn of 1871 regarding the right of the Diet of Bohemia to deal with all matters – except for foreign and military affairs and finance began hopefully but broke down due to the resistance of some influential politicians and the entire German Liberal camp respectively. The historical individuality of the Kingdom of Bohemia stemming from the idea of State Rights was not accepted even in the proposed moderate form.

IV

The result was total Czech negation of the new Austro-Hungarian statehood. It was expressed by Czech absence in all representative institutions, including ostentatious refusal to recognize officially arranged state functions. For example, the Vienna World Exhibition of 1873 was ignored, though many Czechs attended it as private citizens. In the 1870s the *struggle against the state* resulted in the unwillingness to accept this state formally. Of course, already then in the Czech Lands the 'Hungarian way' of resistance was viewed varyingly, and the so-called passive resistance was widely discussed and became an object of strong controversy. It separated the majority of so-called Old Czechs, around Palacký and Rieger, from the faction of Young Czechs, in which some 1848 radical veterans, headed by Karel Sladkovský (1823–1880) played a role. Although the majority of Czech Liberals of both orientations rejected Dualism in the form it was realized, they differed in practical approach to the so-called passive policy. Virtually it meant to give up voluntarily possibilities of actions and not to use conditions offered by the constitutional system. The Young Czechs stood for an active policy in the Diet of Bohemia and were restrained in their criticism of Dualism because they saw in the activation of Hungarian State Rights a precedent for the possible activation of Bohemian State Rights.

The majority of Czechs politicians, and those members of the public who were interested in politics, realized that the political system of the constitutional monarchy created conditions for further development of Czech society – development that had been unthinkable under absolutist conditions. The complex of constitutional laws of December 1867, valid in the Cisleithanian half of the Austro-Hungarian monarchy, ensured a wide range of civil and human rights and liberties, including the right to unhampered national and linguistic development. This complex of laws allowed wide possibilities for self-governing institutions and it gave a voice to public opinion in legislative bodies. Moreover, the December Constitution of 1867 was not creating a strictly centralized state and did not interfere with the historical-political structure. Lands of the Cisleithanian part of the Austro-Hungarian monarchy constituted a complex of 'Kingdoms and Lands, represented in the Reichsrat', that is, the Imperial Parliament. Special organs of state administration and autonomous self-government functioned formally and actually in individual historical lands. The Kingdom of Bohemia, the Margraviate of Moravia and Duchy of Silesia neither lost their identities nor became mere provinces, but retained in many respects elements of independence. The basic and the most important problem was a question of principle. Since the ultimate goal, that is, authentic political independence of the Czech Lands was not reached, everything else was rejected as incorrect, inconsistent and half-hearted. The main line of Czech Liberals up to the end of the 1870s can be characterized succinctly: yes to liberal and democratic changes – but under different state-political and constitutional conditions.

Of course, this passive policy could not continue indefinitely. Czech society was still too weak to achieve its ultimate goal but, on the other hand, it was too strong to stand by and ignore neighbouring events. Apart from endogenous Czech conditions (continuous arguments and conflicts and natural impatience regarding 'doing nothing') wider circumstances and the whole international political situation played an important role in contemplations of further action.

The occupation of Bosnia and Herzegovina in 1878 had a clear influence on changes in the internal political situation of the Cisleithanian part of Austria-Hungary because it affected existing government policy of the constitutionalist German Liberals. The year 1878 also had deeper international consequences for then the Congress of Berlin gave support to Austria-Hungary's occupation and administration of Bosnia and Herzegovina. Up to that time, Czech policy was based on the supposition that the pervasive change of international political relations have a more enduring impact and that they would necessarily affect South-Eastern Europe. Thus in the long run, the Austrian and Czech questions could be activated as open international problems. The Balkans constituted an open question with unpredictable consequences – indeed confirmed in 1914 – but Europe wanted peace for the time being and left its 'solution' for a later time. However, the Congress of Berlin put an end to all speculations regarding possible internationalization of the Czech question and its potential solution within a wide European framework.

The Czech political representatives reacted to these changes in a remarkable way. There was no basic change – the programme for the restoration of Bohemian State Rights was retained – but it was 'shelved' and its realization was put off till a more convenient time in the future. The Czech policy now was to accept the status quo expressed in the willingness to participate in constitutional deliberations and, indeed in a complete turnabout, to back directly the activities of the government. Already in 1878, Czech deputies representing both the Old and the Young Czechs were back in the Diet of Bohemia and, in the autumn of 1879, they entered the Reichsrat in Vienna. There they immediately took part in the formation of a feudal conservative coalition of the so-called 'Iron Ring' on which depended Premier Count Edward Taafe's (1833–1895) government that was in power during 1879–1893.

V

Thus by 1880, Czech policy acquired a distinctly changed character: *the struggle against the Austrian state* was replaced by *the struggle for the Austrian state*. The new activist policy arose from the following premises: the State Rights programme remained the alpha and omega of Czech policy but, because there was no possibility of realization in its maximalist form in the near future, it was put aside temporarily. While the current active policy would utilize existing constitutional conditions, it would not go beyond the limitations in order not to block the road to reach the ultimate goal. The new active policy was to use all existing possibilities and constitutional means to realize even partial concessions. In accordance with this, relevant demands concerned solely with the placing of the Czech and German languages on an equal official footing, especially in the sphere of education, were formulated in four memoranda at the turn of 1879/1880. A number of these demands were fulfilled in the following decade. Prague University was divided in 1882 into two separate, German and Czech, branches (institutions), and several dozens of Czech *gymnasia*, modern secondary schools, industrial training schools, technical schools for a particular trade and other secondary schools were gradually brought under state control or newly founded. Only then the linguistic and cultural endeavours came institutionally into their own and the horizontal and vertical build-up of modern Czech education was completed. Owing to this, illiteracy practically disappeared. At the beginning of the twentieth century more than 96 per cent of Czechs older than six years and similarly 94 per cent of indigenous Germans were literate. These figures greatly exceeded figures for average literacy in the Habsburg monarchy and indicate the relative high general educational and cultural level of the population when modernism arrived at the turn of the century.

The results of active political engagement, even though it was sometimes described derisively as the 'policy of crumbs', indisputably contributed to the growth of Czech self-confidence and brought about changes in the relationship between the Czechs and the Germans in Bohemia. To a certain extent the situation was reversed. If the Czechs had been afraid of Germanization of Bohemia during the previous decades, the Germans now feared Czechization. Over the years both sides had no contact and ignored each other. The placing of the two languages, throughout the Czech Lands, on an equal footing in administrative day-to-day dealing with outside parties was understood on the German side as the frontal Czech line-up. These apprehensions were not unfounded since previously German-educated Czechs would enter the German-speaking milieu and serve as officials more easily than the other way round. From 1886 German deputies refused to participate in the proceedings of the Diet of Bohemia thus imitating the Czech policy of abstention of the 1870s.

But this situation was not to last and the government of Taaffe was interested in its resolution. In January 1890 in Vienna Taaffe started negotiations with the Old Czechs which resulted in a stipulated agreement known as 'punctations' which proved to be a turning point in the history of modern politics at least in two senses.

First, the punctations constituted, in a way, the last 'crumb', an untimely, unsuitable and ill-conceived compromise. Their provisions potentially threatened the territorial integrity of Bohemia by envisaging a separate German-speaking borderland territory and a bilingual interior territory. In itself, the stipulated agreement was not legally binding but was to serve as a basis for proceedings in legislative bodies and, if need be, for the realization of administrative changes via governmental and ministerial decrees respectively. Conducting the negotiations, the Czech representation (still led by the Old Czech Party) behaved like a governmental party, but the majority of the Czech public soon voiced opposition to the proposed partitioning of the Czech Lands. The result was that the Old Czech Party lost its traditional support and failed utterly in the elections to the Reichsrat in 1891. It had to make way for the vigorous Young Czech Party which, with one exception, won all Czech seats in the Imperial Parliament. The policy of the Young Czech Party – later characterized as 'proceeding by stages' or 'positive' – was not linked directly to governmental policy, but it evaluated flexibly the changing situation supporting or opposing the government according to its interests. At the same time, the Young Czech representation placed emphasis on achieving real progress in the executive and jurisdictional sphere, and it did not restrict itself only to activities in the Reichsrat or Diet. Owing to this, the Czech struggle for statehood acquired new and much wider dimensions.

Second, the year 1890 also meant the end of unitary Czech politics, strictly speaking the end of unitary national politics, and the opening of the road to ideological and political pluralism. The era of three decades of 'the leading role of one party' ended, and the political scene acquired a different image and appearance. Initially, the Young Czech Party concentrated all opposition forces and unified different elements, which negated the old. Then the Young Czech Party itself went quickly through a process of disintegration and differentiation when it should have formulated a constructive policy. Under the impact of the emergence of mass political parties and cultural, scientific, artistic and political modernism in the 1890s, also the Czech milieu experienced differentiations and splits along ideological and party political lines. Besides narrow national interests social, professional, *Weltanschauung*, and other aspects were coming to the fore. Besides the Young Czech Party, a relatively strong Czech Agrarian Party, and on the Left the Social Democratic Party, were established before the end of the nineteenth century. From the beginning of the twentieth century the Social Democratic Party was not only the strongest Czech political party, but also belonged to the most powerful socialist parties in Europe. Then, along with these three main parties, ten other parties or party groupings, with their own programmes and parliamentary representations, appeared on the Czech political firmament. The small, but intellectually influential, Realist Party of the Prague University (Czech branch) professor T. G. Masaryk (1850–1937) was among them. Before 1914, owing to its respectable economic base and solid build-up of cultural and educational institutions, Czech society became gradually 'rooted' in Austria and learned to use the existing possibilities of the system.

After 1890, Czech–German relations were subject to constant conflicts and disagreements which, especially in the last three years of the nineteenth century, were turning into a serious inner-political crisis. All attempts to reach an acceptable solution failed and, from the beginning of the century, it was clear that the search for possible solutions was being postponed for another time. The power of tradition, the authority of the dynasty, economic prosperity and relative stability created a special framework of basic certainties, and only intellectual sceptics considered the time of 'order and tidiness' to be a period of 'motionless stagnation'. Europe lived in peace, and it seemed that all questions regarding State Rights, nationalities, social and other problems would be solved rationally and gradually, step by step, without critical shocks of catastrophic dimensions. Modern European civilization presented itself as a world civilization and endeavoured that its values should be accepted on a global scale. Serious conflicts of interests were perhaps thinkable somewhere on the periphery of this civilization. Before 1914 only a few admitted the possibility of a catastrophic break-up in its centre.

VI

It happened after all, and the year 1914 saw the beginning of upheavals with immense consequences not only for Europe but also for the world.

Czech society became totally paralyzed by the war situation. The majority of the Czech population did not share the enthusiasm for war for many reasons, and it adapted more or less passively to realities. In connection with new ambitious plans for the reorganization of Central Europe, hopes for the eventual realization of political independence disappeared, but also the results of three decades of active political engagement were threatened to a large extent. Parliamentary institutions did not function, the political parties stopped most of their activities, and the political press subjected to censorship reflected more or less only official viewpoints. All public, economic, cultural and political life was subordinated to the needs and aims of the war.

Abroad the activities of small groups of Czech émigrés partly substituted for the enforced Czech passivity at home. Among them Masaryk, who represented the Realists in the Viennese Reichsrat, became the leading figure. He assumed the war to be a great conflict between the modern democratic and republican principle and the old aristocratic and monarchistic principle. In this spirit he reformulated, in the summer of 1915, the Czech political programme along decisively maximalist lines. Masaryk took up the original political programme of Palacký and Rieger, he enlarged and modified it to fit the current situation, and he chose active resistance on the side of the Entente instead of passive resistance at home.

For a long time, this programme was only an idea and its realization depended on the result of the war, on the attitude of the victorious parties and on a number of other circumstances. The collapse of Russian tsarism in 1917 and the revolutionary chaos that followed in Russia, influenced pervasively further developments, and also contributed in the end to the fall of the Central European monarchies and their political systems. After 1917, therefore, Czech political activity abroad grew substantially. But, at the same time, the Czech domestic political scene was becoming gradually active and the maximalist political programme was gaining more open followers. By the time of the defeat of the Central Powers in the autumn of 1918, this programme was accepted by all decisive political forces in Czech society.

At the beginning of the war, Czech society found itself in a very complicated situation and in apparent impasse, which could annul the efforts of several generations. At the end of the war new perspectives were being opened for Czech society. They exceeded by far the maximalist State Right programme, which had been formulated fifty years before. The disintegration of Europe and its values was so vehement and so barbarously drastic that it could hardly become the basis of a new stability.

Selected bibliography (excluding texts in Czech)

A. Fuchs, *Geistige Strömungen in Österreich 1867–1918* (Vienna, 1949)

B. M. Garver, *The Young Czech Party 1874–1901 and the Emergence of a Multi-Party System* (New Haven and London, 1978)

D. Good, *The Economic Rise of the Habsburg Empire* (Berkeley, 1984)

M. Hroch, *Social Preconditions of National Revival in Europe A Comparative Analysis of the Social Composition of Patriotic Groups among the Smaller European Nations* (Cambridge, 1985)

W. M. Johnston, *The Austrian Mind* (Berkeley, 1972)

R. A. Kann, *The Multinational Empire* (New York, 1950)

J. Kořalka, *Tschechen im Habsburgerreich und in Europa 1815–1914* (Vienna and Munich, 1991)

J. Křen, *Konfliktgemeinschaft Tschechen und Deutsche in den böhmischen Ländern 1780–1918*
(Munich, 1993)

F. Prinz, *Geschichte Böhmens 1848–1948* (Munich, 1988)

F. Seibt, *Deutschland und die Tschechen*, 2nd edn (Munich, 1993)

G. Stourzh, *Die Gleichberechtigung der Nationalitäten in der Verfassung und Verwaltung Österreichs 1848–1918* (Vienna, 1985)

O. Urban, *Die tschechische Gesellschaft 1848–1918*, 2 vols. (Vienna-Cologne-Weimar,
1994)

A. Wandruszka and P. Urbanitsch (eds.), *Die Habsburgermonarchie*, 6 vols. (Vienna,
1973–1993)

11

The university professors and students in
nineteenth-century Bohemia

JAN HAVRÁNEK

When the Austrian governor of Bohemia, Philipp Weber von Ebenhof, came into conflict with the majority of the German professors at Prague University in 1879, he ironically referred in his report to Vienna to 'Godlike German Professors' (*Gottesähnlichkeit der deutschen Professoren*).[1] Thus for those who came to Prague from Germany we can find both respect and disdain of the high bureaucrat who was not accustomed to having problems with his subordinates, let alone open opposition to his opinion.

The same attitude of society to the *ordinarii* (full university professors) is expressed in the title of Fritz Ringer's well-known book about the end of the German 'Mandarins'.[2] It seems to be fully justified that in the forty-three peaceful years between 1871 and 1914 such expressions were used to characterize the social prestige of the *ordinarii* in Central Europe. In this period their social status was higher than ever before or after. Their prestige was based on two foundations: their academic results and their key role in examining all future civil servants. This was especially true in the field of medicine. During the last pre-war decades the attitude of the public toward the medical sciences changed from scepticism to trust, sometimes even overconfidence. The professors of the faculties of medicine were admired as saviours, and their fees were commensurate with public confidence in their omnipotence. Not by accident, the money lent to Emil Škoda by his uncle, Viennese professor of medicine Josef Škoda, opened the way for him to establish the famous factory in Plzeň. The professors of law faculties were consulted by the state legislatures as well as by private entrepreneurs. What is more, every future lawyer had to come to them as his examiners; nobody could be sure about his success. Marie Červinková-Riegrová, the daughter of the Czech political leader František Ladislav Rieger

(1818–1903), mentioned in her diary that her brother Bohuš, an excellent lawyer and later university professor, was very nervous on the eve of his examination by the professors who were political adversaries of his father, stating that the professor can fail every student.[3]

The high status of professors was typical for the second half of the nineteenth century, even though some features of it existed even earlier – but not before 1810 and Wilhelm von Humboldt's great initiative in Berlin. In the eighteenth century, research (*Forschung*) and teaching (*Lehre*) were rather distinct activities. Research was pursued more successfully in Learned Societies and Academies where the prevailing majority of members were amateur investigators and not university teachers. In Bohemia among them were influential noblemen who were researching in their leisure time and achieved important results such as Ignaz von Born (1742–1791) and the brothers Counts Joachim Sternberg (1755–1808) and Kaspar Sternberg (1761–1838). However, by the 1850s, even rich amateurs could hardly afford the costly apparatus and instruments on which scientific experimentation more and more depended.

By and large there existed three courses of action: (1) experts could accept payment and investments from those who needed the results of scientific research, namely entrepreneurs for their factories, or the state for military purposes; (2) the professionalisation of academies; or (3) the reorientation of the existing universities toward research. Whereas the first alternative was successful in technology and the second in organizing geographic expeditions, the third brough important progress not only in philosophy and the humanities, but also in physics, mathematics, chemistry and other sciences as well. For the purpose of reorientation the model of the Central European universities was adaptable. This was evident from the time of university modernization at Halle and Göttingen in the eighteenth century. In spite of these examples the spirit of innovation proceeded slowly even in German universities. The Catholic establishments were especially conservative.

Prague University was located in two buildings at the time – in the Carolinum and in the Clementinum. The faculties of law and medicine resided in the Carolinum where the professors were laymen. The faculties of philosophy and theology, which were in the hands of the Jesuits up to 1773, were in the Clementinum. 'Two faculties in Clementinum; two in Carolinum. The first ones destroy man's soul; the second ones his body.' Thus in one of his famous epigrams the renowned publicist Karl Havlíček (1820–1856) expressed his opinion about the difference between them. As for the Clementinum, even when Empress Maria Theresa tried to enforce some moderation of the bigotry in education through State Directors of Studies in all faculties, progress was very slow. The only important scientist in the philosophical faculty, the Jesuit mathematician and physicist Josef Stepling (1716–1778), who became the State Director, could not change the conservative tradition of the faculty, which was oriented toward the education of militant Catholic clergy. Even experiments on the phenomena of electricity were arranged as typical church ceremonies.

Not much progress was made in the medical faculty either. The faculty was an organisation incorporating all the doctors practising in Bohemia, and fulfilled the roles of both today's Ministry of Health and the professional representation of doctors. As a teaching institution, it was not too important. Even in the 1820s the number of students in one class was, as a rule, not much higher than ten. Only in the faculty of law did some improvement take place. The reforms, famous under the name of the Superintendent of the University Peter Theodor Birelli, were thoroughly analysed by Karel Kučera.[4]

In the last decades of the eighteenth century, after the dissolution of the Jesuit order (1773), when the Clementinum faculties became state establishments, the process of advancing the authority of Enlightened absolutism reached its most important goal. In 1784 a new syllabus was introduced into all the faculties, and German replaced Latin as the language of instruction. Professors were no longer obliged to take an oath professing their faith, their obedience to the Holy See, and their belief in the immaculate conception of Virgin Mary. Nevertheless their social prestige was not too high; it was stated in the law that all state officials who reached the rank of Royal and Imperial Councillor – and practically all of those who owned University diplomas reached this rank later in their careers – preceded University professors.[5] Even more illustrative was the secondary place assigned to the Rector and the four faculty Deans of the University of Vienna at the Corpus Christi ceremony.[6] The Rector and Deans were below the first in rank, not only in the Corpus Christi processions, but in the daily life of the realm as a whole.

Changes in the social status of university professors

The social position of the university professors improved during the nineteenth century both in their classification among the state officials and in the amount of their salaries, but the rise of their social prestige was even more conspicuous. By 1900 *ordinarii* in the Austro-Hungarian monarchy belonged to the VIth rank class, that is, to the same class as the heads of ministerial departments (*Sektionsräthe*) who had the yearly income of 3,200–4,000 florins.[7] The colonels belonged to the same class as well, but their yearly income was only 3,000 florins.[8] The fact that army officers with

Table 11.1. *The male population of Bohemia, Moravia and Austrian Silesia*
(1781–1850/51)

Year of Census	Clergy	Nobility	Officials and *Honoratiores*	Burghers, Craftsmen and Artists	Peasants	Male Population Over 18	Total Male Population
1781	10,255	2,401	5,697	125,758	211,135	1,257,581	1,935,112
1790	8,568	2,502	6,008	118,627	213,703	1,303,276	2,108,368
1800	6,715	2,487	6,294	121,157	213,123	1,254,406	2,176,591
1810	6,374	2,920	10,032	111,268	216,232	1,200,755	2,238,968
1820	6,275	3,124	14,902	96,857	217,469	1,391,149	2,429,497
1831	6,466	3,392	13,040	57,580	206,600	1,593,176	2,844,191
1843	6,730	3,429	14,781	56,208	205,440	1,819,149	3,101,933
1850/51	6,706	3,314	15,332	52,379	200,934	1,810,837	3,156,049

The statistics above include only the Christian population for 1781–1800. After 1810 the Jewish population is also included.

Source: Česká statistika 1978 [Czech statistics], vol. 13, 'Obyvatelstvo českých zemí v letech 1754–1918' [The population of the Czech Lands in the years 1754–1918], Part I 1754–1865, pp. 61–3; F. Dvořáček, *Soupisy obyvatelstva v Čechách, na Moravě a ve Slezsku v letech 1754–1921* [Censuses of population in Bohemia, Moravia and Silesia in the years 1754–1921] (Prague, 1926), pp. 2, 4, 8–11, 22–5.

such a high rank had a lower income than civil servants is surprising for those who live in the twentieth century, but in the nineteenth these were still mostly noblemen, who were owners of estates which brought them incomes of much more importance than their salaries. On the other hand, of course, the financial needs of officers in the Austrian army at the time were not small. They were ranked two classes higher than District Captains (*Bezirkshauptmänner*), the chief representatives of the state in the administrative districts. Their income and status in 1900 were relatively and absolutely much higher than in the last decades of the eighteenth century.

Income was only one side of the social advancement of the professors. The other, more important part was their position among the 'worthies' (*honoratiores*), largely intellectuals of non-noble origin whose legal position was the same as that of the burghers. One expression of their position was that they obtained the right to vote during the Revolution of 1848 and retained it even after its setback.[9] The professors were not only *honoratiores* but as examiners they also opened or closed the doors for their students to become the privileged ones among the state's students. Passing the state examinations included the qualification for all state officials; while passing the *rigorosum* (doctoral examination) laid the foundation for the career of doctors and lawyers.

Table 11.2. *The percentage of clergy, nobility and 'officials and honoratiores' among the adult male population (1781–1850/51)*

Year of census	Clergy	Nobility	Officials and *honoratiores*
1781	0.82	0.19	0.45
1790	0.66	0.19	0.45
1800	0.45	0.20	0.50
1810	0.53	0.24	0.84
1820	0.45	0.22	1.07
1831	0.40	0.21	0.82
1843	0.37	0.19	0.81
1850/51	0.37	0.18	0.85

Source: Based on table 11.1.

The social importance of those who were obliged to complete their university studies was increasing during the nineteenth century. At the same time, university graduates of a different type came to the fore than had formerly entered into key positions in public affairs. The number of clergymen went down. The dissolution of many monasteries by Joseph II (1780–1790) diminished their number by one third and, at the same time, replaced the monk (who could be an active scholar) with the parish priest with pastoral as well as state servant's duties. The lawyer in state service, or local government service, and the independent solicitor, had more money and more influence than the parish priest, and in the second half of the nineteenth century the importance of doctors in towns grew; later *gymnasium* professors (secondary school teachers) became respected citizens too. The university-educated civil servant was replacing the clergyman.

For the Czech Lands we have data about the distribution of educated people and other social groups from 1762 up to the middle of the nineteenth century (Tables 11.1 and 11.2). For comparison the data of the 1762 census could be employed, even though they are useful only within certain limits.[10] In 1762, 9.234 clergymen were registered (3,550 priests and 5,684 monks) against 2,408 noblemen, and 6,521 officials. The total male Christian population was 1,424,311. In other words: among adult men 1.00 per cent were clergymen, 0.26 per cent noblemen and 0.70 per cent officials. We can conclude therefore that the proportion of clergymen among the population declined between 1762 and 1851 to one third. In the first thirty years of this period – especially during the decade of Joseph's II reforms and his closing of many monasteries – there was a decline of 34 points. In the following

Table 11.3. *Distribution of Prague Charles-Ferdinand University students according to faculties (1784–1913)*

Year	Branch	Theology Number	%	Law Number	%	Medicine Number	%	Philosophy Number	%
1784		596	70	174	21	73	9		
1850		186	14	795	61	328	25		
1890	Czech	197	8	968	40	1095	45	163	7
	German	36	3	525	43	516	43	131	11
1913	Czech	144	4	1754	47	1112	30	684	19
	German	100	5	933	46	726	35	289	14

Since 1882 Charles-Ferdinand University was divided into two separate, Czech and German, branches (institutions).

Source: Jaroš and Job, *Rozvoj* (see note 12), pp. 100–1 (for 1784 and 1850); J. Havránek, 'Počátky a kořeny pokrokového hnuté studentského na počátku devadesátých let 19. století' [The beginnings and roots of the student progressive movement at the beginning of the 1890s], *Acta Universitatis Carolinae-Historia Universitatis Carolinae Pragensis*, 2, 1 (1961), 5–33; J. Havránek, 'Soziale Herkunft, sozialer Rang und Berufsperspektiven der Intelligenz vor 1914 – Böhmen, Galizien, Ungarn und die Slowakei im Vergleich' [*Prepared for publication, in 1988, as part of the Bielefeld University research project Bürgertum, Bürgerlichkeit und bürgerliche Gesellschaft. Das 19. Jahrhundert im europäischen Vergleich*]; this article remained in manuscript. Up to 1850 the philosophical faculty was not a full but a preliminary faculty preparing students for university.

sixty years from 1800 on, the number of clergymen was also stable. In a society with a 50 per cent increase in population, this meant that there was a slow decline of the proportion of clergymen within the society. The proportion of adult noblemen increased a little during the Napoleonic wars, and then a moderate relative decline can be noticed. Compared with neighbouring countries, such as Poland and Hungary, where the nobility accounted for about 5 per cent of population, its percentage was very low.

When we ignore the different data from 1762 and 1820, so different because of instructions given to the statisticians, we may observe a stable increase of officials and *honoratiores* (*honoratiores* were characterized as 'army officers on a pension, doctors, professors and teachers'). In 1850 priests were added to this category, members of whom were entitled to vote in the local elections as electors in the second of three curias. In the 1890s Ings. (Ing. – abbreviation for 'Ingenieur'), that is, the graduates of Technical High Schools (in effect Technical Universities), were included in this category.[11] It seems that the officials formed the overwhelming majority within the category 'officials and *honoratiores*'. The number of men registered as *honoratiores*

Table 11.4. *Gymnasium pupils in the Czech Lands*
(1816–1910)

Year	Number	Percentage
1816	7.267	0.62
1860	9.358	0.73
1900	23.893	1.64
1910	28.317	2.04

Source: Jaroš and Job, *Rozvoj*, pp. 25–8; *Atlas obyvatelstva ČSSR*
[Population atlas of the Czechoslovak Socialist Republic]
(Prague, 1962), p. 35.

in 1781 was only half as large as the number of clergymen. In the 1830s, however, it was twice as large.

In table 11.3 this laicisation of the intellectual strata in Bohemia can be illustrated by comparing the number of students in the faculty of theology of Prague University, on the one hand, with the number enrolled in the faculties of law and medicine, on the other. In 1784, 596 students were enrolled at the faculty of theology, 174 at the faculty of law, and 73 at the faculty of medicine. In 1789, there were 164 students of theology, 197 of law, and 58 of medicine. In 1850/51, 186 students studied theology, 795 law, and 328 medicine.[12] The interest of students in Catholic theology (Catholics constituted 96 per cent of inhabitants of Bohemia in 1900) can be illustrated by comparing the student membership of the three (later four) full faculties with the entire student body.

The differences between 1784 and 1850 are striking. The proportion of clergymen diminished five times whereas that of lawyers increased nearly three times. In the following forty years the proportion of students of medicine increased but, in 1913, students of law were more numerous by 46 per cent. After 1850, on attaining the status of a full university faculty, the faculty of philosophy attracted a growing number of students. It trained them to become *gymnasium* (secondary school) teachers preparing pupils for university, and also to enter cultural professions. After 1900, the proportion of female students at this faculty rose. The results of the analysis of Prague data are identical with those reached by Konrad Jarausch in a publication dealing with the transformation of higher learning in several countries between 1860 and 1930.[13]

The modernization of society brought more professional opportunities for people with university diplomas during the nineteenth century, but the employment situation was not always propitious. After years of expanding recruitment came years when young graduates hardly found jobs available unless they looked for openings abroad. In Prague the graduates of the Technical High School in the 1880s faced such problems. Young doctors and *gymnasium* teachers saw their future in dark colours on the eve of the first World War.

The interest in university careers can be determined by the number of pupils, in the *gymnasiums*. The training in these secondary schools was demanding, especially in Latin. The pupils who passed ('matriculated') were well prepared for university studies, and usually about two thirds of them actually enrolled in an university. It is useful to compare not only the absolute number of *gymnasium* pupils (which are not fully comparable because up to the reforms of 1850 those schools had six classes and after then eight), but also the proportion of students with respect to their cohorts.

The increase in the number of pupils was related to the more intensive efforts of recruitment, filling the *gymnasiums* not only with the sons of teachers and officials along with the sons of the town bourgeoisie, but later also with children from poorer families in the towns where *gymnasiums* were situated, and with second-born sons of peasants. This development influences the social structure of the university student bodies. At the Czech Prague University in 1913, the percentage of sons of those working manually (peasants, cottagers, craftsmen, servants and workers) was rather high – 77 per cent at the faculty of theology, 40 per cent at the faculty of law, 35 per cent at the faculty of medicine, and 41 per cent at the faculty of philosophy.[14] Moreover, one half of them came to Prague from Czech villages. It must be mentioned that living in Prague was relatively cheap for them compared with most German university towns. Those especially who came from villages regularly obtained food from their parents and this was one of the reasons why so many sons of peasants could afford to study in Prague.

Prestige issues

The higher respect for the university diploma in law or medicine in Central Europe resulted in an increase in the social prestige of those who taught legal and medical subjects – university professors. They were desirable candidates not only for seats in the Bohemian and Moravian Diets and the Lower and Upper Houses of the Austrian Parliament (Reichstat) but also for marriages with daughters from well-placed families. In the first decade of the twentieth century, when the first female students came to the lecture halls, some young university teachers were successful in this respect.

Thus the noted musicologist, historian and cultural politician Zdeněk

Nejedlý (1878–1962) married Marie Brichtová, a daughter of one of the established Czech entrepreneurial families. Those teachers who for some reason did not succeed in this way were occasionally ungracious with the young ladies in their lectures. The eminent Czech historian Josef Pekař (1870–1937) remarked once that 'female students wait in the University Library to be greeted by him, a thirty year-old professor, first and formost as young ladies and not as students'!

The importance of the university teaching staff grew after the abolition of the traditional model of a university – the University as the body corporate of doctors. In the list of dignitaries in the Annuals (*Schematismus*) of the Kingdom of Bohemia up to 1850, the university was embodied in the faculties of doctors, who were admitted to these corporations after graduation. These guilds of doctors of theology, law, medicine and philosophy elected the Deans and the Rector of the university. By the reforms of Leo Thun, during 1849–1850, their role in the life of the university was radically diminished in favour of the professorial staffs, and after 1873 they ceased to exist.

The professorial staffs at the faculties and the academic senates (elected by the staffs) became the steering bodies of the universities in 1849. Thus after a forty years' delay the Habsburg monarchy realized Humboldt's idea of the university as an autonomous body of academics oriented to research and teaching. The professor's qualification was primarily judged by his academic (scholarly) activity and demonstrated by published works.

Changes in qualification and coherence

The Ministry of Education in Vienna, established in the spring of 1848, officially outlined these parameters in a decree released on 11 December 1848. The decree set down the scholarly qualification as the first and the ability to teach as the second prerequisite for a professorial appointment.[15] It regulated not only the appointment of university professors, but also of teachers in *gymnasiums* and other schools of the same level.[16]

The decree of 11 December 1848 stipulated the terms of 'habilitation' involving the submission of published scholarly work accessible to specialists for criticism, a colloquium with a commission composed of professors, and the delivery of a model lecture to the faculty staff. It led to a 'docentship' required from those who were aspiring to a university professorship. This process paved the way for real scholarly competition, and thus for a significant improvement of the academic level of universities. In principle for every chair – especially for an important chair – it was possible to choose the best among several persons seeking the job. The faculty was obliged to propose to the Minister of Education three best-qualified candidates for the vacant chair. The Minister of Education, however, was not obliged to respect the wish of the faculty, expressed in its proposal by the order of preference of the three possible candidates. The selection of a professor depended on many things; nevertheless, successful competition in the sciences became an important element in obtaining an appointment and positively contributed to the advancement of sciences. The competition was not limited by state borders – only knowledge of the language of instruction was prescribed. Not all universities had the same prestige or the same level of income. In the income of the professor of a small university the salary prevailed. In larger universities fees and taxes for examinations were for some professors more important. In the provincial capitals of the Habsburg monarchy salaries were simplified by consultants' fees. When this was coupled with differences of cultural and social life in various university towns, it is easy to understand the epigrammatic characterization of the Austrian professor's career: 'Sentenced to Czernowitz, pardoned to Graz, promoted to Vienna'.

The professoriate, especially in smaller university towns, formed a group providing mutual social contacts, friendships, aversions, and sometimes animosities. Not all professors appreciated the accepted customs and proprieties. When in 1911 Albert Einstein became professor at the Prague German University, he found it very boring when he had to introduce himself to the families of all his faculty colleagues. Of course, the mutual relations were not always idyllic, and sometimes the teaching personnel was divided into hostile groups. The Czech philosophical faculty, in the 1880s, split over the authenticity of presumed early medieval Czech poetical works known as the Manuscripts of Králové Dvůr and Zelená Hora. The older generation of Czech professors believed in it whereas younger scholars – the philologist Jan Gebauer (1838–1907), the historian Jaroslav Goll (1846–1929), the philosopher Tomáš Garrigue Masaryk (1850–1937) – put forward arguments proving that the manuscript material was forged. The dispute was conducted in a very temperamental and tenacious way, including personal insults. Under such conditions it was impossible for members of the staff not to be involved in the controversy. Moreover, professional rivalry often led to deadly enmities. With some abuse of Latin grammar, this was expressed in the sentence: *Homo homini lupus, femina feminae lupior, professor professori lupissimus.*

It has to be added that the community of professors had as a feature not only mutual enemies, but also a strong sense of solidarity and common defence against the interference of non-academic bodies in the life of the university.

Reasons for changes in status and function

What underlined the sudden increase in social and moral prestige of university professors in the second half of the nineteenth century? The answer to this question in part is given by the fact that in their youth they had the advantage of obtaining conditions for independent research work, including good access to literature, relatively satisfactory laboratory equipment, and qualified technicians as assistants. Early in their careers they became professors with a stable good income, without the danger of being dismissed. One half of the professors of the medical faculty in Vienna, in its golden era at the end of the nineteenth century, attained their status before they were thirty years old. The same situation prevailed at the Prague Czech philosophical faculty before 1912. Most of its professors 'habilitated' before they were thirty, some even before they were twenty-five, such as the orientalist Rudolf Dvořák and the botanist Karel Domin. Their appointments came for nearly all of them before they were thirty-five, for some before they were thirty (Dvořák, Nejedlý, the philologist Josef Král).

The academic freedom to research and publish was fully respected. A university chair was even used for making political statements, which was tolerated by the state, and attempts to restrain this liberty were as a rule resisted by the academic community as a whole.

Universities in the Habsburg monarchy, where the national language became the language of instruction, won this position in the second half of the nineteenth century. There were five such institutions: the Magyar University of Budapest, the Polish Universities of Cracow and Lwów – these three changed the language of instruction in the sixties; the Croatian University of Zagreb was founded in 1875, and the Czech branch of Prague University became independent in 1882. These universities acquired an extremely high prestige in their national societies, and university professors were accepted as political representatives of their respective nations. It is not surprising that five out of twelve Czechs who became ministers in Austrian cabinets were university professors. In 1918 the professor of medical chemistry at the Czech University, the Ukrainian Ivan Horbaczevski, became the first Minister of Health in Vienna when the last Emperor Charles wished to show good will to his Ukrainian subjects in a desperate effort to preserve the multinational Habsburg monarchy.

Since each nation had only one or two universities, there was less academic competition within one national intelligentsia, although this competition did take extremely sharp forms from time to time when two scholars were fighting for the only accessible chair. In the national context, universities replaced older centres of research (museums, Learned Societies) during the second half of the century as the most authoritative learned corporations. Gradually the university professors acquired the decisive voice in the ruling bodies of the older corporations, and transformed them into organizations for the distribution of scholarships, and subsidies for the publication of scientific books and journals.

If we look for the reasons behind the rise of prestige of the universities, it may be said: (1) they controlled the training of high state officials and free professions, social groups that occupied key positions in public and political life; (2) they became centres of scientific research at a time when the usefulness of science for progress in production and improvement of quality in human life became readily apparent; (3) the secure and relatively independent position of the university professors enabled them to win influence among the students and intellectuals, and therefore to play an active role in politics.

Concluding remarks

At the beginning of the twentieth century, the model of the *Forschung und Lehre* university was dominant, and the prestige of the 'mandarins' was reaching its peak. The professors possessed moral authority among students, and their pronouncements were also accepted as authoritative statements in public affairs by higher state authorities. Nevertheless, signs of crisis of the model of the *Forschung und Lehre* university were becoming apparent. By and large, it was not wealthy enough to provide adequate research facilities for the sciences which needed expensive and specialized equipment. As to humanities and social sciences, many professors were dutifully loyal to the state. They found this obligation more important than any other, and demanded from their students the exact reproduction of the lectures rather than a firm understanding of the underlying problems. This was typical especially for classical philology, assigned a vast role at the *gymnasiums*. The faculties of law followed the instruction given by Emperor Franz I in the 1820s in Ljubljana during a speech to the professors of a local lyceum: 'I do not need scholars, I need obedient state officials.'[17] Nevertheless, the privileged position of the university professor gave those, who were really independent individuals, the opportunity to express their opinions freely and to publicise them broadly. Some were strong personalities who influenced public opinion by their philosophical, moral, aesthetic and political ideas – this was the case of T. G. Masaryk who in 1882 joined the Czech branch of Prague University, as *extraordinarius* professor of philosophy, when it divided linguistically. The university faculties that developed without important external interference and with political ambitions of their professors were the medical faculties – they remained relatively faithful to both research and teaching.

Notes

1 J. Havránek, 'Česká univerzita v jednání rakouských úřadů do roku 1881' [The Czech University in official Austrian acts up to 1881], *Acta Universitatis Carolinae-Historia Universitatis Carolinae Pragensis*, 82, 1 (1982), 48.

2 F. Ringer, *The Decline of the German Mandarins the German Academic Community 1890–1933* (Cambridge, MA, 1969).

3 Havránek, 'Česká univerzita', p. 37.

4 K. Kučera, 'Rannĕosvícenský pokus o reformu pražské university' [An attempt to reform Prague University in the Early Enlightenment], *Acta Universitatis Carolinae-Historia Universitatis Carolinae Pragensis*, 4, 2 (1963), 6–86.

5 J. Kropatschek, *Oestreichs Staatsverfassung* (Vienna, 1794), I, p. 556.

6 Cf. 'Der Rektor der Wiener Universität hat mit den vier Dekanen jedesmal beim Fronleichnamsumgange . . . stets den Rang auf der rechten Seite des Baldachins ausser der Treppe zu nehmen.' *Ibid.* p. 555.

7 A. L. Hickman, *Geographisch-statistischer Taschen-Atlas von Oesterreich-Ungarn* (Vienna and Leipzig, 1900), p. 75.

8 *Ibid.*, p. 71.

9 A Wandruszka (ed.), *Die Habsburgermonarchie 1848–1918*. Vol. II: *Verwaltung und Rechtswesen* (Vienna, 1975), p. 284.

10 There are no exact data at our disposal for the number of men aged eighteen and above. The author established the number by comparison with the data of 1781. The category of officials (*honoratiores* were not mentioned) seems to be a little broader than in 1781 because officials employed by towns and feudal authorities (*städtische und Obrigkeitsbeamte*) are included in this category. See Dvořáček, *Soupisy obyvatelstva*, pp. 2 and 4.

11 Wandruszka (ed.), *Die Habsburgermonarchie*, II, p. 284.

12 K. Jaroš and J. Job, *Rozvoj československého školství v číslech* [The development of Czechoslovak education in numbers] (Prague, 1961), pp. 100–1. The increase in the number of students of law and medicine does not need any commentary. The extreme decline in theology students in the 1780s can be partly explained by the great educational reforms in that decade. For a full comparison for 1850/51, the number of students at the seminaries of Litomĕřice, Hradec Králové and České Budĕjovice bishoprics would be needed even though the numbers there were usually lower than at the faculty of theology in Prague.

13 K. H. Jarausch (ed.), *The Transformation of Higher Learning Expansion, Diversification, Social Opening and Professionalisation in England, Germany, Russia and the United States* (Stuttgart, 1983).

14 Havránek, 'Soziale Herkunft', p. 14.
15 Cf.

> 1. Der Vorschlag zur Wiederbesetzung einer Lehrstelle geht von dem Lehrkörper der Lehranstalt aus, an welcher das Amt erledigt ist, und ist durch das Landespräsidium an das Ministerium zu erstatten. Es ist jedesmal eine Terne vorzulegen. Nur solche Personen können in Vorschlag gebracht werden, für deren wissenschaftliche Befähigung wissenschaftliche Arbeiten, gedruckte oder geschriebene, vorliegen, und deren sonstige Lehrfähigkeit entweder durch wirkliches Lehren oder wenigstens durch eine Probevorlesung bewährt ist. Sie können übrigens wirkliche, in- und ausländische Lehrer und Professoren oder Privatdozenten sein, oder Privatgelehrte, welche noch nicht wirklich gelehrt haben.

Quoted from 'Erlass des Ministeriums für Kultur und Unterricht vom 11. Dezember 1848' in O. Placht and F. Havelka, *Předpisy pro vysoké školy Republiky Československé* [University regulations of the Czechoslovak Republic] (Prague, 1932), pp. 1033–34.

16 Cf. 'Normierung des Verfahrens bei Wiederbesetzung erledigter Lehrkanzeln an Universitäten, Lyzeen, Gymnasien, technischen Instituten und Realschulen'. *Ibid.*, p. 1033.
17 F. Kavka *et al.*, *Stručné dějiny Karlovy University* [A concise history of Charles University] (Prague, 1964), p. 169.

12

Science in a bilingual country

IRENA SEIDLEROVÁ

I

In the preceding chapters of the present volume, the main aspects of the history of Czech society and the formation of the modern Czech nation and its culture up to 1918 have been dealt with. It was in this period that the Czech Lands were gradually finding their place in the world development of science.

Here the nineteenth century saw the specialization and institutionalization in particular branches of science and the creation of criteria for deciding what can be considered original scientific work. It was in the course of the nineteenth century that the notion of science was separated from that of learning and education. Naturally the criteria of originality developed historically.[1] No activity in the field of science and education in the Czech Lands, whatever the historical circumstances and the social function it fulfilled, can avoid being assessed also by these criteria.

We will devote our essay to some specific features exhibited by the development of science in the Czech Lands, where scientific production existed in parallel: in Czech (the language of a small nation) and in German. At the same time, German was (especially in the second half of the nineteenth century) practically the leading language of international science. Even if our interest will be concentrated primarily on the conditions for original scientific work, we cannot avoid dealing with aspects of the organization of scientific life and the formation of corresponding institutions, above all universities. Indeed, it was their existence that offered the only possibilities for scientific work. There were no private scholars in the country, neither did there exist in the nineteenth century any institutions whose single task would be scientific research. Our reflections relate primarily to the situation in the exact sciences and some more theoretical fields of technical sciences, because in these domains the originality of research was already scrutinized in the last century in the most consistent manner. Moreover, their content was to a much lesser degree affected by extra-scientific aspects, for instance political, national and other similar factors. Biological and geological sciences, being connected far into the nineteenth century to a large extent with scientific surveys of the home country, were much less independent of these factors, and the humanities were a different thing altogether. Not only history but even some branches of philology were developed as an integral part of the ideology of national revival or, as the case may be, part of German reaction to this ideology.

II

The transition from Latin as the universal scholarly language to vernacular languages took place in various countries at different periods. Its character was essentially democratizing, being connected with the fact that wider circles, often lacking the corresponding classical education, were becoming consumers of the results of science (as the period understood it) and technology. In the Czech Lands the passage, from Latin as the teaching language of secondary schools and universities to German, was considerably accelerated by the political, centralizing pressure of the absolutist government under Joseph II. The change was ordered in 1784 and led to a number of complications. Although there was a rich tradition of literature and some professional specialist literature in German available educated people, who came from the lower classes and had from childhood been educated in Latin, used German at a rather low level. Their way of using the language made the Czech-speaking background of many of them apparent. Even numerous members of the nobility, albeit for different reasons, had a poor knowledge of German.[2] This was why the realization of the above-mentioned Josephine reform took more time. The teaching language, of course, changed but basic university textbooks for the exact sciences written in German began to appear only in the second decade of the nineteenth century. In the second half of the 1820s, it was still possible in Prague to assign a Latin book as an obligatory university textbook.[3] The situation was influenced also by the fact that Latin continued to be the university language till mid-century not only in several German states but also in Hungary. To get a more complete picture let us mention the then newly revised all-Austrian competition rules for university teachers' appointments; the examination included a lecture, which was assessed partly from the viewpoint of the use of language. Archival sources bear witness that some applicants, especially in technical sciences, were reproved for using nonliterary, 'common' language, and even frequent Czechisms.[4]

The Enlightenment's stress on science led to the foundation of a number of institutions[5] of which the Royal Bohemian Society of Sciences (officially founded in 1784) was of the greatest importance for science.[6] Unlike the analogous 'small academies' that were emerging in the eighteenth century in other countries, it accepted more readily domestic stimuli – the concern of Enlightened Absolutism for matters relevant to practice, as well as the concentration on the 'glorious past' of the homeland motivated by territorial patriotism.[7] The need to adopt Czech as a professional and scientific language was not at that point strongly felt. Of course, this does not mean that occasionally Czech was not used quite pragmatically both in various official educational publications for the general public (e.g. on the cultivation of clover) and at universities when lecturing on pastoral theology or midwifery.[8] A quintessence of the best ideas which the eighteenth century produced regarding science in the Czech Lands can be found in a remarkable lecture by Ch. C. André (1753–1837) in 1806, in which the writer on agricultural and scientific matters, residing in Brno, outlined the programme for the then newly constituted Moravian Society for Agriculture and Science.[9] André called not only for research in the history and natural history of Moravia, but also for the universal dissemination of scientific and technical information, and for the development of indigenous basic and applied research. However, the actual situation of the Austrian monarchy at the beginning of the nineteenth century did not allow the fulfilment of these comprehensive demands.

III

For mathematical and physical sciences the first three decades of the nineteenth century represented a period of substantial progress. None the less, the volume of research was still small – a survey of original results could be put together in a slender booklet; in turn the world's leading journals reprinted the most important papers. In this period natural history was still predominantly descriptive, its content was generally better comprehended, and the boundary between scientific work and amateur collecting was less distinct. The future technical sciences, including chemical technology, were then just an extensive conglomerate of heterogeneous facts. A typical feature of much technical literature was the contrariety of information: a report on an important discovery just next to a handicraft instruction of no significance.

Given the backward general situation of the country, these trends of international science experience considerable modifications. Here we have to point out that in the early decades of the nineteenth century the Lands of the Crown of Bohemia do not represent any specific territory in relation to the problems of science and education. If it is all possible to speak about a certain homogenous enclave in the Habsburg monarchy at that time, it was rather Bohemia together with Lower Austria.

The domestic society, in initiating the process of technical development, was naturally deeply interested in improving the level of education, in particular in technology. However, its approach was narrowly utilitarian: the need was for skilled technicians and state bureaucrats, not for scientists. The main effort was to supply information. Therefore the first Austrian journals, technical as well as scientific, set themselves almost exclusively tasks of a reviewing character, although from the very beginning they did not shut themselves off from attempts at original research.[10] Even more apparent is this tendency in the Prague journal of the Industrial Association, established in 1833, in order to support domestic entrepreneurship.[11] This educational activity was taking place in Bohemia and Moravia in the period when broad strata of the Czech-speaking population began to enter production. It was necessary (taking into account the absence of any Czech universities) to provide basic education for them on a very popular level. Therefore, technical literature written in Czech was quite elementary. Also Czech handbooks of physics, astronomy and chemistry usually were only paraphrases of the corresponding German works, and their authors just tried to develop Czech special terminology.[12] Some natural scientists around the philologist Josef Jungmann (1773–1847) were dissatisfied with this merely mediatory role and, from the 1820s onwards, made attempts at original scientific work in Czech language, primarily oriented to biological problems.[13] However, the possibilities for publication were scarce. After several years, the Bohemian Museum (*České Museum*) (founded 1818) was forced to stop publishing both its Czech and German periodicals (which were intended to have a strictly scientific content) due to the lack of both funds and subscribers.[14] The Journal of the Bohemian Museum (*Časopis Českého Museum*), published in Czech from 1831, was again more or less a popularizing periodical, and natural sciences did not play a major role in it.[15] Four volumes of the educational journal *Krok* chose relatively advanced literature for translating and reviewing, including physics, astronomy and chemistry.[16] None the less, their main contribution was the development of Czech terminology.

Thus in the late thirties the foundations for specialist terminology in the Czech language were laid; however, the more advanced scholarly literature written in Czech did not have a wider circle of consumers. At that time, a Czech-speaking scientific or technical community had not yet been in existence, and actually many tendencies in society hampered its formation in a considerable measure. For example, the possibility of working in research in mathematics or physics was in practice linked with a post as a teacher at an institution of higher learning. However, these posts were filled by competition covering the whole of Austria. Here up to 1848, available posts were far fewer than the number of applicants while whole groups of candidates for professorships at universities, polytechnics and secondary schools of various types (*Realschule*, *Lyzeum*) were coming forward. They then applied for any post from Gorizia to Lemberg, provided its orientation was just remotely relevant to their learning. The number of unsuccessful attempts quite frequently exceeded ten. It is understandable that for these people, coming from all over the Habsburg monarchy, German represented a certain link, and their ties to their original background were in most cases quite loose. Neither was the relatively weak industrial sector able to absorb the rapidly increasing number of graduates of the polytechnics in Prague and Vienna, and therefore a large portion of them were entering the civil service. These circumstances created already at that time a type of Austrian 'state technician' (later especially a railway engineer) who in the course of his life worked in a number of lands of the Habsburg monarchy, and whose goal in life was to finish his career in Vienna. These specialists again were naturally oriented to German. Altogether we can say that the national polarization among educated people in the first half of the nineteenth century was probably not as common as the nationalistically tinged literature of the later period would suggest. The diaries of J. Th. Held document the fact that in pre-March Prague of 1848 a distinguished physician totally untouched by the national problem could live an intensive social life.[17] It seems that some forms of patriotism were not necessarily tightly bound in with the reactionary interests of the nobility, and the naturally neutral notion *böhmisch* was in certain strata of society considered meaningful for a relatively long time.

IV

The 1840s represent a certain turning point in world science, especially in the exact sciences. The scientific journals start to differentiate according to the interests and the level of their readers, and demands on quality of scientific work are increasing. The same phenomenon can be observed in the Czech Lands. First of all, a certain balance of standards between Prague and Vienna had totally disappeared. Universities and institutions of higher learning in the imperial capital definitively assumed the leading role in the Habsburg monarchy. Nevertheless, the Czech Lands had made a considerable step forward. Among professors of university and polytechnic level

appeared a number of individuals who were capable of independent original research. The number of graduates, in particular from the Prague
Polytechnic, increased several times. After thirty years of stagnation, the
Royal Bohemian Society of Sciences resumed its activities, which included
also an increase in the number of its publications. However, brilliant
accomplishments by outstanding individuals (active in Bohemia for a long
or short time), such as the mathematician Bernard Bolzano (1781–1848), the
physicist Christian Doppler (1803–1853) and the physiologist Jan
Evangelista Purkyně (1787–1869), had relatively little scientific connection
with the local environment.

This period brought a substantially greater proportion of Czechs in the
educated classes of the population, while the attraction of the ideals of the
so-called national revival were increasing, and the discrimination against
Czech was painfully felt. Czech national demands also appeared as part of
the general efforts at democratization as manifested especially during the
1848 Revolution. Thus the students' meeting in Prague, on 15 March 1848,
demanded not only liberty of learning and teaching, including admittance
of Jews and Protestants to teaching posts, but also 'the granting of full equality and equal rights to Czech as a language of study and instruction'.[18]
Nevertheless, primitive nationalistic overtones had appeared in the forties
as well. The first among physicists to attempt publishing an original work
written in Czech was F. Petřina (1799–1855), professor at the faculty of philosophy at Prague University. When in 1847 Petřina presented a critique of
Ohm's theory of electric resistance, he stressed that the theory 'had been
discovered by the German Ohm', and that he was addressing the 'Slavonic
public' and the 'Slavonic world of erudition'.[19]

German intellectuals in Bohemia, for the most part of liberal views,
looked at the cultural efforts of the Czechs with a certain sympathy. But the
demand that Czech should also become a university and scholarly language
appeared to them irrational, unnecessary and capable of jeopardizing the
process of integrating indigenous science into the world context. This
impression was only confirmed by some enthusiasts on the Czech side, e.g.
K. S. Amerling (1807–1884) whose devoted educational and cultural activities simultaneously brought to light their lack of scholarly erudition.[20]

However, the beginning of reaction, and the stagnation of the political
and social life in the 1850s did not prevent the implementation of essential reforms in education, projected already in 1848 which, at the same
time, created entirely new prerequisites for the progress of scientific work
in the Habsburg monarchy. Freedom of teaching at universities and polytechnics was connected with new regulations for the appointment of professors. Before 1848, examinations of applicants had only verified their

ability to lecture on the given subject at the required level. The new regulations required the professorial staff to assess the standard of scientific research o˙ the candidate when considering his appointment to a vacancy, as well as ı the course of the newly introduced 'habilitation' proceedings, leading to the grant of lecturing at universities (*venia legendi*). However, it was the reform of secondary education that was of utmost importance. The need of teachers of science subjects at *gymnasia* and *Realschulen* brought hundreds of students to the philosophical faculty. At that time, their curricula were already relatively specialized, and they were expected to be familiar with the latest developments in their field. The vigorous ascendancy of Czech nationality was reflected primarily by a flood of pupils into newly established secondary schools where Czech was the language of instruction. Lectures in Czech at university level, though permitted, remained exceptional.

V

At the end of the 1840s, the Vienna Ac ıdemy of Sciences started its activity. The original composition of the me ıbership reflected the complicated situation in Austria.[21] Besides a number ı f prominent scientists from all over the Habsburg monarchy, there were also influential representatives of social and political life who became members in spite of second-rate or next to no credentials. Also the anxiety to achieve proportional representation of individual provinces was accompanied by numerous extra-scientific aspects: it was necessary in addition to take into account the position of the candidate in his own land. Nevertheless, the prestigious publications of the Vienna Academy offered new opportunities for German-written science.

Liberalization of public life in the 1860s was accompanied by the hasty establishment of various clubs and societies. Among them, there was a number of scientific and professional associations from which some came to be the basis of influential organizations.[22] Let us illustrate the difference in their approach to the development of scientific life by taking a look at several examples.

Lotos, the Prague German natural history society was originally founded as a student club in 1848–9. It set itself the task of joining together the groups of professionals and amateurs for scientific exploration of the country. Its popularizing journal with the same name appeared for the first time in 1851. It is probably not a mere coincidence that this occurred at the same time as the Natural History Board of the Bohemian Museum – initiated by Purkyně – was founded with a similar programme but with a distinctly Czech character.[23] *Lotos* kept up its original orientation for the next thirty years, with the interest in geological problems prevailing. Nationalistic dissensions were only slightly reflected in the pages of the journal, which corresponded with the originally rather passive attitude of Germans in Bohemia. Since the late 1860s, distinguished physicists, etc. began to appear among the lecturers at the society's meetings. Apparently this reflected the situation whereby German professors of the University and Technical High School (*Technische Hochschule*) were gradually driven out of local professional societies, and therefore considered it their duty to support the activities of a German society, even if its scientific orientation was rather remote from their own interests.

The history of the Union of Czech Mathematicians is more typical for the situation in Czech society.[24] Its foundation in 1862 was motivated by shortcomings in the teaching of mathematics and physics at the institutions of higher learning in Prague where the curricula of the obligatory courses were being modernized only slowly and open lectures were scarce. Originally, the intention of students and assistants was to improve their education, beyond the range of the obligatory courses, essentially by self-help activities. However, if we go through the list of lectures that took place in the society duri 1g the first years of its existence, we see that they neces-sarily slipped mc e and more into routine expositions of elementary material. Thus it was understandable that the other aspect of the efforts of the mainly Czech members of the society began to be emphasized: in the subsequent years these lectures primarily supplemented the missing instruc-tion in the Czech language. This gradually isolated Czech students from the German ones, and from the 1870s the Union definitely lost contact with German teachers at the university, the most prominent of them being Ernst Mach (1838–1916). It ceased to be a students' club, becoming instead the main organizer of Czech teachers at secondary schools, and it started to publish series of basic textbooks needed by Czech schools. The Union also took in many technicians, entrepreneurs and corporations for whom membership represented above all a manifestation of their national consciousness. In spite of the efforts of more ambitious authors, the orienta-tion of the Union's journal naturally adapted to the level of members.[25] However, in the international context science in the 1870s already formed a certain entity, and for a scientific work to be included, it was necessary to subject it to critical assessment, and this was possible only if it was published in an international language. There is no doubt that the efforts to create Czech written scientific literature formed a historically necessary stage leading, in the second half of the nineteenth century, to the finalization of Czech specialist terminology; of course, Czech-written work was excluded from the international context. However, the best educated members of the

Union were aware of this, and their awareness was one of the factors that led in the mid-1870s to a temporary and unsuccessful attempt to publish a periodical for mathematics and physics in foreign languages.[26] German mathematicians and physicists in the Czech Lands did not feel a need for a special organization. There was already a rich choice of German textbooks and popular works available. Practically all of the few creative workers in the field were in contact as teachers at Prague institutions of higher learning, and periodicals produced in Vienna and Germany provided sufficient publishing possibilities.

The situation in technical branches was different. The Association of Architects and Engineers in Bohemia, founded in 1866, despite its orientation to professional problems and educational activities, also started to publish a quarterly in a Czech and German version that was to bring out original papers.[27] Naturally, the top intelligentsia represented a very small portion among the hundreds of members of the Association. The majority were practical technicians and entrepreneurs, in particular in construction, who often had not even had higher education. It was primarily a professional corporation, and the tangle of competition and national interests came to the fore from the very beginning. Therefore the Germans left the Association, after three years, when the Czech majority succeeded in forcing them out of all offices in the Association. They founded the German Polytechnical Society (Der deutsche polytechnische Verein) whose membership was much less numerous but much more representative both professionally and socially. Although the German journal of the Society did not usually bring out more important original papers – those were mostly published in Vienna technical periodicals – it retained permanently high standards, mainly thanks to the professors of the Technische Hochschule (in effect Technical University).[28] A pronounced German nationalism, even if in a relatively cultured form, could be seen on its pages already from the 1870s. But the Czech Association of Architects and Engineers desired at first to avoid a total break since part of the members, in particular from entrepreneurial circles, did not wish to start open clashes, and therefore it continued to be formally bilingual, even published its journal in both Czech and German. Nationalism of a chauvinistic orientation in its full swing appeared in the Association only in the mid-1880s when after stormy discussions victory went to the more militant if professionally less significant faction. The Association became a pure Czech institution according to its statutes, and stopped publishing the German version of its periodical. At that time, it also more or less gave up scientific activities, but it became a very important professional and, to a certain extent, also political organization.

VI

In the late 1860s took place the division of the Prague Technical High School into separate Czech and German institutions primarily for pragmatic reasons. The separation created a large number of vacancies. Formally, they were to be filled only according to professional and scientific qualities of the candidates but, in practice, into the process entered a number of personal, local and political aspects. Characteristic for the general situation was the statement of Purkyně in 1865 that his warmest wish was that his successor (as professor at the University of Prague) should defend not only the interests of science but also those of the nation.[29] A candidate for a Czech professorship had to satisfy an important additional condition: to be able to lecture in Czech. In a situation when there was a lack of candidates who could satisfy all criteria, knowledge of Czech paradoxically was the single condition that could not be circumvented. This was why there were persons, among the first teachers at the Czech Technical High School, whose professional level was rather low. The division of the Technical High School was carried out in relative calm and, from time to time, the professorial staff of both Schools even agreed on a joint declaration on professional problems.

More than a decade later (1882), the division of Prague University into two separate, Czech and German, institutions became a first-class political issue, which cannot be analysed here in detail. Let us only note that the problem of the Czech educational system always constituted an important part of Czech politics, because they offered prospects of success that were most real.[30] The division led to a total separation of both teachers and students of the two institutions. While in international science the number of new facts and the cost of experimental equipment were rapidly growing, which led to the foundation of centres concentrating on certain problem areas, and international co-operation was even coming into existence, nationalism in the Czech Lands enforced the reverse process.

The German institutions of higher learning suddenly turned into small and provincial ones;[31] nevertheless, the conditions for scientific work by their professors did not get worse. German professors compensated a certain isolation in the Prague environment by emphasizing their adherence to the greater German culture. In periods of nationalist frictions, scientific activity was also a matter of prestige for them. Moreover, good scientific results raised a professor's chances of getting to higher ranks in the hierarchy of German institutions of higher learning.

Among newly appointed teachers at Czech institutions of higher learning there were personalities who had already successfully started their scientific career and on whose further development considerable hopes were set (for example, the professor of experimental physics Čeněk Strouhal [1850–1922]). Their subsequent long-lasting scientific sterility has sometimes been explained in the literature by their excessive task, connected with establishing and organizing new institutes, as well as by a rather megalomaniac effort to prepare Czech university textbooks in all subjects as soon as possible. Still, it can be seen that during the same periods of time their German colleagues were fulfilling analogous tasks without fatal consequences for their scientific production. On the other hand, we must not neglect consideration of the social conditions in which the Czech University functioned. For professors at the Czech University, their appointment meant reaching the top of their professional career, and Czech society expected from them first and foremost public activity and political involvement, and only this was really appreciated. This was why worthy but scientifically mediocre officers of the Union of Czech Mathematicians were appointed professors at the Technical High School while, for instance, a mathematician of world significance, Matyáš Lerch (1860–1922), was forced to accept a post abroad. The language barrier in addition insulated Czech literary production against critical assessment in an international forum and, on the other hand, made overestimation of its level in the local environment possible. For example, the professor of mathematics at the Czech University, F. J. Studnička (1836–1903), in his reviews sent to world journals did not hesitate to present elementary and survey papers, written and published in Czech in the *Časopis pro pěstování mathematiky a fyziky*, as research work. The authors of the commemorative volume on the occasion of the fiftieth anniversary of the accession of the Emperor Francis Joseph adopted the same approach, presenting practically all scientific literature written in Czech as scientific success.[32] It should be pointed out that the promoting of the status of Czech-written science was practised not only by second-rate authors but that also some top scholars followed this trend out of sincere conviction. For example, the above mentioned M. Lerch published a number of his key mathematical works first in Czech, although there were certainly less than five qualified Czech readers for them. None the less, even in these specific conditions a number of Czech professors were successfully working in research. Many of them were aware of the fact that the prevailing standpoint of the Czech public toward Czech science was misleading: the opinions of this group were reflected in particular by the journal edited by T. G. Masaryk (1850–1937), *Atheneum*. Masaryk considered it the primary duty of Czech scholarship to find its place within the world scientific community. He demanded above all original work from scholars;

concerning textbooks he believed that translations could help to get over the initial period.[33]

VII

During the last two decades of the nineteenth century, there existed in the Czech Lands two scientific communities, a Czech and a German one, whose interaction was practically nil – this, of course, had its impact on other institutions. From the middle of the nineteenth century, the Royal Bohemian Society of Sciences was gradually Czechized losing, as a consequence, its German members. On the other hand, its formal bilingualism discouraged the Czech radicals. The standard of research associated with the Academy of Sciences in Vienna, in the latter half of the nineteenth century, was really high in a number of branches, e.g. in physics. However, its originally intended all-Austrian character had mostly disappeared, and it was growing more and more to be just a Viennese institution. This situation in the Monarchy led to the foundation of other academies, for instance the Polish and Croatian, on the national principle. It is understandable that also in Bohemia the establishment of an academy became a topical issue. Unfortunately, when it was actually founded the two nationalities had become totally alienated.

There were various conceptions, but it was finally the conservative idea of the architect Josef Hlávka (1831–1908) that won.[34] Sponsored by him the Academy of Sciences, Arts and Literature – established in 1891 – admitted as its full members only persons of Czech nationality; Czech was the only language allowed to be used in its meetings and publications.[35] The scientific level of new members was uneven; the members of the natural history section were mostly professors of Czech institutions of higher learning.[36] No doubt the constitution of an academy of such a type was an anachronism but it offered new possibilities for publishing. It was of special importance that already in 1895 the natural history section of the Czech Academy started *faute de mieux* to publish the foreign-language *Bulletin international*, which contained, often very extensive, abstracts of works originally published in Czech.

The German side naturally launched a counterattack and made an attempt to establish a local German academy. It did not succeed; the only result was the establishment of the Society for the Furthering of German Science, Arts and Literature in Bohemia.[37] Although there were excellent scientists in its ranks, the Society's activities emphasized political aspects, which showed up especially in the twentieth century.[38]

The first decades of the twentieth century saw an equilibrium achieved between the Czech and German intellectual communities, at least in the technical and scientific disciplines. The German institutions of higher learning withdrew into a certain isolation, but retained their current standard of scientific work. The Czech institutions of higher learning, already in good shape, became more demanding when selecting new professors. Scientific work was growing more intensive and its results often emerged onto the international stage.

But the separation of Czech and German science and universities was already complete. The situation did not change after the foundation of Czechoslovakia in 1918. This led to the absurd situation whereby in the 1930s a science student at the Czech Charles University in Prague did not know who lectured in his discipline at the German University in Prague, whose building was sometimes less than a hundred metres away. Even Czech university teachers and researchers often had no idea that in their works they actually cited a colleague from the Brno German Technische Hochschule. Not only from the viewpoint of science, this was a very sad affair.

Notes

1 L. Nový, 'K pojetí vědy na počátku průmyslové revoluce' [On the concept of science at the beginning of the Industrial Revolution], *Práce z dějin přírodních věd*, 6 (1978), 126–8.

2 J. Hanuš, *Národní museum a naše obrození* [The National Museum and our national revival], 2 vols. (Prague, 1921, 1923), I, p. 74.

3 Cf. *Personal–Stand der . . . Universität zu Prag und Ordnung der . . . Vorlesungen, welche an derselben in dem Schuljahre 1827 gehalten werden* (Prague, 1826).

4 A wealth of records related to this problem can be found at the State Central Archives (Státní ústřední archiv – SÚA) in Prague, ZV 1791–1873, sg. 85/50/Vb.

5 Cf. V. Orel and A. Verbík, 'Programy učených společností v Brně na přelomu 18. a 19. století' [Programmes of the Learned Societies in Brno at the turn of the eighteenth and nineteenth centuries], Y. Purš (ed.) *200 let České společnosti nauk 1784–1984* (Prague, 1985), pp. 107–12; E. Wondrák,, 'Činnost a osud olomoucké společnosti neznámých učenců' [The activity and fate of the Societas Incognitorum in Olomouc], *ibid.*, pp. 289–90.

6 M. Teich, *Královská česká společnost nauk a počátky vědeckého průzkumu přírody v Čechách* [The Royal Bohemian Society of Sciences and the beginnings of scientific surveys of natural resources in Bohemia] (Prague, 1959).

7 L. Nový, 'Hlavní tendence a etapy institucionálního vývoje československé vědy do vytvoření ČSAV' [The main tendencies and stages of the institutional development of Czechoslovak science up to the establishment of the Czechoslovak Academy of Sciences], *200 let České společnosti nauk*, p. 68.

8 W. W. Tomek, *Geschichte der Prager Universität* (Prague, 1847), p. 339.

9 Cf. V. Orel and A. Verbík, 'Program rozvoje vědy na Moravě na počátky 19. století' [The programme for the development of science in Moravia at the beginning of the nineteenth century], *Dějiny vědy a techniky*, 18 (1985), 153–8.

10 Cf. *Jahrbuch des k.k. polytechnischen Institutes in Wien*, I–XX (1819–1939); *Zeitschrift für Physik und Mathematik*, I–X (1826–1832).

11 *Jahrbuch für Fabrikanten und Gewerbetreibende*, I, II (1839. 1840); *Encyclopädische Zeitschrift*, I–VIII (1841–1848), published by the *Verein zur Ermunterung des Gewerbsgeistes in Böhmen*.

12 See the collective work by J. Folta, Z. Horský, L. Nový, Irena Seidlerová, J. Smolka and M. Teich, *Dějiny exaktních věd v českých zemích do konce 19. století* [History of science in the Czech Lands to the end of the nineteenth century] (Prague, 1961), pp. 168–9, 173–5, 199–202.

13 Cf. Rozsívalová, 'Mladá léta Jana Evangelisty Purkyně' [The youth of Jan Evangelista Purkyně], *Acta Universitatis Carolinae – Historia Universitatis Carolinae Pragensis*, 27, 1 (1987), 43.

14 A. Chalupa, 'Měnící se úloha Národního musea v přírodovědeckém a společenskovědním výzkumu' [The changing role of the National Museum in research in natural and social sciences], *200 let České společnosti nauk*, pp. 373–8.

15 Hanuš, *Národní museum*, II, pp. 375–6, 394.

16 *Krok*, I–IV (1821–1840).

17 Ludmila Hlaváčková, *Jan Theobald Held 1770–1851* (Prague, 1972).

18 V. Kruta, 'Jan N. Czermak profesoru Janu E. Purkyňovi' [Jan N. Czermak to Professor Jan E. Purkyně], *Acta Universitatis Carolinae – Historia Universitatis Carolinae Pragensis*, 15, 1 (1975), 89–104.

19 Folta *et al.*, *Dějiny exaktních věd*, pp. 187–8.

20 Cf. Eva Hoffmannová, *Karel Slavoj Amerling* (Prague, 1982).

21 H. Schlitter, *Gründung der Kaiserlichen Akademie der Wissenschaften* (Vienna, 1921).

22 Jana Mandlerová, *Soupis odborných spolků a vědeckých institucí v českých zemích 1860–1918* [Register of professional associations and scientific institutions in the Czech Lands 1860–1918] (Prague, 1973).

23 L. Niklíček, 'Význam druhého pražského období Jana Evangelisty Purkyně pro dějiny české vědy' [The significance of the second Prague period of Purkyně's life for the history of Czech science], *Acta Universitatis Carolinae – Historica Universitatis Carolinae Pragensis*, 27, 1 (1987), 105.

24 J. Petráň, 'Od spolku pro volné přednášky z matematiky a fysiky k Jednotě českých matematiků a fyziků' [From the Open Lectures Club to the Union of Czech Mathematicians and Physicists], *Jubilejní almanach JČSMF 1862–1987* [Jubilee yearbook of the Union of Czechoslovak Mathematicians and Physicists 1862–1987] (Prague, 1987), pp. 15–29, 211–12.

25 Cf. *Časopis por pěstování matematiky a fysiky* [Journal for the Cultivation of Mathematics and Physics], I (1872)ff.

26 *Archiv mathematiky a fysiky* [Archives for Mathematics and Physics], I–II (1875–1877).

27 *Mittheilungen des Architekten- und Ingenieur-Vereines in Böhmen*, I (1866).

28 Cf. *Technische Blätter*, I (1869)ff.

29 V. Kruta, 'Ke sklonku Purkyňova působení na universitě' (The last years of Purkyně's activity at the University), *Acta Universitatis Carolinae – Historia Universitatis Carolinae Pragensis*, 11 (1970), 54. After 1823 Purkyně speat twenty-seven years as professor of physiology in Breslau before returning to Prague in 1850.

30 Jana Mandlerová, 'K boji za zřízení 2. české university v Brně 1882–1918' [The struggle for establishing the second Czech university in Brno 1882–1918], *Acta Universitratis Carolinae – Historia Universitatis Carolinae Pragensis*, 10, 1 (1969), 95.

31 L. Nový, 'Hlavní etapy vývoje novodobých vědeckých institucí u nás' [The main stages of the development of modern scientific institutions in Czechoslovakia], *Práce z dějin přírodních věd*, 4 (1973), 35.

32 *Památník na oslavu padesátiletého panovnického jubilea J. V. císaře a krále Františka Josefa I.* [Commemorative volume on the occasion of fifty years of the reign of His Majesty Emperor and King Francis Joseph I.] (Prague, 1898).

33 T. G. Masaryk, 'Jak zvelebovati naši literaturu naukovou' [How to improve our scientific literature], *Atheneum*, II (1885), 270–5.

34 L. Nový, 'Podíl Josefa Hlávky na rozvoji vědy a kultury v českých zemích na přelomu 19. a 20. století' [Josef Hlávka's part in the development of science and culture in the Czech Lands at the turn of the nineteenth century], *Rozpravy národního technického musea*, VC (1984), 20–34.

35 J. Beran, 'Vznik České akademie věd a umění v dokumentech' [The establishment of the Czech Academy of Sciences and Arts in documents], *Studia historiae Academiae scientiarum bohemoslovacae*, IIB (1989).

36 J. Beran, 'II. třída ČAVU v letech 1891–1914' [2nd section of the Czech Academy of Sciences and Arts in the years 1891–1914], *Dějiny věd a techniky*, (1971), 193–208.

37 Jana Mandlerová, 'K založení Gesellschaft zur Förderung deutscher Wissenschaft, Kunst und Literatur in Böhmen v roce 1891' [The establishment of the Gesellschaft zur Förderung deutscher Wissenschaft, Kunst uns Literatur in Böhmen in 1891], *Dějiny věd a techniky*, 15 (1982), 13–27.

38 Jana Mandlerová, 'K změnám charakteru Gesellschaft zur Förderung deutscher Wissenschaft, Kunst und Literatur v letech 1900–1910' [On the changing nature of the Gesellschaft zur Förderung deutscher Wissenschaft, Kunst und Literatur in the years 1900–1910], *Sborník historický*, 33 (1986), 89–134.

13

The rise and fall of a democracy

ROBERT KVAČEK

The new state

An independent Czechoslovak state came to be the declared programme of Czech politics only in the course of the Great War. It marked the culmination of Czech constitutional endeavours which until then had been focused mainly on achieving internal adjustments within the framework of the Habsburg monarchy. Considerations of an independent Czech state had either issued forth from political parties with little influence which existed more or less on the fringe of politics, or else, had been kept within the bounds of private political thoughts. During the Great War, and particularly after 1917, the idea of a plausible restructuring of Austria-Hungary virtually disappeared from the Czech political scene. The Czech constitutional programme was definitively transformed to embrace the concept of an independent Czechoslovak state, as formulated and implemented outside the country by the anti-Austrian resistance group headed by Tomáš (Thomas) Garrigue Masaryk (1850–1937). In the course of 1918 it was adopted by the overwhelming majority of Czech politicians. It was also embraced by political leaders in Slovakia who had no constitutional programme of their own; abandoning the tactic of passivity for which they had opted during the war, the most active among them now strove for association with the Czech emancipatory action.

The actual birth of the new state in the wake of the events of October 1918 none the less was received on its future territory with feelings of surprise, as something rather unexpected, even though the manifestations and reasons of such feelings were widely varied. While inwardly Czech society may have matured up to a point where it could aspire to national sovereignty, it still either lacked the courage to make a step beyond the Austrian framework or deemed such a step disadvantageous as well as impracticable. The course and outcome of the Great War, though, virtually called for exactly that kind of action to be taken, having created a fundamental prerequisite there with the military and political defeat of Austria-Hungary and Germany. That alone, however, would have amounted to nothing had it not been for the condition of 'ripeness' for independence which had been attained within society. The Czech nation's euphoria over having 'lived to see' their own statehood, though, gradually died down under the burden of obstacles posed by the new situation in the constitutional, economic and social fields.

In Slovakia, the emergence of Czechoslovakia induced both a shock and a surprise. That country's separation from Hungary even had to be carried out, after an early stage of declarations and accords – which proved to be inadequate – by the military. Slovak society, still lacking much in terms of either internal or external definition and assurance, had no power to act on its own. For quite some time to come, it was even to experience occasional feelings of transience and incompleteness with regard to the newly established constitutional makeup, as something which might revert back to the times of Magyar rule.

The Czechoslovak state was to comprise the entire territory of what had thus far been the Czech Lands. This demarcation of boundaries met with resistance on the part of indigenous Germans who increasingly defined themselves as 'Sudeten Germans'. As early as 21 October 1918 the border regions of the Czech Lands were declared part of the then proclaimed German-Austria (Deutsch-Österreich), an ethnic state being hatched for separation from Habsburg Austria which was in the process of disintegrating or aspiring to form a federation. After all, in October 1918 the Germans and Magyars were ahead of the other nations in the Austro-Hungarian monarchy, in their efforts towards its dismantling. Underlying the adverse reaction of the native German political circles to the declaration of independent Czechoslovakia, was not just disapproval of the historic frontiers of Bohemia coupled with their traditional opposition to the establishment of a Czech state, but also certain new impulses called up by the outcome of the Great War. To expanded German nationalism in Austria, the war defeat equalled the frustration of hopes associated with the idea of waging a victorious war and thereby achieving for the German element a dominant position in Austria and in Central Europe as a whole. Instead, the upper hand was gained by national revolutions and upheavals, and the German element found itself excluded from decision-making in the Central Europe arena. A solution to that was seen – especially by socialist members of the governments in Vienna and Berlin – in a united German state which would have brought together Germany and German-Austria. Only such a framework would have made practicable a Sudeten German attempt to separate the border regions of the Czech Lands from Czechoslovakia, in the form of four provinces, with a view to annexing them to German-Austria. The two most important of those regions were not even geographically linked with Austria. The Czechoslovak government regarded those separatist tendencies as expressing a more general ambition either to prevent the founding of Czechoslovakia altogether, or to surround it from all sides by a 'Greater Germany'; consequently, it ordered a prompt military action to do away with the provinces. This was not a difficult task, given the general post-war turmoil, yet Sudeten German politicians' defiance of Czechoslovakia continued well into the summer of 1919, assuming other forms, even though by then they took part in the country's communal elections.

Tensions, and possibly even conflicts with Sudeten German politics, were something that the Czech founders of Czechoslovakia had actually expected would happen. By no means, however, did that mean they were ready to revise their concept of the new state; rather on the contrary, it reinforced their determination to pursue their aim. Officially, Czechoslovakia was created as a national state – a state of the 'Czechoslovak nation'. Its two branches being constituted by the Czechs and the Slovaks, the nation was conceived primarily as a political phenomenon, and the principle of the Czecho-Slovak union was to serve as a basis for the development of a civil society. It was supposed that the ensuing process would involve the establishment, or 'accomplishment', of ethnic unity, which happened to be the chief premise held notably by the Czech proponents of the 'Czechoslovak' conception. The notion of 'Czechoslovakism' sought its *raison d'être* in the very closeness of Czechs and Slovaks, including similarity of the two languages, as well as in the latter-day history of cooperation in the cultural and other fields, which was promoted particularly by intellectuals. Apart from that, political motives were involved as well: the Czechs constituted half of the new state's total population, and they needed the Slovaks since only together with them they might hope to amount to what could be termed a decisive majority. The Slovaks alone would have ended up in the third place in terms of population numbers. Likewise, the concept of a national state stemmed from the firm belief that the Czechs and Slovaks were rightfully entitled to it, in view of the existence of national states in their neighbourhood, and as it were, in the larger part of Europe.

Under this thesis, Czechoslovaks were considered to be the 'state nation', whereas the state's citizens of other nationalities were regarded as German, Magyar and Polish minorities. Czechoslovakia's ethnic structure was further diversified by the attachment to it of the territory wedged in the Carpathian Bend in the east, which was given the name Subcarpathian Ruthenia. Rather than making a programmatic effort for its acquisition, the Czechoslovak state accepted it in deference to the declared wishes and will of notably expatriate Ruthenes, and in compliance with the decisions of the Peace Conference. Its policies there were concentrated primarily on efforts to raise the state of culture and social development in that wholly neglected region of Europe. At the same time, successive Czechoslovak governments would keep postponing the implementation of the pledge of autonomy for the region, which had been stipulated by the provisions on its attachment; this was due partly to the lack of Subcarpathian Ruthenia's infrastructural development, as well as to the fear that its autonomy might set a precedent for other parts of the state. Czech politics moulded Czechoslovakia as a unitary state, regarding that particular form as the most suitable alternative also with a view to overcoming the postwar hardships and conflicts which accompanied the birth of the new state. This situation was nothing exceptional in Central and Eastern Europe at that time, and was also occasioned by social problems characteristic for a period between war and peace. In the end, Czechoslovakia encountered no really grave problems, though some difficulties did leave imprints in the country's political life, e.g. in relations between the nationalities and in the strength of the communist Left.

The bringing into a common state lands and territories which had been formed by diverse historical processes, whose economies were unequally developed, and whose political and spiritual orientations were different, was viewed with optimism within Czech political circles: there would be enough time for such a development to take its due course. Time which would entail peaceful international relations based on the principal results of the Great War as well as the constant progress of democracy in the world at large, and its further development and consolidation in Czechoslovakia itself. In fact, the Czechoslovak state linked its existence with democracy in a programmatic way. This was also a consequence of changes in the top echelons of Czech politics, changes which were symbolized and personified by the ascendancy of T. G. Masaryk, to the detriment of former Young Czech Party leader Karel Kramář (1860–1937). A conservative liberal and nationalist, Kramář became Czechoslovakia's first Prime Minister, but left after what was only a brief term of office and never returned to a government post. For his part, Masaryk was elected President four times over, staying there for seventeen years. His views of the origin and consequences of the Great War, as well as his concepts of the building of Czechoslovak statehood and his opinions on democracy, ethnic problems and social issues, came to influence strongly the spiritual and ideological complexion of the state. Moreover, Masaryk's political thinking had its polestar in firm adherence to democratic principles. Hence the belief in the democratic applicability of the full civil rights and freedoms to imbue the entire population, including members of minorities, with a positive attitude towards the Czechoslovak state. Owing to its Czech authorship, the constitution codified Czechoslovakia as a democratic parliamentary republic. The democratic republican system was received by Czech society as something quite natural, though in actual fact it laid an entirely new kind of state and political institution before it. However, Czech society tended to overestimate its 'endowments' for democracy, often confusing democracy with plebeian attitudes and folksiness traceable to the loss of its aristocratic component. A negative attitude to authorities, including the authority of the state, was believed to be a manifestation of democratic tradition. Therefore, society as a whole was rather slow in accommodating itself to having become a state-building society. The element of superficiality in the way democracy operated was to some extent attributable to Czech political parties which appropriated what was arguably a disproportionate stake in the life of the state while not always behaving with the necessary degree of responsibility.

Slovakia's first government representatives, who were closely linked with the Czech political establishment, viewed their own country's readiness for democracy critically and with some concern. Immaturity in this direction seemed to them to be one of the reasons for the need of a centralized state and of Czech presence in Slovakia. Their scepticism was excessive, if not entirely unjustified. Democratic development in Slovakia could draw upon comparatively busy social activities – centred on local associations and clubs, while also relying on national cultural traditions. What was decisive was the spirit in which the process of Slovakia's 'Slovakization' would eventually take place.

German-speaking inhabitants of the Czech Lands were neither geographically nor in terms of their 'tribal' affiliation a compact and uniform mass. Their 'unification' had been pushed by their nationalist politicians during the Great War. The war defeat of Austria-Hungary and its constitutional consequences dictated unification efforts comprising, as they did, as a binding element – opposition to the Czechoslovak state. That became instrumental in excluding indigenous German politics from the state's early building endeavours, as well as from participation in drawing up its constitution. Czech politicians welcomed this since, after October 1918, the German stand threatened to complicate the preparation of the constitution. Moreover, they were now able to draft it in accord with their own ideas and interests. That did little good to the constitution, language law provisions, and even less to their practical implementation, though the law did honour

Czechlosvakia's international commitments to her ethnic minorities. As early as the nineteenth century, language had acquired a privileged status within the national movements in Central Europe among the characteristics of a nation; and the issue of official language constituted the most delicate aspect of the national question in Austria. It was by no means easy for the German population to get accustomed to the minority status, notably so with regard to the 'ruling' Czechs. Memories of the 'reverse' situation in Austria were still very much alive on both sides, and were far from conducive to new forms of co-existence. At the same time, a positive effect was generated by the overall democratic atmosphere prevailing in the Czechoslovak state, which was reflected in the extent of the Germans' traditionally rich political and cultural life.

The political system

The making of the political system and administration in Czechoslovakia involved a variety of factors. Postwar social unrest heightened the action and impact of the working-class movement in all parts of the country; that, in its turn, was duly projected into the initial phase of the country's economic and social legislation. An emergent communist current of considerable vigour was to be confronted with policies of social reform. The content and breadth of reform, though, became the subject of political bickering which also concerned divergent views of the state's role in that sphere and its economic policies in general. Liberal conceptions, which were focused on long-term prospects, clashed with immediate social problems, particularly during the economic depression in the early 1930s.

The Czech political establishment entered the new state with its old-time party spectrum intact. Each of the major Czech political parties, with the exception of the Communists, had an Austrian past, and in successive parliamentary elections, all of them managed to retain the degree of influence they had acquired while still operating in Austria. Their quest for models abroad concentrated on the Western democracies from which were taken duly adjusted and interpreted suggestions for the building of a system of constitutional organs. On the whole, while the structure of the political system was rather too complex, it was still valued for its openness based upon the plurality of opinions and competences. The danger of the system growing prone to some degree of formalism was warded off, among other things, by the spiritual climate prevailing throughout the state. This was particularly true of Czech society with its openness to popular contemporary discussions on the content of democracy and progress. Busy political activity had been characteristic for Czech society ever since the mid-nineteenth century, and it experienced further intensification with the foundation of the new state. It was also related to the weight of political party allegiance in state administration and other related spheres, as well as to the dominant role played by parties in the political system as a whole.

A bicameral National Assembly (parliament and senate) was set up as the supreme law-making body, based upon the outcome of elections held according to the principle of proportional representation; women had the franchise right from 1918. That election system was favourable to smaller parties, including those of the ethnic minorities, to whom it could provide easier access to parliament and senate. At the same time, it caused splintering of votes and did not enable any party to come out of the elections with anything like a solid majority. Parties that were strong enough in parliament grouped in coalitions to form governments, and party coalitions became Czechoslovakia's key policy-making institution. Their basic method of functioning came to consist of the search for such solutions, often involving compromise, which would either correspond to the interests expressed and represented by the various parties, or would not threaten them. A prerequisite of accords and verbal agreements reached within the government was a relatively rigid coalition discipline binding the government parties both within their ranks and notably in the National Assembly. Significantly, however, that entailed a serious weakening of the National Assembly's role. Senate was devoid of influence due to its scanty powers while, for its part, parliament found itself unable to stand up to, let alone prevail over, government. Typically, parties grouped in a government coalition would wield a comfortable and disciplined majority in parliament, and anyway parliamentary mandates were considered party property. This may have given the government a feeling of stability, but the political system and political life in general were deprived of a 'loyal' opposition.

Government coalitions were formed chiefly by five major Czech, or Czechoslovak, political parties, some of which exceptionally found themselves relegated to opposition for limited periods of time. Simultaneously, those government parties epitomized Czech society's prompt and profound identification with the Czechoslovak state, the transformation of 'Czech' into 'Czechoslovak'. Thriving in such a national-oriented environment were parties which were neither capable of, nor – given the opportunities available for participation in government – interested in forming a 'normal' opposition which would have been in a position to change government without simultaneously affecting the foundations of the state and the political system. The absence of that particular kind of opposition benefited neither the country's political life nor the parties themselves. At the most, opposition would start to develop, in embryonic forms and half-heartedly, within individual parties; in the course of the 1930s such pockets would also crop up in defiance of the stereotypes set by irreplaceable party bosses losing the ability to address the problems and requirements posed by the period's complex developments. Characteristically, such forays or attempted forays by 'junior' members, or at least attempts at them, could be witnessed practically in all major political parties. Most of the time, parliamentary opposition was filled with a spirit of negation with regard to the state. Its motivation was ideological – as in the Communist Party – or ethnic – as in the German and Magyar nationalist parties.

A specific, if merely occasional, opposition to the government coalitions' conduct would issue from President Masaryk. The powers with which the president was invested by constitution did not define explicitly his actual rights. He was free to limit his functions to representation and be, as a remark of the time had it, 'a monstrance shown to the people', or he could strive to become a political figure of considerable influence. The decisive factor there was his personality. Masaryk's option was unambiguous, especially in the light of the lion's share he had in bringing the state into existence. The authority which he accumulated, at that stage and later while in office as president, enhanced his status up to a level where he was recognized as the symbol of Czechoslovakia and her democracy.

There were various ways in which Masaryk made his presence in political life felt: they included anonymous press items, ground-rule instructions addressed to government ministers, as well as private criticism of governments, their members and political parties, voiced through his confidants and followers occupying top ranks in political parties and influential public bodies. He also made himself the centre of a group of prominent representatives from various walks of life. Thus was gradually formed an entirely distinct political and ideological 'Castle group' (named after the presidential seat in Prague), promoting Masaryk's programme of building a democratic state. The Castle's direct influence was manifest in the orientation of Czechoslovakia's foreign policy and diplomacy. There Masaryk took part in defining strategic guidelines in conjunction with his closest collaborator Edvard Beneš (1884–1948), who was continuously, until 1935, Minister for Foreign Affairs and, indeed, shaped the basic principles of Czechoslovak foreign policy.

His involvement in home politics, outwardly inconspicuous though it was, coupled with the Castle's influence at large, turned Masaryk into a target of attacks which climaxed, in 1927, in the failure to prevent his re-election as president. The then government coalition leader, the chairman of the Agrarian Party Antonín Švehla (1873–1933), aware of Masaryk's importance to the stability of the state and its international reputation, blocked the plan of a section of the Czech and Slovak Right Wing to carry the anti-Masaryk design through. During the 1930s government parties oriented towards programmes of social reform moved ever closer to the Castle. Already by then, Beneš had become the central figure in the Castle group and eventually replaced Masaryk as president in 1935. His election was preceded by yet another abortive attempt at the political elimination of the Castle.

Masaryk associated his presidency with an integrationist mission, not only in politics but also in the overall process of consolidating the state. This was much needed in view of internal divisions rooted in the state's history and its economy, in its civil and spiritual traditions. It appeared that the most solid internal safeguard of Czechoslovakia's continued existence was the formation of a new supranational civil society. At that time, this was merely a vision which, moreover, had received little theoretical analysis. The need to reduce differences was more understood, though the proffered solutions were not always fortunate. Czech society – influenced by politics – aspired to accommodate the state primarily to its perception and image. It knew little about the state's other ethnic and geographical constituents, and was not particularly interested in getting to know more. That gave rise to conflicts and misunderstandings which could have been avoided, or at least diminished and blunted, had there been a greater degree of sensitivity on the Czech part towards the other nationalities.

Underlying these conflicts were also considerable but less readily available economic differences between Czechoslovakia's principal constituent parts.

The economy

Czechoslovakia inherited from Austria-Hungary some 60 to 70 percent of the latter's industrial potential. That would have seemed a magnificent starting asset, and yet it entailed a series of severe burdens and problems. The largest share went to the light industries which now lost some of their former domestic markets. Austria-Hungary's successor states enclosed themselves within a network of customs barriers, and in more than one case confronted one another as political opponents. At the same time, exports and competitiveness of Czechoslovak products on international markets were perhaps the most crucial concern of the country's economy.

The fact of Czechoslovakia's economic inheritance being a mixed blessing was still emphasized by differences between the Czech Lands and the country's other parts. Slovakia was not yet past the initial stage of industrialization, a process that had only just touched, almost imperceptibly as it were, Subcarpathian Ruthenia. Agriculture, the wholly dominant economic sector in the east of the state, still relied on extensive essentially pre-industrial farming methods. The higher development level of the Czech Lands did in the long run augur fair prospects, in particular for the rise of Slovakia. Under conditions of an integrated economy, this was still a matter of a reasonably long-term process. At the start came shocks and blows caused by the new market conditions, coupled with adverse consequences of the severance of some of the previous economic ties.

It was not until the mid-1920s that the economy began to rise above its prewar levels. This occurred in all parts of the Republic. In the domain of exports Czechoslovakia could offer on a small scale quality products, often produced which low labour costs made marketable. Czechoslovakia had always had relatively cheap labour; the boom of the late 1920s did little to change that. It was then, in a world which was already more or less settled economically, that Czechoslovakia took tenth place in terms of its share in the world industrial output, and twelfth place in per capita production. It surpassed middle-ranking European industrial countries, such as Italy, Austria, Norway or Finland. With virtually all of them, she shared the problem of internal economic contrast. The bulk of Czechoslovakia's industrial potential was concentrated in northern and central regions of Bohemia and Moravia, and in Silesia. On the basis of agricultural production, which managed to satisfy the needs of the home market, Czechoslovakia also numbered amongst the ten leading countries.

Well thought-out approaches to the state's economy constituted a rather rare phenomenon in the policies of successive governments. They were applied at the state's inception during its separation from the defunct Austria-Hungary, but afterwards they came up against pressures of everyday politics and sectional conflicts. It was evident, and increasingly manifestly so, that Czech politicians had an inadequate understanding of economic matters, and did not give proper consideration to their significance. They were reminded of that in a drastic way by the terrible economic depression and social crisis of the early 1930s.

The depression forced industrial output down on a wide scale, cutting it by more than a half in some industries, thereby assuming an additional dimension as a structural crisis, as well as bringing about shattering social consequences. The process of recovery in the mid-1930s was relatively slow and incomplete. Government circles were unprepared for the onslaught and at first contented themselves with the role of helpless observers; they responded only to its most dramatic social and political manifestations. Previous years, with their auspicious economic and political outlook, had not prepared them for a similar trial.

Slovaks and Germans

In 1926 Czech political parties succeeded in bringing into government two German parties, along with the Slovak's People's Party which had until then remained in opposition. This was motivated more than anything else by sectional considerations underlying agrarian and Catholic clerical interests; this limitation notwithstanding, it represented an asset for the state – an indication of its acceptance. Thus far it had been accepted wholly and unreservedly – as pointed out earlier – by Czech society. It was only with the existence of Czechoslovakia that Slovaks came into their own as a nation. The political ideology and practice of 'Czechoslovakism' did not prevent this process; on the contrary, it took it as a proof of Slovakia's definitive detachment from Hungary and Magyar influence. But simultaneously this emancipation served as a sign that the moulding of Slovak society into a nation was completed. Its political life was growing richer and branching out. There were Czechoslovak parties, that is, political parties operating across the whole of the state's territory in which the majority of prewar Slovak nationally oriented politicians were active. And there were political parties emphasizing Slovak national interests, such as the People's Party led by the parish priest Andrej Hlinka (1864–1938) which, with its programme of Slovak autonomy, was attracting Catholic sections of the population that had until recently been nationally either inactive or altogether indifferent.

There were good, internal, Czechoslovak reasons and also external ones following the unattractive postwar developments in Germany and Austria, that were speaking for the need to calm down the wild anti-Czechoslovak radicalism of Sudeten German politicians. It was pursued by two parties, the German National Party (DNP) and the German National Socialist Workers Party (DNSAP), while other German parties pragmatically and, as the case may be, boldly or hesitantly looked for ways of cooperation with their Czech counterparts. From the very beginning of the state's existence this co-operation had been encouraged and supported by President Masaryk even though, at an early stage, he irritated the native-born Germans by observing that they originally came to the country as immigrants and colonists. Some Czech parties and individual politicians found it difficult to forget previous ethnic skirmishes under Austrian rule and let memories of these events still reverberate in their contemporary stance. Moreover, day-to-day practice, especially that of the state authorities, was infringing on minorities' rights. On the whole, though, the Czechoslovak state's policy towards the minorities corresponded with its commitments under the Treaty of Saint Germain (1919), on certain points even doing more than was stipulated there. Thus, when Slovakia was part of Hungary the German-speakers there lost their national awareness or lacked it altogether, whereas when Slovakia became part of Czechoslovakia they were able to establish themselves as a minority.

The economic crisis of the early 1930s brought into sharp focus the economic and social content of Czechoslovakia's ethnic issues. The light industries, concentrated in the preponderantly German-speaking border regions of the Czech Lands, suffered from the collapse of foreign trade while Slovakia, for its part, felt the impact of the agrarian crisis. Social disequilibrium affected the country's political life; certain political and ideological interpretations of the roots of the depression put the blame for it on the Czechoslovak state – a line adhered to by German nationalists – or on democracy as such. In fact, democracy was then under pressure from adversaries world-wide. The hopes in Czechoslovakia for a continuing advance of democracy were not being fulfilled – the scope for democracy was actually shrinking.

The vacuum of values caused by the Great War was exploited by two radical, antagonistic, political movements: fascism and communism. For the time being fascism proved to be the more successful of the two; it did not 'uproot' society at its foundations. It pandered to various social strata, and it was outspokenly nationalistic. Riding on the same wave were further attacks on democracy by the right wing, close to fascism, which headed for setting up corporative states and installing authoritarian regimes.

Among Czechoslovakia's neighbour states, democracy was gradually crushed. Czechoslovakia was not unaffected. Here the most severe effect was felt in connection with developments in Germany. Democratic Germany was generally believed to be a condition and safeguard for a 'new' Central Europe and for providing sufficient time to make possible the development of peaceful co-existence between the new states in the area. The Nazi 'cure' for the depression in Germany was gaining ground among the Sudeten Germans who were finding new leaders and a new nationalist programme: it strove, first of all, to bring Germans in Bohemia and Moravia under a single banner. To this end the Sudeten German Patriotic Front (SHF), headed by Konrad Henlein (1898–1945), was brought into being in 1933. It looked upon democracy solely as a favourable environment in which it could come into existence and become active. It successfully exploited social ills, promising to remedy them depending on the control of the border regions' administration which it sought. Once again, heightened national consciousness started to turn against the Czechoslovak state. Democratically minded indigenous German parties were on the defensive and saw their influence dwindle.

In Slovakia broader consequences of the economic depression brought to light the complexity of its amalgamation with the Czech Lands. Once again government policies were confronted with opposition put up by the People's Party which proclaimed itself the sole representative of the Slovak nation, despite gaining less than 30 percent of the Slovak vote in elections. This self-promotion was opening up a way for its development into an authoritarian, totalitarian party, a trend that was underlined by its sharply critical attitude towards democracy and liberalism. The autonomous Slovakia championed by that party was to be given a new spiritual face, different from that of the Czech Lands, one that would have been based upon an ideology of nationalism and – in view of the Slovak population's high religiosity – clerical Catholicism. The younger generation of People's Party politicians sought models in the authoritarian regimes which had by then managed to do away with democracy. It has to be said that the party's leader, Andrej Hlinka, was pushing for Slovak autonomy within the framework of the Czechoslovak state. But the claims to autonomy continued to be rejected by government coalitions, including their Slovak members; they still saw in it a threat to the Republic's integrity, as well as a precedent with respect to the Sudeten Germans. Some consideration was given only to an extension of existing administrative powers, which the People's Party would not seriously discuss. Neither had the more accommodating neo-activist tendency among the Germans in Bohemia any reason to be satisfied, as it was meeting with political and bureaucratic inertia and small-mindedness.

Foreign policy

Czech political parties did not offer a particularly fertile soil for right-wing radicalism. Some of them would make occasional attempts at turning it into a vehicle for a political breakthrough, but to no avail. Nor did its long-established symbiosis with nationalism yield anything like the expected political gains either; instead, it merely demonstrated that Czech nationalism too could be aggressive, chauvinistic and anti-democratic. What was more serious, though, was the fact that the political winds from the Right blowing across Europe had their effect also on the new leadership of the Agrarian Party which started to contemplate shifts towards the Right in the government and in the top echelons of the state. From such moves it expected easier agreement with Czechoslovakia's neighbours and enhancement of the country's internal and external security. However, it managed neither to prevent Edvard Beneš being elected president in 1935 (which would have eliminated the Castle from its position of power) nor to reach an accord with right-wing parties on the other side of the ethnic spectrum.

Czech society proved on the whole rather unwilling to show understanding for such government shifts. The feeling of existential threat being posed to the state was associated with the growth of right-wing anti-democratic tendencies in the country's neighbourhood and at home. Fascism was overwhelmingly rejected by the Czechs – primarily because of its rule in Germany which they looked upon from the national standpoint. The Nazi brand of fascism was regarded as yet another manifestation of pan-Germanism and as a lasting German threat. Its imminence had its effect on Czech society's attitude to the development of the situation inside the country. While finding solutions for ethnic problems was getting increasingly difficult, democracy itself was being reappraised and upgraded. Traditionally much concerned with politics, Czech society had been even more politicized since the mid-1930s. As the character of government and regime in Czechoslovakia was dependent on democracy's condition and its decisions, it was largely up to Czech democracy to preserve the democratic face of the state. Throughout the 1930s Czechoslovakia remained Central Europe's sole democracy. By then this isolated position came to entail unfavourable international consequences for the country.

While still under Habsburg rule, Czech society had shown extraordinary regard for the international framework of its potential activities and their impact in Austria itself. The birth of the Czechoslovak state was made possible only thanks to a propitious international situation; its maintenance was then paramount to Czechoslovakia's continued existence. That demanded the preservation of the Peace Treaties which had created a new international order and defined Czechoslovakia's borders. The Versailles system, though, was clearly an instance of peace achieved by the use of force; it could become fragile should that force prove to be vulnerable and slackening. It represented a big-power dictate imposed by the Great War's victors yet, at the same time, it was intended to strengthen democracy in Europe in the wake of the fall of three non-democratic empires to democracy. This was also exactly how the Versailles system was evaluated and defended by Czechoslovak foreign policy, guided by the principle that peace was possible only through the application of democracy.

Among the victorious powers, France was the one with which Czechoslovakia found the strongest links; it was France, after all, which had done the most to obtain international recognition for Czechoslovakia and included it in its own *cordon sanitaire*. Czechoslovakia accepted and upheld France's leading position on the European continent, regarding it as a practical guarantee of the Versailles system. However, its orientation towards France, reaffirmed in 1924 by a Treaty of Alliance was not intended to be either uncritically conformist or exclusive. Czechoslovakia proclaimed its vital interest to be the preservation of the Franco-British Entente in which it saw the key to the solution of the European situation and to the safe-guarding of peace for decades to come. Foreign Minister Beneš even tried to mediate between Paris and London when their 'entente cordiale' showed signs of losing some of its cordiality. He did not succeed there and proved equally unable to awaken British interest in Czechoslovak opinion about Central Europe and its future.

Czechoslovakia strove to play a more independent role in this area, which it defined as territory 'between Russia and Germany', including their weak-ened international position. What Czechoslovakia wished to achieve was to pacify, rebuild and consolidate Central Europe to convince other small states of its approach which relied, in general terms, on the existing peace treaties and the influence of France as a Great Power. The basis for such a broadly conceived Central Europe was to be supplied by the creation of the Little Entente, an alliance involving Czechoslovakia, Yugoslavia and Romania (1933). Gradually, it became obvious that the Little Entente had too many weak points and could not fulfill its aspirations. It was unanimous in orchestrating opposition to a restoration of the Habsburg rule, and in confronting Hungary in defence of the Treaty of Trianon (1920) which defined her post-1918 borders. Apart from that, the Little Entente member states proved unable to establish adequate mutual economic links, and their internal political systems also developed in different directions, with Yugoslavia and Romania heading for authoritarian monarchies in whose eyes democratic methods of government and institutions were hardly any-thing other than unnecessary burdens. Both countries were concerned more with Balkan affairs than with Central Europe and at the same time, each had to tackle its own international problems which also detracted attention from Central European issues.

Proving to be equally questionable was another Czechoslovak notion, namely, that democratic tendencies would also prevail in Austria and in Hungary, and this would facilitate accord with these states that were finding it extremely hard to come to terms with the consequences of the end of Austria-Hungary. Czechoslovakia did not draw back from providing both explicit and latent encouragement to such development, but to little avail. It was only in its relations with Austria that some kind of accommodation was eventually reached, though it lacked warmth. Moreover, in terms of its internal and international orientation, Austria had since the late 1920s pro-gressively distanced itself from Central European co-operation projected in Prague and in Paris. As for Admiral Miklós Horthy's Hungary, whose declared top priority was the revision, or more precisely, nullification of the Treaty of Trianon – it offered no hope whatsoever for finding a common language with Czechoslovakia. In effect, it long regarded Czechoslovakia as its principal adversary. Thus the sole option was to wait for favourable

7. The Little Entente.

changes to take place in Hungary's policies. No such changes were in the offing; rather, the existing differences grew deeper. Czechoslovakia's relations with Poland, one of its most important neighbours, had been burdened from the very start by a territorial dispute to which political discord was added since the mid-1920s. Underlying their frictions were also the rival ambitions of the two states in the area 'between Germany and Russia', Czechoslovakia's 'caution' *vis-à-vis* the conflictory Polish–German relations, as well as Poland's internal political inharmoniousness in the wake of Józef Piłsudski's (1867–1935) coup which deflected Poland from democracy (1926).

The military defeat of Germany and the elimination of influence in Central Europe had made possible the foundation of Czechoslovakia. The establishment of the Weimar Republic was labelled in Prague as 'a war victory for Germany' which as a nationally cohesive republic was considered to be better suited to pursue democratic and peaceful policies. Czechoslovakia sought to lay the foundations to her relations with Germany at a period when the latter was more than anything else an object of international politics; Czechoslovakia did not identify completely with the early-1920s French tactic of increasing pressure on Germany, even though in many respects it did comply with it. According to Czechoslovak thinking, Germany was to emerge from isolation with the consent of the West and through a system of agreements with the West would also bring to Central Europe. While the mutual guarantee convention signed with Germany in October 1925 could not fully satisfy Czechoslovakia, the two states had no outstanding territorial or other bilateral disputes. Democratic Germany did not represent a threat, yet her internal developments continued to be closely watched, and during all negotiations between the West and Germany it was necessary to give due consideration to the interests of the smaller states.

Czechoslovakia linked the constant emphasis on democratization of international relations with the principle of collective security. There also she came to play an active part in the League of Nations. In 1924 Czechoslovakia was among the initiators of the Geneva Protocol which sought to endow the League of Nations with more effective powers against disturbers of international order and peace. Czechoslovakia even ratified the Protocol though it eventually failed to be ratified by the League of Nations. Foreign Minister Beneš was involved in the search for a viable correlation between disarmament and security. Altogether his activities transgressed the boundaries of the state which he represented; while they took into account France's standpoints, they did not merely interpret or reflect them. Czechoslovakia's primary alignment with France, none the less, continued especially as Benito Mussolini (1883–1945) brought into international relations the impulse to revise the peace treaties, including distribution of spheres of influence between the Great Powers. That was to be achieved through a Four-Power Pact between Italy, Germany, France and Britain which would have considerably damaged the spirit and letter of the Versailles system. Proposed in 1933, the idea entered international politics and stayed there. Five years from then Czechoslovakia was to be given a fatal proof of that in the shape of the Munich Agreement.

Efforts for revision of the peace treaties gained momentum by becoming initially the centrepiece of Nazi Germany's foreign policy. It became evident that to attack and to render ineffective obligations stemming from the Treaty of Versailles, was no longer difficult or hazardous as for various reasons the ranks of those who kept watch had thinned out and those that remained were continually getting weaker. The advent to power of National Socialists in Germany introduced tensions into international relations. The toppling of the Weimar Republic in 1933 had wide-ranging repercussions. World democracy suffered a defeat which was exacerbated by the impact of Nazism on the growth of anti-democratic forces. While initially the Germany of Adolf Hitler (1889–1945) had to put up a fight against sanctions and isolation and offered to enter into deals, the German threat was re-emerging. Nazi and other forms of militarism signalled the danger of a new war, and that was what everybody in the West dreaded. The human, economic, political and spiritual consequences of the previous world conflagration were still too deeply felt and made the safeguarding of the Versailles system problematic.

Isolation

The new international tendencies affected Czechoslovakia's external status as well as her internal situation. Of special significance, Czechoslovakia's relations with Germany became more and more uneasy. The assessment that Germany was a principal adversary was totally justified. Hitler's attitude towards Czechoslovakia was unequivocally hostile. Even before he came to power he would readily talk of seizing the Czech Lands and expelling the Czech nation from them. According to Nazi geopolitical designs, the Czech Lands were to become part of the 'steel core' of the future Great German Reich. Czechoslovakia found itself in disfavour with the Nazis because of its democratic regime *per se*. It remained a steadfast ally of France, willing to intervene militarily on its side against Germany. In turn, Czechoslovakia occupied a permanent place in German military thinking as a hostile entity. As early as 1935, the German High Command had worked on plans for pre-emptive war against Czechoslovakia. Hitler intended to make it the first Central European state he would do away with provided, of course, Czechoslovakia's political and military isolation were in place.

The country's international disqualification and internal instability were to be increased by the activities of Henlein's Sudeten German Party, which came into existence in 1935 with its transformation from the Sudeten German Patriotic Front. Successes scored by Nazi Germany were instrumental in the fascization of what had initially been a conglomerate nationalist party. At the end of 1937, its leaders made a definitive decision to assist Germany in bringing about the destruction of the Czechoslovak state. From that time, any domestic talks on Sudeten German issues were doomed to failure. The Sudeten German Party's official autonomist programme and negotiations on it with the government in 1938 were turned into a means of fomenting an atmosphere of crisis which was to be exploited by Germany in its activities against Czechoslovakia. In addition to that, the Sudeten German Party sought allies among the nationalist parties of the Magyar and Polish minorities. That also corresponded with the anti-Czechoslovak policies pursued by Hungary and Poland, policies which set the guidelines for those parties. In the course of 1938, Hungary and Poland helped Germany to achieve the isolation of Czechoslovakia, by whose extinction they wanted to profit territorially and politically. They only hoped that it would not set a pretext for war, at least, not on a large scale.

For its part, the People's Party in Slovakia stepped up its campaign for Slovak autonomy though still keeping it within the constitutional limits of the Czechoslovak state. Actually, the People's Party resisted an alternative under which Slovakia would have been once again incorporated into Hungary, which was the aim of Hungary. But its leadership considered the option under which, in case of German attack on Czechoslovakia, it would try to attach Slovakia to Poland with whose government it had maintained long-standing contacts based on ideological affinities.

Czechoslovakia hoped it would not stand alone against Germany, either politically or in case of a military conflict. It continued to rely on its alliance with France in the firm belief that France could not sacrifice Czechoslovakia, as that would have wiped out French influence in Central Europe. Britain, too, was expected to take into account Czechoslovakia's relevance to the West and to democracy in Europe at large. At the same time, there was plentiful evidence of the West being on the defensive, of its international losses and constant concessions – both political and economic – in its political confrontations with the fascist powers which sought to disrupt the postwar peace system and to change the world. Czechoslovakia, however, did not respond to that by any substantial realignment of its foreign policy, nor would it have been able to do so anyway, as long as it did not wish to undergo internal changes as well. None the less, it did advise

Germany of her willingness to reach a new accord, which would certainly have had an effect on Czechoslovak foreign policy. But Hitler would not have any non-aggression treaty-type agreement, loth as he was to enter into binding obligations involving any Czech political grouping. His sole interest at that point was to destabilize and unsettle Czechoslovakia both externally and internally. German propaganda assailed Czechoslovakia with campaigns designed to demonstrate oppression of ethnic minorities and danger of bolshevism. The propaganda met with international response where it suited one's own enmity towards Czechoslovakia, or where it could be used to bring political pressure to bear on its government.

In 1935 Czechoslovakia, as the only small European state, concluded a Pact of Non-Aggression and of Mutual Assistance against Unprovoked Aggression with the Soviet Union. It was derived from the Franco-Soviet Pact (concluded about the same time) and was contingent on it. Moreover, it represented a vestige of a broader attempt at setting up a regional system of collective security in Central and Eastern Europe, which had been rejected by Germany and Poland. Czechoslovakia intended the treaty with the Soviets to have a mainly political effect, with a view to keeping Germany at bay while contributing to a rapprochement between the West and the USSR which had seemed to be a contribution to the development of international relations, and with regards to the situation inside the Soviet Union. In this instance as in several other cases, Czechoslovak foreign policy based its action largely on hypotheses and wishful thinking; acting on its own, it could not achieve more. Underlying its concepts and estimates was Beneš's, by then, familiar political optimism: it defied political reality while, at the same time, reflecting it imprecisely. It persisted well into the hardest times beginning in the spring of 1938 when Germany, encouraged by the smooth annexation of Austria, started to direct the brunt of her political and military threats against Czechoslovakia.

The Munich Agreement

Czechoslovakia had braced itself for that danger for years, and not just militarily. Even though not entirely obvious on the surface, the danger profoundly marked the life of the country. Accordingly, the history of the First Republic appears to have been split into two distinct parts: the first, covering the 1920s, involved the building of the state whereas the second, embracing the 1930s, with obstacles to the systematic continuation of that process, saw the emergence of existential problems.

The imminence of that threat posed by Nazi Germany had since the spring of 1938 united the Czech nation, whose awareness was heightened toward what was generally regarded as a danger to national identity. It identified with Czechoslovakia as its state and one which was well worth defending. But thinking along national lines also prevailed among the majority of the country's German-speaking population, which desired the incorporation of the Czech Lands' border regions into Germany. Guided by the national criterion, the German-speaking population saw in Nazism the embodiment and extension of the Great German idea. The situation in Slovakia was influenced by several factors. Ethnically, the 'Czechoslovak nation' had not been formed; on the contrary, the democratic and cultural climate aided the maturation of Slovak national society. It was not as acutely aware of the 'German' danger as was the Czech nation because it lacked the former's historical experience in that respect. While it did not worry as deeply as its Czech counterpart, it did not question the *raison d'être* of the Czechoslovak state either, and showed understanding for the need to defend itself. The notion of a union with Poland hedged within the People's Party was kept secret – merely as an option should the war turn out to go badly.

In 1938 Czechoslovakia suffered a defeat in what was a political war. In its course Germany resorted to military threats while on the propaganda front it pushed to the fore its own interpretation of the Sudeten German question, intensifying it to a point of raising territorial claims. The West officially accepted the interpretation of the tensions between Germany and Czechoslovakia as resulting from the ethnic policies of the Czechoslovak government, and compelled it to make concessions to the orchestrated pressures of Germany and her agents in the Sudeten German Party. The president and cabinet decided to agree with the granting of autonomy to the Sudeten, although they were apprehensive about the regions' administration passing into the hands of a fascist party. They wanted at all costs to maintain political links with the West and to secure its continued interest in the fate of the Czechoslovak state; pursuing that goal they also appealed to common spiritual values. By their conduct in the negotiations on the Sudeten German issue they strove to give proof to the West, and the world at large, that to Germany the matter was nothing but a pretext for the liquidation of Czechoslovakia.

But the 'appeasement' governments of Great Britain and France concentrated on finding political accord with Germany which would prevent war. While the initial stakes appeared to be limited to the border regions of the Czech Lands, they eventually proved to be much higher and indeed drastic. Czechoslovakia was then prepared to put up military resistance to Germany, provided it could rely on assistance from its French ally. Hence also its hopes for the creation of a broader-based anti-German coalition and for the League of Nations' positive response to its self-defence. Such hopes were frustrated as France reneged on its alliance treaty with Czechoslovakia.

Mitteilungen
des Sudetendeutfchen Hauptverbandes der Induftrie

XIX. Jahrgang.	Reichenberg, am 6. Oktober 1938.	Folge 40.

Unfere fudetendeutfchen Gaue kehren heim ins Deutfche Reich.

Ein Siegerdiktat glaubte trennen zu können, was durch Blut, Sprache und Kultur Einheit ift. Gerechtigkeit und die ewigen Gefetze der Natur erwiefen fich ftärker.

Die Sehnfucht eines Jahrtaufendes ift erfüllt: Ein mächtiges einiges Großdeutfchland.

Schwer lafteten 20 Jahre Fremdherrfchaft auf unferer Heimat. Aus Stätten emfiger Arbeit wurden Induftriefriedhöfe, unzählige Volksgenoffen mußten in Arbeitslofigkeit darben und unfere Befchwerden blieben ungehört.

Nach hartem Kampfe liegt nun der Weg in eine beffere Zukunft offen. Erft jetzt ift die wahre Befriedung Europas möglich. Unfere Heimat wird eingefügt in den mächtigen Lebensftrom der deutfchen Wirtfchaft und die fchweren Wunden werden heilen.

In diefen Stunden weltgefchichtlichen Gefchehens find wir uns der Pflichten bewußt, die uns der fieghafte Geift des nationalfozialiftifchen Deutfchland in Volks- und Betriebsgemeinfchaft auferlegt. Mit neuem Mute und frifcher Tatkraft fchreiten wir an den Wiederaufbau und geloben, einträchtig alle Kräfte einzufetzen zum Wohle der Gemeinfchaft, in fozialem Verftehen und unerfchütterlicher Treue zu Staat und Volk.

Das fei unfer aus tiefftem Herzen kommender Dank an unferen Führer.

Heil Hitler!
Sudetendeutfcher Hauptverband der Induftrie.

8. The Sudeten German Industrial Association thanks the Führer on 6 October 1938.

This contributed more than anything to Czechoslovakia's acceptance, on 30 September 1938, of the conditions imposed upon it by the Munich Agreement. There was more to it than depriving Czechoslovakia of a part of its territory. The blow dealt to Czechoslovakia at Munich had as a consequence the setting off an internal transformation which marked the end of democracy in Czechoslovakia. 'Munich' also badly hit Czechoslovakia's economy and robbed it of independent foreign policy. Reaching beyond the Czechoslovak context, 'Munich' did severe damage to democracy worldwide and finally disrupted the international order established after 1918. In the climate 'Munich' had ushered in, Germany had no difficulty in destroying Czechoslovakia completely in March 1939.

Selected bibliography

K. Bosl (ed.), *Die demokratisch-parlamentarische Struktur der Ersten Tschechoslowakischen Republik* (Munich-Vienna, 1975)

K. Bosl and F. Seibt (eds.) *Kultur und Gesellschaft in der Ersten Tschechoslowakischen Republik* (Munich, 1982)

E. Broklová, *Československá demokracie Politický system ČSR 1918–1938* [Czechoslovak democracy The political system of the Czechoslovak Republic 1918–1938] (Prague, 1992)

J. W. Brügel, *Tschechen und Deutsche 1918–1938*, 2 vols. (Munich, 1967, 1974)

Z. Deyl, *Sociální vývoj Československa 1918–1938* [Social development of Czechoslovakia 1918–1938] (Prague, 1986)

Alena Gajanová, *ČSR a středoevropská politika velmocí (1918–1938)* [The Czechoslovak Republic and the Central European policy of the Great Powers (1918–1938)] (Prague, 1967)

J. K. Hoensch, *Geschichte der Tschechoslowakischen Republik*, 3rd edn (Stuttgart-Berlin-Cologne, 1992)

V. Kural, *Konflikt místo společenství? Češi a Němci v československém státě (1918–1938)* [Conflict instead of sociality? Czechs and Germans in the Czechoslovak state (1918–1938)] (Prague, 1993)

R. Kvaček, *Nad Evropou zataženo Československo a Evropa 1933–1937* [Clouds over Europe Czechoslovakia and Europe 1933–1937] (Prague, 1966)

V. S. Mamatey and R. Luža (eds.), *A History of the Czechoslovak Republic 1918–1948* (Princeton, 1973)

Věra Olivová, *The Doomed Democracy Czechoslovakia in a Disrupted Europe 1914–1938* (London, 1972)

Alice Teichova, *The Czechoslovak Economy 1918–1980* (London and New York, 1988)

W. W. Wallace, *Czechoslovakia* (London, 1977)

Z. Zeman, *The Masaryks The Making of Czechoslovakia*, repr. (London, 1990)

Slovensko v politickom systéme Československa. Materiály z vedeckého sympózia [Slovakia in the political system of Czechoslovakia Symposium materials] (Bratislava, 1992)

14

The Protectorate of Bohemia and Moravia (1939–1945): the economic dimension

ALICE TEICHOVA

Introduction

From its foundation on 28 October 19 8 to its dismemberment after the Czechoslovak government's acceptance of the Munich Agreement on 30 September 1938 the Republic of Czech slovakia remained an independent state. At the same time, its political and economic system was influenced by complex financial and diplomatic relations. In the League of Nations' order of developed economies, inter-war Czechoslovakia ranked among the ten largest per capita producers of industrial goods[1] and the seven largest suppliers of armaments in the world, as well as among those European countries most dependent on exports. International business was attracted to the Czechoslovak economy because of its relatively high concentration in industry and banking, the comparatively low level of wages and the stable political conditions of the country's democratic system of government.

Between the wars the Czechoslovak economy became an important link between Western, especially British and French economic interests, and South-east Europe. At the same time it became an area of complicated competitive struggles, above all, between Western Europe and Germany. Within this framework competition in the country itself between Czechoslovak and German groups continuously sharpened. German capital endeavoured to capture economic positions in Czechoslovakia and tried to sever the economic and political ties between Czechoslovakia and the Western powers as well as between the states of the Little Entente.[2]

As a result of the *Anschluß* of Austria to Germany (11 March 1938) the threat to Czechoslovakia's independence became imminent. Half a year later the Munich Agreement sealed the fate of the First Republic

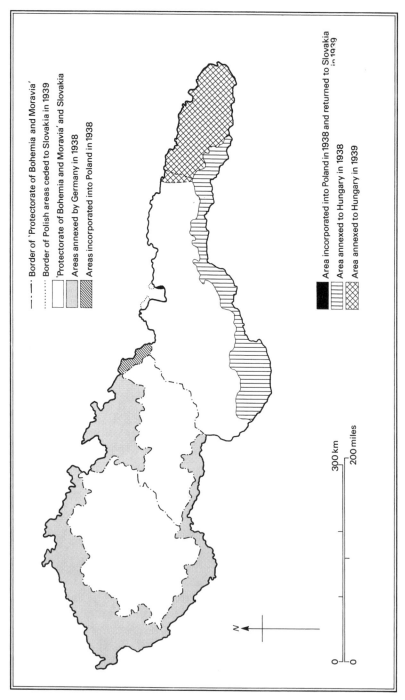

Border of 'Protectorate of Bohemia and Moravia'
Border of Polish areas ceded to Slovakia in 1939
'Protectorate of Bohemia and Moravia' and Slovakia
Areas annexed by Germany in 1938
Areas incorporated into Poland in 1938

Area incorporated into Poland in 1938 and returned to Slovakia in 1939
Area annexed to Hungary in 1938
Area annexed to Hungary in 1939

300 km
200 miles

N

0
0

9. The dismemberment of Czechoslovakia, 1938–39.

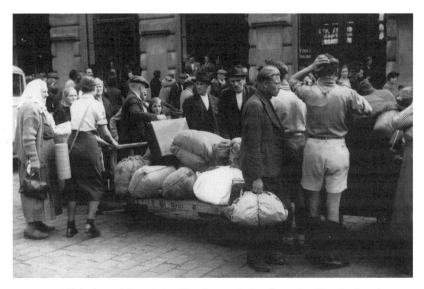

10. Flight/expulsion of the Czech population from the Czechoslovak
border regions in 1938.

of Czechoslovakia. It led to the annexation of extensive border regions of
Czechoslovakia to Germany, Poland and Hungary (see fig. 9). As a
result Czechoslovakia lost 30 per cent of her territory and more than a third
of her population at the same time as about 450,000 inhabitants were
expelled or fled from their homes in the borderlands into the interior of the
country.[3] Severe losses of industrial and agricultural capacity were incurred
as well as vital fortifications were forfeited in the border regions which
Germany annexed (see fig. 11). Under these circumstances the life of the
rump of the state's territory, the so-called Second Republic of Czechoslovakia, was doomed. (After the proclamation of Slovak autonomy on 6
October 1938, Czechoslovakia became Czecho-Slovakia). In the short
period between 30 September 1938 and the occupation of Bohemia and
Moravia by the German army on 15 March 1939 Czechoslovakia's role in
the international economy was destroyed, her territory divided into different parts which, ultimately, served the war economy of National Socialist
Germany. Of the total industrial production of the former Czechoslovakia,
92 per cent was concentrated in the territories incorporated into the Reich:
70 per cent in Bohemia and Moravia, the occupied Protectorate, and 22 per
cent in the border regions annexed to Germany. The remaining 8 per cent
was located in Slovakia which had seceded from the Second Republic of
Czechoslovakia and declared its independence on 14 March 1939.[4]

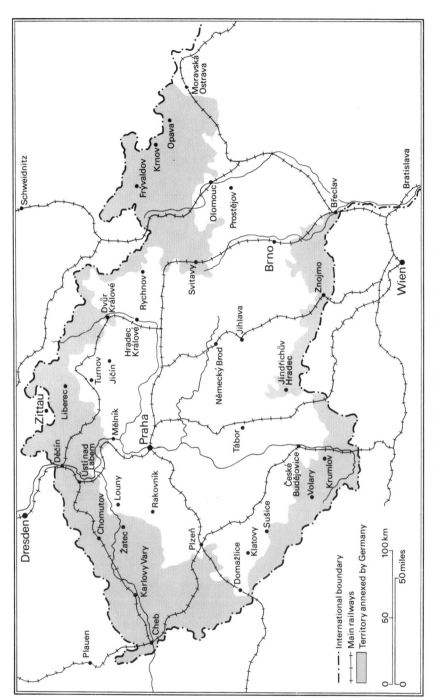

11. Borders of Czech Lands, 21 November 1938.

Schweidnitz

Moravská
Ostrava

Frývaldov
Krnov
Opava

Bratislava

Olomouc
Prostějov

Dvůr
Králové
Rychnov

Hradec
Králové

Svitavy

Brno

Znojmo

Zittau

Liberec

Turnov
Jičín

Jihlava

Německý Brod

Jindřichův
Hradec

Wien

Dresden

Děčín

Ústí nad
Labem

Mělník

Praha

Chomutov
Louny
Rakovník

Tábor

Žatec

Plzeň

Karlovy Vary

Klatovy
Sušice

Domažlice

České
Budějovice
Volary
Krumlov

Cheb

Plauen

International boundary
Main railways
Territory annexed by Germany

50
100 km

50 miles

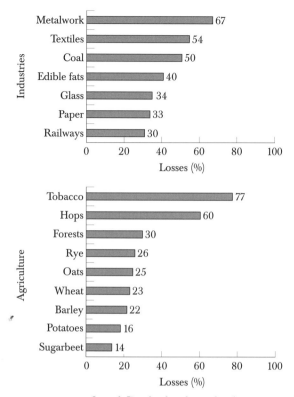

12. Losses as percentage of total Czechoslovak production as a result of the
Munich Agreement, 1938.

For National Socialist Germany's preparations for war the Protectorate
was of great importance, because there the decisive part of former
Czechoslovakia's total production of the iron-and-steel and mechanical
engineering industries was situated, while in the annexed border areas the
share of consumer goods industries, such as textiles and glass, etc., was relatively greater.

In this chapter, attention is focused on the German occupation of the
Czech Lands, Bohemia and Moravia, the so-called Protectorate.

Character and structure of the occupation regime –
administration as an instrument of economic control

Officially, the date of the invasion of the Czech Lands by the German army
is 15 March 1939. But the starting signal for crossing the frontier into north

Moravia demonstrates the importance National Socialist Germany attached to Czechoslovakia's heavy industry. On the afternoon of 14 March, Adolf Hitler (1889–1945) issued an order to General Wilhelm Keitel, the Chief of High Command, to occupy the largest Central European iron-and-steel works, the Vítkovice Mining and Foundry Works in Ostrava, before the general military invasion of the Czech Lands on 15 March 1939, to prevent Poland from seizing the rolling mills before the arrival of the German army.[5]

The constitutional position of the Czech Lands remained intentionally vague as the German government took into account that the military conquest of non-German territory was happening in peace time and, in order to reap benefits from the expected spoils, a smoke screen of legality would have to be observed. The leading Slovak politician Monsignor Dr Jozef Tiso (1887–1947),[6] at a hastily convened meeting with Hitler on 13 March 1939, agreed that the secession of Slovakia from the Second Republic of Czechoslovakia and the establishment of a Slovak state under his premiership was to be announced on 14 March 1939. However, Emil Hácha (1872–1945),[7] the President of Czechoslovakia, was kept in the dark. Although Hitler had not replied to Hácha's urgent requests to be received, Hácha decided on his own accord to travel to Berlin on 14 March to find out from Hitler himself about his intentions concerning Slovakia and the Czechoslovak state in general.[8] When he was eventually received at the Reich Chancellery in Berlin on the afternoon of 15 March 1939, Slovakia had declared independence, his government in Prague had tendered its provisional resignation and the invasion of Bohemia and Moravia by the German army was in full swing. During this humiliating visit Hácha signed a declaration placing 'the fate of the Czech nation in full confidence into the hands of the Führer of the German nation'[9] and in return, received Hitler's nebulous promise that Germany would guarantee the Czech nation's 'autonomous development of its national life according to its character'.[10]

The next day, 16 March 1939, Hitler decreed the establishment of the 'Protectorate of Bohemia and Moravia as an integral part of the German Reich'. Colonial status was conferred upon the Czech Lands – thus the designation of 'Protectorate' – according to the model of the French–Tunisian agreement of 1881 which, to a certain extent, provided a basis for the structure of the occupied territory's administration.[11] Czechs became citizens of the Protectorate at the same time as all Czechoslovak citizens of German nationality received citizenship of the German Reich.[12] This was greeted by Germans in the Protectorate with extravagant demonstrations of joy similar to the hysterical celebrations when former

Czechoslovak citizens of German nationality became citizens of the German Reich after the annexation of the Czechoslovak border regions in October 1938.[13] At the same time the Sudeten German Party which, between 1933 and 1938/9, had considered itself to be the representative of all Germans in Bohemia and Moravia, was dissolved and merged with the National Socialist Workers Party (NSDAP – Nationalsozialistische Deutsche Arbeiterpartei). In the course of implementing German rule through the administration in the Protectorate, this move carried seeds of frictions between indigenous Germans and Germans from the Reich.

Schema 1 shows the institutional structure of the German Occupation Authority and its relation to the Czech Protectorate government which functioned, except for minor changes, from 16 March 1939 to 20 August 1943. It contained organizational elements of dualist government which, if needed by the German authority, could be activated. On the eve of war and during the heady period of Germany's military successes it was expected that Hácha's government guarantee social peace and order as the economy was rapidly geared to war production. However, the last remnants of this euphemistic autonomy were liquidated in the summer of 1943 when victory slipped ever further out of Hitler's grasp.

In response to the German invasion of Bohemia and Moravia Edvard Beneš (1884–1948), the former President of Czechoslovakia living abroad, returned into politics, first forming a National Committee and then, after the fall of France, the Czechoslovak government in exile in London, which was recognized by the British government on 21 July 1940.[14] The contacts it established with resistance groups at home and with the Protectorate government led to severe persecutions by the German occupation authority.[15]

From the very beginning German rule was headed by the Reichsprotektor, whose authority was strengthened, as he was directly responsible to Hitler. The first to be appointed Reichsprotektor, after a short interregnum under the leader of the Sudeten German Party (SdP – Sudetendeutsche Partei) Konrad Henlein (1898–1945), was Konstantin von Neurath (1873–1956), described as a diplomat of the old school but capable of imposing the brutal Nazi dictatorship without scruples. Karl Hermann Frank (1898–1946), an ambitious and violently anti-Czech leading functionary of the Sudeten German Party, was appointed State Secretary and Deputy Reichsprotektor. Unlike in Germany and in the unrestrained post-*Anschluß* period in Austria, the activities of the NSDAP in the Protectorate were strictly separated from the executive authority of the Reichsprotektor.

Never the less, claims of the *Gauleiters*, the heads of NSDAP's regional party organizations, to have a say in the affairs of the Protectorate led to competition within the National Socialist hierarchy on questions of anti-Czech policy and Aryanization[16] and, in particular, on attempts to change the territorial organization of the Protectorate. The latter emanated from the differences in the administrative and political borders between the NSDAP and the Protectorate. Instead of the expectations of Konrad Henlein's Sudeten German Party that all the territories annexed to Germany in October 1938 would be included in an undivided administrative whole called Sudetenland, ten districts of the NSDAP were formed in the Protectorate and subordinated organizationally to the four neighbouring German *Gaue* (Sudetenland, Bayerische Ostmark, Oberdonau, Niederdonau). Some of these *Gaue* included large areas inhabited also by Czechs, as for instance the *Gau* Oberdonau which reached almost as far as Prague. Leading functionaries of the NSDAP in southern Germany and in the Ostmark (Austria) applied pressure on Berlin to liquidate the autonomy of the Czech government in the Protectorate, together with the office of the Reichsprotektor, and include Bohemia and Moravia in the German Reich's *Gau*-system. While the Reichsprotektor, sensing a restriction of his powers, opposed such schemes as they arose, Hitler prevaricated and as late as 1943 let it be known that the last word about this had not yet been spoken.[17]

Further down the line of the German administration of the Protectorate, twenty Oberlandräte (OLR) (twelve in Bohemia and eight in Moravia) were appointed on 22 April 1939. Subordinate to both the Reichsprotektor and the State Secretary, they were charged with the control of the Czech organs at district and communal level. President Hácha and his government had, on the basis of Hitler's promise, expected to head an autonomous Czech administration but the decisive posts were kept firmly in the hands of German high officials (see Schema 1).

Ostensibly, the national Czech administration was an autonomous government of the Protectorate. In reality, it was autonomous in name only and had to get permission for all its actions from the Reichsprotektor and the State Secretary. Parliament was dissolved and political parties were prohibited. In the Protectorate government's subservient statement of intent, it pledged to use all organs of state at its disposal, especially police and gendarmerie, to ensure social peace and order on the whole territory of the Protectorate, including prevention of disturbances of any kind. Further, it declared that all acts of sabotage which disrupted or paralysed normal public life, especially economic life, were actions inimical to the Reich and as such would be prosecuted and most severely punished.[18] The President was allowed to keep a small symbolic 'government army' enabling him to retain the title of Chief Commander but the word 'Czech' in the official name of this army was not permitted.[19] The character of the Czech

Protectorate government was described in a German programmatic document thus: 'We need a weak Czech government able to re-organize the Czech nation in such a way that it would never rebel against Germany, but that the government should be strong enough to prevent an opposition from taking power'.[20]

The Czech administration was very large. Although entirely subordinate to German control and steering, it was kept as a fictitious autonomous organism in order to ensure that Czechs fulfilled the needs of the German war effort. Figures quoted in situation reports from Prague to Berlin mention *c.* 400,000 Czech personnel, whilst German civil servants amounted to *c.* 2,000.[21] Indeed, the co-operation of the Czech government, whose main policy was to ensure compliance in order to maintain its 'autonomous' status, enabled the German regime of occupation to economise on its own civil servants. The Czech civil service respected, accepted and obeyed Hácha and his government, as did the leading personnel in industry, transport, police and in the government army. Opportunism reigned from the centre in Prague down to Czech local authorities on the basis of the attitude 'if it is not us it would be a worse outfit'.[22] Generally, the Czech population did not share this feeling and practised various forms of passive resistance to the regime of occupation, as well as forms of active resistance which were cruelly suppressed.[23]

While the civil administration in Bohemia and Moravia continued to work smoothly the German authority could keep the numbers of its own civil service low and concentrate on the personnel of the occupation army, the German police, the SS ('Schutzstaffel'), the feared Gestapo and the security service (SD – Sicherheitsdienst). In the attempt to create a colonial-type Protectorate, a few hundred thousand Germans became the governing strata over millions of Czechs who were now second-class citizens in every respect.

In fact, the German occupation authority could not act as a 'classical' colonial regime, for it imposed itself on a society and economy in the heart of Europe which had a structure as advanced as Germany itself. Thus, the occupation regime's policy could not consist merely of mindless primitive plunder but concerned more complicated and sophisticated methods of exploitation to ensure the utilization of advanced technology and capacity in Czech heavy industry and, above all, the employment of skilled labour, qualified technicians and an educated workforce – all of which became increasingly important in Germany's war effort.

Two main views affected the administration of the Protectorate and led to conflicts between the Office of the Reichsprotektor and that of the State Secretary – until Reinhard Heydrich (1904–1942), the chief of the Reich security service, succeeded von Neurath as Deputy Reichsprotektor on 28 September 1941. One view represented by von Neurath and supported by the army and diplomacy, espoused a traditional imperialist policy based on collaboration with domestic elements and exploitation of economic resources of the Czech Lands. The other, Karl Hermann Frank's view, was based on a dictatorship of terror and brutality. It emanated from chauvinist circles of the former Sudeten German Party and was based on their claim to a leading role in the Protectorate. Frank favoured a complete denationalization of Czechs (*die vollkommene Enttschechisierung*) by forced Germanization (*Eindeutschung*), expulsion and physical liquidation (see further) and the total incorporation of Bohemia and Moravia as one of the German provinces into the Thousand Year Reich.[24] But this view, as mentioned above, had to compete with the claims of leading Reich German circles, and it was these claims which prevailed. Although Hitler endorsed Frank's detailed proposal in principle as a long-term solution, he decided in the autumn of 1940 that, in the short term, the status of the Protectorate under supreme authority of the Reich ('Reichsgewalt') was to be maintained in the interest of the war effort (cf. Document 1 in the appendix to this chapter).[25]

Compared with other occupied areas, the economic realities of the Czech case set certain limits to mass terror and the barbarian extermination policy. Without doubt, economic considerations were paramount, but the regime of occupation also reaped psychological advantages due to the presence of former Czechoslovak citizens of German nationality (who had automatically gained German citizenship) in the leadership of the Protectorate and who intimately knew the Czech environment. This made an impact on the occupation authority's tactics which could and were, if needed, adapted to the specific behavioural pattern of the Czech nation. In this connection knowledge of the mood, historical experiences and tradition of the Czech population became a useful instrument of rule especially during the depressive period following the Munich Agreement.

Occupation policies were, of course, strongly influenced both by the international and domestic situation and, therefore, distinct phases are recognizable: 1. 15 March 39 to the outbreak of war, Czech autonomy was instrumentalized for German gains in the world market. 2. After Nazi victories in Europe, restrictions on autonomy were stepped up and, with Heydrich's arrival in Prague, 28 September 1941, the implementation of the New Order was more vigorously pursued. 3. From the defeat of the German army at Moscow in the winter of 1941/2 and Heydrich's assassination, 27 May 1942, terror and brutality was let loose until 20 August 1943 when dualist government was liquidated. 4. At that time, the up-keep of war production in the Protectorate demanded greater restraints from the occupation regime, but also the resistance movement gained strength and reached its peak in the Slovak Uprising in 1944 and the Prague Rising in 1945.

German economic policy and instruments of economic exploitation in Bohemia and Moravia

Foreign exchange and exports

The immediate concern of Hermann Göring (1893–1946) as Plenipotentiary for the Four Year Plan was expressed in his urgent dispatch of 16 March 1939 – the very day Hitler decreed the establishment of the Protectorate – which was sent to every Reichsminister, to the Reichsprotektor and to all civil service chiefs in Bohemia and Moravia. In this dispatch he insisted on greater centralized control in the process of incorporating the occupied territory into the German *Wirtschaftsraum* than had been necessary in the former Czechoslovak border regions (Sudetenland) or in Austria (Ostmark). He therefore reserved decision-making on all fundamental economic questions to himself. In particular, he pointed to the well-known export orientation of Czechoslovak industry and stressed the urgent necessity of maintaining this export for the purpose of gaining foreign exchange. He urged the Reich Economics Minister to take all suitable measures to achieve this aim, and he stressed that all current foreign contracts of Bohemian and Moravian enterprises should be fulfilled punctually in order to secure the proceeds in foreign exchange ('Devisenerlös') for the whole German economy. In the same dispatch he warned against a rush of German buyers wanting to acquire Czech assets at knock-down prices, as well as against unauthorized capital transfers and 'wild' Aryanization. To ensure an orderly transfer from peace to war production he demanded strict discipline and the maintenance of the local price and wage levels.[26]

Without delay the German occupation authority initiated a rigorous inventory of all foreign exchange and gold reserves at banks and savings institutes in Bohemia and Moravia. At the same time, the Czech National Bank was ordered to transfer its gold reserves deposited in London to the Reichsbank. On 24 March 1939 it was confirmed by the Bank for International Settlements that the transfer of gold on its account for Czechoslovakia valued at Kč 739,740,596 had taken place.[27] Concurrently, the Reichsbank received further gold reserves from the Škoda Works and the Czech Armaments Works in Brno for the purchase of raw material supplies for both the German and Czech armament industry. In many cases of foreign debt and interest payments to Czech creditors, the Reichsbank was able to collect hard currency. However, the British government blocked Czech gold, currency and shares deposited in British banks; negotiations about their transfer to the Reich were terminated with the outbreak of war.[28]

An early example of Germany's adaptation of occupation policy to economic gain – in the interest of acquiring foreign exchange by maintaining Czech exports – is the matter of the Customs Union where, for a time, Czech and German interests coincided. The decree of 16 March 1939 establishing the Protectorate states in point 9: 'The Protectorate belongs to the customs area of the German Reich and is subordinated to its customs sovereignty'. While German business circles strongly advocated the liquidation of customs borders, the Czech business community expected customs and exchange autonomy. In April 1939, the Czech National Bank and the autonomous Czech ministries in a Memorandum – intended as a basis of negotiations – for the German Economics Ministry entitled 'Preconditions of economic development of the Protectorate Bohemia and Moravia' argued for customs, financial and exchange autonomy. They pleaded for the retention of customs sovereignty on the grounds that the sudden establishment of a Customs Union between Germany and the Protectorate would threaten export possibilities because of rising raw material prices and loss of traditional foreign markets, on the one hand, and a too-rapid adaptation of price and wages levels to the Reich would reduce the advantages of Czech exports, on the other. Moreover, the advantages, accruing to Germany, of the unrealistically underrated Czech Crown (K) to the German Mark (RM) as 1:10 (the real rate was 1:6) would be wiped out. On 12 May 1939 Walther Funk, the Reich Economics Minister, in his reply to the Czech Memorandum, agreed for the present to retain customs and exchange autonomy but added that 'no assurances can be given for the future'.[29]

Germany did reap substantial advantages from large export surpluses of the Czech economy while peace lasted. Czech business co-operated in an export programme under the direction of the largest concerns, above all, the Škoda Works and the Czech Armaments Works in Brno. The Škoda Works produced a list of uncompleted export orders for peace-products on 1 April 1939 in which their calculated value was just under half a milliard crowns (K 478,491,400); of this total 37 per cent were destined for Germany, while the greater part of 63 per cent was to be payable in hard currency. The list substantiates the world-wide destinations of Škoda exports: it shows fifty client countries, of which India, Iran, the Soviet Union and Yugoslavia held the leading places. Until 1940 the Armaments Works in Brno produced mainly for export to Romania, Yugoslavia and Turkey.[30] In the concept of the future export policy of the *Großraumwirtschaft* ('large space economy'),

Czech industrial capacity played a significant part: the Protectorate works were to be given preference in the Southeast European market because of their more favourable geographical transport position, while German works were to supply the West European market. Under German occupation Czech business, as partner in the German export drive, was able to penetrate the Southeast European market more successfully than before Munich. As a result the structure of the destination of Czech exports changed dramatically in a short time: by April 1940 70 per cent of total exports of the Protectorate were received by countries of Southeast Europe (of which 30 per cent went to Yugoslavia, 22 per cent to Slovakia, 15 per cent to Romania and 3 per cent to Hungary).[31] At the same time the reorientation of Czech exports towards the German market, while bringing numerous advantages for the Czech business community, changed the proportions of Czech trade with hard currency countries and clearing countries. Between the end of 1937 and May 1939 trade with hard currency countries fell from 61.5 per cent to 29 per cent, and trade with clearing countries rose from 38.5 to 71 per cent. In spite of this reversal the Protectorate's balance of trade with free market countries remained active (the balance was still more than half a milliard crowns in surplus at the end of 1939) during the period customs borders with Germany lasted. As the Czech business community joined its fate with the German economy, its role in international trade declined rapidly.[32]

But in the aftermath of the German conquests in Europe in the first year of the war, the advantages for Germany's balance of payment derived from separate customs territories outweighed the disadvantages: by the end of 1940 the Protectorate's trade with Germany had reached 80 per cent of total imports and 71 per cent of total exports.[33] Despite requests, indeed entreaties, by the Czech government of Premier Alois Eliáš (1890–1942), the Customs Union was introduced on 1 October 1940 and the Czech Lands were included in the Clearing Centre in Berlin. Its records show that during the occupation regime the Czech National Bank was credited with K 24.4 billion of which K 11.6 billion were paid out for supplies from third countries. The balance remained with the German Reich, never to be returned. At the same time, the National Bank in Prague paid Czech entrepreneurs export premiums in Czech Crowns (K) which acted as a substantial interest-free loan to the German Reich.[34]

Enforcement of war economy

Regulations of the transition from a market economy to a centrally controlled and administered economy were introduced in quick succession during the spring and summer months of 1939 in order to tighten controls and, above all, to incorporate the world-renowned war industries situated in Bohemia and Moravia into the German war machine. The instruments of transition from a peace-time to a war economy were operated both by the Czech administration and the occupation regime. In May 1939 the Supreme Price Office ('Nejvyšší úřad cenový') was established by Government Order. At the same time, conscription of the workforce on the Reich model was introduced by Order of the Ministry of Industry, Commerce and Trades. In June 1939 a State Order regulating wages and workers' duties was issued. This was followed in July 1939 by the Order of the 'organic construction of the economy' adapting the organization to the *Führerprinzip*. In its wake, labour exchanges were entrusted with the conscription and distribution of the work force.[35] In August 1939 the corporate system on the German model was established.[36] With regards to industry it consisted of the Central Association of Industry for Bohemia and Moravia (membership of both Czech and German industrialists was compulsory). In addition, there was a separate German Society for the Economy in Bohemia and Moravia ('Deutsche Gesellschaft für Wirtschaft in Böhmen und Mähren') which pursued the Germanization of the economy. Associations under central organization were: Trades, Transport, Financial Institutes, Insurance, Agriculture and Forestry, each controlled by the appropriate economic ministry. Further, the Control Office for Exports and Imports began to function. A tight grip on all economic activity was held by the decisive organs in the occupation administration: The Office of the Reichsprotektor, Sector Economy, Armaments Commission, Armament Inspection, Central Office for War Orders.

National Socialist Germany's ruthless domination over the Czechs, who were regarded as a racially inferior population, was tempered only by the crucial importance of the contributions the Czechs were capable of making to the German war effort. This is clearly substantiated by overwhelming documentary evidence. None is more revealing than the frenzied memorandum by K. H. Frank, addressed to Hitler on 28 August 1940, on 'The treatment of the Czech problem and the future organization of the Bohemian-Moravian area' (of this more later) in which he writes that certain considerations inhibited progress towards solving the Czech problem.[37] Because of this necessity, better wages and larger rations were apportioned to Czech workers in armament factories, and the liquidation of Czech nationhood was not held to be a realistic option during the war.

Never the less, an increasingly brutal regime was imposed on Bohemia and Moravia with the appointment of Reinhard Heydrich, the chief of the security service, as Deputy Reichsprotektor in Prague on 28 September

Table 14.1. *Index of industrial employment (Czech Lands 1939–1945) (Annual average – March 1939=100)*

Year	Industry total	Metallurgy & metalworking	Other branches
1939	104.9	107.9	103.9
1941	115.9	136.3	100.5
1942	117.6	150.9	94.5
1943	130.9	186.7	96.0
1994	141.9	223.8	93.6
1945/March	138.9	223.9	89.3

Source: Statistický zpravodaj, 1–2 (1945), 8.

1941. During his short reign, the Czech Lands were completely integrated into the Reich, the Czech Protectorate's government's authority crippled, and its Prime Minister Alois Eliáš was arrested a few hours after Heydrich's arrival in Prague on 27 September 1941[38] on account of his connections with the Czechoslovak government in exile. During the wave of terror after Heydrich's assassination, Eliáš was executed (19 June 1942) with thousands of other Czechs.[39] The Czech government as a collective organ was dissolved and only a few ministries were retained, most importantly the Ministry of Economics and Labour under Walter Bertsch, who came from the Reich. During this period war production as well as searches and persecution of persons suspected of sabotage or opposition were stepped up. On 21 March 1942 Hitler issued a Decree threatening heavy penalties (prison and death sentences) for false or withheld information about labour supply, material reserves, production targets and important raw materials, as well as products, machines and equipment needed for war production.[40] Heydrich and his successor Kurt Daluege who, with Frank, presided over the sacking of the villages Lidice and Ležáky and the murder of its male population,[41] pursued a stick-and-carrot ('Zuckerbrot und Peitsche') policy, as they reiterated in their reports to Berlin, in order to enforce submission and order and to ensure the continuation of war production.

The realization of Germany's economic policy in the Protectorate brought about changes in the structure of industrial employment. Table 14.1 shows the dramatic increase in employment in the metallurgical and metalworking industries which more than doubled between March 1939 and March 1945, while employment in other branches fell from an index figure of 103.9 to 89.3. This is borne out in table 14.2 which shows the percentage increase in industries essential to the war effort as against the fall of employ-

Table 14.2. *Industrial employment in 'Protectorate Bohemia and Moravia' (thousands)*

Industries	Sept. 1941	Average 1942	Average 1943	Average 1944	March 1945	Percentage change 1941–44
Metallurgy and metal working	314	347	429	514	512	+63
Chemicals	32	37	42	44	41	+37
Wood, sawmills and paper	60	61	66	63	62	+5
Textiles, leather and clothing	130	128	125	117	113	–10
Pottery, ceramics and glass	66	53	50	48	40	–27
Other industries and building	128	119	118	115	112	–10
Total industrial employment[a]	730	745	830	901	880	+23

[a] Excluding mining, electricity, gas and water.

Source: Report of Czechoslovak Finance Ministry in Budget Speech of Dr Vavro Šrobár (Prague, 1946).

Table 14.3. *'Großdeutschland', including 'Protectorate': Industrial employment 1941–1944*

	Percentage change 1941–1944	Percentage share of total	
		1941	1944
Germany: 1937 area	−1	86	82
Austria	+22	5	6
Czech Lands	+40	9	12
of which: Protectorate	+23	7	8
Sudetenland	+89	2	4
Total	+4	100	100

Source: Cited by E. A. Radice, 'The development of industry', in M. C. Kaser and E. A. Radice (eds.), *The Economic History of Eastern Europe 1919–1975* (Oxford, 1986), II, p. 424.

ment in consumer goods industries from September 1941 to March 1945.

During these years the significance of the Czech Lands rose as an area of relative safety from Allied bombing to which industrial capacity could be transferred and production maintained. This emerges from estimates based on employment figures contained in table 14.3 which demonstrate that the Czech regions contributed between 9 and 12 per cent to total 'Greater German' industrial production, and that their share increased relatively more than that of any other area of *Großdeutschland* between 1941 and 1944, although generally productivity fell.

The policy of Germanization[42] as an instrument of control and exploitation of Bohemia and Moravia

The instruments of economic control and exploitation employed in the Protectorate of Bohemia and Moravia by the German occupation regime have to be assessed in the context of the 'radical solution to the Czech problem'. The question of how to deal with the Czech nation had exercised the minds of the leadership of the Sudeten German Party for a long time, but practical proposals were put forward only after the fortunes of war had turned in Germany's favour. K. H. Frank's Memorandum ('Denkschrift') to Hitler of 18 August 1940 became the basis for policy decisions in Berlin and Prague.[43] Reading the language of the relevant documents, one could regard the horrendous ideas as the chimera of extremists were it not the case that the German authorities had already begun to implement them.

In the long term the Germanization of the Czech Lands was to be achieved by liquidating Czech nationhood. The following methods were to be applied: first, assimilation of the 40 to 50 per cent of the Czech population considered to be racially suitable to be Germanized. For this purpose the occupation regime established 'Health Care Commissions' which, in co-operation with the SS-Racial and Settlement Office, began their work of selection. Identity cards ('Kennkarten') were distributed to those considered as possible German material on the basis of racial research, and lists ('Volkslisten') were compiled. The attack on Czech intellectuals and learning was stepped up. Czech universities had been closed in November 1939 and the Germanization of the school system was taken in hand, especially the introduction of German as compulsory language.[44] The second method was to consist of deportation, removal and expulsion. This was to be postponed after victory, as no suitable region was deemed to be available as yet for large population movements. The third and most drastic method of solving the Czech problem was through special treatment ('Sonderbehandlung'), which meant physical liquidation. During periods of brutal terror, especially after the assassination of Reinhard Heydrich, progress was made by this method but, while the war required ever more workers both in the Protectorate and in Germany, mass extermination was unrealistic. An estimated 250,000 Czechoslovak citizens, of whom two thirds came from Bohemia and Moravia, lost their lives in concentration camps, or through executions and death during imprisonment between 1939 and 1945. As compared to other occupied countries, e.g. Poland, less Czech lives were lost due, above all, to the crucial economic role of the Czech Lands in German war production. As already pointed out, these plans were not the result of the nationalistic ravings of K. H. Frank alone but were approved policy decisions agreed with Hitler and conveyed to the Reichsprotektor from Berlin (cf. Document 1 in appendix). First and foremost the Czech problem was to be tackled by Germanization in the economic field: transfers of property into German hands, Aryanization and settlement of Germans on Czech soil.

Institutionalized economic exploitation by transfers of capital

The transfer of property in the Czech Lands into German hands was carried out speedily by the occupiers. In the short run, this policy aimed at making the industry and, indeed, the whole economy of the Protectorate available for Germany's mobilization for war. In the long term, the Germanization of capital was one of the important steps in the direction of the complete solution of the Czech problem. Let us deal with the historical reality of the short term.

As mentioned above, Göring in his dispatch of 16 March 1939 immediately reserved decision-making about the economic integration of Bohemia and Moravia into the German economy ('Wirtschaftsraum') to himself. In particular he demanded an orderly transfer of properties of great economic value, such as large estates, industrial enterprises, majority shareholdings and capital participations. For that reason he laid down that, for the time being, his personal approval was required to acquisitions of all larger objects valued at more than half a million.[45] This was followed up by Göring on 20 March 1939 authorizing the chief official ('Generalreferent') in the Economics Ministry, Hans Kehrl, to acquire the Czech Armament Works in Brno, the Škoda Works in Plzeň and the Vítkovice Mining and Foundry Works with their subsidiary enterprises.[46]

By his peremptory intervention Göring dashed the hopes of the Czech government and the leading Czech bankers and industrialists that the takeover of the great Bohemian-Moravian armament complex by Germany could be avoided. During the last months of the existence of the Second Czechoslovak Republic the government of Premier Rudolf Beran (1887–1957) carried out the privatization of the state's share in the capital of the Škoda Works and the Czech Armament Works Brno which stood at the head of a complicated structure of intertwined banking and industrial subsidiary companies. In this way a powerful armaments concern with vertical and horizontal linkages in the entire heavy industry of Czechoslovakia was formed under the leadership of a Czech syndicate on the eve of the German occupation of Bohemia and Moravia. The Czech government and business circles expected this armament complex to survive in Czech hands, because they based this erroneous belief on the experiences of Austria after the *Anschluß* where private property, as long as it was not in Jewish possession, had apparently been respected.[47] The arrival of Hans Kehrl in Prague, who was concurrently Plenipotentiary for the integration of Austria and the Sudetenland and who proceded to incorporate the Czech armament combine into the Third Reich, put an end to these expectations.[48]

Historians have researched and published widely on the acquisition of industrial assets and direct capital participations in occupied Czech territories in the course of the Germanization of properties. Above all, the contributions of Dietrich Eichholtz and Richard Overy[49] provide a detailed insight into the historical context and the mechanisms of property transfers. Václav Král devoted the second volume of his trilogy to reconstructing the acquisition of each of the largest Czech industrial and

Table 14.4. *Direct foreign capital investment in industrial, commercial and banking enterprises (in %)*

Country of origin	Czechoslovakia (31.12.1937)	'Protectorate Bohemia and and Moravia' (31.12.1940)
Great Britain	30.8	34
France	21.4	1.5
Austria	13.1	–
Holland	8.8	–
Germany	7.2	47
Belgium	7.1	–
Switzerland	4.5	7
USA	3.5	4
Italy	2.2	–
Sweden	0.9	1.2
Hungary	0.5	–
Slovakia	–	1.3
Other countries	–	4
Total	100.0	100.0

Sources: For Czechoslovakia, A. Teichova, *An economic background to Munich International business and Czechoslovakia 1918–1938* (Cambridge 1974), pp. 40–49; for the Protectorate, Archiv Státního úřadu statistického (ASÚA) – Koncernové šetření (Inquiry into combines).

banking concerns and cooperatives by German big business and leading banks.[50] Also the scramble for the spoils among business circles of Sudeten Germans and Reich Germans as well as among German private and state enterprises is well evidenced. The ways and means of this process varied from the appointment of trustees ('Treuhänder'), over transfers affected under constraint, to confiscations under the pretext of sentences for political and economic offences and, last but not least, to Aryanization of Jewish property (see below). I confine myself here to presenting a general picture of German acquisitions of industrial assets in the Protectorate by 1940/41 based on investigations conducted by the German Occupation Authority.

Changes in the structure of foreign investments and the increase in German direct capital participations are shown in tables 14.4 and 14.5. While Europe was still at peace, representatives of Reich German banks, industrial companies and government agencies conducted negotiations, mainly in France and Britain, about the purchase of equity owned by foreign firms in large enterprises of the former Czechoslovakia. However,

Table 14.5. *German direct capital investment on territory of the 'Protectorate Bohemia and Moravia' 1938 and 1945 (in Kč)*

Year	Total	Index
1938 (post-Munich)	208,528,000	100
1945 (by end of war)	1,884,242,000	903

Source: ASÚS – Cizí účasti (Inquiry of the State Statistical Office into foreign participation), 1945.

as soon as war had broken out these capital participations were acquired as enemy property by German private and state enterprises in various ways. In table 14.4 the results of estimates of direct foreign capital investment in Czechoslovak enterprises at the end of 1937 according to countries of origin are compared with the results, in table 14.5, of a statistical survey of the countries of origin of direct foreign investment in industry and banking in the Protectorate at the end of 1940. Within two years the ranking of countries of origin of foreign investments was reversed: At the end of 1937, Britain and France took up first and second place among the countries which invested in the economy of Czechoslovakia (Britain 30.8 per cent and France 21.4 per cent, together 52.2 per cent of total foreign direct investment), while Germany held fifth place. At the end of 1940 the German Reich had moved to the leading place holding 47 per cent of total direct foreign investments in Bohemia and Moravia. Also the 34 per cent which in table 14.5 is allocated to Britain came as enemy property into the hands of German trustees, mainly under the management of the Hermann Göring Werke. By that time, the Göring Works controlled 80 enterprises and employed 150,000 workers in the Protectorate.[51]

A further inquiry about Reich German direct industrial investment in Bohemia and Moravia, conducted by the economic department of the Deputy Reichsprotektor's Office in Prague, showing the amount of German participations in percentages in each branch of industry by May 1941, is reproduced in table 14.6.

The decisive part played by German participation in the majority of the branches of industry investigated provides evidence of the strong penetration of German capital into industrial production of the occupied territory. By the autumn of 1941 the Germanization of the ownership of large enterprises had made great strides. It was implemented not only by direct takeovers of Czech enterprises but also by placing Germans on boards of

Table 14.6. *German direct capital investment in enterprises by branch of industry on territory of the 'Protectorate Bohemia and Moravia' (May 1941 – in % of total equity)*

Industry	%
Hard coal	90
Mineral oil	100
Chemicals	30–40
Clothing	30
Garments, Linen	50
Wool	60
Spinning	20–30
Dyeing	50
Hosiery	20–30
Weaving of linen	75
Glass	20–25
Cement	90
Bricks	30
Paper	almost 100

Source: Extracted from Report of Gruppe Wirtschaft to K. H. Frank, 9 May 1941, Frank Archive cited by V. Král, *Otázky hospodářského a sociálního vývoje v českých zemích v letech 1938–1945* [Problems of economic and social development in the Czech Lands in the years 1938–1945] (Prague, 1957), I, p. 54.

directors and appointing them as general managers which left Czech entrepreneurs a certain, if subordinate, role in the running of business.[52]

The pace of Germanization of small businesses, although an ongoing process, was slower in the Protectorate than in the border regions annexed to the Reich, in Sudetenland and in south Bohemia, where the expulsion of Czech entrepreneurs and peasants who refused to opt for German nationality was enforced.[53] Yet, the policy of Germanization was pursued everywhere under all circumstances. Undeterred by the Soviet counteroffensive, the military set-backs in North Africa and the entry of the USA into the war after Pearl Harbour, the militarization of the Protectorate economy intensified. On the whole, the liquidation of small enterprises owned by Czechs continued, albeit at a slower pace. It affected mainly factories and workshops not deemed essential for the war effort: thus more than 300 Czech enterprises were closed down during 1942.[54]

Concurrently with the Germanization of Czech business, the Germanization of Jewish property was speedily and vigorously enforced. By 1942 this drive was so thorough that the limit of Aryanization had been reached.

Final solution ('Endlösung') of the Jewish problem – Germanization as part of Aryanization in the Protectorate of Bohemia and Moravia

Immediately after the invasion on 15 March 1939, the Czech government of Rudolf Beran attempted to take the initiative in Aryanization to forestall the German occupation authority and to secure Czech rather than German influence in Jewish enterprises. An Order was issued on 21 March 1939[55] empowering the Czech government to appoint trustees to administer Jewish enterprises 'in the public interest'. For this purpose lists of Jewish properties and of proposed Aryanizers/commissaries were hastily made up. The occupation authorities rejected outright all Czech proposals regarding the transfer of Jewish property under the threat of having offenders arrested by the Gestapo. Aryanization was kept entirely in German hands.

Anti-Jewish measures were taken in the first days of the occupation by the German military authority who had taken over the administration of Bohemia and Moravia.[56] The Order of 20 March 1939 forbade (a) the appointment of commissaries or administrators in Jewish enterprises, (b) the purchase, lease or donation of enterprises which either wholly or partially belong to Jews.

Because anti-Jewish legislation had strong Germanizing aims in the Czech Lands, its impact was directed both against Jews and Czechs. Aryanization was intended to bring as many Germans as possible from the Reich into Bohemia and Moravia and to transfer as many Jewish enterprises as possible into their hands. A further Order issued on 29 March 1939 enacted the prohibition of disposing of economic enterprises, equity or property of all description which were wholly or partially in Jewish possession. The Reichsprotektor commanded that all matters of Aryanization were to be conducted by his Office and reserved the right to appoint trustees for Jewish enterprises to himself; they were in all cases Germans.[57]

The most important and wide-ranging decree concerning Jewish property was issued by the Reichsprotektor on 21 June 1939. In it the definition of a 'Jewish enterprise' was very broadly conceived. Aryanization was to apply if the proprietor or just one of the partners of an enterprise was Jewish; a joint-stock company was declared as Jewish if one of the board members was Jewish, or a quarter of the equity was in Jewish hands. Further the Reichsprotektor was empowered to appoint trustees he considered suitable. This could also be applied to Czech enterprises.[58] Protests by President

Hácha were countered with the statement that the Reichsprotektor's decree only confirmed the Order issued by the Czech government earlier on 21 March 1939. From 4 July 1939 the Nuremberg laws against Jews were enforced in the Protectorate.[59]

Further orders regulating Aryanization followed in brutal succession: By order of 23 January 1940 Jews had to deposit their securities with banks from which they could draw only with the Ministry of Finance's permission. Formally Jewish property was transferred to the Property Office ('Vermögensamt') or Emigration Funds ('Auswanderungsfond'). The Centre for Jewish Emigration granted Jews permission to emigrate after they had relinquished their property. By the end of 1940 exit visas had been granted to 27,000 Jewish emigrants.

German banks (especially the Böhmische Escompte Bank as branch of the Dresdner Bank) were to be given preference in Aryanization deals.[60] Large German concerns acquired Jewish shares out of Aryanization, while the German petty bourgeoisie acquired Jewish shops and workshops. Jews lost all civil rights, all property and ultimately their lives.

According to provision 6 of the Order of 29 March 1940 Aryanized were to be: all joint-stock and limited companies employing more than 100 persons and showing an annual turnover of 3 million K, as well as banks, insurance companies and enterprises in the food and wood industries. All bonds and securities owned by Jews had to be registered. Equally, by Order of 19 September 1940, their property in gold, silver, jewels, art objects and collections of any kind valued at more than 10,000 K had to be registered. Until the end of 1940 Jews had to liquidate their savings books at savings institutions and banks. From 5 February 1941 they had to give up their stamp collections.

The main wave of racial persecution was initiated by Heydrich as part of the Germanization drive in the Czech Lands. Mass deportations of Jews to concentration camps began on 1 October 1941. Before deportation to concentration camps Jews were to be used as forced labour, however, in groups separated from other workers. On 16 February 1941 the Ghetto of Terezín was established by decree of the Reichsprotektor. During the last stage of the final solution of the Jewish question Jews from Bohemia and Moravia passed through Terezín on their way to the extermination camps, mainly in Poland.

Losses in lives and health cannot be enumerated precisely.[61] However, the value of confiscated Jewish property in Bohemia and Moravia was carefully accounted for in German agencies and reported to the Reichsbank.

Table 14.7 contains the first report of the Agency for the Protection of Foreign Exchange ('Devisenschutzkommando') to the German Reichsbank which describes and evaluates the amounts of cash, foreign exchange,

Table 14.7. *First Report concerning confiscated Jewish property in 'Protectorate Bohemia and Moravia' to 14 October 1942*

Description of assets (a)	Value in K (b)
savings deposits and cash	804,982,361.80
cash in German Marks (in K)	3,398,065.00
foreign exchange (in K)	11,400,051.22
securities	910,524,717.16
other values	19,430,660.15
Total	1,749,735,856.32

Notes:
(a) Immovable assets not included.
(b) K=Protectorate Crown
Source: Report of Devisenschutzkommando to Reichsbank, 14 October 1941, cited in Král, I, p. 76.

savings deposits and securities confiscated by 14 October 1941 totalling 1,749,735,856.32 in Czech Crowns (i.e. over 1 and $^3/_4$ billion K). By 1 July 1942 a second report concerning confiscated Jewish property drawn up by the Property Office contains the summary of the value of movable and immovable assets, which had reached over 6 billion Czech crowns (cf. table 14.8). Among 'building sites' were listed 234 big enterprises, valued at almost 1.5 billion K, and 190 small enterprises, the estimated value of which was 114 million K. These figures do not include confiscated Jewish properties held by the Gestapo, nor undefined and unregistered transfers into German hands by various semi-legal and illegal means. But by the end of 1942 there was nothing left to Aryanize.

In the case of advancing Germanization through Aryanization the targets of the final solution of the Jewish question in the Protectorate were met. At the same time the exclusion of Czech business circles from benefiting in the course of Aryanization was upheld which corresponded to German economic policy in Bohemia and Moravia.

The Germanization of the Czech Lands[62]

The intensive agriculture in the Czech Lands was expected to assist in solving the problems of food provision for Germany. In a very short period after 15 March 1939 thorough and penetrating measures were imposed which changed agriculture into a controlled sector of the economy. By

Table 14.8. *Second Report concerning confiscated Jewish property in 'Protectorate Bohemia and Moravia' until 1 July 1942*

Description of assets	Value in K
1. Value of bank accounts	2,063,534,075.66
2. Value of confiscated enterprises	1,603,238,112.05[a]
3. Value of landed property	
a) building sites	830,863,747.00
b) arable land	413,084,000.00
4. Confiscated cash and receipts from sale of immovable assets	42,808,074.00
5. Special possessions	1,075,276,925.90
Total	6,025,804,934.61

[a] Consisting of 234 big enterprises valued at
K 1,489,238,112.05 and 190 small enterprises valued at
K 114,000,000.00.
Source: *Vermögensamt: Zusammenfassung der bis zum 1. Juli 1942 beschlagnahmten und eingezogenen Vermögenswerte*. This does not include confiscated property held by the Gestapo in the Auswanderungsfond, cf. Král, I, p. 76.

31 March 1939 agricultural workers were not allowed to leave their employment without permission from the District Authority. An Order of 23 June 1939 empowered authorities to force workers into agricultural labour. Lack of agricultural labour became critical from 1943 on.

Controls modelled on the organization of German agriculture were further imposed by the Order of 18 September 1939 giving the Ministry of Agriculture sweeping authority over the whole chain of agriculture from production to consumption. Similar as in industry the corporate system was introduced in agriculture with compulsory membership of producers in eight associations.

Agricultural policy has to be seen in the context of Germanization which aimed to expel Czech peasants and replace them on their land with German settlers. Plans were prepared by the SS-Rassen und Siedlungsamt with the German Settlement Society ('Deutsche Ansiedlungsgesellschaft') (cf. Schema 2 in appendix) and the Land Office in Prague. They included maps showing the location of isles of German villages to be placed in Czech rural areas of Bohemia and Moravia. These villages, newly settled by repatriated Germans from Eastern Europe or by Germans from the Reich, were to be expanded and, in due course, joined together after ousting the Czech population as envisaged by the 'total solution of the Czech question'.[63] Plans for model villages were minutely worked out (see plan of village for German settlers in Schema 3 in appendix). A model peasant farmyard ('Bauernhof'), as proposed by the Bohemian-Moravian Land Society ('Böhmisch-Mährische Landgesellschaft)' (a branch of the Deutsche Ansiedlungsgesellschaft), was to be made available to German settlers (cf. Schema 3).

Plans for resettlement were started in accordance with overall Germanization criteria: assimilation, evacuation and physical liquidation. While the war lasted this could not be realized to the full. Expulsion of Czech villagers did take place, especially in cases where contingents by peasants were not met. During the period of occupation 16,000 holdings over an area totalling *c*. 500,000 ha (1,359,000 acres) were confiscated in Bohemia and Moravia for allocation to German settlers (cf. Schema 3). Czech peasants on Protectorate territory were also evacuated from large areas which were made available to German armed forces; these areas were to be resettled by Germans after victory (consisting of 245 local authorities with a total area of 80,000 ha – 197,680 acres).

The last available Report of the Land Office on this subject to K. H. Frank, dated 1 March 1944, shows the importance of Special Courts ('Sondergerichte') for the increase in German colonization. It reports an absolute increase in the transfer of Czech agricultural holdings to the administration of the Land Office: by 31.12.1943 the number of enterprises managed by the Land Office had increased from 76 (2.26 per cent) over an area of 46,000 ha to 273 (6.41 per cent) over an area of 57,000 ha (16.8 per cent). The increase in numbers comes to 260 per cent and in land to 24 per cent. This was reported to be partly the result of increased depossessions following sentences of Special Courts.[64]

Conclusion

In this contribution the significance of the Protectorate of Bohemia and Moravia in National Socialist Germany's economy in its preparation for war and, subsequently, during the war is examined. As the subjugation of Bohemia and Moravia to German rule progressed the author discusses the contradictory nature of the colonial-type status of the Protectorate and assesses the relationship between the 'autonomous' Czech government and the German occupation regime under the supreme authority of the Reichsprotektor. Economic control and exploitation of the Czech Lands developed in the context of the changing international and domestic situation. Fundamentally, economic realities – the crucial importance of Czech war production – set limits to mass terror and, in conjunction with ruthless strikes against opposition and resistance, led to a stick-and-carrot policy. The main part of the chapter argues that throughout Germanization is employed by the occupation regime as a most potent instrument of economic control and exploitation. This is brought out in the examination of the transfer of capital from Czech into German hands, in the Aryanization of Jewish property to the benefit of the German occupiers, and in the confiscation of land to colonize Bohemia and Moravia with German settlers.

Appendix

Document 1

322.   *Die Grundsätze der geplanten Liquidation der tschechischen Nation waren: ein Teil der Tschechen wird über Deutschland zerstreut und germanisiert, der andere Teil wird ausgesiedelt, die oppositionellen Elemente werden ausgerottet.*

a) *Der Vertreter der Wehrmacht beim Reichsprotektor in Prag an das Oberkommando der Wehrmacht am 15. 10. 1940.*

Geheime Kommandosache
  Der Wehrmachtbevollmächtigte
beim Reichsprotektor in Böhmen und Mähren
                                        Prag, den 15. Oktober 1940.
Nr. 22/40 g. Kdos.
                          Chefsache! (Nur durch Offizier zu behandeln)
Betr.: Grundsätze der Politick im Protektorat   4 Ausfertigungen
                                                         1. Ausfertigung
– 1 – Anlage   Chefsache! Nur durch Offizier!

Das Amt des Reichsprotektors hat am 9. 10. l. J. eine Dienstbesprechung abgehalten, in der Staaatssekretär SS-Gruppenführer K. H. Frank dem Sinne nach etwa folgendes ausführte:

Seit Schaffung des Protektorats Böhmen und Mähren haben sowohl Parteidienststellen, als auch Wirtschaftskreise, sowie zentrale Behördendienststellen Berlins Erwägungen über die Lösung des tschechischen Problems angestellt.

Der Reichsprotektor hat zu den verschiedentlichen Planungen nach reiflicher Prüfung in einer Denkschrift Stellung genommen. In dieser wurden 3 Lösungsmöglichkeiten aufgezeigt:

a) deutsche Durchdringung Mährens und Rückbau des tschechischen Volksteiles auf ein Restböhmen.

Diese Lösung wird, da ja das tschechische Problem, wenn auch verkleinert, weiter bestehen bleibt, als nicht befriedigend bezeichnet.

b) Gegen die an sich totalste Lösung, nämlich die Aussiedlung der gesamten Tschechen, sprechen mannigfaltige Gründe. Die Denkschrift kommt daher zum Ergebnis, daß sie in absehbarer Zeit undurchführbar ist.

c) Assimilierung des Tschechentums, d. h. Aufsaugen etwa der Hälfte des tschechischen Volksteiles im Deutschtum, insoweit diese blut- und sonst wertmäßig Bedeutung hat. Diese wird u. a. auch durch vermehrten Arbeitseinsatz von Tschechen im Reichsgebiet (ausgenommen die sudetendeutschen Grenzgebiete), also durch Zerstreuung des geschlossenen tschechischen Volksteiles erfolgen. Die andere Hälfte des tschech. Volksteiles muß auf die verschiedensten Arten entmachtet, ausgeschaltet und außer Landes gebracht werden. Dies gilt besonders für die rassisch mongoloiden Teile und den Großteil der intellektuellen Schicht. Letztere ist sowohl stimmungsmäßig kaum zu gewinnen und andererseits dadurch, daß sie immer wieder Führungsansprüche gegenüber den anderen tschechischen Volksteilen anmelden und damit eine möglichst rasche Assimilierung stören würde, eine Belastung.

Elemente, die der beabsichtigten Germanisierung entgegenarbeiten, müssen scharf angefaßt und ausgeschaltet werden. Die aufgezeigte Entwicklung setzt naturgemäß ein vermehrtes Hereinströmen Deutscher aus dem Reichsgebiet in das Protektorat voraus.

Der Führer hat nach Vortrag als Richtlinie für die Lösung des tschechischen Problems die Lösung nach c) (Assimilierung) gegeben und entschieden, daß bei äußerer Beibehaltung der Autonomie des Protektorats die Germanisierung noch Jahre einheitlich vom Amt des Reichsprotektors wahrgenommen werden müsse.

Von seiten der Wehrmacht ergeben sich aus Obigem keine wesentlichen Folgerungen. Es ist die Richtung, die von hier stets vertreten wurde. Ich nehme in diesem Zusammenhange Bezug auf meine an den Herrn Chef des Oberkommandos der Wehrmacht am 12. 7. 1939 unter Zahl 6/39 g.Kdos. verfaßte Denkschrift: „Das Tschechische Problem". (Liegt als Anlage zu.)[1]

> Der Wehrmachtbevollmächtigte
> beim Reichsprotektor in Böhmen und Mähren
> Friderici, General der Infanterie

b) *Der Vertreter des Auswärtigen Amtes beim Reichsprotektor in Prag an das Auswärtige Amt Berlin am 14. 10. 1940.*

Der Reichsprotektor in Böhmen und Mähren   Prag, den 14. Okt. 1940.
Der Vertreter des A. A.   Geheime Reichssache.
                 Ganz geheim. Nur zu striktester persönlicher Information!
Inhalt: Die Entscheidung des Führers.

Staatssekretär Frank hat am 12. Oktober d. J. nochmals den Führer gesprochen. Nach der Schilderung des Staatssekretärs billigt der Führer völlig die Gedankengänge der bekannten Denkschrift. Es bleibt also, zumindestens für die Kriegsdauer, bei der Aufrechterhaltung des Protektorats einschließlich des Amtes des Reichsprotektors, anderseits soll die in Aussicht genommene Verdeutschung des Raumes und der Menschen vorbereitet werden. Die Regierung des Ministerpräsidenten Eliáš wird

---

[1] Hier nicht abgedruckt.

weiter geduldet; die Abrechnung mit der Widerstandsbewegung und den kompromittierten tschechischen Persönlichkeiten erfolgt später.

Der Führer hat ferner entschieden, daß Staatspräsident Hácha nicht auf ihn vereidigt wird, da ein solcher Eid mehr ihn selbst als den Dr. Hácha verpflichten würde.

Staatssekretär Frank wird in 2–3 Wochen Richtlinien für die spätere Durchführung der Denkschrift aufstellen lassen.

Ziemke

SÚA – Reichsprotektor.

Document 2

Schema 1

Institutional structure of the German Occupation Authority and Czech 'autonomous' government of the 'Protectorate Bohemia and Moravia' (16 March 1939–5 April 1945).

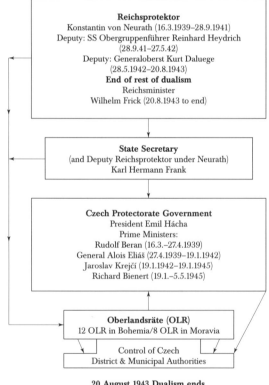

Reshuffles are closely connected with international situation and fortunes/ misfortunes of Germans in theatres of war: (1) March–September 1939 (elements of autonomy allowed to Czech government); (2) September 1939 to 27 May 1942 (conquest of Poland to Fall of Paris, attack on Soviet Union, advance on Eastern Front halted December 1941 before Moscow led to curbing autonomy, intensifying control of labour and germanization in flush of victory-Heydrich assassinated 27 May 1942); (3) May 1942 to autumn 1942 terror unleashed; (4) From Winter 1942 (Stalingrad) in framework of total war-drive policy in Protectorate changes to 'not to do anything which might harm victory, and to do everything which serves victory', therefore 'unpoliticizing the Czech population' and to pursue germanization with more subtle methods. Coincides with end of dualism and dictatorship of K. F. Frank from 20 August 1943.

Schema 2

Organizational structure of Deutsche Ansiedlungsgesellschaft
(30 April 1943).

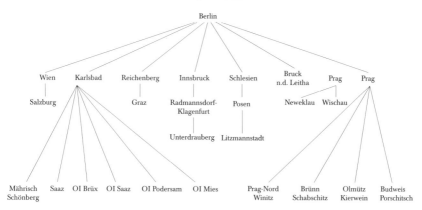

OI = Oberinspektorat

Schema 3

Model of German *Bauernhof* proposed by Böhmisch-Mährische
Landgesellschaft.

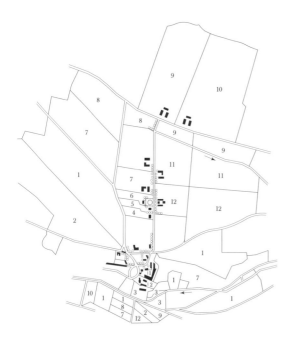

Plan of village for German
settlers after evacuation of
Czech inhabitants. From Státní
ústředni archiv [State Central
Archive], Prague, fond
Pozemkový úřad [Land Office].
Note: during the period of
occupation 16 March 1939–9
May 1945 16,000 Czech farms
(total area *c.* 550,000
ha=1,359,000 acres) were
confiscated.

Size of peasant holdings from 20–50 hectares
(1 ha = 2.471 acres) (49.5 = 123.5 acres)

1 = 50 ha	7 = 21 ha
2 = 21 ha	8 = 21 ha
3 = 3 ha (Gardener)	9 = 30 ha
4 = 1.5 ha (Agricultural labourer)	10 = 30 ha
5 = 1.5 ha (Agricultural labourer)	11 = 20 ha
6 = 1.5 ha (Agricultural labourer)	12 = 20 ha

Notes

The auf hor wishes to thank Professor Richard J. Overy for granting permission to draw on her paper 'Instruments of Economic Control and Exploitation The German Occupation of Bohemia and Moravia (1939–1945)' presented at the Second Workshop of the European Science Foundation (ESF) Network on the National Socialist Occupation Policy in World War II which was convened at King's College, University of London, 22–23 April 1996. I am very grateful to Professor Jaroslav Pátek of Charles University, Prague, for providing archive material and for sending me his publications. I appreciated greatly the helpful comments of Dr Michael John of Johannes Kepler University of Linz.

1 Measured by volume of national income per capita Czechoslovakia ranked fourteenth among European countries, according to *Economic Survey of Europe in 1948* (Geneva, 1949), p. 235.

2 Cf. A. Teichova, *An Economic Background to Munich. International Business and Czechoslovakia 1918–1938* (Cambridge, 1974).

3 Cf. V. Průcha, 'Hospodářský vývoj českých zemí v letech 1938–1945' [Economic development of the Czech Lands in the years 1938–1945] in I. Smolka and J. Folta (eds.), *Studie o technice v českých zemích* [Studies in technology in the Czech Lands] (Prague, 1995), V, part 1, p. 35.

4 A. Teichova and R. Waller, 'Der ts hechoslowakische Unternehmer am Vorabend und zu Beginn des Zweiten Weltkrieges', in Waclaw Długoborski (ed.), *Zweiter Weltkrieg und sozialer Wandel Achsenmächte und besetzte Länder* (Göttingen, 1981), p. 288.

5 Cf. Keitel's testimony, International Military Tribunal (IMT), 1400–1700, 5 April 1946.

6 During the existence of the Second Republic of Czechoslovakia Monsignor Dr Jozef Tiso held the office of Prime Minister of the Slovak autonomous government from 7 October 1938 to 9 March 1939. He regained the premiership with Hitler's blessing on 14 March 1939 after his visit at the Reich Chancellery in Berlin when the 'independence' of the vassal Slovak state was announced.

7 Emil Hácha (1872–1945) was elected President of the Second Republic of Czechoslovakia on 30 November 1938 and, after signing away the freedom of his nation and country in Berlin on 15 March 1939, he became President of the Protectorate Bohemia and Moravia until the defeat of Germany in May 1945. On 13 May 1945 Hácha was transferred from the presidential country seat in Lány to the prison hospital in Pankrác/Prague where he died on 27 June 1945.

8 Cf. D. Tomášek and R. Kvaček, *Causa Emil Hácha* (Prague, 1995), pp. 30–8.

9 Cited in *ibid.*, p. 38.

10 Protocol of Hácha's visit at the Reich Chancellery in Berlin on 15 March 1939, cited by E. Sobota, *Co to byl protektorát* [What was the Protectorate] (Prague, 1946), pp. 21–2.

11 *Ibid.*, pp. 30–1.

12 Hitler's decree concerning the *Protektorat Böhmen und Mähren* of 16 March 1939 contains the following wording:

Die von den deutschen Truppen besetzten Landesteile der ehemaligen ČSR gehören von jetzt ab zum Gebiet des Großdeutschen Reiches und treten als 'Protektorat Böhmen und Mähren' unter dessen Schutz . . . Die volksdeutschen Bewohner des Protektorates werden deutsche Staatsangehörige. Die übrigen Bewohner von Böhmen und Mähren werden Staatsangehörige des Protektorates . . . Das Protektorat Böhmen und Mähren ist autonom und verwaltet sich selbst'.

Die faschistische Okkupationspolitik in Österreich und der Tschechoslowakei (1938–1945). Dokumentenedition (Cologne, 1988), p. 103.

See also M. John, 'Aspekte der Enteignung, Vertreibung und Deportation der jüdischen Bevölkerung aus Oberösterreich und Südböhmen' in *Aktuelle Forschungen zur nationalen Frage und Vertreibungspolitik in der Tschechoslowakei und Österreich 1937–1948* (Vienna, 1996). The full text in Czech is in *Sbírka zákonů a nařízení* (hereafter Sb. z. a n.=Collection of laws and orders), 1939/part 28 of 17 March 1939.

13 Konrad Henlein's Sudeten German Party's popular slogan 'Heim in's Reich' was enthusiastically supported by a large number of Czechoslovak citizens of German nationality who 'overjoyously exchanged their affiliation to a free and democratic Czechoslovak Republic for citizenship to Nazi Germany'. Cf. E. Hahnová, *Sudetoněmecký problem: obtížné loučení s minulostí* [The Sudeto German problem: difficult parting with the past] (Prague, 1996), pp. 15–16. The irony of the slogan 'Heim in's Reich' is that indigenous German citizens of Bohemia and Moravia overnight became citizens of Germany for the first time in history. Although close relationships existed with neighbouring Bavaria, Saxony and Silesia, they had not shared a common citizenship (i.e. until October 1938 and March 1939). *Ibid.*, p. 53.

14 The Czechoslovak emigré government in London under the presidency of Dr Edvard Beneš was headed by Monsignor Dr Jan Šrámek (1870–1955) and consisted of a Centre-Left coalition.

15 Cf. Křen, *Do emigrace* [Into emigration] (Prague, 1963), p. 177, cites Jan Masaryk's (the Czechoslovak Foreign Minister in exile) letter to Beneš of 26 June 1939 in which he reports Eliáš's (the Prime Minister of the Protectorate government) pledge that he is fully available and that he joined the government only to protect the people from Frank. The contacts between the Czechoslovak government in London and the Protectorate government are examined by D. Brandes in his comprehensive account *Die Tschechen unter deutschem Protektorat Besatzungspolitik, Kollaboration und Widerstand im Protektorat Böhmen und Mähren bis Heydrichs Tod (1939–1942)*, vols. I and II, (Munich and Vienna, 1969, 1975).

16 Cf. John, 'Aspekte der Enteignung', p. 11.

17 Cf. M. John, 'Südböhmen, Oberösterreich und das Dritte Reich Der Raum Krum[m]au-Kaplitz/Český Krumlov-Kaplice als Beispiel von internen

Kolonialismus', in T. Winkelbauer (ed.), *Kontakte und Konflikte Böhmen, Mähren und Österreich Aspekte eines Jahrtausends gemeinsamer Geschichte* (Horn-Waidhofen an der Thaya, 1993), pp. 461, 465–6. On plans regarding changes of the *Gau* system, cf. also Brandes, *Die Tschechen* I, pp. 127–36.

18 Statement of Protectorate government (Summer 1939 – no exact date) Státní ústřední archiv (SÚA) [Czechoslovak Central State Archive] – MPOŽ – No. 75680–39–I/B.

19 Tomášek and Kvaček, *Causa Emil Hácha*, p. 59.

20 Cited by V. Olivová in *Dějiny Československa*, IV [History of Czechoslovakia] (Prague, 1967), p. 354.

21 By May 1942, after the reorganization of the occupation administration under Reinhard Heydrich (1904–1942), the number of Germans in the civil service was reduced. One sixth of German officials employed in the Protectorate was freed for service in the Wehrmacht. Heydrich's situation report to Hitler's official deputy Martin Bormann (18 May 1942), cited by V. Král, *Otázky hospodářského a sociálního vývoje v českých zemích v letech 1938–1945* [Problems of economic and social development in the Czech Lands in the years 1938–1945], I, p. 23.

22 Tomášek and Kvaček, *Causa Emil Hácha* p. 97. The authors comment, 'while this attitude was logical, from the point of view of history it cannot be used as a convincing apologetic argument'.

23 As early as 28 October 1939, demonstrators in Prague commemorating the 21st anniversary of establishing Czechoslovakia as an independent state were shot at which led to the death of the medical student Jan Opletal. His funeral prompted further mass demonstrations by students which were brutally answered by the German authorities. On 17 November 1939 nine officials of the Czech Students Union were shot without trial, over 1,000 students living in halls of residence in Prague and Brno were dragged away into concentrations camps, and all Czech universities were closed for the duration of the war. The date 17 November became International Students Day. For the full story and its consequences cf. *17. listopad 1939 po 55 letech* [17 November 1939 after 55 years] edited by the Committee of the History Group 17 November 1939 (Brno, 1994).

24 The complete solution of the Czech question is discussed in a Report 7760/D.Pol.2.g. by Ziemke, the representative of the Reich German Ministry of Foreign Affairs at the Office of the Reichsprotektor, to his Ministry in Berlin on 8 July 1940, in which the options of the strategy of the 'total de-Czechization of the Bohemian-Moravian space' are examined. For the full text see Doc. 95 in *Sborník k problematice dějin imperialismu* 21 (Collection of documents concerning the problems of the history of imperialism). (Prague, 1987), p. 242. K. H. Frank proposed his own solution of the Czech question to Adolf Hitler (18 August 1940): 'D. Eigene Stellungnahme. Das Ziel der Reichspolitik in Böhmen und Mähren muß die restlose Germanisierung von Raum und Menschen sein . . .', 'Denkschrift über die Behandlung des Tschechen-Problems und die zukünftige Gestaltung des böhmisch-mährischen Raumes', Doc. 315 in *Acta Occupationis Bohemiae et Moraviae. Die Deutschen in der Tschechoslowakei 1933–1947* (Prague, 1964),

pp. 419. See also M. John, 'Südböhmen', about regional planning with the policy of integration (*Eingliederung*) and Germanization (*Germanisierung*), pp. 455–6.

25 Cf. *Acta occupationis Bohemiae et Moraviae. Die Deutschen in der Tschechoslowakei 1933–1947*, Doc. 320 (5 October 1940), p. 426; especially 'Grundsätze der Politik im Protektorat' and 'Die Entscheidung des Führers' Doc. 322 (14 and 15 October 1940), pp. 247–8 (cf. Doc. 1.).

26 Doc. 52, Göring's express dispatch, dated 16 March 1939, in *Sborník k problematice dějin imperialismu* 21, pp. 129–31.

27 Cf. L. Chmela, *Hospodářská okupace Československa, její metody a důsledky* [The economic occupation of Czechoslovakia, its methods and results], (Prague, 1946), pp. 43–5.

28 Some of the 'Czech gold' in Britain was returned to the Czechoslovak government in exile and later to the re-established Czechoslovak Republic.

29 Excerpts of the Memorandum and of Funk's reaction to it cited by Král, *Otázky*, I, pp. 128–9, 131–2.

30 Bundesarchiv/Militärarchiv (further BA/MA), Freiburg, RW46/2. Discussed in Teichova and Waller, 'Der tschechoslowakische Unternehmer', pp. 298–9.

31 *Ibid.*

32 Figures in this paragraph are calculated from *Statistická ročenka Protektorátu Čechy a Morava* [Statistical Yearbook of the Protectorate Bohemia and Moravia] (1941), pp. 84–6: V. Průcha *et al.* (eds.), *Hospodářské dějiny Československa v 19. a 20. století* [The economic history of Czechoslovakia in the 19th and 20th centuries] (Prague, 1974), pp. 506–507, and Král, *Otázky*, I, pp. 134, 152. After the occupation of Bohemia and Moravia, Czech trade declined in foreign markets as the most favoured nation clause lapsed in agreements with the former Czechoslovakia, the Czech Crown was not allowed to be traded on foreign stock exchanges, payments of outstanding invoices were blocked in Britain and Brasil, a boycott on German goods was extended to Czech goods not only by Jewish entrepreneurs but generally in France, England, USA and Scandinavia.

33 Estimated from table 9 in Průcha *et al.*, (eds.), *Hospodářské dějiny*, p. 509.

34 Cf. Chmela, *Hopodářská okupace*, pp. 37–8, 159f.

35 Government Order on regulation of prices No. 121/1939 Sb.z. a n.; Order of Ministry of Industry etc. on conscription of workforce No. I/D-45383/1939; State order regulating wages etc. No. 149/1939 Sb.z. a n.; Order on Labour exchanges, August 1939: No. 193/1939 Sb.z. a n.

36 Order No. 168/1939, Sb.z. a n.

37 '. . . weil die Notwendigkeit des Protektorratsbeitrages zu kriegswichtigen Leistungen (Erzeugungsschlacht, Waffen- und Munitionsfabrikationen, Funktionieren von Handel und Verkehr) den Angriff gegen tschechisches Volkstum wegen eventuell auftretender Störungen des Werkfriedens auf die Kriegsdauer verbietet' (Frank's *Denkschrift*, in *Acta occupationis*, Doc. 315, p. 417).

38 Cf. Brandes, *Die Tschechen*, I, p. 213.

39 The political life and the execution of Eliáš is described in D. Tomášek and R. Kvaček, *Generál Alois Eliáš Jeden český osud* [General Alois Eliáš A Czech destiny]

(Prague, 1996). Eliáš's indictment prepared by the Prague Gestapo dated 29 September 1941 is published on pp. 87–8.

40 *Reichsgesetzblatt*, I, (1942), p. 165.

41 Cf. full report of Daluege to Martin Bormann on the destruction of the villages Lidice (10 June 1942) and Ležáky (18 June 1942), the murder of their male population, the deportation of the women into concentration camps and the placement of children into homes is contained in 'Abschulußbericht über den Mordanschlag auf SS-Obergruppenführer Heydrich', *Acta Occupationis*, Doc. 385, pp. 486–9.

42 The policy of Germanization of the Czech nation in the context of National Socialist racial theory is discussed by Petr Němec, 'Český národ a nacistická teorie germanizace prostoru' [The Czech nation and the Nazi theory of Germanization of space], in *Český časopis historický*, 4, 88 (1990), 535–58; in German translation, Peter Němec, 'Das tschechische Volk und die nationalsozialistische Germanisierung des Raumes' in *Bohemia* 2, 32 (1991), 424–55.

43 Cf. 'Denkschrift über die Behandlung des Tschechen-Problems und die zukünftige Gestaltung des böhmisch-mährischen Raumes, in *Acta Occupationis*, Doc. 315, pp. 417–20. The political implications of Frank's *Denkschrift* are discussed by Brandes, *Die Tschechen*, I, pp. 130–3.

44 Cf. J. Doležal, *Česká kultura za Protektorátu Školství, písemnictví, kinematografie* [Czech culture during the Protectorate Education, literature, cinematography] (Prague, 1996), pp. 47–58.

45 3. Der Besitzwechsel bei grossen wirtschaftlichen Werten, insbesondere bei Grundbesitz, Gewerbetreibenden, Aktienmehrheiten, Beteiligungen, usw., muß in einer den Belangen der deutschen Wirtschaft entsprechenden Weise geordnet werden. Deshalb behalte ich mir einstweilen die Zustimmung bei allen größeren Objekten (ab 1/2 Million) vor. Ich bitte den Herrn Reichwirtschaftsminister, dafür zur sorgen, daß die entsprechenden Anzeigepflichten und Genehmigungsvorbehalte eingeführt werden, damit eine laufende Kontrolle über die Besitzumschichtungen möglich wird.
Sborník k problematice dějin imperialismu, Doc. 52, p. 130.

46 Ministerpräsident Generalfeldmarshall Göring
Bauftragter für den Vierjahresplan
Vollmacht
Ich beauftrage hiermit den Generalreferenten im Reichswirtschaftsministerium, Hans Kehrl, als Treuhänder einer von mir zu benennenden Stelle oder Rechtsperson die Aktienmehrheit
1. der Waffenwerke Brünn,
2. der Skoda-Werke Pilsen,
3. des Eisenwerkes Witkowitz
und ihrer Tochtergesellschaften zu erwerben und alle ihm hiebei zweckmäßig erscheinenden Verhandlungen zu führen und Maßnahmen zu treffen, soweit die erworbenen Werte zu verwalten, Umgruppierungen in den

Beteiligungsverhältnissen der genannten Gesellschaften und der direkt oder indirekt abhängigen oder verbundenen Firmen vorzunehmen, soweit ihm diese notwendig oder zweckmäßig erscheinen.

Soweit hierzu Rechtsgeschäfte mit Dritten erforderlich werden oder Verbindlichkeiten einzugehen sind, ist er bevollmächtigt, in Gemeinschaft mit Dr. Rasche die noch benennende Stelle oder Rechtsperson zu vertreten und alle zur Durchführung dieses Auftrages ihm zweckmäßig erscheinenden Rechtsgeschäfte abzuschliessen und Willenserklärungen abzugeben.

Sofern bei diesen Rechtsgeschäften und Willenserklärungen der Reichsfiskus verpflichtet werden soll, ist zu ihrer Rechtswirksamkeit die Zustimmung des Herrn Reichsministers der Finanzen einzuholen.

gez. Göring

Doc. 53, *Sborník k problematice dějin imperialismu*, pp. 131–2.

47 These events are related in more detail in Teichova and Waller, 'Der tschechoslowakische Unternehmer', pp. 295–7.

48 Cf. Military Tribunal IV, Case No. 11, Exh. 3812, NID12510, DB167, E19, 25–26.

49 Cf. D. Eichholtz, *Geschichte der deutschen Kriegswirtschaft*, 2 vols. (Berlin, 1984, 1985); R. J. Overy, *War and the Economy in the Third Reich* (Oxford, 1994).

50 Král, *Otázky*, II (Prague, 1958).

51 *Ibid.*, pp. 34–6.

52 In Heydrich's situation report of 18 May 1942 to Bormann the implementation of the policy of ensuring German influence in Czech business by takeovers of equity, taking up seats on boards of directors and appointments as managers is conveyed to Berlin. Cited from sources in the Archives of the Czechoslovak Ministry of the Interior in Král, *Otázky*, II, p. 51.

53 *Acta Occupationis*, Doc. 303, 'Rundschreiben des Reichsministers des Innern vom 19.3.1940' empowers local government in Sudetenland and Südböhmen to expel Czechs living in occupied border areas (pp. 400–1).

54 Cf. Olivová, *Dějiny Československa*, p. 163.

55 Government Order No. 87/1939, Sb.z. a n.

56 The part of this paper on Aryanization draws from documents in *Sborník k problematice dějin imperialismu*, 21, pp. 133–57, and on the problem of connections between Germanization and the final solution of both the Jewish and the Czech question from documents in *Acta Occupationis Die Deutschen in der Tschechoslowakei, passim*.

57 This led to discontent among indigenous Germans who complained that Reich Germans get all advantages from Aryanization. Submissions to *Landräte* contain objections to the enrichment of big German concerns while indigenous Germans do not have enough capital to obtain small and medium enterprises from Aryanization.

58 'Die Einsetzung der Treuhänder kann vom Reichsprotektor sowohl in jüdischen wie auch in nicht-jüdischen Betrieben angeordnet werden', *Der Neue Tag*, 21 June 1939.

59 Ladislav Feierabend, who was Minister of Agriculture in the government of the

Protectorate and later fled abroad, maintains that Hácha and his government refused to decree the Nuremberg anti-Jewish laws. See his memoirs *Ve vládě protektorátu* [In the government of the Protectorate] (New York, 1962), p. 44.

60 Cf. Ch. Kopper, *Zwischen Marktwirtschaft und Dirigismus* (Bonn, 1995), p. 338.

61 The wider implications of Aryanization and Germanization are discussed in M. Kárný, 'Poznámky ke genocidní politice německého fašismu' [Comments concerning the genocidal politics of German fascism] in *Sborník k problematice dějin imperialismu*, 13 (1982), *passim*.

62 I wish to thank Professor Jaroslav Pátek of Charles University, Prague, for sending me his publications on agriculture during the occupation as well as source material from the archive of the Pozemkový úřad (Land Office) in Prague. I have drawn on his article 'Zemědělství za okupace' [Agriculture during the occupation] in *Dějepis ve škole* [History in Schools] (1965), pp. 180–183, and his manuscript 'Deutsche Siedlungspolitik am Gebiet des "Protektorats Böhmen und Mähren" (1939–1945)'.

63 Discussing various views of German administrators concerning the strengthening of Germanhood in the Protectorate, voiced by Frank, the Reichsprotektor, Oberlandräte, Gauleiters and the military, Brandes mentions the building of a German 'Landbrücke' (land bridge) to reach from the North to Prague, which was agreed between the Office of the Reichsprotektor and the Oberlandräte on 6 March 1940. Cf. Brandes, *Die Tschechen* I, p. 169.

64 'Die Erscheinung ist z.T. auf die gesteigerten Einziehungen infolge Urteilsspruchs der Sondergerichte zurückzuführen' (Doc. 425, in *Acta Occupationis*, p. 519). Brandes remarks 'den Boden für seine Siedlungsaufgaben bekam das Amt (Bodenamt [Land Office]– A.T.) u.a. durch Einziehung von Vermögen auf Grund von Sondergerichten und durch "Arisierungen"'. Cf. *Die Tschechen*, I, p. 35.

15

Czechoslovakia behind the Iron Curtain (1945–1989)

MILAN OTÁHAL

The struggle for political power (1945–1948)

The Second World War changed not only the face of the world but also its character. The Axis Powers' totalitarianism was defeated, the breaking-up of colonialism accelerated, communism, socialism and the Christian world outlook became the main ideologies in Europe, and Soviet totalitarianism ceased to be limited to a single country. In the Central and East European states, later on also in some Asian countries, Communist Parties usually with direct Soviet support gained a monopoly of power as a basic prerequisite of the Soviet model of socialism.

The day of Czechoslovakia's liberation from Nazi rule was a turning point in its history. After a six-year occupation, Czechoslovakia was again an independent state in its pre-1938 borders. That is, with the exception of Subcarpathian Ruthenia, which was ceded to the Soviet Union and became Transcarpathian Ukraine. But its social system was altered and Czechoslovakia set out on a path of socialist changes. An historic contradiction was hidden in this decision – a contradiction that influenced the development of the next forty-five years. With the fall of the First Republic in 1938 a number of prominent Czechoslovak personalities began to contemplate its causes and analyze its internal factors. The weak points were found in the unresolved national and social question as well as in the political system that was marked by rampant partisanship. Many arrived at the conclusion that structural changes in all spheres of social life were necessary in order to prevent similar disasters. The left-oriented movements and the civil democratic stream in Czech politics led by Edvard Beneš (1884–1948) – who had continued the ideas of T. G. Masaryk – moved closer to each other in recognition that these changes should have a socializing or socialist character. The common approach of the main political forces to post-war social problems was an inner condition for establishing a coalition between the centre of emigration in London and the communist leadership in Moscow, personified by Edvard Beneš and Klement Gottwald (1896–1953) respectively. The first government programme announced in Košice (eastern Slovakia) on 3 April 1945, had been the result of their mutual agreement. It proclaimed structural reforms to be the aim of all political parties that were to govern in the new Republic. Yet it also enabled the existence of a comparatively democratic regime during 1945–1948. Another part of the agreement was a division of power in which the Communists, who occupied the key posts, ensured their hegemony – an indispensable condition for their success in the struggle for power.

The result of the 1946 general election underlined the orientation to far-reaching social reforms in accord with the feelings and interests of many strata of the population whose fundamental life experience was not only the Munich Agreement and occupation, but also the existential uncertainty connected with the economic crisis of the early 1930s. While the Communists and Social Democrats just barely gained the absolute majority in the election, the vast majority of the population by voting for the parties of the National Front expressed the support for the Košice government programme. The attitude of the voters was also influenced by the fact that they considered the Soviet Union – a socialist country – to be their liberator from Nazi rule, and that the Communist Party presented itself as a national and not only as a left-wing force.

The nature of the changes was influenced in a decisive way by the Soviet Union in whose sphere Czechoslovakia was included. Through the Communist Party of Czechoslovakia, the Soviet Union soon suppressed endeavours for a democratic socialism as advanced by some resistance groups and as the structural reforms were understood by other political forces after 1945, and it enforced its own model of socialism. Czech and Slovak society was gradually excluded from the world of Western civilization and began to conform to Soviet society. The individual stages of the realization of this aim also depended on the relation between both super powers, and on Stalin's strategy of 'world revolution' that had, for only a short period after the war, taken into account the existence of the anti-Hitler coalition; that is, cooperation between the Western democracies and the Soviet Union. The Soviet Union was also the external factor that had allowed for the conclusion of the agreement between both Czechoslovak resistance centres abroad. Even at that time, Stalin was mainly pursuing a policy of 'breaking out of the imperialistic encirclement of the USSR' part of which was the creation of a zone of states where the Communists would be the sole ruling force. In Czechoslovakia the Communists could reach this goal only by smashing the civil society that had been the basis of Czechoslovak democracy as well as of a certain stability of values on which Czechoslovak society, in spite of all the traumas, had based itself.

The instrument became the structural reforms which were in harmony with the postwar attitudes of Czechoslovak society, but were used by the Communists as a means of polarization. In the beginning the changes could be accommodated within a national and even a democratic framework. But they gradually took on a class character since they were directed against the forces that were defying the Communists endeavouring to implement Stalinism in the country.

The question of nationalities, after the war, was to be resolved in the concept of a national state of Czechs and Slovaks, agreed by all the dominating political forces. The concept presumed the recognition of the Slovaks as a nation with equal rights as well as the transfer of the Germans, who had formed more than one fourth of the population. However, they were not a mere minority but an organic part and co-creator of all the values made on the state's territory. The transfer the idea of which had evolved from the resistance movement, and was approved by the Great Powers at the Potsdam Conference, had in one blow dramatically resolved a long-standing conflict between Czechs and Germans. Based as it was on the principle of collective guilt, it proved that the Czech political leadership was unable and unwilling to solve the question of coexistence with Germans in a humanitarian and democratic way. Its moral and structural consequences were long-term and are visible to the present day. The transfer bound Czechoslovakia even more firmly to the Soviet Union, which guaranteed not only the transfer's realization but also Czechoslovakia's security from potential German revisionism. These apprehensions became an important socio-psychological instrument in the sovietization of Czechoslovakia.

The relationship between Czechs and Slovaks was established according to the 'asymmetrical' model: Slovakia was organized on the principle of nationality with its own organs of national administration, whereas the Czech Lands worked on the territorial principle and were run by a government authorized for the whole state. The extent and powers of the Slovak authorities were determined, according to the situation, by 'settlements' in Prague resulting in the main from discussions between the Czech political parties. However, after the 1946 election these powers were greatly limited since in Slovakia the Democratic Party – the main opponent of the Communist Party and distrusted even by the Czech non-Communist parties – had won the majority of seats. The 'Slovak question' was one of the most serious issues in the entire postwar period in Czechoslovakia.

The socio-economic measures such as land reform and nationalization of large industries, mines, and banks deeply affected the structure of society. The political parties expressed support for these measures since in their opinion they removed one of the weak points of the prewar Republic; only some spoke out against their extent. The Communists skilfully used the reforms for their own political ends because they could use them to satisfy the needs of the poorest social strata, for example, with transfers of land, and thus gain their support. These measures, in the initial stage, had national motives since the property of Germans, traitors, and collaborators was confiscated, and full use was made of Czech and Slovak nationalism that increased greatly after the war. The reforms changed Czechoslovak society qualitatively; an economy of three sectors had its roots in them. The capitalist, i.e., the private sector was severely limited and the state became the main economic force as well as the biggest employer. A 'new middle peasant', who obtained his plot of land predominantly in the border regions became a central figure in the village. A general levelling of society, i.e., an effort to do away with extremes, predominantly in the social sphere, was another consequence of this process.

The political system changed substantially. The National Front, a coalition of all political parties, limited to four in the Czech Lands (Communists, Social Democrats, National Socialists, People's Party), to two and later to four in Slovakia (Communists, Democrats, Labour Party, Freedom Party), became its core and most important element. The creation of potential new parties had to be approved by the National Front, and opposition acting outside it was not permitted. Hence, there came into existence a 'closed pluralistic system' which represented one of the limitations of the regulated democracy. There was no voting in its organs and consensus was required. Resolutions, once passed, were binding on all levels, for Cabinet members as well as for members of Parliament. This unconstitutional and unelected organ was, in fact, superimposed upon the supreme executive organs as well as upon the legislature. This was another important weak point of the new democracy. The National Front was the decisive political force even in the sense that it was active in all affairs of the state, involving state policy as well as the day by day business of the government. In a sense the National Front resumed the practice of the unconstitutional organs of five coalition parties (National Democrats, Agrarians, Social Democrats, National Socialists, Christian-Socials) during the First Republic. But in comparison with the role of the so-called Five (*Pětka*), its importance and real power increased greatly: it became the most serious obstacle to pluralistic democracy.

Mid-1947 formed a certain turning point in postwar development. The Western powers, the USA above all, adopted the policy of containment of

communism, aimed at the reduction and even discontinuation of co-
operation with the Soviet Union. This tendency was expressed quite clearly
by Winston Churchill in his renowned Fulton speech (5 March 1946) where
he had characterized the division of Europe with the term 'iron curtain'.
Another expression of this policy was the Truman doctrine, aimed at help
for Greece and Turkey, the states most endangered by the Soviet Union and,
at the same time, strategically key states from the point of view of the
Western powers. The Marshall Plan, the main aim of which was to gain
economic, social and political stability in West European countries as well
as to try to undermine positions of the Communist Parties in East European
Peoples' Democracies, represented another expression of the policy. At that
time, Stalin came to the conclusion that the potentialities provided by the
anti-Hitler coalition were already exhausted. It led to the establishment of
the Cominform, in September 1947, by delegates of nine Communist
Parties at a meeting in Sklarska Poreba (Poland). There the world was
divided, according to new criteria, into the 'imperialist' camp led by the
United States of America, and the 'socialist' camp led by the Soviet Union.
The necessary precondition for forming a monolithic Soviet bloc was the
liquidation of the 'internal enemy' and the establishment of the power
monopoly of the Communist Parties.

The period of 'specific roads to socialism' came to an end, and the Soviet
model became obligatory. The direct intervention of the Soviet Union in
the internal affairs of the satellite states increased, for example, at the time
of the Czechoslovak government decision about the possible acceptance of
the Marshall Plan (July 1947). Then, the first hints of economic difficulties
and political crises, such as the disintegration of the National Front para-
lyzing the whole political system and leading to the formation of political
blocs within it, began to manifest themselves in Czechoslovakia. The
Communist Party of Czechoslovakia made use of the situation to 'complete
the revolution', that is, to undermine totally its adversaries' remaining positions in the economic as well as political spheres. The Communist Party of
Czechoslovakia continued to put limitations on the private sector and, by
making use of confiscated property, it appeased the discontented. By extra-
parliamentary means it mobilized broad social groups against the alleged
threat of 'reaction'. The struggle for power was ended by 25 February 1948
with the victory of the Communists and the removal from power of those
representatives of political parties who tried to stop the communist advance
with quite inadequate means. That is, by relying on elections, on the parliament and on USA support.

In May 1948 elections were carried out with a single list of candidates,
composed predominantly of Communists. The result was a parliament

completely subordinated to the Communists. Klement Gottwald (1896–1953) replaced Edvard Beneš in the presidential function, and power at all levels went fully to the Communists so that nothing stood in their way when they began to implement Soviet totalitarianism.

The establishment of the Soviet model and its failure

In the period immediately following February 1948, the Communist Party began to restructure the political system so that it served its needs and enabled its Presidium to gain control over all spheres of social life. The last remnants of democracy, the pluralist system and the parliament (independent to a certain degree), were liquidated; there was a merger of state power with the ruling party. In the economic sphere the capitalist sector and gradually even the small-scale production sector, and thus elements of market economy were disposed of. The so-called 'mechanical engineering' concept was enforced according to which the main task of the Czechoslovak economy was to help in the industrialization of the other countries in the Soviet bloc. The extraordinary demands of this programme on energy and raw materials which Czechoslovakia had to import from abroad, and the militarization of the economy that was connected to Stalin's orientation to a new world war, soon exhausted the resources of the Czechoslovak economy so that it went through periodic crises. The leadership of the Communist Party tried to solve them by partial economic reforms directed not at restructuring the economy or at least renewing elements of market economy, but only at its centralized control and administration. The thoroughly collectivized agriculture, too, was going through a deep crisis. In the end, however, it was this sector of the economy that was quite successfully stabilized so that it could, in contrast to industry and services, cover the basic needs of consumption.

The economic difficulties affected many strata of the population and provoked discontent which manifested itself most strikingly at the time of the currency reform in 1953: strikes occurred in a number of works and some of them turned into street demonstrations (Plzeň). The 'workers state' had to use armed forces against them, thus exposing its real character and leading to disillusionment.

For a time shortly after February 1948, some groups expressed their disapproval regarding the situation on various occasions, for example, at Beneš's funeral and earlier at the general rally of the gymnastic organization Sokol (Falcon). These fading manifestations were soon suppressed. The Communist leadership realized that it was not enough just to control the economy and state power; it was also necessary to complete the smashing of civil society. That is why many clubs and civic organizations were closed down, mass organizations – if not already before – were changed into 'transmission belts from the Party to the masses' and freedom of speech and assembly and other civil and human rights were suppressed. An important role was played by the political trials which, in view of the tradition of civil society in Czechoslovakia, were brutal and extensive.

The enforcement of the Soviet model, so foreign to Czech and Slovak traditions, by police state methods led to a gradual widening of the gulf between the intimidated, indifferent, citizens on the one hand, and the power elite on the other. The social crisis became almost permanent and the Communist Party leadership succeeded only temporarily in softening it by various partial measures. The most realistic alternative for overcoming this crisis was a reform of the Soviet model that would make socialism more attractive for the people. In the Communist Party a reform movement came into being because, owing to its power monopoly, only Communists could and had to be the main actors in the experiment. A portion of the socialist-oriented intellectuals participated in an active way in this process. They began to reflect on the social responsibility, attempted a revision of dog-matic Marxism and, together with some politicians, worked out both a plan for economic reform with elements of market economy, and principles of a new political system putting the relationship between the Party and the state on a more democratic basis. The Communist Party of Slovakia became an important component of the reform movement. It got into conflict with the leadership of the Communist Party led by the First Secretary and President of the Republic, Antonín Novotný (1904–1975), owing to his endeavour to make Czechoslovakia a centralist state and limit as much as possible the powers of Slovak national organs of self-government. This tendency was realized in 1960 in the Constitution of the – newly renamed – Czechoslovak Socialist Republic.

The XXth Congress of the Communist Party of the Soviet Union in 1956 represents a turning point in the history of Soviet-type socialism. It sub-jected Stalinism to a crushing though not fundamental criticism, discarded some of the old values but did not create new ones. Under the influence of the XXth Congress there occurred in Poland and Hungary attempts at reform and even first endeavours to remove the Soviet totalitarian system. In Czechoslovakia the leadership of the Communist Party succeeded – as a consequence of having achieved a certain economic and political stabiliza-tion – in forestalling these tendencies and neutralizing or suppressing dis-content in the Party and outside it. In the beginning of the 1960s, however, the crisis erupted again. The Presidium and the Central Committee of the Communist Party of Czechoslovakia were compelled – despite opposition from the dogmatic wing – to accept economic reform suggested by the reform wing as a means to overcome the economic decline and stagnation. The question of the political trials in the 1950s became a serious Party and social issue. Above all, the younger generation of functionaries held the leading officials responsible and demanded their resignation. The Slovak question reemerged. The antagonisms ceased to be the concern of only a part of the Party and reached ever wider strata of society which became politically active. The leadership of the Communist Party failed to suppress the reform stream entirely. When it tried to apply a strong-hand policy against rebellious intellectuals it failed because the Party had split from within. After the Czech reform stream, aiming at liberalization of the system, merged with efforts of Slovak Communists to restore equality of rights for Slovakia, the fate of Antonín Novotný was sealed. In January 1968 he was replaced in the capacity of First Secretary of the Central Committee of the Communist Party of Czechoslovakia by Alexander Dubček (1921–1992), the head of the Communist Party of Slovakia up to then. A short period of the attempt to build up 'a socialism with a human face' began.

The Prague Spring

The Prague Spring tried to resolve the social crisis rooted in the confrontation between the Czechoslovak idea of socialism and the Soviet model, and in the conflict between the Czechoslovak democratic tradition and Communist Party power monopoly. In 1968 these problems found reflection in three essential questions.

The first question was about state sovereignty, that is, about a new arrangement between Czechoslovakia and the Soviet Union. For years since the end of the Second World War Czechoslovakia was not able – and altogether its leadership was not even willing – to pursue national goals. Its foreign military and domestic policy was subordinate to interests and needs of the Soviet Union to the point that even the rule of the Communist Party in its own country was limited. A closer alliance with Yugoslavia and Romania, states considerably independent of the Soviet Union, could have been a way out of the situation. But even in this respect the Dubček leadership was not successful. What was at stake was to enforce the principle of non-intervention in the internal affairs by the Soviet Union and the states of the Warsaw Pact. Its realization required the limitation of the Communist Party power monopoly as well as the general support of the public. The Communist Parties of the Warsaw Pact states opposed resolutely such moves, feeling that they were endangering their position in their own countries and weakening the Soviet bloc power – a guarantee of their rule.

The reformers in the leadership of the Communist Party of Czechoslovakia did not make up their mind to defend state sovereignty though they had the unanimous support of the population in this respect. They did not, in fact, take sufficiently into account the possibility of Soviet intervention nor made it clear that they would do everything possible to defend state independence.

The second question the reform leadership had to deal with was the promulgation of the constitutional law to readjust the relationship between Czechs and Slovaks. There were the essential Slovak claims crystallized during the 1960s: the rehabilitation of the so-called Slovak bourgeois nationalists, among them Gustav Husák (about whom more is to come); the revaluation of modern Slovak history, including the Slovak National Uprising in 1944; and the establishment of a Federation based on the principle of equal rights for the Czech and Slovak constituent parts of the Republic. Realization of these claims was not only a concern of the Slovaks; the Czech Communist intellectuals participated very actively both in the question of rehabilitation and revaluation of the Slovak National Uprising. In 1968 the issue of the Federation came to the fore. While in Slovakia national demands were prevailing, the reformers in the Czech Lands were pushing for certain liberalization and democratization of society, including of course the national demands of Slovaks.

Both streams which, in January 1968, jointly caused the fall of Antonín Novotný and opened the process of reforming socialism, pursued effectively somewhat different aims, and the efforts to unite their paths never really succeeded. After the occupation of Czechoslovakia by military forces of five states of the Warsaw Pact on 21 August 1968 (Soviet Union, German Democratic Republic, Poland, Hungary, Bulgaria) the new leadership of the Communist Party of Czechoslovakia headed by Gustav Husák (1913–1991) became a Soviet instrument of suppression of the reform movement. In the process the Communist Party leadership made use even of the essentially justifiable Slovak demands by giving them a one-sided national slant. The passing of the law regarding the Federation, on 28 October 1968, did not solve the issue of the relationship between Czechs and Slovaks because the asymmetrical model persisted, particularly in the Communist Party, and the old bureaucratic centralism was restored.

Thirdly, the relationship between the Communist Party and the state was an issue of no less importance. Most of the reformers thought that it could be solved by democratizing the Party, by changing the principle of democratic centralism – in other words by removing the dictate of the Politburo and the apparatus of the Party. In this respect the draft of new Party statutes represented considerable progress since it conceded to the minority the right to its opinion after a vote was taken. In fact, it sanctioned the existence of factions.

A further key issue concerned the leading role of the Party. The reformers attempted to define it in a new way. The Action Programme of the Communist Party of Czechoslovakia, published in April 1968, did not dispense with this principle. It only rejected its application by administrative means and the power of command, and recommended to Communists to gain authority by their activity for the benefit of society. In the spirit of these principles, the Action Programme did not allow concentration of power in the hands of any Party organ or any individual, and presumed the restoration of independence for the legislature and governmental administration. The state and its institutions were henceforward not to be steered by the Party directly but by the Communists working in their agencies.

It must be admitted that the Action Programme did not solve the basic problems of the relationship between the Communist Party and the state but it impaired the power monopoly and slightly opened the door to democratization of the political system. In comparison with the Soviet system the Action Programme represented significant progress and could – under favourable international conditions – have become the starting point of further weakening of the police-administrative model.

The non-Communist intelligentsia realized that democratization of the Communist Party was not an assurance of democracy in society since it did not prevent misuse of power. But only a few critics perceived the guarantee to rest on a really pluralist political system in which society could control the Communist Party through further political actors. Even the majority of the reformers opposed an authentic pluralist system because they saw the Communist Party as the guarantee of socialist development. Though the Dubček leadership conceded the emergence of several new organizations, for example, the Club of Committed Non-Party Members (KAN – Klub angažovaných nestraníků) or the K-231 (a pressure group of political prisoners), it did not allow the establishment of the Social Democratic Party or another political party. A pluralist system was not realized and Communist Party power could be controlled only by the Party itself. Historical experience showed, however, that this way was not a sufficient guarantee of democracy. Only further development could have demonstrated whether the reformers would have been able to go in this direction and exceed the limitations of the Action Programme. Neither were they successful in solving fundamentally the issue of the relationship between Party and state on the basis of consistent democratic principles.

A centrally directed economy was an important part of the Communist Party control of society. The reformers regarded the economic crisis as a reflection of the general crisis in society. In order to deal with it they suggested structural changes that would reduce the economy's exacting demands on energy and raw materials, and allow a development of its prospective branches. They also put forward principles of socialist entrepreneurship to be realized primarily in autonomous enterprises, relatively independent of state organs, and in utilization of elements of market economy under socialism. Workers Councils were to guarantee the influence of employees on production the control of which was not to be kept exclusively in the hands of technocrats and managers. Though these measures would have led to ending the economy's subordination to the omnipotent centre it would not have resolved the basic issue of every democratic society, that is, plurality of forms of proprietorship and restoration of private ownership of the means of production.

An elimination of the Party's domination of the sphere of culture and ideology was also included in the programme of 'a socialism with a human face'. The communist intelligentsia attempted the restoration of continuity with the past, with the tradition of legal security, with democratic humanism connected with the name of T. G. Masaryk, and with the binding character of truth demonstrated by the condemnation of political trials and other actions of the Communist Party regarded as immoral. They wished to create a social structure in which confidence would dominate and the human being would be at the heart of affairs. An atmosphere of non-violence was a distinctive feature of this process – the demands of the Prague Spring were being realized by legal means. The mass media played an important role and, after freedom of speech was gained, they grew into an independent political force which shattered the hitherto uncontrollable regime in its very foundations.

Democratization of society met with opposition from conservatives and dogmatists in the Party. Their positions were not negligible so that the Dubček leadership had to employ tactics and retreat. The reformers alone could not ensure transition from totalitarianism to democracy since they were incapable of overcoming certain established communist principles, such as the leading role of the Party that was preventing and precluding the formation of a really pluralistic democratic political system. But the pursuit of reform of the Soviet model as expressed in the Action Programe was, under the historical circumstances, the only viable way to attain this goal. In this the party leadership was supported by a civic movement which, at times, was more radical and was pushing it to take more decisive measures. Thus the Prague Spring resulted from reforms from above and pressure from below. The causes of the defeat of this experiment were not rooted in 'internal' factors but in the armed intervention from outside. In spite of it a lesson of the experiment of 1968 was learned to the effect that it was not possible to overcome totalitarianism Soviet style by a reform under the aegis of Communists but only by an opposition fighting the Communist Party and its power monopoly.

The aftermath

The military intervention in Czechoslovakia and the subsequent signing of the Moscow Protocol (26 August 1968) created conditions to 'normalization' of the situation. Its main aim was to restore the authority of the Communist Party, obedient to Moscow directives, as the decisive factor of the post-Stalinist system. In the first stage the new political team, led by Gustav Husák, became executor of Soviet policy in Czechoslovakia and focused its attention on regaining control of the key positions in the Party and state apparatus, in the mass media and other institutions. In the course of this process the new team took away positions and Party membership from the chief representatives of the Prague Spring, from activists and others who refused to dissociate themselves from the ideas of 'a socialism with a human face' and to approve the occupation. Not only the Prague Spring but all attempts at reform were condemned as counter-revolutionary actions in a Party document called: *The Lesson from the Period of Crisis in the Party and Society after the XIIIth Congress of the Communist Party of Czechoslovakia* (1970). The thesis about counter-revolution underlay the position of the new state and Party leadership, which based its legitimacy on it, and could remain in power for as long as it was capable of defending it, and was supported by the Soviet leadership.

The reformers who, under Soviet pressure, signed the Moscow Protocol, and who at the sitting of the Central Committee of the Communist Party of Czechoslovakia in April 1969 helped to vote in Gustav Husák as First Secretary, thus paved the way for him – he became President in 1976 – and his group to control the Party and state. This particular attitude of the reformers, after August 1968, proved that they were not the historical force capable of defeating totalitarianism.

The 'divide et impera' rule became the leading principle of the new leadership. It was applied in the constitutional sphere with respect to the relationship between Czechs and Slovaks. Slovak interests were favoured and the new leadership appropriated the credit for establishing the Federation of Czech Socialist and Slovak Socialist Republics (1 January 1969). That is why Slovaks tended to support Husák's policies while Czech sentiments began to be rather anti-Slovak. In Slovakia mass purges did not occur. Hence there a numerous group of persecuted citizens, not enjoying equal rights and turning into opposition, was not created. This was why opposition in Slovakia did not play such a role as it did in the Czech Lands.

Here to a certain extent, in accordance with the slogan 'he, who is not for us, is against us', people divided into those with privileges and those who did not enjoy full rights as citizens. The first group included the 'nomenklatura', that is, persons wielding all power and using it for their own benefit. The second-class citizens were composed of persons got rid of during the purges. But there was also the rest of the population, in effect the non-homogeneous majority, on which the fate of normalization depended first and foremost. The aim of the new leadership was to strengthen its power base by building up a consumerist communism which would satisfy the existential and material needs of the majority. In the main, it succeeded in stabilizing the economy so that in the years of normalization in Czechoslovakia no serious social conflicts occurred and no strong oppositional workers movement conditioned by bad living standards arose, as it happened in Poland.

A 'parallel' or 'black' economy grew in importance and even played an irreplaceable role in the service sector. Some engaged in it enjoyed high earnings and even the problem arose how to realize the increasing amount of savings. The human as well as material dependency of the majority of the population on the 'state of really existing socialism' constituted – as pointed out by the dissident Milan Šimečka – the basic reason for the stability of the normalization system. By way of exchange for a share in economic stability, the regime demanded from the population an apolitical attitude. The regime enabled the population to realize themselves in the private instead of in the public sphere. To spend the days off in small houses in rural areas ('cottage subculture') became a characteristic feature of Czechoslovak social life. The regime did not ask the population to believe in socialist ideology, only to display publicly its positive attitude to it. Thus a contradiction arose between reality, as it existed and was seen by the individual, and illusion of reality suggested by the regime. Naturally this contradiction concerned the majority of population but it became a really vital issue primarily for a certain group of intellectuals. Thus it was Václav Havel (born 1936) who analysed the system of normalization from this point of view in his dramas and essays. Havel was interested predominantly in the individual who, according to him, constituted the basic element of society. Havel's demand for authenticity and identity was related to the individual, and not to the nation or society as a whole. Havel treated the social crisis as a crisis of morals which should be overcome in the existential sphere, and not in the political sphere, by a return to 'living in truth'. In the given state of affairs he rejected politics as an instrument of struggle for power, as a means for social changes, and took it as a means to search for truth. Thus he came to articulate the principles of 'antipolitics' characterizing the attitude of the majority of intellectuals towards social problems.

A specifically Czech approach of oppositionist intellectuals to social problems was expressed by Charter 77, which definitely dissociated itself from politics proclaiming that it did not wish to be a basis of opposition activity. Charter 77 was an expression of antipolitics as well as an attempt at authentic living. In its first proclamation (1 January 1977) it demanded restoration and respect of human and civil rights which the Czechoslovak government had pledged to observe. The moral radicalism of Charter 77 was – beside an unprecedented persecution of the signatories and their family members and the deterring effect on the rest of the population – the reason why it remained restricted to a small group: it was signed by about 2,000 men and women up to November 1989. Its significance related not to the sphere of real politics but to the sphere of ethics because Charter 77 attempted to say the truth aloud at the time when political opposition was not possible.

The collapse

Mikhail Gorbachev's coming into power (1985) in the Soviet Union and his policy of *glasnost* and *perestroika* also gradually changed the situation in Czechoslovakia. The state and Party leadership because of the new Soviet policy got into international isolation, which deepened even more owing to developments in other countries. The mass exodus of East Germans in the autumn of 1989 was also of psychological importance. Adoption of Gorbachev's reform course which solely could gain certain popular support would lead necessarily to the fall of the very political representation that had based its existence precisely on the struggle against any reform attempts. This is why the Party leadership (since 1987 headed by Miloš Jakeš) liquidated sporadic attempts by some functionaries to follow Gorbachev's policies. Thus the leadership also got into internal isolation and deadlock – power became powerless. A real possibility of passing from 'existential' to democratic revolution arose. Together with it the importance of the opposition increased which was to stand at the forefront at the emergent civic movement and give it a political programme. Because Charter 77 and Václav Havel were still rejecting political means of struggle, new initiatives rehabilitating politics were arising. They were putting forward definite political demands that endangered the very grounds of the normalization regime, such as the removal of the Party's leading role from the

Constitution. Petitions the signing of which was also influenced by popular artists – the best known was called 'A Few Sentences' (*Několik vět*) – and demonstrations which acquired mass character particularly in January 1989, on the occasion of the twentieth anniversary of the student Jan Palach burning himself to death (16 January 1969), became the form of such struggle.

The impulse to a decisive attack on the totalitarian regime was not initiated by the traditional opposition but by independent students who, together with other young people, formed the core of protesters. From the beginning of 1989 students began coming up with their own demands, such as the removal of Marxism-Leninism classes at universities and public support of persecuted colleagues. Many independent students came from families of dissidents but they did not want to be merely their instrument, and endeavoured to make their own contribution to the forthcoming clash. Students represented a new generation, no longer influenced by the Prague Spring or deformed by the oppressiveness of Husák's policies at the outset of normalization. They saw in the 'bolshevik', that is, in the whole communist system the cause of the universal malaise – and they hated it.

The demonstration organized by independent students, together with the Municipal University Council of the Socialist Youth Organization on the occasion of the fiftieth anniversary of the execution of Czech students by the Nazis (17 November 1939) became the direct cause of the clash with the regime. The brutal intervention of armed police against the procession caused great outrage even among Party members since their children were also beaten up in Národní třída (one of the main streets in the centre of Prague). The next day indignation escalated due to misinformation about the death of one student, leading to spontaneous demonstrations especially in Prague. Students placed themselves at the head of the movement having already proclaimed on 18 November a general strike in support of demands related mainly to the events of the previous day. They were immediately joined by numerous artists and, especially, by actors. Also some opposition groups as well as individual dissidents voiced their support on this very day. The opposition as such took action on 19 November when the Civic Forum was established at a meeting of its representatives with several officials of existing satellite political parties and organizations.

All independent streams united in the Civic Forum, dominated by the group around Václav Havel who grew into a charismatic personality in this situation. The Civic Forum, proclaiming itself to be the sole representative of discontented people, based its concept of the solution of the crisis on two principles: dialogue and non-violence. The dissidents had envisaged a dialogue already in the first proclamation of Charter 77 and their attitude to

13. Dubček and Havel in the days of the 'Velvet Revolution'
(November 1989).

this form of struggle was clearly influenced also by experiences of 'round tables' in Poland and Hungary. But the changes in Czechoslovakia were taking place under a new situation abroad and at home. The regime, for international reasons, did not dare to use violence because the meeting of the American President George Bush and Gorbachev at Malta was near at hand. Also the leadership itself lacked the self-assurance necessary to proceed with such a policy. Its behaviour was characterized by fear, indecisiveness and search for alibis. It lost all authority even with the Communists and was so compromised that nobody, including the Civic Forum, wished to negotiate with it. Thus the Communist Party was disqualified as an independent political force. The Prime Minister of the Federal Government and a Member of the Presidium of the Central Committee of the Communist Party, Ladislav Adamec, who attempted to form a second centre of state power, undertook the task of trying to save the position of Communists. It was with him, owing to his reputation as a reformer, that the spokesmen of the Civic Forum opened a dialogue regarding the reorganization of the Federal government which represented, after the Party leadership's retreat, the main factor of power. At the time of negotiations with Adamec, the representatives of the Civic Forum clearly did not wish to assume responsibility for future development – for quite a while they did not put forward their own proposals for the composition of the government. It was only when Adamec's attempt to form a government with a great majority of Communists (15:5) foundered under the pressure of the popular protests, that the representatives of the Civic Forum assumed all initiative in the negotiations which followed. By 9 December the Civic Forum took power in forming a Government of National Understanding headed by Marian Čalfa, a Slovak who in January 1990 resigned from the Communist Party), and a day later Gustav Husák gave up the Presidency.

An opposition group known as the Czechoslovak Democratic Initiative, which had established itself as an independent political party in September 1989, suggested an alternative to solve the crisis. In its proclamation of 19 November it called for the resignation of the government led by Adamec, by 25 November, and the formation of a new one composed of former reform Communists representing the Prague Spring, representatives of the opposition headed by Václav Havel, and uncompromised members of the Communist Party – amounting to a coalition government composed of the chief political forces in the country. Its task was to be the preparation of elections to be held at the beginning of February 1990, which were to complete the takeover in the legislative sphere. Thus the Democratic Initiative was the sole force that as early as 19 November unequivocally demanded an effective share of power for the opposition. But its influence was insignificant and the Civic Forum did not accept its proposals.

The collapse of the compromised ruling set-up allowed the election of Václav Havel as President of the Republic on 29 December 1989. The Czech and Slovak national governments were reorganized; at the Federal, national and regional levels power passed into the hands of the opposition in a non-violent way in all spheres of state administration. Thus the first stage of the antitotalitarian revolution was completed. The more difficult part, that is, the creating of a basis for a democratic system lay ahead for the new political representation.

The period 1945–1989 constitutes quite an exceptional chapter in the history of Czechoslovakia. With the effort of an initially large part of the population as well as some non-communist political forces an attempt was made to create a state based on social justice. This attempt ended, however, in a tragic way by the establishment of a totalitarian system of Soviet type. Conditions under which Czech and Slovak society developed meant also that the attempt by Communist reformers to build 'a socialism with a human face' failed. The responsibility for the future fate of the country passed to a small group of intellectuals-dissidents, who decisively influenced the manner of the takeover in the November days of 1989. Thus a path opened for Czech and Slovak society to return to Western civilization to whose framework it belongs in view of its spiritual and social developments.

Selected bibliography

T. G. Ash, *We the People The Revolution of 89* (Cambridge, 1990)
   The Uses of Adversity Essays on the Fate of Central Europe, revised and updated (Cambridge, 1991).
V. Havel, *Living in Truth: Twenty-two Essays Published on the Occasion of the Award of the Erasmus Prize to Václav Havel* (Amsterdam-London-Boston, 1986).
   Power of the Powerless: Citizens against the State in Central Europe (London, 1988).
Barbara Wolfe Jancar, *Czechoslovakia and the Absolute Monopoly of Power. A Study of Political Power in a Communist System* (New York, 1971).
K. Kaplan, *Die politische Persekution in der Tschechoslowakei 1948–1972* (Cologne, 1983).
   The Communist Party in Power (London, 1987).
R. Littell (ed.), *The Czech Black Book. An Eyewitness, Documented Account of the Invasion of Czechoslovakia Prepared by the Institute of History, Czechoslovak Academy of Sciences* (New York–Washington–London, 1969).
J. Pelikán (ed.), *Le congrès clandestin: protocol secret et document du 14e Congrès extraordinaire du P.C. tchèchoslovaque* (Paris, 1970).
   Das unterdrückte Dossier: Bericht der Kommission des ZK der KPTsch über politische Prozesse und Rehabilitierungen in der Tschechoslowakei (Vienna-Frankfort/M-Curych, 1970).
M. Otáhhal, *Der rauhe Weg zur 'samtenen Revolution'. Vorgeschichte, Verlauf und Akteure der antitotalitären Wende in der Tschechoslowakei. Berichte des Bundesinstituts für ost-wissenschaftliche und internationale Studien*, 25 (Cologne, 1992).
G. Skilling, *Czechoslovakia's Interrupted Revolution* (Princeton, 1976).
M. Šimečka, *The Restoration of Order: The Normalization of Czechoslovakia* (London, 1984).
   Das Ende der Unbeweglichkeit: Ein politisches Tagebuch (Frankfort/M., 1990).
E. Táborský, *Communism in Czechoslovakia 1949–1960* (Princeton, 1961).

16

Changes in identity: Germans in Bohemia and Moravia in the nineteenth and twentieth centuries

JAN KŘEN

A historical picture of the Czech Lands would not be complete if the indigenous German population was not considered. According to contemporary statistics Germans, at the turn of the century, formed approximately one third of the inhabitants in Bohemia, a quarter in Moravia and a half in Austrian Silesia. At first, the majority of Jews opted for German nationality but, since the turn of the century, more than a half inclined to be Czechs.[1]

The literature on Czech–German relations, on the whole, has focused on Czechs whose development and rise are generally considered to be at the core of the problem. This chapter takes the opposite approach: it concentrates rather on Germans, particularly on Germans in Bohemia (*Deutschböhmen, Sudetendeutsche*), and on the uncertainties, splits and changeability of their national identity connected, as they were, with turns in the national-political programme. There were more twists and turns in their development than in that of the Czechs – one of the underestimated causes of domestic nationality conflicts.

Separation of nationalities

At the turn of the eighteenth century, modernization and emancipation introduced movement both in society and in its information network, transforming profoundly the national landscape of the Czech Lands. The era of national vagueness and exclusive estate-based territorial-political nations was over. Linguistic and ethnic differences, which were not so important earlier, gained importance with the coming of new social forces and a new spiritual environment. The modern nation-forming process, which engulfed all Central European ethnic groups (the largest groups – Germans – was the first), prevented the creation of a political 'Habsburg' nation, linked by common state citizenship and by a common – German – state language. Instead, linguistic and ethnic nations began to form, a typical model was the Czech national revival.[2]

Like the Czechs, the Germans were traditionally committed to territorial patriotism and, indeed, had constituted its leading element for the previous 150 years. They found themselves at the intersection of various nation-forming streams flowing within the Czech Lands, with sources also in Germany and Austria. Until then, they had not developed into a 'neo-German' tribe (such as German Silesians) and from the beginning, their identity was extremely complicated, multilayered, changeable and vaccilating. In many respects, it was irritated as well as irritating. A considerable part of the population in the Czech Lands, above all in both the Czech and German countryside, remained passive as regards the national question. Moreover, those in the most elevated and most conservative circles – aristocracy, Church and parts of the bureaucracy – held on (for as long as possible) to traditional Habsburg-oriented territorial patriotism. The centre of the new national ferment was found in the new, modern (or at least modern *in spe*) strata, subsumed largely under the German expression *Bildungsbürgertum*.

But for a long time, the national consciousness of these German strata in Bohemia and Moravia was not strongly developed. It was marked by various co-existing (and conflicting) tendencies: the idea of belonging to a German-wide cultural community clashed both with the consciousness of belonging to the Czech Lands and with loyalty to the Habsburg monarchy. In contrast to Czechs who were quickly becoming nationally active, the nation-forming stimulus among indigenous Germans remained latent for some time. At that time, they viewed Bohemia and Moravia as two of the many German-Austrian 'historical-political entities' whose character did not affect the ethnically different Czech population in the slightest. It was looked upon as a folklore group whose cultural uniqueness was at times even seen positively as an element enriching Germanhood. This non-national and pre-national concept of nationality expressed, for example, in the early works of Prague German poets and inspired by Czech motifs (Mortiz Hartmann, Alfred Meissner and others), survived among Germans in Bohemia until the 1840s, and among Germans in Moravia even longer.[3]

The change was initiated by democratic emigrés who lived in politically and nationally more awakened Germany. Since 1843 Franz Schuselka (1811–1886), a native of Budějovice writing in the *Allgemeine Zeitung* (Augsburg) and elsewhere, rejected the hitherto accepted *Bohemismus* and pledged for a nationally conscious attitude: either German or Czech. Three years later Karel Havlíček's (1821–1856) article 'The Czech and the Slav' in *Pražské noviny* [Prague News] became the Czech counterpart. In it, contrary to the older vague notion of Slav Czechdom, emphasis was given to a clear-cut nationally conceived Czechdom. On the intellectual horizon of Bohemia – in Moravia, this process started at least one generation later – a new nationality terminology appears. A sharper distinction began to be drawn between 'Czechoslavs' and 'Deutschböhmen', that is, between 'Bohemians' who spoke Czech and German respectively.[4]

Although Czechs in Bohemia and Moravia constituted the majority, Germans did not consider themselves as a minority. They felt at home, at least in the whole Western part of the Habsburg monarchy which, since the time of Maria Theresa (1740–1780), had been consistently formed as an integrated and German-bonded entity – the Austrian unitary state (*Einheitsstaat*). The entire state administration, social life and a greater part of cultural life used the German language as means of communication. German was spoken by all upper social strata who, at that time, solely constituted the nation. Moreover those engaged in commerce conducted their activities in German. As to emerging industry, it was centred – well into the second half of the nineteenth century – on border regions settled by Germans. Czech, the language of the population's majority and only gradually gaining the qualities of a modern language, occupied an inferior position. Except for the thin stratum of nationally conscious Czech intelligentsia (who for that matter had a German higher education and were altogether bilingual), Czech was the means of communication for the rural population in the interior of the country and for the lower urban strata, who occasionally employed a kind of pidgin German ('kucheldeutsch'). Because of their indisputably leading position and awareness of links with the other Germans in Austria, Germans in the Czech Lands undoubtedly felt nationally secure and self-confident. This in turn gave rise to a kind of saturated and superior lukewarmness which was altogether typical for Austria as a whole.

In this respect the Revolution of 1848 brought many changes, the most far-reaching being the rapid activation of the Czech element and significant Czechization of all social life. The German facade was torn down and what surfaced was the ethnic reality of a country with a Czech majority. This did not prevent a joint stand against Metternichian gerontocracy in the spring of 1848 but, immediately afterwards, the paths of both national entities started to separate. With the ascendancy of radical democratic and liberal elements among Germans in Bohemia, as in Austria (less so in Moravia), resistance to absolutism grew into opposition to the Habsburg monarchy as a whole. Their thinking was bound up with the vision of German national statehood, embodied by the Frankfurt National Assembly. Other sections of the German-Czech (*deutschböhmisch*) community lacking interest in the national cause, for example the peasantry, stayed loyal to the monarchy but were pushed into the political background.[5]

Because Czechs rejected the unification of the Czech Lands with a nationally united Germany, both national groups, that is their political representatives, found themselves in a conflict. Both sides claimed national self-determination (first called for in the Czech milieu) but the two demands were in effect mutually exclusive. The politically most active and also democratic wing, representing the Germans in Bohemia (this tendency was far weaker in Moravia), desired unification with Germany and campaigned for elections to the Frankfurt Parliament. The leading liberal Czech group, together with the 'historical' Czech aristocracy, was oriented towards autonomy for the country (Lands of the Crown) of Bohemia and concentrated on elections to the Diet of Bohemia. Ultimately, the only elections had concerned the Austrian Imperial Parliament (Reichsrat) to which deputies representing Czechs as well as Germans were sent.

Meanwhile the situation on the German side became complex as well as more transparent. The Great German (*großdeutsch*) vision was to replace the existing German Confederation (*Bund*), which was to contain the Habsburg domains (including the Czech Lands). This vision faced more and more obstacles. In Frankfurt the Little German (*kleindeutsch*) notion prevailed: unification of Germany centred on Prussia which excluded the Habsburg monarchy. Although a significant number of German deputies from Bohemia was attracted to Great German thinking, they had to accept the actual situation, all the more so since the Habsburg monarchy showed greater vitality than was expected. The result was a kind of 'return' to Austria which they, however, wished to transform into a constitutional monarchy which observed Bohemian State Rights. More or less independently, the German Ludwig von Löhner as well as the Czech František Palacký (1798–1867) started to ponder the transformation of the Habsburg monarchy into a number of national 'substates'. They were to include a German-Austrian substate containing the Habsburg hereditary domains (*Erblande*) and the German-speaking border region of Bohemia and Moravia, and a Czech substate or a Czechoslovak substate respectively, made up of the Czech-speaking inland of Bohemia and Moravia and Upper Hungary, that is, Slovakia. None of these projects succeeded nor did the compromise reached in the Constituent Assembly at the small Moravian town Kroměříž where the first Imperial Parliament (Reichstag) was moved from revolutionary Vienna (1848–9): subdivision of historically established parts of the Habsburg

monarchy into national regions. The *rapprochement* between the political representatives of Czechs and Germans in Bohemia and Moravia did not prevent
defeat – the Parliament was forcibly dissolved by the army (7 March 1849).
The first great chance for a solution based on the new foundation of a balanced compromise between two ethnic nationalisms came to nothing.[6]

The liberal era

Not before the 1860s another such chance occurred when Liberals replaced
the idealistic radicals of 1848 in the leadership of the bourgeois camp in the
Habsburg monarchy. They were led by Germans from Bohemia, Moravia
and Silesia which industrially and capitalistically belonged to the most
advanced parts of Austria. But this domestic liberalism differed from the
classical liberal position which approached the national question by com-
promising with traditional political forces and adopting their state ideology.
While pressing for a thorough realization of liberal ideas in the political
sphere, Germans – above all from Bohemia – supported Viennese centralism which not only secured their hegemony in the country but also the
national link with their Austrian kinsmen. As a whole, Austrian liberalism
took a cool attitude to Great German conceptions which, at that time,
became the domain of traditional forces – above all, the efforts of the
Habsburg dynasty to maintain its hegemony in the *Bund*. If it is at all possible to rationalize and simplify the contemporary most contradictory and
confusing notions, liberal Germans (and liberal Czechs) would most probably have been willing to accept the Prussian Little German solution, especially if it were to stop at the Mainz border and preserve the 'third'
Germany. In the 'fratricidal' war of 1866 between Prussia and Austria, the
Czech and German Liberals stood firmly behind Austria.[7]

After the exclusion of Austria from the German *Bund* (1866), the situation
of German-Austrians became complicated. The Dualism negotiated, in
1867, between the Imperial Crown and Hungary set other nations, including Germans, aside. However, in the western half of the monarchy
(Cisleithania) Germans were compensated constitutionally by the transfer
of power to them. Because the majority of Liberal cabinet ministers in
Vienna were Germans from Bohemia and Moravia, they, too, felt satisfied.
The golden era of Austrian liberalism was their golden era as well. When
they returned to power after the conservative episode of 1870–1, during
which the attempt to reach a compromise with the Czechs failed,[8] they
again imposed centralized rule. By then, however, different conditions
obtained. The crisis in 1873 shook the liberal order while the government
was unsuccessful in restoring the state of affairs before 1866.

On the contrary, Bismarckian Prussian-led Germany grew to become the leading continental power whose rise strongly influenced the Austrian political scene. While Austrian conservative parties remained faithful to the Habsburg monarchy, the liberal camp proved to be more perceptive towards the changed situation. The younger generation, especially Germans in Bohemia influenced by the alluring successes of the Bismarckian Reich, started to form a more nationalistically oriented group of Young Liberals (analogous to the Young Czechs) whose platform was geared towards a new conception of Austria as a second German state. One expression of this conception was the demand to establish German by law as the state language. In the programme formulated 1868 in the small Austrian spa town of Aussee, the idea which came to play an important role in the German national movement appeared for the first time, that is, the separation of Dalmatia, Galicia and Bukovina from Cisleithania (the western half of Austria-Hungary) – they were to be only loosely connected to it through the person of the sovereign.[9] This seemingly defensive concept concealed a nationalistic expansive agenda: in reduced Cisleithania Germans would have a guaranteed majority. Germans in Bohemia would have benefited considerably from this solution because despite of their generally superior status they were at least potentially endangered by the Czech majority. Their position in Bohemia as well as their links with other Germans in Austria would be strengthened. But this apparently, in retrospect, premature programme found little backing from Germans in Bohemia. They had few contacts with their kinsmen in the Reich whose national consciousness was developing in the nation-state context. There, the public and also the government kept their distance from the nationally conscious German-Austrians who found support only from fringe nationalist clubs.

Official Berlin gave definite priority to a prospective alliance with the Habsburg monarchy (concluded 1879 with a Conservative and not a Liberal government) and adhered to its policy of non-interference. It was not willing to engage on behalf of German-Austrians considered to be strong enough to defend their position within the Habsburg monarchy – for that matter, the German-Austrians felt so themselves. Regarding Czechs, even Germans in Bohemia were confident of their political supremacy in view of the liberal monopoly of power in Vienna in which they participated extensively.[10]

Never the less, at the end of the 1870s, the Liberal government in Vienna fell and the power in the state passed into the hands of the Conservative imperial cabinet of Count Edward Taaffe (1833–1895). In the years which followed Premier Taaffe would rely on the so-called 'Iron Ring', a right-wing coalition of Poles, Czechs and Austrian clerical conservatives

('Hohenwart Club'), who were not as nationally engaged as the Liberals. There was evidence around this time of the unstable basis of German hegemony in Austria, as well as of the lability of the links between Germans in Bohemia and other Germans in Austria. Centred on German as the *de facto* exclusive state language and on the monopoly of German Liberal cabinets, they were dependent on the swings of political shifts. During Taaffe's rule, the pendulum swung widely indeed. Czechs now participated in exercising power and, moreover, they gained ground in particular regarding the language question. Czech began to be employed in the administration of the Czech Lands whose almost exclusive German character had begun to change. Bohemia ceased to be a German domain: under Taaffe's regime, Germans lost definitively their majority in the Diet.

Whereas German political supremacy remained unchallenged in Moravia and in the ethnically mixed Austrian domains, Germans in Bohemia suddenly had to face the prospect of being a minority. This prospect emerged as a result of the fall of the Liberal government to which they were particularly attached. Losses in Bohemia also weakened the German position in Austrian politics where Germans became in effect a minority. Engaged in a contest with the Czechs, they were left to depend on outside support from Austria, and eventually from Germany. This was even reflected in the mentality of Germans in Bohemia: a sense of superiority was being replaced by anxious defensive psychosis (although in Moravia they continued to feel secure for a long time to come). Their national existence was, in fact, not under threat, but this first retreat from taken-for-granted privileges and positions was already exciting a sense of national endangerment. The reaction was the establishment of German national associations for the defence of every possible issue. This became the source of the notorious 'petty war' between Czechs and Germans which, in the future, would come to charge and poison the atmosphere in the Czech Lands and would become a hindrance to any agreement between them.[11]

The democratic era

The era of traditional elitist liberalism, with which Germans in Bohemia and Moravia were deeply linked, was drawing to a close. Social strata not enjoying full rights – the petty bourgeoisie, the working class and the peasantry – were placing the political scene under pressure and demanding political participation. The new generation of German–Austrian politicians was forced to look for novel approaches to the national question. The first step in this direction was what came to be known as the Linz Programme (1882). It was definitely directed against liberalism and favoured democratic changes. The foremost initiators were to become the future leaders of mass parties – Victor Adler (Social Democratic Party) and Robert Pattai (Christian Social Party) as well as the pan-Germanist Georg v. Schönerer. Moreover, the national doctrine was undergoing change. In Linz there was a return to half-forgotten ideas of the Aussee platform, which were gradually broadened with the demand for a customs union with Germany and a constitutionally laid down alliance with Germany (the so-called Whitsun Programme of 1899). This alliance was to endow the union with the character of a special German–German relationship.[12]

Missing among the leading authors of the Linz Programme were Germans from Bohemia who continued as guardians of liberalism. At the time of the elections in 1891, almost their entire representation in the Reichsrat was still controlled by the 'progressivists' (Deutsche Fortschrittspartei), the succession party of old liberalism. Never the less, half of the German mandate in the Diet in the 1880s already belonged to the new nationalistic parties (Deutsche Nationalpartei, Deutsche Volkspartei). Furthermore, the All-German Movement (related to the Alldeutscher Verband) found its focal point in the Czech Lands. German political circles saw the emergence of a new national programme which went back to the ideas of 1848 and called for a division of the country along national lines and for the creation of a so-called German closed linguistic area. At first, this was meant to be only an administrative measure (a division of districts based on a national key and sectioning of territorial administration along national lines). Later, the project was extended by the demand for total rupture, that is the creation of Deutschböhmen (German-Bohemia) as a separate Crownland.

On the one hand, liberalism did not succeed in solving the national conflict in the Czech Lands; on the other, it did provide a basis for future attempts. From the 1880s until the First World War the idea of national separation (effectively, national autonomy) was the starting point and the basis of all efforts by the Germans in Bohemia to reach a settlement with respect to the national question.[13] These negotiations were successful in 1905 only in Moravia where a Czech could vote only for Czechs and a German only for Germans in elections to the Diet of Brno. The proposition for a self-contained German linguistic area in Moravia was considered even less realistic than in the case of Bohemia. The Moravian Compromise (as it is sometimes called)[14] revealed for the first time discrepancies in political attitude between Germans in Moravia and Germans in Austria. German representatives from ethnically mixed Austrian domains resolutely opposed division into constituencies according to nationality (Slovenians, Italians).

Germans in Moravia also differed in their political profile from their Austrian kinsmen. Among Germans in Moravia, as among Czechs, the Agrarian Party became more influential than the Christian-Social Party which was so important in Austria.

Moreover, the bloc of nationalistic parties, to whose policies liberal pro-gressivists gradually were drawn, had stronger positions in Bohemia than in the Austrian lands. This was a reflection of deeper differences between these two groups of Austrian Germanhood which exceeded the dimensions of territorial articulations so characteristic of Austrian conditions. In many respects, the Germans in Moravia were more like the Czechs than their Austrian kinsmen to whom, however, they were closer than to the Germans from the Reich.[15] In times of violent national conflict, as for instance in connection with the so-called Badeni Language Ordinances of 1897, Austrian solidarity did, in fact, emerge. The Language Ordinances named after the Premier Casimir Badeni (1846–1909) and designed to meet the Czechs halfway, were toppled by the combined opposition of all German parties in Austria (including the Social Democratic Party). Simultaneously, the national question in the Czech Lands experienced a new factor. This consisted of attempts to internationalize the hitherto localized internal Austrian conflict b involving Germans from the Reich. From there support emanated from the nationalistic wing which, in the Wilheminian era, had gained in importance.[16] Until that time Germans in the Czech Lands – especially in Moravia – had looked towards Austria where their inclination lay. In the course of this new development, the nationalistic camp of Germans in the Czech Lands provided a gateway for Great German nation-alism to return, in its modernized, imperialist garb, into the German environment in Austria.

However, this was not the only line of movement pursued by Germans in Bohemia and Moravia. After the Badeni riots the Social Democratic Party reverted to a more moderate national policy, while the strengthened Agrarian Party also inclined towards restraint in national politics. Difference of opinion also proceeded in the nationalistic camp similar to that (but less pronounced) which occurred among Czechs. At the same time, anti-Semitism generally grew and induced a considerable number of Jews to draw more closely to the Czech side which, noticeably, weakened the Germans. Concurrently, in the nationalistic camp of Germans in the Czech Lands and in Austria a radical chauvinist wing gained strength which was driven by visions of All- or Great German unification and which pursued, in the beginning, a strongly separatist and anti-Habsburg line (*Germania irre-denta*). Among Germans in Bohemia – not in Moravia – parties of this hew (joined at the beginning of the twentieth century by the predecessor of

Hitler's party, the DNSAP – Deutsche Nationalsozialistische Arbeiterpartei) were stronger than in the Austrian lands. Although still a minority among Germans in Bohemia, their aggressiveness held nationally more moderate parties often at bay.

War conflict

The dramatic experience of war, nationalistically conceived as a conflict between Teutons and Slavs, acted as a serious factor in moulding national consciousness both for Germans in the Czech Lands and Germans in Austria and brought about a further change in their national-political development. The alliance with Germany and endorsement of her war aims – to establish a Great German *Mitteleuropa* by a close union with the Habsburg monarchy – augmented in German consciousness the Great German euphoria without its anti-Austrian sting: Austria could now be counted on, but only as a kind of new German *Ostmark*. Regardless of the former anti-Prussian sentiment, especially characteristic for Austrian clericals, this feeling also engulfed them and, perhaps even more so, affected Social Democracy where Great German leanings had deeper roots. The leadership of German politics in Austria passed into the hands of the nationalistic bloc where nationalist Germans from Bohemia and Moravia played a particularly active role. *Mitteleuropa* seemed to them the optimal solution to their long-standing problems. Their aims exceeded the mere expectations of acquiring power by regaining domination over the Czech Lands – at last there loomed the hope of resolving the persistently and agonizingly perceived split in their national identity between 'Austrianess' and 'Germaness'. This, incidentally, applied to all Austrian nationalists who considered war to be the long-yearned-for opportunity for fundamental change and the enforcement of all their long-time claims. Indeed the escalation of these demands was, obviously, to compensate for the frustration caused by the compromises of Austrian *fortwursteln* (muddling through).[17] In 1916, after the Central Powers' successes in the war, the nationalists victoriously brandished their detailed programmatic statement 'Forderungen der Deutschen Österreichs' (Demands of Germans in Austria). In the spirit of the new Great Germany they professed their allegiance to *Mitteleuropa* and to a special German-German relationship with the Wilhelminian Reich. Following the old prescription they laid out their new aim: by the separation of Galicia and further 'secondary lands', a new West- or Little Austria was to be created where they would be the exclusive masters. With the unconcealed arrogance of victors they proclaimed the 'Forderungen' as the basis for German policy giving absolute priority to their own national needs without concern for other nations, above all for the Slovenes and the Czechs. For them a certain residual principle was to apply: only those national rights were to be extended to them which would not trouble the Germans. In the Czech Lands, to which the greatest attention was paid, this objective was to be achieved by extra-parliamentary measures concerning the nationality compromise about which negotiations had taken place before the war.[18] This seemingly moderate attitude was, however, just as deceitful as the great-Germanness advanced through *Kleinösterreich* (Little Austria). After long years of struggle and repeatedly deflected negotiations, the details of the balance had been punctiliously worked out in the proposed compromise. In the new situation, however, the balance was thoroughly reversed as the remaining controversial issues were to be resolved in favour of the Germans within the framework of a German *Mitteleuropa* and a violent, undemocratic and dictatorial scenario. Despite possessing the characteristics of a dynamic, modern, sovereign nation with the qualities entitling to claim statehood, the Czechs were to be confined to the role of an island in a German sea, to be a tolerated minority equipped with elementary rights only allowing for a mere cringing folkloristic existence.

Thus during the war German policy lost the last traces of its former superior latitude characteristic for the era of liberal hegemony – and even that was very far from the idea of *primi inter pares*. Driven by the maximalistic and war-inspired militant spirit of self-determination the Germans in Bohemia and Moravia claimed the same national status as their kinsmen in purely German countries which induced an equal maximalism on the Czech side. An irreconcilable and confrontational atmosphere of animosity was thus created in which the conflicting constellation was determined by the question 'who will win': nationalistic tension escalated to the extreme no longer permitting reconciliation and compromise but only capitulation of the opponent.

The boom of German extreme nationalism, supplemented by the Austrian military clique's attempts at dictatorship, did not last long. At the very moment of its realization, it was thwarted by the external shock of the February Revolution of 1917 in Russia. The Vienna Court, fearing a 'Russian' crisis in Austria, hesitated and the militant German national front disintegrated. However, the bellicose and confrontational constellation repeated itself once more at the end of the war. After the Peace of Brest Litovsk, in 1918, it seemed that the Central Powers stood at the threshold of victory. Moreover, weakened Vienna had to accept a vassal-type protectorate from Germany and, in the Czech Lands German nationalists extorted the consent, at least, to the first steps towards the division of the territory. However, both the new German order in the Czech Lands as well as the whole German *Mitteleuropa* were merely still-born fetuses. Defeat in the war sealed the dissolution of the Habsburg monarchy. The Czech Lands became the core of the new successor state – Czechoslovakia.

For indigenous Germans – whether they were from Bohemia or Moravia – this meant a deep shock with far-reaching repercussions: not only their extremely heightened hopes of the war years but, essentially, also the basis of their entire hitherto declared national-political doctrine collapsed. The worst scenario, feared for years, had become reality: they became virtually a minority, moreover, in a state of their long-standing rivals. They tried to resist their fate of 'servants of their former servants' by a desperate escape forward, that is by an attempt to rescue the rest of their war aims. Activating the slogan of self-determination they had rejected only the day before, their various political units again formed a united block which decisively refused to be incorporated into the Republic of Czechoslovakia (ČSR). In the border regions of Bohemia and Moravia they proclaimed the establishment of four German provinces all of which were to become part of the newly created German-Austria (*Deutsch-Österreich*). Two of the largest of these territorially unconnected provinces in northern Bohemia and Moravia were, however, separated from Austria by a wide area of Czech settlement. Their existence would, therefore, only have been possible on the condition of an *Anschluß* of Austria to Germany which, at that time, was desired by their Austrian kinsmen.[19] None of these expectations was realized: Austria's *Anschluß* was prevented by the victorious Entente, and the phantom attempts of gaining independence for the above-mentioned provinces was foiled by the Czech army which occupied them quickly without encountering any perceptible resistance. The failure of the Germans in Bohemia and Moravia was completed by disinterestedness in Germany which, after her defeat, had enough troubles of her own and was neither willing to annex Austria nor the Czech-German provinces: indeed, the Reich's diplomacy advised their leaders to accept the new reality and to try and secure for themselves the strongest possible position in the new Republic of Czechoslovakia.[20]

Sudeten Germans

The establishment of Czechoslovakia confronted the Germans in Bohemia and Moravia with an entirely novel national constellation: traditional ties with their Austrian kinsmen were severed and little German-Austria, itself in the grip of a traumatic existential crisis, ceased to be the centre of attraction. A new national terminology reflected the change: for the Germans in Bohemia and Moravia a new collective name – Sudeten Germans

(*Sudetendeutsche*) – came quickly into common use.[21] This signalled a new phase in the process of nation-building – like the Austrians, the Germans in Czechoslovakia experienced the forming of a new, common national identity which included Germans in Moravia and in Silesia. In Slovakia where democratic conditions were remarkably vitalized, the local German minority (*Karpatendeutsche*) was only marginally affected.

Conditions for the life of Germans in the ČSR became complicated: the relatively decent minorities regime, one of the most liberal in Europe, did not satisfy them. In numbers and social potential they exceeded the usual dimensions of other national minorities: they still retained their social advantage compared to the Czechs and they were also strong in the cultural sphere although they suffered a continuous drain of talent. In the new Czechoslovakia the loss of their previous privileges and benefits seriously affected them psychologically although, in reality, it was not so serious as to threaten their livelihood. Of greater significance were, possibly, objective difficulties which, in the structure of the new state, became more pronounced. Light industries (textiles, glass) which constituted the basis of their economy had already previously passed their peak and, due to the shrunken capacity of the Czechoslovak market, they became export-orientated and faced great obstacles, not least because of strong competition from the Reich. Also the advantages gained by Sudeten Germans in the course of greater democratic freedoms after the revolutionary change in 1918 were, in their minds, invalidated by the lack of collective national rights, above all, by the fact that they had not been granted territorial autonomy.[22]

However, the negativism of German nationalistic parties, which rejected integration into Czechoslovakia, soon led them into a blind alley similarly as had happened to the Czechs fifty years earlier when they pursued their unsuccessful policy against Austria. While the Czechs had kept up their defiance almost twenty years, the Germans changed their stance remarkably quickly. Already at the beginning of the 1920s, a change can be observed in their policy similar to that resorted to by the Czechs towards Austria at the turn of the 1870s and 1880s. The protagonists of this new positive orientation, which became known as 'activism', were the traditionally less nationalistic parties (German Social Democratic Party, German Agrarian Party and German Christian Socialist Party) which, in the elections of the 1920s, gained three times as many votes as the nationalists. The political concept of German activism strongly resembled that of the Czechs before the war, that is, to compensate the lack of local national autonomy by participating in central government. Thus from 1926 German parties were represented in all government coalitions in Czechoslovakia and the importance of the Sudeten Germans grew. Although dissatisfied in many respects, they showed remarkable vitality and led, on the whole, a tolerable existence, similar to that of the Czechs in the old Austria; but their feelings for Czechoslovakia were harsher than corresponded with reality – just as the Czechs' feelings for Austria had been in the past.[23]

Nazism and Sudeten Germans

As a result of the shock of the world economic crisis (border regions inhabited largely by Germans experienced greater hardships than the interior inhabited by Czechs) and because of the impact of the rise of Nazism in neighbouring Germany this hopeful trend was completely reversed. In 1933 Konrad Henlein's (1898–1945) united nationalistic party, the Sudeten-deutsche Partei (SdP), was founded and as early as 1935, when it fought its first election, it received two thirds of the German vote. In the following years it was able to strengthen its leading position further. Nevertheless, difficult twists and turns were concealed behind this seemingly straightforward development. Only part of the German nationalists embraced Hitler's Nazism immediately. The majority in the leadership of the new Sudeten rallying movement (*Sammelbewegung*), which was to replace the forbidden Nazi organizations, consisted rather of followers of a more traditional nationalism similar to that in contemporary Austria under Dollfuß. The SdP's leader Henlein (previously known as the head of the German Gymnastic Federation), and the majority of his companions professed the conservative, authoritative teaching of the Viennese Professor Othmar Spann whose concept of Germanhood was based on traditional ideas of a plural entity in which Germans in Austria and German minorities elsewhere were to safeguard their individuality and independent role. Henlein's original programme corresponded with this concept: authoritative, not democratic, autonomy. Gradually, the attraction of Hitler Germany and the pressure of its followers in Henlein's ranks brought about change: followers of Spann were ousted and Henlein himself joined the Nazis and subordinated the SdP to Hitler. During the years of appeasement leading to Munich the SdP, financed from Germany, totally subscribed to the Nazi doctrine.[24] At the same time, the SdP's ideas on the national perspectives of Sudeten Germans changed. From a movement aiming at the greatest possible autonomy within the Czechoslovak state emerged the vanguard of Hitlerism, Germany's fifth column, whose objectives the political representation of Henlein had fully adopted. Their priority was not the 'liberation' of the Sudeten and its integration into Germany but the liquidation of Czechoslovakia and the direct annexation of Bohemia and Moravia by Germany. Together with Austria these territories were to become part of the 'steel core' of Hitler's Great German Reich. This aberrant vision provided the Sudeten Germans with an apparent solution of their problems – the final harbour of their national identity was to be integration into Germany. A particular attraction of this vision was the expectation that, in this way, the long-lasting rivalry with the Czechs would be resolved in their favour and their former domination over the Czech Lands would return to them. Furthermore, they hoped that their significance in Germany would be enhanced and they would, in future, represent more than a mere marginal grouping.

Only once in their history, during the Munich crisis, were Sudeten Germans to play a prominent historical role performing a special heroic act in the proscenium of the theatre of European politics. In reality it was all semblance and deception in which they were pawns in Hitler's game and for which they had to pay heavily and enduringly. Thus they became both objects and victims,[25] first of Hitler, then of the Allies and the Czechs. However, this interpretation usually resorted to in Sudeten German historiography is not flawless. Pawns are not totally negligible chess pieces and that applies also to the case of the Sudeten Germans at the time of Munich. Indeed, Henlein's contemporary representatives played this role eagerly, enthusiastically and authentically, last but not least, thanks to the massive, demonstrative support by the Sudeten German public. Their success was truly crushing and suicidal – the anti-Fascist world and, above all, the second victim of German aggression, the Czechs, would in future regard them as the makers of their misfortune.

The Sudeten Germans' benefits were short-lived. Many of their exalted wishes were not fulfilled. On the contrary, the first victim were they themselves, that is, their 'tribal' unity, for they did not remain a whole unit in the Reich. Although the north Bohemian and north Moravian border areas were merged to create a new Reich county, the *Sudetengau*, other parts, by no means insignificant, were cut off and simply integrated into neighbouring German provinces. Equally, hopes for domination over the 'Protectorate of Bohemia and Moravia' faded away as Henlein headed its administration only for one month, but the appointed 'Reichsprotektor', Konstantin von Neurath, and all his successors came from the Reich. While the Protectorate became the domain of the SS, the *Sudetengau* became the model domain of the Nazi Party. Speedily all distinctive Sudeten German institutions were abolished, including the democratic organizations which had been an inalienable component of Sudeten German public fabric. Autonomy, the wide network of associations (clubs) and ramified culture were degraded to a mere 'transmission belt' for the totalitarian Nazi machine in which the Sudeten Germans themselves played a secondary role. National 'liberation' and 'unification' degenerated under the Nazi regime and deprived the Sudeten Germans not only of the expelled Jews, active Social Democrats, Communists, Catholics and other opponents, but also of many non-Nazi nationalists, including some of Henlein's former companions. These grave losses at the expense of the Sudeten German national sub-stratum did not seem so great as long as they were overshadowed by triumphs in the war and certain economic advantages, such as the liquidation of unemployment. Whether and to what extent the Sudeten Germans sobered up from their initial euphoria is not clear. Not only Czech but also Sudeten German historiography has its lacunae to which the fate of the Sudeten in the Nazi era belongs. Meticulous efforts to reconstruct local resistance does not fill this gap satisfactorily; apparently resistance was stronger than in the Reich but not evident enough to signal a break with Nazism.[26] It could, perhaps, be conjectured that in face of the inevitably looming defeat many would have liked to change the slogan 'Heim in's Reich' to 'Heim in die Tschechoslowakei' but no such change was visible. Desperate efforts to revitalize local resistance by means of injections from abroad (for instance, paratroopers sent by Social Democrats from the West and Communists from Moscow) failed. For a long time illusions were held about a possible turn for the better in the theatres of war. Even stronger were the effects of Nazi pressure, of habitual obedience and of fears of Czech revenge. At least on the surface the Nazi regime remained untouched and firm – the Sudeten were occupied by the Allies at the very end of the war.

Sudeten Germans and the future?

The postwar fate of the Sudeten Germans began as a veritable calvary. As the war drew to its end, first the Nazis, carried out ruthless evacuations, then escapes and suicides took place. After the war had ended, the Czechs started spontaneously to take brutal revenge and to expel the Sudeten Germans. These actions were stopped when the Potsdam Conference approved the evacuation of the entire German population, a move which – with regards to Czechoslovakia – was put into effect in 1946.[27]

Sudeten Germans as a group ceased to exist. Scattered over the whole of Germany, both over West Germany and East Germany (and partly also over Austria) they were integrated into local society. In this arduous and painful process they felt doubly afflicted: by total defeat like all Germans at that time but, in addition, by the loss of their homes. During that time the contribution of these expellees to the reconstruction of Germany belongs, doubtlessly, to their greatest historical achievements and is, consequently, highly appreciated. Many had difficulties in accepting their fate. Therefore, all the

14. Expatriated German population from the Czechoslovak border regions
waiting for transfer after the end of the Nazi occupation in 1945.

more, needs to be recognized that they did not become an institutionalized
source of instability and revenge in – let us say – a Palestinian manner. The
majority, however, did accept their new homes, familiarized themselves with
them and settled down.[28]

Is this the final act of their century-long existence? By becoming German
citizens and being absorbed in Germany did they finally achieve self-
determination and find their long-searched for identity? Were those exalted
hopes of the Munich period fulfilled in this paradoxical and tragic form
which had found expression in Henlein's slogan 'Es kommt der Tag' (The
day will come)? The relevant lines in the poem of Ferdinand Freiligrath, *O
lieb, so lang du lieben kannst!* (1838), which might have inspired this slogan, read
ominously:

> Die Stunde kommt, die Stunde kommt,
> Wo du an Gräbern stehst und klagst.
> [The hour will come, the hour will come
> When standing at graves, you will cry]

Did Sudeten German national consciousness find rest in the arms of
mother Germany? Was it a grave or a beginning or both?

Much bears witness to this unhappy–happy ending and much speaks against it. As far as a fair number of very active cultural and political institutions are concerned, which keep Sudeten German memory and cultural existence alive, no such funereal impression can be perceived. Their achievements, including honorable efforts by many to reach an understanding with Czechs, belong legitimately to the structure and diversity of Europeanism. Equally organically they belong to German reality. Germans have never been, and neither are they to this day, a nation like the French *une et indivisible* and, thus, the Sudeten German element is a not ommisible part of this fruitful plurality.

A more complicated question is the political existence of the Sudeten Germans. The greatest number of them settled in Bavaria where they are acknowledged as one of the constituent 'tribes'. There they and their political organizations found a natural refuge. As early as 1950, one of their most well-known political organizations, the Sudetendeutsche Landsmannschaft, rejected revenge in a special declaration. At the same time, the Potsdam decision has so far not been accepted and the restitution of *status quo ante* is sought.[29] This is also the reason for their rejection of the latest Treaty of Friendship and Good Neighbourly Relations between the Federal Republic of Germany and the former Czechoslovak Federal Republic. Claims for the revision of the resettlement and restitution of property rights to Sudeten Germans in Czechoslovakia have recently been put forward in an emphatic manner. Certain Sudeten German elements connect these demands, in a not altogether European spirit, with the vision that the return from Germany of the remaining German minority to the Czech state could lead to the revival of their previous status. Repercussions of these claims on the German political scene have not made themselves greatly felt so far. However, the majority of the Czech public rejects them and even those representatives of the state most critical of the postwar evacuation do not view these attempts favourably.

Viewed from the perspective of the Czech Republic's future membership in the European Community (which the Federal Republic of Germany in the above-mentioned treaty is pledged to support) things would look somewhat differently, for within the Community freedom of movement and settlement would have to be guaranteed. Here it will be necessary to take into account long periods of time which makes a more extensive renewal of a German entity in the Czech state unlikely, although this cannot be ruled out entirely, at least not as a means of pressure on Czech governments. Sudeten Germanhood and its influence on future Czech–German co-existence still remains, at least, somewhat an open question.

Notes

1 Cf. J. Heřman, *Evolution of the Jewish Population in Bohemia and Moravia 1754–1953* (Jerusalem, 1974).

2 M. Hroch, *Die Vorkämpfer der nationalen Bewegung bei den kleinen Völkern Europas* (Prague, 1965), pp. 41–62; J. Chłebowczyk, *Procesy narodotwórcze w wschodniej Europie środkowej w dobie kapitalizmu* [Nation-building processes in East Central Europe during the period of capitalism] (Warsaw, 1975), pp. 122–238.

3 J. Křen, *Konfliktní společenství Češi a Němci 1790–1918* [Society in conflict Czechs and Germans 1790–1918] (Prague, 1991), pp. 33–9; G. Pirchen (ed.), *Das Sudetendeutschtum* (Brno, 1937), p. 428.

4 Křen, *Konfliktní společenství*, pp. 73–6; J. Kořalka, *Tschechen im Habsburgerreich und in Europa 1815–1914* (Munich, 1991), pp. 27–31, 37–40, 47–8, 56–8, 64–9.

5 F. Seibt, *Deutschland und die Tschechen Geschichte einer Nachbarschaft in der Mitte Europas* (Munich, 1974), pp. 144–6; A. Klíma, *Češi a Němci v revoluci 1848–1849* [Czechs and Germans in the Revolution of 1848–1849] (Prague, 1988), pp. 99–119.

6 Kořalka, *Tschechen im Habsburgerreich*, pp. 190–94; Klíma, *Češi a Němci*, pp. 385–98.

7 E. v. Plener, *Erinnerungen, II* (Stuttgart, 1919), p. 20; H. Lades, *Die Tschechen und die deutsche Frage* (Erlangen, 1938), p. 208.

8 A. O. Zeithammer, *Zur Geschichte der böhmischen Ausgleichsversuche (1865–1871)* (Prague, 1912), I.

9 B. Sutter, 'Die politische und rechtliche Stellung der Deutschen in Österreich 1848 bis 1918' in A. Wandruszka and P. Urbamitsch (eds.), *Die Habsburger-monarchie 1848–1918*, vol. III/1: *Die Völker des Reiches*, pp. 208, 213–214.

10 E. Wiskemann, *Czechs and Germans. A Study of the Struggle in the Historic Provinces of Bohemia and Moravia* (London, 1967), p. 35.

11 K. Bosl (ed.) *Handbuch der Geschichte der böhmischen Länder* (Munich, 1967), III, pp. 157–63; J. Křen, *Konfliktní společenství*, pp. 218–24.

12 R. A. Kann, *Geschichte des Habsburgerreiches 1526 bis 1918* (Vienna, 1967), pp. 390–91; the same, *Das Nationalitätenproblem der Habsburgermonarchie*, (Graz, Cologne, 1964), I, pp. 98–9, 294; Bosl (ed.), *Handbuch*, III, pp. 156–57.

13 Kořalka, *Tschechen im Habsburgerreich*, pp. 152–73.

14 H. Glassl, *Der mährische Ausgleich* (Munich, 1967); R. R. Luft, 'Die Mittelpartei des mährischen Großgrundbesitzes 1879 bis 1918', in F. Seibt (ed.), *Die Chance der Verständigung* (Munich, 1987), pp. 216–20, 230–6.

15 Křen, 'Češi a Němci na přelomu století. Pokus o historickou bilanci' [Czechs and Germans at the turn of the century. An essay in historical evaluation] in *Historické studie*, 8 (1981), 3–83.

16 O. Urban, *Česká společnost 1848–1918* [Czech society 1848–1918] (Prague, 1982), pp. 456–72.

17 Bosl (ed.), *Handbuch*, III, pp. 280–8.

18 *Forderungen der Deutschen Österreichs zur Neuordnung nach dem Kriege* (Basle, 1916).

19 J. K. Hoensch, *Geschichte der Tschechoslowakei* (Stuttgart–Berlin–Cologne, 1992), pp. 32–4; R. Hilf, *Deutsche und Tschechen* (Opladen, 1986), pp. 63–7.

20 M. Alexander (ed.), *Deutsche Gesandtschaftsberichte aus Prag*, (Vienna–Munich, 1983), I, pp. 217–19.

21 It is doubtful that the term was used for the first time in 1902, as claimed by Franz Jesser, a German politician from Moravia, in his memoir *Volkstumskampf und Ausgleich im Herzen Europas. Erinnerungen eines sudetendeutschen Politikers, Veröffentlichung des Sudetendeutschen Archivs in München* (Nuremberg, 1983), XVII, p. 37. The author of the Foreword, Heinrich Kuhn, had doubts about Jesser's claim pointintg out that Jesser himself employed the term rarely before 1918. See *ibid.*, pp. 7, 123. Be that as it may, the term was very seldom used before 1918. Cf. E. Pscheidt, '80 Jahre "sudetendeutsch"?', *Mitteilungen des Sudetendeutschen Archives*, 73 (1983), 1f.

22 F. Seibt, *Deutschland und die Tschechen*, pp. 209–11; R. Hilf, *Deutsche und Tschechen*, pp. 76–8.

23 J. Křen, 'Nationale Selbstbehauptung im Vielvölkerstaat. Politische Konzeptionen des tschechischen Nationalismus 1890–1938', in D. Beyrau (ed.), *Integration oder Ausgrenzung. Deutsche und Tschechen 1890–1945* (Bremen, 1986), pp. 42–50; H. Neuwirth, 'Der Weg der Sudetendeutschen von der Entstehung des Tschechoslowakischen Staates bis zum Vertrag von München', in *Die Sudetenfrage in europäischer Sicht, Veröffentlichungen des Collegium Carolinum*, 12 (1962), 122–179.

24 O. Novák, *Henleinovci proti Československu Z historie sudetoněmeckého fašismu v letech 1933–1938* (Henlein's followers against Czechoslovakia On the history of Sudeten German Fascism 1933–1938) (Prague, 1987); R. Jaworski, 'Die Sudetendeutschen als Minderheit in der Tschechoslowakei 1918–1938', in W. Benz (ed.), *Die Vertreibung der Deutschen aus dem Osten* (Frankfurt/M., 1985), pp. 29–38.

25 G. Bareš *et al.*, *Odboj a revoluce* [Resistance and revolution] (Prague, 1965), pp. 44–8; R. Luža, *The Transfer of the Sudeten Germans* (London, 1964), pp. 155–6.

26 L. Grünwald, *Sudetendeutsche – Opfer und Täter* (Vienna, 1983), pp. 41–55.

27 T. Staněk, *Odsun Němců z Československa 1945–1947* [The transfer of the Germans from Czechoslovakia 1945–1947] (Prague, 1991, pp. 52–86, 98–116, 169–254; Luža, *The Transfer of the Sudeten Germans*, pp. 267–300; Th. Schieder (ed.), *Dokumentation der Vertreibung der deutschen Bevölkerung aus der Tschechoslowakei* (Munich, 1984).

28 F. P. Habel, *Die Sudetendeutschen* (Munich, 1992), pp. 103–43; H. Raschhofer and O. Kimmich, *Die Sudetenfrage* (Munich, 1988), pp. 281–98, 303–44.

29 J. Křen, 'Smlouva, Němci a my' [The treaty, Germans and us] in *Přítomnost*, 2, no. 12 (1991), 2–3; and 'Vergebung, Entschuldigung und Blick in die Zukunft', in *Ztracené dějiny aneb zemie oszyskanie? Verlorene Geschichte oder wiedergewonnenes Land?* (Prague, 1992).

17

Czechs and Jews

HELENA KREJČOVÁ

I

Ask a non-Czech what he knows about Jews in Bohemia and he will probably answer, 'Nothing'. When asked if he knows anything about Prague
Jews, he might smile and reply, 'Well, Franz Kafka'. At most he might add
the Golem and Rabbi Loew. Most Czechs, indeed, know very little about
the topic. A Czech might add, possibly making a subconscious and somewhat anti-Semitic allusion, that the Jews were the ones who carried out
Germanization and industrialization in Bohemia and Moravia. Most
Czechs, in fact, have never known an indigenous Jew: that is, they do not
know that the person they are talking to or about is actually a Jew. This is
both paradoxical and tragic.

In 1968, the dwindling community of Jews left in the Czech Lands com-
memorated its millennium – 1,000 years since the founding of the first
Jewish settlement in the area of Bohemia and Moravia.[1] The anniversary
took place less than thirty years after the Jews of this Central European
region had been massacred in a way whose manner and scope are unparal-
leled. The Jews as a people, who before the Second World War formed
approximately 1 per cent of the population of Bohemia, Moravia and
Silesia, almost did not survive the Nazis' 'final solution'. Approximately
80,000 native Jews died in Nazi concentration camps and thousands of
others died on the front-lines. Only about 15,000 managed to survive, and
of that number an estimated 5,000 remained in Bohemia and Moravia after
1948. This devastation of native Jewry is not, however, only a Jewish tragedy,
but in many ways a tragedy of the Czech nation too, not only because
Czechs were thereby deprived of a significant cultural potential (and the
word cultural should be understood in the broadest context), but also

because at the same time there occurred a moral devastation so profound that the Czechs have still not been able to come to terms with it and are likely to face it for many years to come. One of the outstanding Czech-Jewish writers (who declared himself to be of Czech nationality), Karel Poláček (1892–1944), expressed this fact poignantly when he told Karel Čapek's widow shortly before leaving forever with a Nazi transport, 'A chain with one link broken can never be what it once was'.

When one speaks of indigenous Jews, one is actually always speaking about Jews from Prague. 'Prague Jew', 'the Jewish community of Prague', are actually synonymous terms meaning a Jew from Bohemia or Moravia. This is the result of Prague being the metropolis of the Kingdom of Bohemia where there had long been a very large Jewish population and the fact that the Jewish community of Prague was by far the biggest in Bohemia and Moravia (in the latter, Mikulov, whose ghetto remnants are still visible today, had a similar function but was smaller). Thus Prague became the natural cultural, social, and religious centre of both the country and, in terms of size, all of Central Europe; in some historical periods it was even the centre of European Jewry. Owing to its geographical position, Prague was predestined to become the crossroads of trade routes that connected Eastern and Western, as well as Southern and Northern Europe. It also became the crossroads of spiritual currents, ideas, and concepts, which came to Prague, intermixed, were transformed, and then went out and infiltrated the world. The Jews, who dedicated themselves to trade and commerce much more intensively than the Christian population, became the importers and exporters of goods, as well as the importers and exporters of spiritual impulses and values, education, and art, especially in the period when European civilization was detaching itself from narrowly conceived, unambiguously religious points of view.

To call Prague the centre of Central Europe is rather a misnomer. Prague is located near the border of West European and East European civilization (the region known as Moravian Slovakia is considered the dividing line between these cultural zones). Spiritually and in terms of education, Bohemia and Moravia are drawn to the Western cultural zone but through their language and Slavonic roots they are also drawn to Eastern Europe. This geographically determined area of the mixing of two basic versions of European civilization was specifically enriched and at the same time given strength by its Jewish cosmopolitan settlement. All nationalities who came into contact and confrontation here left their imprint on Prague, giving it a unique, somehow mysterious atmosphere which it radiates and with which it captures the attention of tourists and its inhabitants.

A significant part of this atmosphere is not only the Old Jewish Cemetery, unique in the world, but also the oldest synagogue in Europe and the oldest European Jewish town hall. They have been witness to the glory and suffering of the Prague ghetto which was razed at the turn of the last century to make way for the needs of the new age (which we now find to be problematic), more specifically, to make way for a potentially bustling, modern commercial district, which, in fact, never came to pass.

II

The history of the Prague ghetto is a history of clashes and conflicts, both in the good and bad senses of the words. With few exceptions, Jews in Bohemia were tolerated by the powers that be – most of all as a source of income for the rulers: in exchange for being allowed to settle on Bohemian territory, they had to pay high annual taxes to the dukes/kings of Bohemia. Until the twelfth century, they remained, in their own way, free people, albeit not fully equal with Christians, and could settle without restriction in the Christian environment. They earned their living mainly by trade and finance (which Christians were prohibited from participating in).[2] During the thirteenth century, though, the long period of the Jews' relatively free existence in Bohemia and Moravia ended. While inhabitants of towns acquired rights, the old legal status of the Jewish quarter still obtained. Jews, up to that point free merchants, continued to be excluded from medieval economic life which was becoming increasingly connected to manufacturing and organized into guilds (from which Jews were prohibited). They became increasingly a 'fringe' social stratum, and Prague's Jewish Town changed into an enclosed ghetto. Social hatred was now added to the ever popular religious hatred against the Jews, who were now perceived as people who, rather than work in workshops or farm the land, were only wheeler-dealers. In the collective consciousness, a Jew was a being marked with a stigma.

Nevertheless, in the same century something unprecedented happened. The Czech King Přemysl Otakar II (1253–1278) proclaimed a new law, in 1254, which was to regulate the coexistence of Jews and Christians for many centuries. This law granted Jews, as individuals, protection against attacks by Christians. In this respect, they had the same rights as their Christian counterparts. The Jewish community as a whole, however, was not protected by this law. Succeeding rulers confirmed the privilege granted by Přemysl Otakar II, but Jewish rights had been increasingly restricted by various decrees. The Jewish Town, therefore, went through alternating periods of calm and riots. There were attacks on the ghetto, Jew-baiting and even the total expulsion of all Jews from Bohemia; an example occurred during the reign of Maria Theresa (1740–1780).

The Jewish community inside the ghetto was not at all a homogeneous entity. There was a small group of rich people, some of whom, particularly during the rule of the first Habsburgs, became the royal bankers; and there was a large group of the utterly destitute. The Jews, forced to live in a walled-in area, found themselves in increasingly desperate conditions as the Jewish Town was unable to grow in size – basically, there was no land left – while its population increased. Pogroms, fires, and plagues threatened the ghetto inhabitants constantly. The fact of being separated from, and outcast by, the society around them did not, however, give the Jews a sense of isolation or spiritual impoverishment, nor did it lead to stagnation in their community.

Jewish society in the days of the ghetto was cosmopolitan. The continuous movement of inhabitants, a result of the Jewish immigration from Germany, Poland, the Balkans, Russia and, in the period of the Inquisition, from Spain and Portugal, alternated with waves of departures – expulsions; all this formed an ever-changing conglomerate of European and especially Central European Jews in the Czech Lands. But it was not only the waves of emigration and immigration which prevented the Jewish Town from living in perpetual poverty and perishing on the edge of society while being dependent on the capriciousness of Christian neighbours. The main Jewish professions – commerce and money lending – played an important role here and enabled lively, intensive contact with the rest of Prague society and the busy operations of merchants all over Europe. Thanks to this constant movement, Jews not only got to know foreign countries but also met with new experiences, new ways of manufacturing and new sources of spirituality, ideas which they absorbed, transformed, and then passed on to the neighbouring society.

In the sixteenth century, the ghetto became known throughout Europe as a centre of Jewish culture. Thanks to Jewish bankers,[3] it enjoyed the imperial court's protection and was thus able to create a modern economic foundation. 'Manufactory' forms of production, largely based on division of manual labour, were gradually coming to life. Jews bought surplus from aristocratic estates and traded it all over Europe (Jews had the monopoly of the feather, wool and fur trades). The aristocracy, for whom this kind of trade was very profitable, provided Jews with houses in which to establish workshops. In a similar way, Jews began to conclude contracts with guilds in Prague and the rest of the country and in many cases tried to obtain all of their production for their own business. The most courageous were those who started their own workshops right inside the ghetto, with Jewish and Christian employees working side by side. At that time, they specialized in textile and leather processing, which enabled them to switch over to the making of uniforms – another source of huge financial profits, which led to the creation of their own large manufactories.

Sections of society in Bohemia began to sense that the indigenous Jews were vital for economic growth. When Maria Theresa expelled the Jews from Prague and the rest of Bohemia in 1745, her decision was met not only by panic in the Jewish community but also by the indignation and protests of the aristocracy and most Prague merchants and craftsmen. This alone confirms that the Jews had grown to be a significant and increasingly accepted part of both Bohemia's population and economic development. They were not yet perceived as competitors, but as an enriching and necessary part of society.

The history of the ghetto, as of every community forced to live inside a closed zone, is also a history of remarkable learning and culture. This is a frequent occurrence, in the history of ghettos, whether medieval, Renaissance, or modern. The walls of the ghetto were not impenetrable but permeable. The Prague community, as the dominating and privileged Jewish centre, did not represent the Jews just of Bohemia but its standing was also recognized in the whole Ashkenazi diaspora. This came about thanks mainly to the extent and quality of Prague Jewish culture which found its expression in the Hebrew literature that had been developing there since the beginning of the Jewish settlement. The high level of education in the ghetto can be demonstrated by the fact that most if not all ghetto inhabitants were able to read and write (in Hebrew). This basic educational provision for children inside the ghetto contrasted sharply with the situation outside. The Torah and Talmudic studies were the basis of further Jewish education. This was the reason, so closely connected with the destiny of this nation in the diaspora, why literature written in Hebrew dealt in most cases with topics of religion and ritual. It is interesting to note how expressions from other languages spoken here crept into the Hebrew literature of the ghetto. By virtue of the ceaseless movement of its inhabitants, Prague's Jewish Town was a linguistic Babel. Nevertheless, from the thirteenth to the fifteenth century, the most important subsidiary means of communication was naturally the Czech language; from the sixteenth century to seventeenth, it was Yiddish; from the eighteenth to the nineteenth century, German; and from the mid nineteenth century onwards, Czech regained its place beside German as one of the two primary languages. This was not, however, the case in the days of the classic ghetto.

The Prague ghetto at the end of the twelfth century and the beginning of the thirteenth, saw the establishment of the famous Tosaphist school where the specialization was Talmudic studies.[4] The commentaries, interpretations and modifications of the Torah and Talmud by the Prague Talmudic scholars were valid for centuries and were the most widely recognized by Jews throughout the world. The school attracted a wide range of scholars from all over Europe. Many of them settled here and were elected as chief rabbis of Bohemia and rectors of Prague Talmudic schools.[5] Many of the Jewish scholars from Prague, authors of religious-philosophical tracts and books, were acknowledged authorities throughout the Jewish world. Two examples are Jehuda Liva ben Bacalel (better known as Rabbi Loew, (1512–1609), who became one of the most celebrated personages of the Prague ghetto, and Jom Tov Lipman Heller (1575–1654), whose commentaries on the Talmud are still studied and respected in conservative rabbinic circles.[6] Similarly, the works of Ezekiel Landau (1713–1793),[7] who in the eighteenth century represented the conservative trend in traditional rabbinical scholarship in the diaspora, are still studied today.

Prague Jewish culture and its dissemination were dependent on the Hebrew typography of Prague,[8] which was highly regarded even outside the Czech Lands. Publications that came out of Hebrew publishing houses in Prague were among the foremost works of European typography. The respect paid to books as well as the technology that allowed for their production enabled Rabbi David Oppenheimer (1664–1736) to gather an extensive collection of prints and manuscripts (approximately 7,000 titles), which is now a part of the Bodleian Library in Oxford.

Along with the crystallization of ideas on nature, man and society in the world around the ghetto, there was an increasing differentiation of points of view in the closed-in Jewish community between advocates of an orthodox, conservative trend and the gradually growing liberal movement which started to gain influence at the end of the eighteenth century and the beginning of the nineteenth. One of the leading liberal representatives was the Chief Rabbi of Prague, Solomon Judah Rapaport (1790–1867), for whom Hebrew literature was not only the source for Torah and Talmudic studies but was also becoming an increasingly distinct source for the study of Jewish history and culture.

Thanks to the liberals, the works of the Renaissance scientist David Gans (1541–1613) could see the light of day. Gans had been in contact with Tycho Brahe and Johannes Kepler during the calm and tolerant times at the end of the sixteenth and beginning of the seventeenth century. In his work *Nechmad we naim* [Pleasant and kind] he summarized the available knowledge of Jewish and non-Jewish authors on geography and astronomy. Gans was also the author of the first truly historical work to have been written in the Central European diaspora.[9] His work was the first secular literary work of Prague Hebrew literature.

III

The liberal trend, an important and irreplaceable link in the Jewish Enlightenment, was connected to the spiritual trends of the Enlightenment in the rest of Europe and played a part in the social changes taking place throughout the area. It was these Prague liberals who by means of their printing houses could spread the ideas of enlightenment and emancipation not only through Bohemia and Moravia but throughout the Austrian monarchy, as well.

Jews in Bohemia of liberal orientation identified naturally with the reforming ideas of Emperor Joseph II (1780–1790) on the future of the Habsburg monarchy. On the basis of his Enlightened reforms Jews in the Czech Lands began to attain equal status with non-Jews. In exchange for opening up the ghetto, the Jews were required to accept the Emperor's policy of Germanization and the Jewish community to become one of the pillars of the Germanizing efforts of the Austrian rulers in the Czech Lands. This, however, had far-reaching effects, because it was precisely this Germanization, along with other persisting differences linked with ritual, customs and earning a living in the ghetto, that was to bring large and complex problems for the Jews in Bohemia years later.

Joseph II was one of the first European rulers to make a serious attempt at the cultural and economic improvement of his multinational Empire. His reforms meant a fundamental intervention in Jewish society; he forced it to change its attitude towards the world and increased demands on it. In exchange for their Germanization the Jews received a considerable extension of rights. The ghetto was open during the day, and the Jews were allowed to move about freely within Christian society. They could invest in and establish firms and wholesale companies and, indeed, were even invited by the government to do so. They were obliged to attend public (state-run) schools and to learn subjects which in the ghetto had been unknown or were considered unnecessary. They could study at the universities though they were not allowed to work as members of the state administration. They were allowed to cultivate the land though they were not allowed to purchase it (unless they were willing to convert to Catholicism). They were still forbidden to trade grain, and the familial law which determined the maximum number of Jewish families allowed to settle in Bohemia and Moravia remained valid.[10] Jews took advantage of the government's efforts to centralize the administration and to expand the economy, in particular by participating in the industrialization of the country and the development of banking and wholesale business.[11]

The nearly seventy years between the Patent of (religious) Toleration of

1781 and the Revolution of 1848 formed the key period for clarifying opinions, amongst Jews and Christians, on the Jewish question. The Jews in Bohemia, that is to say mainly in Prague, were not of one mind as far as the changes were concerned. The division into two streams, liberal and conservative, deepened and acquired immediate importance. The conservatives feared that Joseph II wanted to separate Jews from their religion and make them convert to Christianity. The fact that Yiddish was to be replaced by German was, they felt, a threat to communication with the rest of the European Jewish community and would lead to their exclusion and isolation. They feared that if their children studied at public schools, they would be diverted from studying the Holy Scripture which had traditionally been the basis of Jewish education. The fear that integration into the surrounding society would affect Jewish ritual life, such as observing the Sabbath, holidays, and making sure that food was kosher, was also prevalent.

Young liberals spoke out against these conservative tendencies. They had adopted impulses from abroad, above all from Germany, whose culture and ways of thinking they had come to know more intensely through Germanization. They realized that they were not alone in their desire for emancipation as a necessary condition for obtaining equal rights. They were influenced by the German Enlighteners and Romantics who were beginning to discuss ideas such as the brotherhood of man, regardless of differences of religion. Of no small importance was the spreading of Moses Mendelssohn's ideas on Jewish emancipation, which he propagated by means of his translation of the Holy Scripture into German but printed in Hebrew characters. Mendelssohn's hope was that studying his translation would help Jews develop their knowledge of German. Although the Chief Rabbi of Prague, Ezekiel Landau, declared anathema the translations of this reformer, for many people who were full of expectations of social change there was no turning back.

At the same time, however, Christian society was also manifesting differences in opinion on the Jewish question, although not with the same intensity as Jewish society. Many Christians protested against their children attending school with Jewish children, fearing that it could lead them away from the Christian faith. The estates of Bohemia and, above all, craftsmen and the guilds, began to defend their interests in the face of a Jewish competition which they felt was becoming a dangerous threat. They even offered the Emperor suggestions on how to ruin the Jews in one fell swoop by economic means.

On the other hand, the Christians voices in support of Jewish emancipation began to be heard. They were usually young men of letters who in the

1830s and 1840s, influenced by the ideological trends coming from Western Europe, used to meet with their Jewish contemporaries and were enthusiastic supporters of equality, brotherhood and liberty. They linked the awaited liberation of mankind with the emancipation and free development of Jewry.

The decisive voice in support of the Jews had, however, been heard many years earlier, from an unexpected quarter in Bohemia. A Catholic priest and professor of the philosophy of religion at the University of Prague and brilliant mathematician to boot, Bernard Bolzano (1781–1848), dealt with the Jewish theme in one of his regular addresses to students and the public in 1809. He asked whether Jewish destiny and the negative sides of the Jewish community were actually the results of Christian conduct; every Christian, he believed, should not only approach the Jew as a human being but should also oneself begin to correct centuries-old injustices. According to Bolzano, everybody had to overcome prejudices both in himself and his surroundings. He assumed that this necessary and beneficial change would be possible only by just and enlightened legislation and that Christians had to be prepared for it.

The loosening of restrictions on the Jews initiated a period in which opinions began to crystallize. Christian and Jewish intellectuals refused to continue in the old ways. As in Germany, liberal circles in Austria – journalists, writers, and students – called for equality, emancipation and liberty. They worked together in groups in which Jews met Czechs and Germans, that is to say, their Christian colleagues who were not yet divided along national lines.[12] For Jewish intellectuals, the ghetto was too small. Only about 240 families, mostly bankers, manufacturers and wholesalers, were allowed to live outside the ghetto – albeit to the great displeasure of their Christian neighbours. Intellectuals, artists and traders moved in Christian society during the day, often with great success, but, as if bound by an umbilical cord, returned to the ghetto at night. Rich Jews, even with aristocratic titles and huge properties, remained tied to the ghetto, because, to the vast majority of the non-Jewish public, they were not yet fully acceptable. Population migration, however, extended communication, between Jews and gentiles and this led to mutual acquaintance and, for a significant number of intellectuals, to mutual tolerance. At the same time, it often created grudges and exacerbated anti-Jewish sentiment amongst the lower strata of Christian society.

IV

Questions raised during the Enlightenment and the emancipation trends related to it led to questions regarding the assimilation problem. For this issue to be discussed, however, the ghetto had to be opened. In the first half of the nineteenth century the possibility of this ripened in Jewish and Christian society. Jews in Bohemia could henceforth live and move freely among Czechs. They began to exist within this larger community, and this closer contact produced not only increasingly intensive mutual influence, but also encounters of three – Czech, German and Jewish – cultures. This tendency came to a head in the 1848 Revolution, when a new era of Jewish history began.

The Jews at this time actively took part in the events; many of them stood in the forefront of the Revolution and died on the barricades or were imprisoned and executed. The longing for change and freedom linked both communities, Christians and Jews, in the first joint struggle for a common aim in the region. It happened first in Vienna, where many Jews from the Czech Lands were studying or were employed as journalists, followed by Prague where the population responded sensitively and enthusiastically to the events in Vienna. Jewish representatives for Prague and Vienna, led by their rabbis, rejected as limited the demands of their congregations. These demands were to be in the form of a petition presented to the Emperor. The representatives considered common and civic demands, as well as Austrian and Czech patriotic demands, to be more important than the narrowly defined Jewish interest in emancipation. The Revolution of 1848 represented a unique but missed opportunity for the multinational Habsburg monarchy.

Cooperation between members of the intellectual elite was manifested in the activity of the first Austrian Imperial Parliament (Reichstag) convened in Vienna (1848) where Jews were also members. At the same time, this understanding among intellectuals became weakened because of anti-Semitic demonstrations by the mob which, in Vienna and above all in Prague, looted Jewish homes and shops and attacked Jewish fellow citizens. Prague's Jewish Town had to be protected by the National Guard which itself was concerned for its own safety. Also the middle, burgher, strata were dissatisfied with the fact that the Jews would have equal rights. The fear of competition, fed for centuries by clericalism (although the Archbishop of Prague and many burghers dissociated themselves from the anti-Jewish demonstrations), led a significant part of the Jewish community to request the reestablishment of the ghetto, and even Jews who had left it long before returned to the ghetto. Hope and subsequent disappointment resulted in a sharp increase in Jewish emigration to America.

As the Revolution of 1848 showed, Bolzano's desire and appeal to Christians that they be prepared to incorporate Jews into society was left unheeded. The willingness of the Jews to overcome mutual problems on the basis of civil society was met by Christian unpreparedness to do the same. It took a long time for the Christians to come to terms with this fact; they understood the opening of the ghettos as a revolution for the Jews and as a revolution stolen from them, which may have been the main reason for the anti-Semitic demonstrations.

Revolutionary changes in Austria were suppressed by force during 1848–9. A great opportunity was wasted because of short tempers and anger, but it was not a lost revolution. Nevertheless, recently-won civil liberties also brought with them nationalistically based hatred that was felt not only by Czechs and Germans but, surprisingly though naturally, also by Jews.

The national question in the Kingdom of Bohemia was not a problem only for the Czechs and Germans. By the beginning of the 1870s, it had also become a problem for the Jews who were now split into two strongly opposing Czech Jewish and German Jewish camps. Lacking respect for beliefs other than one's own, this kind of Jewish intolerance was moderated because recurring anti-Jewish demonstrations from time to time revived the awareness of togetherness.

The development of political events and the ever growing rift between the Czechs and Germans in Bohemia since the time of the German National Assembly at Frankfurt (1848) resulted in Jews from Bohemia and Moravia siding with liberal Germans who, at the time, were truly free-thinking, progressive and willing to defend the ideas which the Jews admired, and which they had often identified with in the past. Many Jews stepped to the forefront of the German liberal movement in Bohemia and actually became its exponents (mostly as journalists); at the same time they had a significant influence upon the development of the economy. The Jewish pro-German trend was strengthened by the Jews' gratitude to the government for the December Constitution (1867), which granted them equal rights before the law. The Germans in Bohemia, moreover, won the Jews' great appreciation because they had participated in this legislation while the Czech parliamentarians at the time were boycotting the Reichsrat (Imperial Parliament) in Vienna. The Germans in Bohemia, of course, took advantage of the strong anti-Jewish antagonism current among Czechs. Anti-Semitism also existed in their society, initially rooted in social and economic factors and later taking on a more and more racialist form. All the same, the Germans in Bohemia were ready to grant the Jews all benefits of the state, including the right to function as an autonomous community. The aim was to commit the Jews to the German national cause and with their help to counter growing Czech competition.

V

It seemed, then, that the Jewish assimilation problem in Bohemia and Moravia was solved once and for all in favour of the Germans. That this did not in fact happen was due to several circumstances. First of all, the pressure of Germanization had long since disappeared. The opening of the ghettos resulted in a situation where inhabitants of tightly closed enclaves, dependent on intensive social intercourse between themselves, dispersed throughout Bohemia and Moravia. Furthermore, the Czech language – still considered more a means of communication than a bearer of cultural and spiritual values – gradually made its way into Jewish families. Another very important factor was that Jews were allowed to purchase land; the relationship to the land, immovable property, developed a feeling of being rooted and belonging not only to a certain place but also to the surrounding neighbourhood. All these external factors contributed to the gradual incorporation of a growing number of Jews into Czech society and the development of Czech awareness of the difference between Jews and Germans. This awareness sharpened when Jews took concrete steps to assist Czechs at the expense of Germans, for example, by helping them win important parliamentary seats. As a result of this political success, Czech influence increased in the Chambers of Trade and Commerce, and clearly helped to strengthen the role of Czechs in economic life.

It is possible to look here for the social roots of the Czech–Jewish assimilation movement, which contained not only general but also specific features of assimilation. The general features include the decision of Jews to become a part of the nation in which they had been born and lived. This decision resulted from their willingness to adopt the language of that particular nation and to co-create a common culture, economy and politics. Another general feature was that the Jews had to overcome barriers of prejudice within both their society and the one surrounding it; they had to demolish the strongest of ghettos – the ghetto in their souls.

Czech–Jewish assimilation, however, had its own specific features. Jews in Bohemia did not assimilate from the original ghetto; they no longer used their original language but gave up a language and culture which they had only recently embraced. The exponents of Czech–Jewish assimilation were mainly students who were familiar with and understood the problem of both ethnic entities. Moreover, since these Jews were educated, Czech society found them more acceptable. The Czech–Jewish movement was extraordinary and in its way unique, in the sense that Jews in Bohemia had decided to assimilate to the oppressed nation. To this day it testifies to the fact that the strength of their conviction really stemmed from their feeling of being part of the Czech world. This makes it all the more tragic, then, to hear the reproaches of Czechs claiming, then as now, that the Jews had joined them only for personal gain.

The founding generation of this movement in its first phase, which lasted approximately until the end of the century, strengthened the movement in terms of its organization and programme. They understood the Czech–Jewish question as national and cultural assimilation on the basis of language. The members of the next Czech–Jewish generation, however, born into already assimilated families, did not see any reason for living in a world of 'empty flag-waving'; they felt their own Czechness and Jewishness as natural and intrinsic. The Czech way of understanding reality became second nature, but they realized all the more that their lives had somehow become complicated. They found themselves facing the Czech–Jewish question as a matter of religion and ethics. They no longer comprehended being Czech as a problem of language but saw its essence in the content, the spiritual level, culture and *raison d'être* of the Czech nation. In their own way, they themselves posed the same questions which the Czech nation had been forced to pose and answer for itself. The youngest and unfortunately last Czech–Jewish generation, the generation of the First Czechoslovak Republic, understood that the Czech–Jewish movement could not restrict itself to national tasks or be concerned only with statehood and democracy but had to be concerned as well, and perhaps above all, with cooperation between nations. This generation did not consider assimilation a phenomenon linked only with the Jewish mentality but rather something which reached far beyond the local Jewish settings. They believed that by working for the rapprochement of Jews with other nations they would in essence be building something for all humanity. Their aim, which at the time was totally utopian, today a little less so, was stated in the motto: 'With the Czech nation towards peace among all nations'. This generation understood its Jewishness as a duty to show others the way from isolation to higher structures to the dream of a parliament of mankind, a 'palace of nations' – a European and, later, a world-wide federation of all mankind.

These ideas were close to the thinking of Jews who had assimilated to the Germans in Bohemia. It seemed that their problems with the pursuit of identity were not as complicated as those the Czech Jews faced. But, in the 1890s, anti-Semitism, which was growing in Austria, even became a part of programmes of certain German political parties and was accompanied by the Czech nation's increasing national self-confidence. Jews who had assimilated to Germans became a [Jewish] minority within a [German] minority. Nevertheless, no ghettoization occurred because, thanks simply to their German mother tongue, they had strong ties to Jewish society in Vienna and

Berlin. This joint effect of pressure and linkage, perhaps led finally to a major flowering of German–Jewish culture and to the significant development of German–Jewish capital and industry.

VI

'Prague German Jews' are words connected with an inseparable and irreplaceable part of modern Western civilization. It is a paradox, then, that the feeling of modern man in society, this 'apostolate of existentialism', which is expressed in the works of Prague German-writing Jews and is now widespread, was inadvertently co-created by the Czechs. While Prague German Jews – as real Central Europeans – were natural links, as it were, between the cultural and intellectual life of Prague, Vienna and Berlin, they were increasingly becoming foreigners twice over in their own country the more Czech society flourished nationally. This feeling of estrangement, resulting from being Jewish, was intensified by the even more justified feeling that they were strangers because of their German language, too. It was Prague Jews who came up with the theory of the 'triple ghetto' (racial, national and social) which shaped their view of the world.[13]

Prague German society was a society of elites, a patriarchate, which lacked the broader German strata that lived mainly in the border regions where both German nationalism and anti-Semitism had been on the rise since the 1880s. This fact caused an even greater rift between successful, economically powerful German residents of Prague and the countryside. Prague German society, including its Jews, was dependent on itself, isolated, and thus tightly linked to, and integrated by, linguistic, cultural, economic and personal ties. As a result, this society did not experience racial differences and was not anti-Semitic. On the contrary, all its members met with Czech anti-Semitism which was connected with anti-Germanism, because Czech society did not much differentiate between these two forms of antagonism. This was another factor which bound together Prague German society. It was manifested in an extreme form at the end of the nineteenth century when nationally tinged anti-Semitism, whose growth can be traced back to the beginning of the 1890s, culminated in the 'December riots' after the fall of the Badeni government,[14] when the resistance of the German population made it impossible to meet Czech demands for increased language rights. Spontaneous anti-German demonstrations took on an almost purely anti-Semitic form and resulted in the looting of Jewish property and physical assaults of such proportions that it was necessary to deploy military units. Similar excesses took place not only in Prague but across the Bohemian and Moravian countryside. The groundswell of anti-Semitism turned into anti-Jewish mistrust. One product of this was the charge of ritual murder laid against Leopold Hilsner – a scandal which had many features in common with the great anti-Semitic trials in Europe at the time.[15]

The anti-Semitic manifestations of the Czech nation at the turn of the century represent some of the more disgraceful moments in Czech history. Although they were but episodes, they had enormous consequences. Many Jews lost hope of the possibility of peaceful coexistence with Czechs. After this reminder, it was difficult to believe that what had happened once would not happen again. This was a new experience of an old theme. On the Czech side, these events were a show of contempt for moral positions. They led to the strengthening of false national self-confidence which in many persons tended to the worst kind of chauvinism. The nation demonstrated both that it accepted a scapegoat for its failures and that it was able to face this scapegoat uncompromisingly. As elsewhere, in Czech society there were citizens who risked their reputation, career and even lives to defend reason, truth, and the law, such as Tomáš (Thomas) Garrigue Masaryk (1850–1937). The very fact that he became President of the Czechoslovak Republic in 1918 became a guarantee and sign of a better future for all Jews in Bohemia, and especially for German-speaking Jews.

VII

The search for Czech or German identity was, of course, not the only chance for Jews in the multinational Austro-Hungarian monarchy. In the second half of the 1890s, another word was heard in the vocabulary of Jewish striving – Zionism. The Zionist movement presented the Jewish population with the problem of its own awareness of Jewish national identity and, in its final consequences, struggled for a return to the ancient homeland. According to Zionists, Jews had to create and develop their own specific cultural and spiritual values and it was a mistake to have adopted them from their host nations.

At first, Zionism was not strongly represented in the Czech Lands; indeed, many Jews distanced themselves from it and found it as foreign as aspirations for a Czech state or for a 'Großdeutschland'. The turning point came during the first decades of the next century, when for some members of the Jewish community Zionism became a way out of the disillusionment caused by Czech and German national intolerance. Opinions were crystallized with the help of the Prague lectures of Martin Buber (1878–1965).[16] A Russian Yiddish theatre company's performances especially helped to increase the younger generation's interest in Judaism, authentic Jewish culture and studies. In the initial period, Zionism intrigued mainly German-speaking Jews; Czech-speaking Jews joined the movement later, and its influence grew in direct relation to the rise of Nazism and the threat this posed to the Czechoslovak Republic.

Jewish society in the Czech Lands had been divided since the end of the century into three, more or less mutually irreconcilable movements which covered a wide spectrum of solutions to the Jewish question, from 'local' faith in the Czech nation to integration into the intellectually and culturally rich German-language region and to the world-wide national emancipation of Jewry. It was not yet clear at this time which trend would be the most attractive or vital for the Jews of the Czech Lands. The solution to the question of assimilation or Zionism was in a way also in the hands of the Czech nation. But the Czechs were reluctant to solve it. At times they did not know how to solve it, or felt they did not need to solve it. In the end, they were unable to solve it.

VIII

When Czechoslovakia was first established the Jewish community experienced anti-Jewish violence incited by Czech anti-Semitic elements.[17] Nevertheless, it can still be said that but for some small excesses Czechoslovakia became an 'oasis for Jews' in Central Europe. Jews in Bohemia and Subcarpathian Moravia assisted actively in the building of the new state. Their community was strengthened by the large number of Jews living in Slovakia and Ruthenia. Despite affinities, there were also tensions between those who had inherited the Eastern orthodox tradition and those of liberal views that were deeply rooted in the Jewish culture of Bohemia and Moravia. There was a massive influx of Jews to Prague which, as a culturally and socially attractive capital with administrative financial and industrial centres, provided more opportunitieis for better life. Here Jews accounted for nearly 5 per cent of the population and their part in the development of the modern state became visible. They were significantly involved in many fields. In the political arena they were active as ministers in the government,[18] members of parliament, in the diplomatic service and in town councils. They were markedly present in industry, banking and commerce and also represented in the agricultural sector. Jews contributed to science and scholarship, to theatre, music and fine arts, and they gained international recognition as writers, translators and journalists.[19]

By means of their creative activities and above all as Czechoslovak citizens, the Jews in the Czech Lands embodied a natural link between the Czech, German and Jewish worlds, and became builders of bridges not only between Czechs and Germans, but also between Czechoslovakia and the world. It was Czechoslovak Jews who presented Czechoslovakia to the world as the country of democracy and tolerance upon which European Jewry, endangered by Nazism, set their sights and hopes. They strove to make all Jewry accept the fact that 'the fall of Czechoslovakia or even its undermining would endanger a universal pillar of human rights which, after all is said and done, Jews in every civilized country lean on'.[20] Democratic Czechoslovakia did not let down either its own Jews or the threatened Jews of the rest of Europe; it took them in and defended them until the moment of its own dismemberment and occupation by Germany.

IX

As a result of the Munich Agreement of 29/30 September 1938 and the German occupation of 15 March 1939, there occurred not only the temporary discontinuation of the Czechoslovak Republic but also the holocaust of Jews from Bohemia and Moravia. They lost their citizenship and human rights; they were stigmatized again and dispossessed – and it should be pointed out that not only the German occupiers but also a number of Czechs participated in their pauperization. The one thing no one could deprive the Jews of – except by death – was their cultural potential.

In 1941, a ghetto was established about seventy kilometres northwest of Prague in Terezín. Built in the eighteenth century as a military fortress, it bore the name of Empress Maria Theresa, who in 1744–6 had embarked on a policy of expelling all Jews from the Czech Lands. Thus in a paradoxical and fatal way this Austrian monarch was again linked 200 years later to further anti-Jewish measures, which this time did not mean merely eviction but the transport eastward to the concentration camps – measures of a magnitude she could never have imagined. Terezín was a transfer point to death for many Jews not only from the Czech Lands. The living conditions in the Terezín ghetto returned its Jewish population to the Middle Ages, but these modern Jews of the mid twentieth century found themselves in a situation much worse than their medieval ancestors. Leaving the ghetto did not mean commerce and success but rather transports and death camps. People in Terezín, living on the line between life and death, resisted their fate – with a unique dedication and intensity – by means of culture. Participation in scholarly activity and especially in arts had to be surreptitious. That the inmates gave lectures, performed plays, operas and concerts is remarkable enough, but in Terezín totally new works of art were created in nearly all spheres; the fine arts, literature and music all had an unprecedented efflorescence here. The diverse creative activities which burgeoned in such

15. Terezín Ghetto 1941–1945. Cardboard boxes for human ashes and tray with human bones. The lines of the original image have been enhanced on the photographic print.

oppressive conditions and in such a short period were extraordinary both for their time and when seen on the scale of all human civilization.

In Terezín the creative human spirit was honoured and celebrated. The unimaginable discrimination, devastation and frustration countered as it was by celebration of life and the victory of the human spirit, handed down the legacy that the ghetto damages not least those who happen to be outside its walls.

Notes

1 The first news about Jews in the Czech Lands is in Ibrahim ibn Jacob's description of Prague (*c.* 960–970). For a Czech version, see J. Benda and J. Hánl (eds.), *Dějiny v pramenech* [History in sources], vol. I (Prague, 1956), pp. 27f.

2 Jews had the status of foreign merchants, and therefore made use of all rights and duties that followed from that status.

3 The most famous of them was Mordechai Mayzl (sometimes written Maisl,

Maisel) (1580–1630); he was the first Jew in the Czech Lands to be elevated to the aristocracy and was granted the title von Treuenberg.

4 Among them were Abraham ben Azriel and Izak ben Moshe Or Zarua.

5 For example, Avigdor Kara (d. 1439), Jom Tov Lipman Mülhausen (*c.* 1350–*c.* 1450), Eliezer ben Elij a Ashkenazi (1512–1586), Mordechai ben Abraham Jafe (1530–1612), Shimon Bacharach (1607–1670), Shelmo Juda Rapaport (1790–1867).

6 The six-volume *Tosaphot Jim Tov* [Addenda of Jom Tov].

7 The collection of responses *Noda bi-Jehuda* [Known in Juda].

8 The most important of the many printing offices was the workshop established by Gershon Kohn, in 1527; another was the printing office of the Bak family. Among later noted printers and publishers was the grandson of Rabbi Landau, Israel Landau (1788–1852).

9 The chronicle *Gemach David* [The bough of David] (1592).

10 The familial edict of 1726 and 1727 set the precise number of Jewish families in Bohemia at 8,541 and in Moravia at 5,106, and stated that only the first-born son was allowed to marry. The law was rescinded in 1848.

11 Among the famous Jewish entrepreneurs and bankers are Leopold Epstein, Moizhish Porges von Portheim and his brother Juda Leopold Porges, Israel Hoenig von Hoenigsburg, Shimon Lämel and his son Leopold von Lämel, Morzic Zdekauer and his son Friedrich von Treuenkron.

12 The most important of those clubs was 'Mladá Čechie' [Young Bohemia], whose members included Siegfried Kapper (1821–1879), Alfred Meissner (1822–1888), Moritz Hartmann (1821–1872), Isidor Heller (1816–1879), and Ludwig August Frankl (1810–1894).

13 The first to come up with the theory of the 'triple ghetto' was Oskar Wiener (1873–1944) in the foreword to the anthology *Deutsche Dichter aus Prag* (1919). Pavel Eisner (1889–1958), Willy Haas (1891–1973), Max Brod (1884–1968) and Johannes Urzidil (1896–1970), among others, developed the idea.

14 The cabinet of Count Casimir Badeni resigned at the end of November 1897.

15 On 1 April 1899, the body of a murdered girl from the town of Polná, Anežka Hrůzová, was discovered. The suspect was Leopold Hilsner, a vagrant and simple-minded Jew. He was accused of ritual murder and after two trials sentenced to death. Emperor Francis Joseph I mitigated the verdict to life imprisonment. Both trials were connected with great anti-Semitic riots.

16 The celebrated *Drei Reden über das Judentum* given in the Prague Zionist club, Bar Kochba, in 1909.

17 Reverberations of the wartime anti-Jewish demonstrations aimed first against Jews fleeing from Galicia, grew into a general, anti-Jewish riot. In 1920, when Alfred Meissner became the third Jew in the cabinet, Czechs protested against the 'Hebraized government'.

18 For example, Adolf Stránský (1860–1932), Lev Winter (1876–1935), Alfred Meissner (1871–1952) and Ludwig Czech (1870–1942).

19 The composers include Ervín Schulhof (1894–1942), Hans Krása (1899–1944),

Karel Reiner (1910–1979). The better known conductors were Karel Ančerl (1908–1978), Walter Süsskind (1913–1980), Georg Singer (1906–1980). Artists include the sculptor Otto Gutfreund (1889–1927), the painters Alfred Justitz (1879–1934), Emil Orlik (1870–1932) and Robert Guttmann (1880–1934). Authors writing in Czech include František Gellner (1881–1914), Karel Poláček (1892–1944), Vojtěch Rakous (1862–1935), Richard Weiner (1884–1943), František Langer (1888–1965), Pavel Eisner (1889–1958), Jiří Mordechai Langer (1894–1943), Jiří Orten (1919–1941), Egon Hostovský (1908–1973), Alfred Fuchs (1892–1941) and Hanuš Bonn (1913–1941). Those writing in German became part of the renowned Prague German literary scene: Franz Kafka (1883–1924), Hugo Salus (1866–1929), Oskar Baum (1883–1941), Felix Weltsch (1884–1964), Max Brod (1884–1968), Franz Werfel (1890–1945), Paul Kornfeld (1889–1942), Willy Haas (1891–1973) and Egon Erwin Kisch (1885–1948).

20 E. Neumann, *Práce, program a cíl Svazu Čechů židů v ČSR* [The work, programme and aim of the Association of Czechs Jews in the Czechoslovak Republic] (Prague, 1937), p. 17.

18

Czechs and Slovaks in modern history

DUŠAN KOVÁČ

Czechs and Slovaks are two distinct nations with many similarities. This phenomenon not only plays a significant role in their present relationship but has also played a principal role in their historical development. This relationship is virtually unique in European history.

Czech and Slovak are two distinct languages easily comprehensible to both nations. Despite their separate historical development the two nations have maintained continuous close contact and their cultures have contained the same or similar elements.

The Czech formed themselves into a nation on the basis of an independent statehood which, though lost to the Habsburgs in the seventeenth century, remained alive as an idea. The Slovaks formed a nation in the Hungarian state, a state which they helped to create in the Middle Ages. They separated from this state when it became dominated by the Magyars, and the Hungarian government began a systematic denationalization of the Slovaks towards the end of the nineteenth century. Thus, despite the ethnic and linguistic affinities between Czechs and Slovaks, each has been subject to a historically separate development.

Moreover from 1526 to 1918, Czechs and Slovaks lived in a common state – the Habsburg monarchy – from which Hungary was able to retain a certain degree of independence. Links between Czechs and Slovaks were quite intensive at times. Co-operation became particularly strong from the end of the nineteenth century when German influence in Austria-Hungary exercised an unfavourable pressure on both nations. Out of their co-operation during the First World War evolved the idea of forming a common state. This was realised from 1918 until 1939 and from 1945 to 1992.

The formation of the Czech and Slovak nations

The process of formation of Czechs and Slovaks into modern nations began at the end of the eighteenth century and was called the 'national revival'. Though historically incorrect this term is still in use. The term 'revival' relates to the idea that the nation is an eternal entity. It was created at the dawn of history and after years of hybernation it came to life again. A detailed analysis of the 'revival' reveals that since the end of the eighteenth century both Czechs and Slovaks became gradually conscious of their national make-up, and this acquisition of national consciousness became a prerequisite of their existence as modern nations. Begun by a small group of intelligentsia in both nations, this process affected large sections of the population by the middle of the nineteenth century.

The beginnings of both Czech and Slovak national movements were connected with social changes under the reign of Maria Theresa (1740–1780) and Joseph II (1780–1790) in the second half of the eighteenth century. The spiritual roots of the national movement may also be traced to the ideas of the French Enlightenment and German philosophy. The works of Herder and Hegel were of great importance.

The national consciousness of both nations developed at the same speed and had comparable results. At times it was a common process. Ján Kollár (1723–1852) and Pavol Jozef Šafárik (1795–1861) were important Slovak representatives of both Czech and Slovak national movements in the first half of the nineteenth century.

The highly centralized state of Maria Theresa and Joseph II contributed to the close cooperation between the Czech and Slovak 'revivalists'. According to Herder, a nation was a linguistic and cultural community. There followed a national debate over whether Czechs and Slovaks were one nation, two separate nations, or just one branch of a Slavonic tribe, as conceived by Ján Kollár.[1]

Language was an important element in the development of both national consciousness. Both Czech and Slovak possess numerous dialects. The literary language originated in the translated version of the Bible, known as that of Kralice. This literary language was later modified and finally replaced by the modern nineteenth-century version. Slovak Protestants also used the Czech language of the Kralice Bible in their liturgical and in some of their secular writings. But Slovak Catholics, composing 75 per cent of the Slovak population, used Latin in their mass and local dialects in their sermons. Latin was in widespread use as the literary language in all Hungary. But by the end of the eighteenth century Latin was being replaced by Magyar, German and several Slovak dialects. Slovak was already in use in literary and scholarly writing. The transformation of archaic into modern languages happened during the first half of the nineteenth century. The Czechs discarded the archaic language of the Bible for the commonly spoken Czech. However, in Slovakia the living language was Slovak. The attempts of Kollár and his followers to Slovakize the Czech language of the Bible were rejected by the Czech intelligentsia. Neither did they solve the basic question of how to make use of a universally understandable language in order to bring the national movement and national literture to the attention of the wider public. The codification of standard Slovak was a political inevitability and a natural development, and it advanced the transformation of Slovaks into an independent nation. Anton Bernolák, a Catholic priest, standardized Slovak at the end of the eighteenth century.[2] It was natural that the codification of the Slovak language began among Catholics because they did not employ the biblical Czech style. The Catholics and the Protestants represented two different national conceptions in the first phase of the Slovak 'revival'. Whereas the Protestants largely supported the idea of a unitary Czecho-Slovak nation, the Catholics favoured Slovak identity.

Standard literary Slovak and the development of the Slovak national movement

At the beginning of the nineteenth century, during the Napoleonic wars, the programmes of both the Czechs and the Slovaks took on a political dimension which became evident in the 1830s. The political agenda in Bohemia concentrated on the restoration of Czech statehood – which was argued to be a historical right. At the same time, Slovaks began to demand cultural and political recognition albeit from a defensive posture.[3] The Hungarian state was administered predominantly by Magyars. The development of a nationally monolithic, i.e. Magyar, state resulted in the degradation of all other nations to collectives, deprived of rights and exposed to linguistic and cultural assimilation. A political agenda of national identity developed in reaction to the constraints placed upon Slovak linguistic, educational and cultural demands. Such a programme came into being during the 1848–9 Revolution.

The political struggle presupposed that the national movement would spread from the small circle of nationally conscious intelligentsia. Success was dependent on its strength in the general public. Miroslav Hroch called this the phase of patriotic agitation.[4] A general national consciousness was formed and national forces gathered around the centre and its personalities to fight for its political programme.

The Czechs and the Slovaks had different goals in their political struggle because the two nations lived in different parts of the Habsburg monarchy. For a short time in the 1830s, Ján Kollár's idea of pan-Slavic reciprocity pushed these different political goals into the background. However, it was seriously damaged when the Russian Tsar's army crushed the Polish Uprising in 1831. By then it had become clear that each nation had to concentrate on its own concrete political agenda. Although the Czechs and the Slovaks co-operated closely, in reality they remained on separate fronts. The primary task for each was to unify the nation at every level of society on the basis of a specific national programme, i.e., to develop a programme of modern nationalism.

Slovaks were in a less advantageous position in this struggle. They lacked the tradition of statehood, a unifying urban centre, and a codified common language. On the other hand, Czechs had a history of self-government, an established capital in Prague, and a standardized literary tongue. A major stumbling block for Slovaks was that Bernolák's standard Slovak was not accepted by Slovak Protestants. In 1843, Ľudovít Štúr (1815–1856), a leader of the young Slovak Protestant intelligentsia, codified standard Slovak based on the central Slovakian dialect.[5] This was both a cultural and a political accomplishment. It enabled the publication of books and periodicals in Slovak which accelerated the growth of national consciousness. The common literary tongue became a strategic unifying element without which patriotic agitation would hardly have been possible.

In 1848 patriotic ferment became embodied in heavily armed struggles, especially in western and central Slovakia, as well as in the ideas of separatism – Slovakia from Hungary – and integrationism – Slovakia into the Czech Lands. Czechs were active in organizing and commanding Slovak armed sorties. The Slovak leaders were active in the organization of the Slav Congress, including the manning of the Prague barricades, in June 1848. This brief period of Czech–Slovak co-operation ceased with the defeat of the Revolution.

Then followed a period of neo-absolutism in which Slovaks, their hopes shattered, concentrated on national unification. However, even with the Magyar position weakened, only few significant language concessions resulted. One was the extension of Slovak as the language of instruction in elementary and secondary schools. A second was the toleration of Slovak as the official language in Slovak regions. This period of neo-Absolutism and the ensuing years revealed to Slovaks the importance of their literary language as a factor of their unification.

However, the introduction of standard literary Slovak was not accepted positively by everybody. There were Slovak supporters of Czechoslovak national unity, led by Ján Kollár, who opposed Štúr's literary codification in a polemic tract in the collection *Hlasové o potřebě jednoty společného jazyka pro Čechy, Moravany a Slováky* [Voices supporting the need of a common language for Czechs, Moravians and Slovaks].[6] There was an almost complete repudiation of standard literary Slovak by the Czech side. It was considered to be an *act of Slovak separatism*. The introduction of standard literary Slovak led to the first serious conflict and misunderstanding between Czechs and Slovaks in modern history, and resulted in a cooling down of their relations during the second half of the nineteenth century.

The Czech reproach to the Slovaks was in the form of the rhetorical question: why have you separated? It was an inaccurate interpretation from both a material and a historical point of view. In fact, even the Czech literary tongue deviated from the classical style of the Kralice Bible, with its use of the living spoken language. However, for Slovaks the spoken language was Slovak, and not Czech, also the transition to literary Slovak could not be accomplished in any other way but with making use of a living Slovak style.

Continued development of the Slovak national movement gave credence to the position of Štúr and his friends. Standard literary Slovak, accepted equally by Catholics and Protestants, helped spread national consciousness rapidly among Slovaks. This was true even of regions which had been less affected by the national movement. There followed a great upsurge in the use of Slovak in national literature and in learned and specialist publications.

In spite of this success, the Czechs by and large continued to misunderstand the Slovak question. The Czech general public became less interested in Slovak development because of the cooled relations between the two peoples. The codification of literary Slovak resulted in two stereotypes by Czechs that in a certain sense have survived until the present. One is the 'Slovak betrayal' and the other is the 'Slovak separatism'.

The Czech intelligentsia has returned sporadically to the question of Slovak language secession and has continued to regard this situation only as temporary. Even as late as 1895, at the occasion of the Ethnographical Exhibition in Prague, Czech followers of ideas of Czechoslovak national unity addressed the Slovak cultural representatives with a questionnaire regarding the return to the use of literary Czech. Frequently mentioned at the time was the idea that Slovak should be used at most in belle lettres and there should be a 'return' to Czech in learned and specialist writings. However, the organizers were very disappointed with the results of their questionnaire. Most answers were negative or, less commonly, no answer was given at all, even in cases where a positive answer had been expected. For example, there were negative answers even from some former Prague students of supporters of close Czech–Slovak cooperation. The notion of Czech–Slovak linguistic and cultural national unity was not endorsed. The historical development and, above all, the political programme of the Czech as well as the Slovak national movement sustained the natural differentiation of both nations, which had lived and evolved under different historical conditions and circumstances. It was most evident in the political programmes of both national movements.

The conceptual origin of political Czechoslovakism

The theory of political Czechoslovakism began to emerge at the end of the nineteenth century. This was about the time when the idea of a linguistically and culturally unitary Czecho–Slovak nation dissolved. It was the difficult situation of both nations which provided the external impulse for the origin of this theory. It surfaced as a product of Austro-Hungarian Compromise (1867) resulting in a dualistic system in the division of political power in the Habsburg monarchy between the Austro-German and Magyar ruling strata.[7] The second important moment significantly affecting the development of national movements was the Dual Alliance treaty between Germany and Austria-Hungary in 1879. Germany greatly increased its influence in Central Europe as a result of this treaty. The treaty also affected the internal situation in the Austro-Hungarian Empire. German nationalism strengthened in the Austrian part (Cisleithania) and the efforts for centralization and Magyarization intensified in the Hungarian part (Transleithania).

Influences from Germany affected the development of the two parts of the Habsburg monarchy in different ways. Although there was an increase in German nationalism in the Austrian part, more liberal conditions enabled the growth of a mass movement of Czechs, including the establishment of a strong economic base and an educational and cultural infrastructure. Since the time of Bismarck, Germany had clearly supported Magyar centralistic efforts in Hungary. A strong centralistic Hungary was regarded as a reliable pillar of the Dual Alliance. Thus German foreign policy offered support to Magyarizing endeavours even though they resulted in the Magyarization of more than two million ethnic Germans living in Hungary.[8] Under these circumstances Slovaks, in contrast to Czechs, fell under brutal governmental pressure. They gradually lost all their institutions, including elementary schools which employed Slovak as the language of instruction.

The German pressure in Central Europe created a condition that encouraged closer Czech and Slovak cooperation. There was renewed interest in Slovakia by the Czech intelligentsia and public. Gradually increased co-operation resulted in a common though not clearly specified political programme. Tomáš (Thomas) Garrigue Masaryk (1850–1937), who was Czech of his own chosing even though his father was Slovak, was the main initiator of 'Czechoslovakism'. This was in spite of the fact that he published almost nothing about it and left no rounded off work which defined his theory or demonstrated his conception.[9] This fact also indicates that political Czechoslovakism was less a theory and more a pragmatic political programme.

Masaryk's path to Czechoslovakism developed through a criticism of Czech politics which concentrated on the restoration of historical Czech State Rights. This idea was very vivid among the Czech public and was part of the national movement. At the end of the nineteenth century, in a complicated situation, it manifested itself not seldom in a radical form. The radicalism of the press and of some politicians documented the fact that the State Rights concept was in a state of crisis and impasse. Masaryk, who became well aware of this situation, was not satisfied with mere criticism of radicalism. Instead, he began a search for a realistic way out. He became conscious that even if the historical Bohemian State Rights could be restored, it was not an acceptable solution. For one thing, such a state would be surrounded by unfriendly neighbours and one third of its inhabitants would be German. For another thing, if the Magyars were successful in their Magyarization plan, it would close off the Czech basin from the East and this would be a disaster for the Czech nation. For the Czechs, therefore, an alliance with the Slovaks was important. It provided them with an outlet to the East and also created a certain counterbalance against the Germans. Helping Slovakia thus constituted a part of positive realistic Czech policy.

Slovaks were grateful for this assistance. They were facing planned governmental denationalization, and Czech aid was one of the few real ways out. But except for a small group of young intelligentsia supporting the journal *Hlas* (Voice),[10] Slovaks were not prepared to discuss the question of national unity with Czechs. For Slovaks, this question had been resolved – to give up their national identity was an impossibility. Their recent historical experiences led Slovaks to reject the theory of a political nation. Moreover, the Magyar theory of a unitary Hungarian nation was, in substance, a political theory. This umbrella covered brutal linguistic and ethnic denationalization. The Slovaks were also repudiating Czechoslovakism because, applied in practice, such a theory required the link-up of two equal subjects. After the Austro-Hungarian Compromise in 1867, the Slovaks were weaker not only in number but also economically and culturally.

Political Czechoslovakism in the years before the First World War emerged only as a *potential* idea. In practice, Czech–Slovak cooperation had been furthered by the Czechoslovak Union which had organized annual Czech–Slovak conferences in the Moravian spa Luhačovice near the Hungarian border since 1908.[11] The goal of these meetings was to bring the two nations closer together but the deliberations did not result in any common political agenda. Thus, political Czechoslovakism existed only as an unarticulated, hidden and latent concept.

After his first visit to Slovakia in 1887, Masaryk came to the conclusion that Slovak leaders, above all Svetozár Hurban Vajanský (1847–1916) and Jozef Škultéty (1853–1948), considered the issues of the language and Slovak national identity to be resolved. Masaryk considered Czech–Slovak cooperation inevitable so he did not consider it appropriate, regarding Czech–Slovak relations, to raise the linguistic and national topic respectively. Thus the theory of political Czechoslovakism came into existence but it was yet to be publicly documented. It was kept alive by some Czech political representatives and *Hlas* supporters in Slovakia, but the state of affairs in Austria-Hungary and the international situation made its realization impossible.

The struggle for a common state

Following the outbreak of the First World War, a new international situation in Central Europe arose. Before the war, Czechs and Slovaks could not expect their political programme to be fulfilled. The Czech programme of restoration of State Rights was as unrealistic as the Slovak programme of autonomy within Hungary, originally proclaimed in 1861.[12] However unrealistic Slovak hopes of self-determination within the state governed by the Magyars, the Slovaks still kept to their programme. The idea of a common Czech–Slovak statehood – largely within a federalized Austria–Hungary – was occasionally discussed before the war. Considering the situation at the time, the idea was little more than an implicit desire, much less a political programme. However, intensive Czech–Slovak cooperation and Czech aid for Slovakia before the War laid the groundwork for a potential agreement between the two nations.

The First World War created several prerequisites for a potential realization of the Czech as well as the Slovak political programme. It depended understandably on the developments during the war and its eventual result. Hitherto, existing experiences with the Habsburgs demonstrated that government concessions were possible only if the Czechs and the Slovaks stood up and resisted. The Habsburgs had little appreciation for loyalty and gave in only when facing open force. This was also the experience with respect to the Austro-Hungarian Compromise and the policy which followed it. This broadly was the case for the Czech and Slovak resistance

movement. It surfaced spontaneously abroad but also at home in unwillingness to join the army and later in desertions from the army which saw entire
units of soldiers going over to the Russians. Moreover, Czech and Slovak
soldiers participated in military riots and mutinies.

From the outset of the war, the resistance movement had an agenda. It
was a very flexible programme that adapted to the situation as the war
developed, but in principle the conjoining of Czechs and Slovaks into one
state constituted its core. In November 1914 Masaryk presented this plan to
his British contact R. W. Seton-Watson (who made a name for himself by
writing on the national problems of Hungary and on the Southern Slavs)
and he later formulated it in the memorandum *Independent Bohemia*.[13]
Masaryk's programme was evolving and adjusting but its basic concept, the
bringing together of Czechs and Slovaks into one state, remained constant.
From the beginning of the war, the resistance organized around this plan
was the logical continuation of Masaryk's prewar policy. Czechs and
Slovaks living in the USA, Russia, France and also in neutral Switzerland
gave financial support to the resistance. Spontaneously, or on the basis of
the Cleveland Agreement, they began to organize resistance groups and
later combat units to fight against Germany and Austria-Hungary on the
side of the Entente. (The Cleveland Agreement of October 1915 was a
declaration of joint efforts between Czechs and Slovaks living in the USA).[14]
The defeat of Germany and Austria-Hungary was the main precondition
for realizing the maximalist goal of the resistance: the creation of the
common state of Czechs and Slovaks.

The idea of a common Czecho–Slovak state was also winning more and
more support at home – in the Czech Lands and in Slovakia. For the Czechs,
joining Slovakia represented the most advantageous option for realizing
their programme of State Rights. Theoretically, Slovaks were offered
several alternatives for the solution of the Slovak question. The traditional
Slovak programme – autonomy within Hungary – was one option. Other
possibilities were to link up in some form with either Poland or Russia. But
the best alternative remained to join with the Czechs within a common
state. Because of the history of severe national oppression, no sufficient
economic, cultural and administrative infrastructure existed to support an
independent state, so the idea was not even mooted.

At home, Czechs and Slovaks gradually accepted Masaryk's programme
of a common state and began to work in its favour. In May 1917, at the first
war-time session of the reopened Imperial Parliament (Reichsrat), Czech
members demanded union of the Czech Lands with Slovakia.[15] During
1918 this agenda and the struggle for its becoming reality received widespread support.

Slovaks were in a poor bargaining position. The Hungarian government forcibly prohibited any public manifestations. But the idea of a common state with the Czechs gradually gained ground among Slovak representatives. This was also due to successes of the resistance abroad in which Slovaks were active participants. On 1 May 1918 the first public demonstration in favour of a common state took place in a meeting in the central Slovakian town of Liptovský Svätý Mikuláš. It took the form of a resolution authored by Vavro Šrobár (1867–1950). The decision to establish the common state of Czechs and Slovaks was reached at a secret meeting of representatives of Slovak political life on 24 May 1918. They confirmed this decision when they met officially as the Slovak National Committee in Turčiansky Svätý Martin (the so-called Martin Declaration of 30 October 1918).[16]

The common state had become an optimal solution of the Czech and Slovak questions. The struggle for a common state pushed into the background some of the issues on the nature of the future state that divided Czechs and Slovaks. So complex was the path that many details were not addressed until the autumn of 1918. Each nation entered the union with different historical experiences, at a different stage of economic and cultural development and, most importantly, with different conceptions of Czech–Slovak statehood.

The Czech nation interpreted it virtually as an extension and transmutation of the traditional Czech statehood. From the outset, Czech society considered the new, Czechoslovak, state to be its own and immediately identified with it. Its establishment amounted, in effect, to the implementation of the Czech State Rights programme in an 'improved' form. The Czech citizen sank his Czech identity in Czechoslovak identity. He did not feel it as a restraint and he did not consider it to be a violation. Simply stated, the Czech citizen had no use for a hyphen in the name of the state.

Slovakia, on the other hand, was entering the common state with a totally different conception of common statehood. The majority of the Slovaks and, indeed, many Slovak Czechoslovakists regarded the establishment of the common state as an act of mutual agreement by two parties. It was not an extension or a follow up of an old State Rights programme. A mutual relationship had been developed over the years but no political programme. Inasmuch as we refer to the course of events in 1918 as an 'overthrow' (*prevrat*), the change associated with it was more fundamental and revolutionary for Slovakia. Slovakia had been a part of Hungary for 1,000 years and the Slovaks took part in the building of the Hungarian state, it was their state. They separated from it only after it stopped protecting their national interests and tried hard to denationalize them. That is, after the originally multi-ethnic state became dominated by a single, Magyar, ethnicity. For Slovaks, the separation from the Hungarian state was something quite deep and fundamental. In the Slovak case there was no question of an extension of a State Rights programme – the scission was a sharp one. As one of the prominent Slovak leaders, Andrej Hlinka (1864–1938), put it at the consultative meeting in Turčiansky Svätý Martin in May 1918: 'Let us not avoid the question and admit frankly that we are for the Czechoslovak orientation. The thousand years' marriage with the Magyars has been a failure. We have to part.'[17] With respect to Slovaks, what was in reality a totally new state came into being due to an agreement between two parties, and was composed of two independent entities. That is, to put it again simply, it was a state with a hyphen. Naturally, the differences in positions regarding the common state cannot be taken to be absolute. Especially in Slovakia, there was a group of prominent politicians who accepted the idea of a centralized state.

It should be added that these differences did not manifest themselves immediately. But gradually they became a source of political problems for the First Czechoslovak Republic.

Centralism and autonomy

In the Czech view the common state was to be more or less centralized and unitary. In the Slovak view it was to be a decentralized state with a significant degree of autonomy. That is, political autonomy – which Slovaks vainly strove for in the Hungarian state – remained a traditional Slovak programme. During the first decade of the Czechoslovak Republic the demand for autonomy was not presented very forcefully and did not constitute an internal political problem. At the time when the political and administrative system was being formed, the majority of Slovak politicians accepted the centralized model as an inevitable but temporary solution. The priority for Slovaks was to free themselves from Magyar administration and influence. During the war, when the future structure of the common state was sporadically discussed by leaders of the resistance at home and abroad, the thinking usually assumed a transition period of ten years. Indeed, it was not until the second decade of the Czechoslovak Republic that the idea of autonomy began to dominate Slovak political life more and more.

From its inception, the Czechoslovak Republic found itself in a difficult international situation, and politicians, be they Czech or Slovak, were aware of this fact. Just as the independent state represented a significant achievement with a promising future, it was in the interest of both nations to preserve it. In a precarious international situation only an internally strong state could survive. But opinions differed on what constituted an internally strong state. Whereas for the Czech side centralization was of paramount importance, in Slovakia autonomy – its tide running strongly – was seen as something the Republic could not do without.

Both the domestic and the international situation of Czechoslovakia was complicated. Serious enough in itself, the Slovak issue was overshadowed by the German question. Not only were there more Germans than Slovaks in Czechoslovakia but they were supported by a neighbouring German state which became quite open after Hitler's accession to power. In such a situation, to solve the Slovak question, and not the German one, would have been difficult. The equivocalness of the Czech–Slovak relationship, however, was creating an atmosphere of mistrust. Czechs accused Slovaks of separatism and Slovaks reproached Czechs for breaking mutual accords, such as the Pittsburgh Agreement, which had been signed by Masaryk and representatives of Slovaks living in America in the closing stage of the First World War.[18]

While the brief span of existence of the First Czechoslovak Republic was a time of rapid economic and mainly cultural development for both nations, the rate of development was more intensive in Slovakia. In a short period of time a whole school system, from the elementary level to university, including the cultural infrastructure, was built up. Connected with the rapid evolution of industrial and banking capital, Slovak entrepreneurs, having been held back in former Hungary, came into their own. From the Slovak point of view, in contrast to the previous situation in Hungary, the possibility of developing within a democratic political system was indeed a major step forward. The majority of Slovaks voted during the years of pre-Munich Czechoslovakia for the first time. The participation in local elections was of particular significance because the voter had the opportunity to observe the impact of his particular preference at first hand and thus see the democratic system functioning. The germs of a civil society began to grow in Slovakia.

Thus in the years of the First Republic a paradoxical situation unfolded. Objectively, both nations were developing under favourable conditions and these were utilized in the interests of the qualitative build-up of both national communities. At the same time, failure to solve the Slovak question was coupled with a policy which underwrote the theory of political Czechoslovakism as the dominant state ideology. This adversely affected the relations between Czechs and Slovaks. The traditional Slovak political programme – autonomy within a wider political entity – had not been fulfilled in pre-Munich Czechoslovakia. The official state doctrine – the theory of a unitary Czechoslovak nation – was not an obstacle to the cultural develop-

ment of Slovakia. To all intents and purposes, Slovakia lacked an established intelligentsia with the consequence that a large number of Czech
teachers and officials came to fill vacancies in schools and administration.
The majority learned to speak Slovak and participated in the development
of Slovak culture. But the Slovaks, who came to think that they had already
qualified as a nation under the Hungarian rule, claimed that they were
entitled to political rights. The political aspect of Czech–Slovak relations
has remained the dominant issue ever since.

From autonomy to federation

The development of Czech–Slovak relations during 1938–1948 was significantly influenced by the contemporaneous changes in the power and political situation in Europe. Following the Munich Dictate, Hitler, aided
momentously by the appeasement policy of the Western Great Powers,
annexed the border areas of Bohemia and Moravia. Soon after Munich, on
6 October 1938, autonomy was proclaimed in Slovakia and accepted by the
Prague government. Given the international situation, little enthusiasm
greeted the birth of autonomy, amounting as it did to a formal realization
of the Slovak historical programme. Pushed through by Hlinka's Slovak
People's Party (named after its deceased founder), Slovak autonomy
acquired a bitter flavour after 2 November 1938 when Hitler and Mussolini
decided that Slovakia was to cede its southern border areas to Hungary
(Vienna Award). Nazi Germany became the dominant power in Central
Europe and controlled developments in this area. On 14 March 1939, under
Hitler's direct pressure, the Slovak Republic was proclaimed and Czecho-
Slovakia became defunct.[19]

During the years of the Second World War the Slovak general public
came to show increasingly dissatisfaction with the regime of the Slovak state
and its one-sided orientation to Nazi Germany. A Slovak resistance movement developed, and its activities culminated in the Slovak National
Uprising in August 1944. One of the main points of its programme was the
renewal of the Czecho-Slovak state, but the goal was not merely the restoration of prewar conditions. The status of the relationship between the two
nations in the common state was to be redefined on the basis of complete
parity and equality.

The break-up of the Czecho-Slovak Republic and the separation of
Slovakia and the Protectorate of Bohemia and Moravia left deep wounds
on the future relationship between Czechs and Slovaks. The democratic
Slovak public demanded the restoration of Czecho-Slovak statehood albeit
on new principles, including the acceptance of Slovak political subjectivity.

The Czech public also aimed at the resurrection of the common statehood. But during the war years a considerable section of the Czech public came to believe the incorrect interpretation of the break-up, disseminated by Edvard Beneš (1884–1948) abroad and through broadcasts at home. It was the 'stab-in-the-back' theory according to which members of Hlinka's Slovak People's Party (often confused with all Slovaks) destroyed the common state of Czechs and Slovaks. In the light of historical facts this interpretation is obviously incorrect. The erroneous slant on historical events at the time when the Czech Lands were suffering under Nazi occupation caused serious damage to Czech–Slovak relations. The stereotypes 'Slovak betrayal' and 'Slovak separatism' which, as we have shown, had deeper historical roots, found a receptive audience among the Czech public.

After the Second World War the Czechoslovak Republic was restored within her pre-Munich boundaries, with the exception of Subcarpathian Ruthenia (Transcarpathian Ukraine) which had been ceded to the Soviet Union. The settling of Czech and Slovak relations in the restored state became a serious internal political issue. Indeed, in the wake of the Second World War, there was a historical opportunity to make a fresh start and to rebuild the Czech–Slovak relations on a new basis. There was the Slovak Uprising with the programme of restructuring of Czecho-Slovakia on the basis of complete national parity and equality. Externally there was a new international situation, and internally the German question had ceased to be the decisive issue. E. Beneš missed the opportunity to build a state on the principles of Czech–Slovak equality manifested in the programme of the Slovak National Uprising in favour, essentially, of a return to the Prague centralism prevailing before Munich.

Following the Communist takeover in February 1948, the centralizing tendencies were reinforced. Certain formal concessions *vis-à-vis* the Slovak demands were gradually abrogated, and the form the state assumed was a centralized unitary regime. As Slovak demands could not be voiced openly during the Stalinist reign of terror in the totalitarian system, they surfaced covertly.

During the Prague Spring of 1968 the federative state form was agreed upon. But the constitutional change became distinctly tainted by 'normalization' because the Federation of Czech Socialist and Slovak Socialist Republics was proclaimed after the entry of the Warsaw Pact troops in August 1968.[20] The outwardly federative regime did not concern itself with coming to grips with the mutual relationship of the two Republics. The Slovak parliament and government were virtually powerless and functioned only formally. Between 1969 and 1989 the relations between the Czechs and Slovaks were not openly discussed. The topic was taboo but in reality these relations were continuously deteriorating. The fateful legacy revealed itself fully when the activities of democratic institutions were restored after November 1989. It was not only the constitutional issue but the question of mutual relations in general that contributed to the deep crisis that arose between Czechs and Slovaks and the dissolution of the common state in 1992.[21]

Notes

1 J. Kollár, *Ueber die literarische Wechselseitigkeit zwischen den verschiedenen Stämmen und Mundarten der slawischen Nation* (Pest, 1837). This conception was developed by Kollár also in his poetical work *Slávy dcera* [Daughter of Sláva] (Pest, 1832).

2 A. Bernolák (1762–1873) codified the Slovak language in these works: *Dissertatio philologico-critica de literis Slavorum* (Posonium [Bratislava], 1790); *Slovár slovenskí česko-latinsko-nemecko-uherskí 1–6* [Slovak-German-Czech-Latin-Hungarian Dictionary] (Buda, 1825–7).

3 *Obrany* [Apologies] were a frequent literary genre by means of which Slovaks defended their national identity, mainly against attacks from the Magyar side. The first major *Apology* was published in 1728 by Ján Baltazár Magin followed by others, including Ľ. Štúr. See J. Tibenský, *Chvály a obrany slovenského národa* [Praises and apologies of the Slovak nation] (Bratislava, 1965).

4 M. Hroch, *Evropská narodní hnutí v 19. století* [European national movements in the 19th century] (Prague, 1986); M. Hroch, *Social Preconditions of National Revival in Europe* (Cambridge, 1985).

5 For Štúr's primary works on codification, see: *Nárečja slovenskô alebo potreba písaňja v tomto nárečí* [The Slovak language or the need to write in this language] (Prešporok [Bratislava], 1846); and *Nauka reči slovenskej* [The grammar of the Slovak language] (Prešporok, 1846).

6 The collection was published in Prague in 1846.

7 On the Austro-Hungarian Compromise, see also *Der österreichisch-ungarische Ausgleich 1867* (Bratislava, 1971).

8 For more on this, see D. Kováč, 'Die Ungarndeutsche in der Politik des deutschen Imperialismus bis 1914', *Zeitschrift für Geschichtswissenschaft*, 2 (1991), 113–16.

9 Indications of this theory may be found in Masaryk's correspondence and in some of his works: *Česká otázka Snahy a tužby národního obrození* [The Czech Question The strivings and aspirations of the national revival] (1895); *Naše nynější krise Pád Strany staročeské a počátkové směrů nových* [Our present crisis The fall of the Old Czech Party and the beginnings of new trends] (1895); *Karel Havlíček Snahy a tužby politického probuzení* [Karel Havlíček, The strivings and aspirations of political awakening] (1896).

10 *Hlas* was published in the years 1898–1904. The group of young intelligentsia which gathered around the magazine was known as *Hlasisti*. The group con-

sisted mostly of Slovak students who studied in Prague. Among the leaders were the physician Vavro Šrobár and the astronomer Milan Rastislav Štefánik (the latter became an airman in the French army during the First World War and eventually the first Czechoslovak Minister of War).

11 J. Vochala, *Luhačovské sněmy československé* [Czechoslovak meetings at Luhačovice] (Prague-Luhačovice, 1936).

12 'Memorandum of the Slovak Nation', in F. Bokes (ed.), *Dokumenty k slovenskému narodnémunm hnutiu v rokoch 1848–1918* [Documents on the Slovak national movement 1848–1918], vol. 1 (Bratislava, 1962), pp. 313–80.

13 E. Beneš, *Světová válka a naše revoluce* [World war and our revolution] (Prague, 1928), III, p. 220.

14 The Czechoslovak Army, i.e. Czechoslovak Legions were organized by the Czechoslovak National Council established in Paris in February 1916.

15 J. Galandauer, *Vznik Československé republiky 1918* [The origin of the Czechoslovak Republic in 1918] (Prague, 1988), p. 288.

16 On Slovakia's share in the establishment of the common state, see M. Hronský, *Slovensko pri zrode Československa* [Slovakia at the birth of Czechoslovakia] Bratislava, 1988); D. Kováč, *Myšlienka československej štátnosti Jej vznik a realizácia* [The idea of Czechoslovak statehood Its origin and realization] (Bratislava, 1988), pp. 241–352.

17 Literary archives of *Matica Slovenská* in Martin: Collection Slovak National Council, p. 564, II/4–a.

18 The agreement between Slovak and Czech organizations in the USA, signed on 30 May 1918. According to it, Slovakia should have had an autonomous position. Cf. K. A. Medvecký, *Slovenský prevrat* [The overthrow in Slovakia], Vol. II (Trnava, 1930), p. 80.

19 On 15 March 1939, German troops invaded Bohemia and Moravia and Hitler proclaimed them to be the German 'Protectorate of Bohemia and Moravia'.

20 The Federation was proclaimed at the parliamentary session on 27 October 1968.

21 On the relation of the historical development to the crisis in Czech–Slovak relations (before the split), see D. Kováč, 'Tschechen und Slowaken – das Ende oder ein neuer Anfang der ČSFR?', *Bundesinstitut für ostwissenschaftliche und internationale Studien. Aktuelle Analysen.* No. 39 (12 July 1991).

Index